The Seasons of the Italian Kitchen

ALSO BY DIANE DARROW AND TOM MARESCA

La Tavola Italiana

ALSO BY TOM MARESCA

The Right Wine

Mastering Wine

ATLANTIC MONTHLY PRESS

NEW YORK

THE SEASONS

OF THE

ITALIAN

KITCHEN

· *Diane Darrow and Tom Maresca* ·

Some of the prose and recipes in this book have appeared, in
slightly different forms, in other publications: *Attenzione*, *Bon
Appétit*, *Diversion*, *Food & Wine*, *New York Daily News*, and *Wine & Spirit*.

Atlantic Monthly Press
841 Broadway
New York, NY 10003

Manufactured in the United States of America
Published simultaneously in Canada

Library of Congress Cataloging-in-Publication Data
Darrow, Diane.
The seasons of the Italian kitchen / Diane Darrow and Tom Maresca.—1st ed.
Includes index.
ISBN 0-87113-575-2
1. Cookery, Italian. 2. Seasons. I. Maresca, Tom. II. Title.
TX723.D286   1994   641.5945—dc20   93-46761

Designed by Liney Li

First Edition

1 3 5 7 9 10 8 6 4 2

FOR

MARY DARROW

ROGER DARROW

AND

CONSTANCE MARESCA

Acknowledgments

This cookbook and the lore we've distilled into it are the result of years of reading, writing, and conversation with cooks and eaters and winemakers beyond counting, in Italy and in America. We owe debts to nameless waiters in little trattorias who told us, from years of seeing it done, exactly what the cook put into the sauce; to modest housewives and their mothers and their aunts and the cousins of their aunts, who told us how their ancestresses (and occasionally ancestors), who were the *real* cooks, handled the pasta or seasoned the veal. We've profited from every writer who came before us, from Platina and Pietro de' Crescenzi and Vincenzo Corrado down to Anna Gosetti della Salda and Ada Boni and Vincenzo Buonassisi. Such debts can never be tallied and never repaid: they can only be acknowledged, and we gratefully do so here.

Among our friends and colleagues, some names call for specific mention for their long-term support and unfailing cooperation. We especially want to thank: Walt Bode and Felicia Eth, for the enthusiasm and expertise that they gave unstintingly to this book; Frank de Falco, for the warmth of his encouragement and the pertinence of his advice; Doreen Schmid, whilom American representative of the Chianti Classico Consortium, for unfailing faith in us and unending aid in prosecuting our plans; Tom Verdillo, resident genius of Tommaso's restaurant in Brooklyn, for his bottomless and freely shared treasury of Italian culinary lore; and, finally, the staff of the Italian Trade Commission, from receptionists to Dr. Giorgio Lulli, for cooperation and help that never slackened. Without all these unindicted co-conspirators, this book might never have been begun. Without them, it surely would never have been finished. *Grazie a tutti.*

Contents

Introduction: In Season
1

Primavera · Spring
1 3

Estate · Summer
1 1 7

Autunno · Fall
2 1 5

Inverno · Winter
3 2 1

Menus
4 2 3

About Wine
4 3 3

Index
4 5 5

The Seasons of the Italian Kitchen

Introduction: In Season

All things have their season: and in their times all things pass under heaven. A time to be born, and a time to die. A time to plant, and a time to pluck that which is planted. . . . And I have known that there was no better thing than to rejoice and to do well in this life. For every man that eateth and drinketh, and seeth good of his labor, that is the gift of God.

—ECCLESIASTES 3

Anyone who has traveled in Italy and seen Italians at table notices the gusto with which they approach food and the endlessly renewed pleasure they take in it. Food in Italy is an occasion, a subject, an experience, a theme, an artifact, a celebration. You don't just eat in Italy: you look, you smell, you savor, you admire, you discuss, you deplore, you praise, you pass plates, you taste one another's dishes, you compare how they make the lasagna here with how your mother made it, or how the restaurant around the corner makes it, you argue, you order another dish, you cross-examine the waiter, you make him show you another fish or suggest a better wine, you all talk at once, you call for more bread, or more lemons, or extra-virgin olive oil, you prolong the dinner far beyond the ever-so-rational length of time Americans allot for fueling their systems, and because everybody is having such a good time, on the spur of the moment you order a bottle of Asti Spumante to finish up with, and you and everyone with you loves every nutritionally and dietetically excessive moment of it. Tomorrow you will probably make a *magro* dinner of frittata and green salad, but tonight you are seeing the good of your labor.

The rhythm and the spirit of Italian life grow out of a long-ingrained, deep-in-the-soul awareness of the truth of Ecclesiastes' ancient wisdom, whose simplicity and starkness much of twentieth-century activity, at least in this country, seems bent on evading. Americans pursue one health chimera after another, apparently persuading themselves that if they eat enough fiber and jog enough miles they will live forever, or if they forego butter and wine and the pleasures of the table in the days of their youth, they will prolong their tedious, toothless old age of flavorless food and perpetual boredom into an eternity of the same.

Even the current fad for "the Mediterranean diet" gets it all wrong: it's not just what you eat, but how you eat, how you live. It isn't simply a balance of fresh fruits and vegetables, lots of fish and little meat, that keeps Mediterranean peoples safe from heart attacks and strokes: worrying about such balances is in fact just another mistake, another element of stress in American life, one more thing to make your life a constant misery instead of a steady pleasure. What makes "the Mediterranean diet" work is pleasure: stepping out of the rat race long enough to realize that the delicacy of this trout—the cool, acid tang of this glass of Verdicchio—the gush of sweet nectar from this huge, golden pear—is exactly what you've been working for, that putting this simple, straightforward goodness on the table to share with your family and friends is the fruit of your labor, and it is worth it.

THE SEASONS

Seasonality is the heart and soul of Italian cooking. Whatever the region, local cooks throughout the peninsula depend on the simplest—and for Americans the hardest to guarantee—factor of all for the success of their dishes: fresh ingredients bursting with flavor. No agribusiness tomatoes in the middle of winter or mushy McIntoshes in July, but cherries and strawberries in the spring, and wild mushrooms and wild game in the fall, and all things between in their own time. Each season brings its impatiently anticipated pleasures, the sharp, clear flavors that are all the better for being rare: the year's first tiny peas or its first glistening purple eggplants, spring's baby lambs or the hearty, warming polentas of winter. We know a little of that in this country, mostly in summer, and mostly from our own gardens or nearby farm stands. Remember how your mouth waters for the first real tomato of summer, still smelling of the vine, its scarlet skin glowing like a tiny sun. Remember how you anticipate the first, fresh-picked corn of the summer, the plump, moist kernels marshaled in their perfect platoons, each bursting with sweetness and just begging for its supererogatory slatherings of butter and salt. Those kinds of pleasures—the sharpness of anticipation, the keen, clean, distinct taste of a vegetable or fish or fruit or flesh that is absolutely and perfectly itself—those are what seasonality in the kitchen is all about.

In Italy, each season has its characteristic flavors, tastes, and smells that are unmistakably its own. For instance: early summer for us is forever captured in the memory of the unexpected heat of a June day on a highway south of Rome, the sun white-hot in a cloudless sky, the saving shade of a grove of umbrella pines, the welcome chill of a carafe of pale, young Frascati, and the succulence of a *panino ripieno con porchetta*—a firm-crusted roll filled with juicy slices of white pork and translucent amber cracklings carved before our eyes from the herb-stuffed torso of a pig that was turning over wood embers, patiently tended by the same cheerful, unshaven factotum who fixed our sandwiches, fetched our wine, and in general presided over the merest excuse for a roadside restaurant that was clearly, for him, the finest dining place on earth. In those beautiful Frascati hills and that clear June light, who could disagree with him?

Italian cooking at its best doesn't just reflect the flavors of the changing season: it embodies and glorifies them. What Americans instinctively respond to in the Italian culinary style is its presentation of the purest, freshest foods as simply and with as little interference as possible—the great art of concealing art translated to the kitchen and the dinner table. That is also what makes Italian cooking so easily accessible to ordinary home cooks. It is not an haute cuisine in the sense of needing special training or unusual skills. What Italian cooking demands—working taste buds and a reasonable degree of attention—is well within the range of all but the palatally tone-deaf. What Italian cooking gives in return is the haute cuisine of every day, of every season: the fleeting flavors of nature's annual roll call of ingredients caught in their seasonal passage and fixed in dishes as delicious and diverse as the varying moods and weathers of nature itself.

The Seasons of the Italian Kitchen is designed to make those flavors available to American cooks. None of our recipes requires any special expertise, and most ingredients are supermarket-available. But our up-front advice is this: take the time to shop well for your fixings. If there is only one butcher shop in your town or neighborhood that sells really young, pale veal, patronize it. If there is only one greengrocer who carries fragrant leafy celery, unblemished artichokes, crisp spinach and green beans, firm young zucchini—patronize it. What you start with in Italian cooking determines what you end with. There are no disguises here—no sugars to homogenize flavors, no elaborate, concentrated sauces to disguise blandness. This is honest cookery: what you see is what you get.

Happy shopping, and happy dining!

THE SEASONINGS
OF THE ITALIAN KITCHEN

As we were working on the recipes for this book and loaning them out to friends to try for us, we often got what seemed to us a strange response from experienced cooks and food lovers—something on the order of "But there's nothing *in* this recipe! Where are all the seasonings? Why are there no spices?" They found it hard to believe that a dish could really taste good with so few ingredients, and so ordinary-sounding ones, as most of the recipes in this book use. Making the recipes quickly changed their minds, and the pleasant surprise often led to an epiphany about Italian cookery, quickly followed by a conversion. It was a real conversion, too, because these recipes derive from a fundamentally different style of cooking than the ones most serious American cooks are familiar with.

Contemporary American and European cooking styles tend toward conspicuous complexity, dishes with a variety of strong flavors that join each other only on the plate. A meat will be braised with something, set in a pool of a separately made sauce whose ingredients are completely different from the meat's braising liquid, and both will be served with an equally independent garnish. The flavors don't mingle until they're in your mouth, and even then you are supposed to taste them as separate strands, not as a harmonious unity. Traditional Italian cooking, which most of our dishes are, takes mostly the opposite stance. Relatively small numbers of flavorings cook together and blend together to achieve a whole that may resemble either a rich orchestral symphony or a concerto highlighting one of the instruments—but never simultaneous solos from all the voices. The genius of Italian cooking clarifies and concentrates flavors rather than complicates them, which is one reason why it is a great everyday cuisine and always satisfying.

Here's a rundown of the major spices, herbs, and other seasonings you'll want to have on hand for making the recipes in this book and in most traditional Italian cooking.

THE SPICE RACK

In a way it's odd that Italian cooking is so sparing and conservative with spices, since so much of Italy's early wealth was founded on the spice trade with the Orient. Salt and black pepper, of course; red pepper, rarely in its ground forms (cayenne or paprika, for instance), more often flaked (in that state frequently used as a table condiment), but preferably dried whole, which moves it out of what we would consider the spice category (see below under "other").

Nutmeg appears quite often in Italian recipes, and not primarily in the dessert category. A fresh grating of *noce moscato* is frequently used to accent risotti, gnocchi, cooked greens, and braised meats. In the same way, Venetian and Genovese cooking make a fair use of cinnamon and cloves in recipes for meats or fowl. These are usually survivals from the glory days of both former republics, when between them they dominated the spice trade. And anywhere in the north you may find recipes calling for berries from the juniper bush, which occurs in the native forests. Saffron makes a virtuoso appearance in *risotto alla milanese*, and not much anywhere else.

THE HERB GARDEN

More than spices, Italians love herbs (i.e., plants in which the foliage is used for seasoning, not the seeds, bark, or other anatomical parts) in cooking, and that mostly means herbs grown at home or picked in the wild. You see very few formal herb gardens in Italy, but it seems that almost every house with a bit of land around it has garden borders or hedges made of rosemary and bay laurel shrubs. (When a thirty-foot hedge of rosemary blooms, the bees go mad with joy!) Aromatic rosemary is more conspicuous in recipes than bay leaf, but both are very common.

Basil is of course the most glamorous of Italian cooking herbs. It's so loved that it often goes beyond flavoring to become an ingredient, as in pesto or in our *rigatoni al basilico*. But for us, the one absolutely indispensable culinary herb is flat-leaf parsley. Those who know parsley only as a frilly dab of emerald-green shrubbery that you push to the edge of the plate before you begin eating have a pleasant surprise in store. "Real" parsley (as we think of the flat-leaf variety) has a less chlorophylly, more foodlike flavor that plays an important supporting role in innumerable Italian dishes.

Leaves of sage (especially with veal dishes), mint (especially in Roman cooking), and the oregano-marjoram-thyme family (ubiquitous) round out the Italian herb garden. Tarragon is an oddity in the cooking of Siena. Lavender is grown everywhere in Italy but is used for its scent, not in cooking. (Thankfully, there's nothing in Italy like some of the French herbes provençaux mixtures that are desperately heavy on lavender.)

Herbs are almost always used fresh—or at worst, this year's crop freshly dried. They are never purchased already powdered or ground, which destroys their flavor almost immediately. We feel strongly about this: You *cannot* use powdered sage, oregano, etc., in any of our recipes. They don't work. In fact, any dried herb you may have that has started to smell like tea leaves—even if it was once lovely—is too old and should be discarded forthwith.

FATS

Our highly reactionary sentiments on the subject of fats in cooking are elaborated in About Frying in Olive Oil, in the Summer section. All we'll add here is that the flavors of Italian dishes depend very strongly on the varying effects of different cooking fats. Generally, butter is commoner in the north and oil in the south, though crossovers are not unusual. But other fats have their specific purposes and lend their specific flavors to dishes too: especially lard and pancetta and prosciutto fat. As always in Italy, regional differences in cooking practices make emotions run high; a great Neapolitan chef we know says that Tuscans are crazy to cook beans in olive oil; that the true secret of *pasta e fagiole* is that you must cook the beans in lard.

It's a pity that the scientific voodoo of nutritional theory still hasn't reversed its excommunication of lard, as over the years it has recanted on olive oil and even butter. Whatever your convictions, we urge you, in using our recipes, not to assume that corn oil or peanut oil are perfectly good all-purpose cooking fats. Sure, they are—from the purely chemical standpoint. But not if you care about the taste of your food.

OTHER SEASONINGS

God is in the details, said Mies van der Rohe. As with architecture, so it is with cooking. The magic of most Italian recipes is in the use of small quantities of intense or aromatic ingredients of many kinds. Thus, under the heading of "seasonings" can be included:

- Cured meats: chopped salame and prosciutto (see About Prosciutto in the Winter section).
- Cheeses, usually grated (see About Parmigiano in the Winter section).
- Dried funghi porcini (see About Mushrooms in the Fall section).
- Dried peperoncino rosso (See About Peppers in the Fall section).
- Capers, the pungent bud of an exotic-flowered plant, packed in brine or salt and used extensively in southern Italian dishes, often in combination with:
- Olives, green or black, whole or chopped, in dozens of local varieties (though our recipes call most often for Gaetas, a luscious purple-to-black olive grown in a stretch of coastal country between Rome and Naples).

- Anchovies—good varieties of which, packed in salt, are clean and light-fleshed, nothing like the slimy, fishy-smelling morsels rightly abhorred by so many people.
- Garlic—firm, moist, white-fleshed, and not for you to be intimidated by. Garlic's intensity is easily controlled by the state in which you use it: a whole garlic clove cooked in a dish for a long time blends imperceptibly into the background; that same clove chopped and tossed in the pan at the end of cooking dominates the dish.
- Onion, celery, carrot—the first two, at least, indispensable for the *battuto* or *soffrito*, which is a mince of aromatic vegetables (usually including parsley and garlic, sometimes also meat), that is sautéed and used as the base for innumerable pasta sauces and meat dishes.
- Tomato paste—small quantities of which give body and acidity to sauces that might otherwise be fat and flaccid.
- Lemons—the yellow zest even more commonly than the juice.
- Wine and wine vinegar (yes, vinegar in cooking, not just to dress salads).

When you add a seasoning ingredient to a dish is also important in Italian cooking. The difference between, say, basil shredded and stirred into a stew two minutes before serving and whole basil leaves simmered along with the meat and its juices for two hours is highly significant: they're practically two different creatures.

That, in fact, is how Italian cooking controls the effect of many strong flavors, like garlic, anchovy, tomato paste, or peperoncino rosso, but it's equally true of milder-flavored ingredients. It's also one of the reasons that you can have three or four Italian recipes with almost-identical ingredient lists that nevertheless produce dishes of totally different character. Thus, when our recipes say to dress a dish at table with freshly ground pepper, grated parmigiano or pecorino, or olive oil, please don't regard those items as optional condiments, like ketchup on a hamburger. They're important last-minute ingredients of the dish.

HOW THIS BOOK WORKS

The Seasons of the Italian Kitchen is organized in several ways to help you think about these dishes and their place in your meal.

First, and inescapably, we've divided things up according to the four seasons. Each seasonal section highlights the characteristic foods of that time of year and the typical ways of cooking them at that time. The changes of weather not only bring different meats and fishes and vegetables to the Italian table, but they also change the ways Italian cooks go about their preparation. Hence:

- Spring—*Primavera*—evokes the excitement of newly awakened nature—new appetites, an interest in trying new food ideas, nontraditional combinations, experimental preparations. Spring weather lends itself to a broad range of cooking techniques, both stove-top and oven, and our recipes reflect that diversity.
- Summer—*Estate*—being usually a carefree, relaxed time, you'll find mostly simple preparations here—cold dishes, salads, make-aheads for picnics, things to be grilled on an outdoor barbecue, and casual dishes that weekend guests can pitch in and help make after a lazy day at the beach.
- With the return of crisp weather in autumn—*Autunno*—we get back to serious cooking and eating. Interest is rekindled in heartier foods like polenta and gnocchi, roast meats, cheeses, pies. This kind of eating lends itself to more formal entertaining and more elaborate preparations—and so do our recipes.
- Finally comes winter—*Inverno*—with all its ancient atavisms—the time to hunker down, provide, protect, gather around the fire, stoke the human furnace with solid foods: robust soups, stews, large cuts of meat for baking and boiling, and humble cuts like oxtails and tripe. In this section, we emphasize time-honored regional and peasant dishes, together with traditional family holiday fare.

Second, within each season, we present our recipes according to the courses of an Italian meal: antipasto, *primo, secondo, contorno, dolce*. There is a rhythm in Italian dining that differs in some key respects from traditional American service and from the sequence of the classic haute cuisine. A meal in Italy tends to be composed of several courses about equal in size and importance, rather than having one or more minor or introductory courses leading up to a pièce de résistance, a large meat course.

Antipasto roughly corresponds to an hors d'oeuvre, but it may be omitted altogether (especially in home dining) or it may (in restaurants or on festive occasions) be multiplied into what amounts to an elaborate buffet. Antipasto dishes are the wild cards in the deck: sometimes they can be served as secondi, sometimes as light lunches, sometimes as appetizers. The appearance and importance of many Italian dishes—where they occur in the meal and how great a percentage of that meal they constitute—depend not so much on a rigid notion of "correct" dining as on the desires of the diners and the nature of the occasion.

The primo is what non-Italians think of as the essence of Italian cooking, and it's probably the course that Italians as well as non-Italians love most. The primo embraces all the pasta and risotto dishes, all the gnocchi and polenta, minestre and minestrone, even pizza. In its placement after the antipasto, the primo corresponds very loosely to a soup course (and so Italians will never eat soup and pasta at the same meal), but in the Italian repertory the basic idea of soup—good things in a flavorful liquid—has been enlarged to take in all sorts of grains and farinaceous products served with the enhancement of a sauce.

If you were to judge by the ingredients that predominate in them, secondi should be the stars of the Italian meal. This is the course that features the fish or flesh or fowl or the most elaborately prepared dish of the day—but portions tend to be small, as we've said, since the edge has already been taken off most appetites by the primo. Diners used to American service or the progression of the French haute cuisine often find Italian secondi anticlimactic—not because the dishes are uninteresting but because the drama has been evenly spread throughout the meal rather than focused in one spot. French and American fine dining are structured like tragedy, with everything building to one grand moment of revelation. Italian dining is operatic: a great aria can occur anywhere in the meal.

Contorni literally provide the contours of a meal, rounding its sharp corners and filling in its missing links. Contorni are vegetable dishes, and in a formal service they may appear, as salad (which is one of their varieties) always does, after the secondo. Many Italians of the older generation find the common European and American custom of serving several vegetables on the same plate as the meat or fish vulgar, even upsetting. They prefer that the effects of the different foods be kept distinct, with no promiscuous mixing of juices and tastes. This is an extreme example of the Italian passion for presenting the natural flavors of honest ingredients directly, with minimal culinary obfuscation. It's also an evidence of the polymorphous nature of many contorni, which may themselves become the secondi—of a magro Lenten dinner, for instance—or antipasti or luncheon dishes in their own right. Italians esteem vegetables and treat them seriously, and you need look no further for proof than the aesthetic role assigned them in the meal by the name of their course.

Dolci are desserts. They are rarely elaborate, and many are not at all sweet. At home, a meal most often ends with a piece or two of fresh fruit—according to the season, of course—or a fruit salad, a macedonia. Dessert is often preceded, and sometimes replaced, by a cheese course, especially if there is some wine to be finished. In restaurants, dolci may be more elaborate, but they are not often the sugary confections that Americans think of as "Italian pastry." Italians do eat things like that—but usually with a cup of espresso or cappuccino at a midmorning or midafternoon coffee break, very rarely after dinner.

Dinner in Italy features yet one more course, though it is rarely recognized as such: *vino*. Wine in Italy is not regarded as an intoxicant. It is a food, and it goes with food. Actually, it's part of a team, the liquid components of an Italian meal—wine and mineral water. In the simplest eating places, your choices are always binary: *bianco or rosso?* (white or red?) for the wine and *gassata o liscia?* (carbonated or still?) for the water. It is unthinkable that you would dine, however simply or inexpensively, without those two necessary lubricants to complete the flavors and prompt the digestion.

Just how bred-in-the-bone is the necessity of wine with meals in Italy was brought home to us once on our first visit to Pienza, a beautifully preserved Renaissance walled town in Tuscany, in the heart of the Sienese Chianti zone. We had decided to dine at Il Prato, a pleasant-looking rustic trattoria just outside the fifteenth-century city gate. (Clearly, the restaurant had been named "the field" because, originally, that's where it was.)

The entire staff of the establishment proved to be Mamma in the kitchen, Pappa at the bar, a twelve-year-old daughter, and an eight-year-old son. Climbing a steep flight of stairs to the *sala da pranzo*, we found ourselves in sole possession of a sizable dining room. Presently the daughter of the house appeared, an expression of great concentration on her face, menus in her hand, and a bottle of red wine under her arm. As she explained, the mineral water was kept up here but the wine was downstairs, and since we were of course going to want red wine, it was just common sense to save herself an extra trip. She was right, and the wine was lovely.

Italian wines have grown up over centuries with Italian foods, and many of the pairings are exquisite—not matters of finicky expertise, but everyday happy marriages of flavors that are, quite literally, made for each other. Since many Americans are still unfamiliar with Italian wines beyond a narrow (and often stereotyped) range, we've tried to facilitate your exploration of this aspect of Italian dining by providing a wine recommendation with every recipe.

Obviously, seasons in the United States are not the same thing as the seasons in Italy. Indeed, seasons in Minnesota are not the same thing as the seasons in Louisiana, nor is midwinter in Manhattan at all like January in San Diego. Add to those regional differences the differences due to produce shipped here from other countries and often another hemisphere, and the result is—for many of us—an out-of-season availability of some ingredients that comes close to their in-season best. Where that is the case, take advantage of it: the heavens will not crumble if you make a spring dish in the fall or vice versa. The key to dining in an authentically Italian manner is to pick the best-flavored ingredients available to you. It may be midsummer and the height of zucchini season, but if it's been raining for a week, Italian shoppers will pass by the bloated, jade-green ninepins offered in the markets, knowing they'd be buying water rather than flavor. If there is an out-of-season fruiting of raspberries or of wood mushrooms, by all means grab the opportunity for an unexpected pleasure. That is shopping and eating in a spirit truly Italian. We ran into an occasion of that one early June in Rome, when for some inexplicable reason, all the restaurants were displaying baskets of huge, fresh porcini, a mushroom that theoretically doesn't fruit until the fall. (You couldn't miss them. Three steps into the restaurant and your nose would catch their scent, even if your eyes were busy elsewhere.) A serving of those mushrooms cost more than the most expensive meat dishes on the menu, but by the end of the evening the basket was always empty.

One last word on the full-scale Italian meal. No one in Italy eats the full-battery meal all the time, every day. If Italians make a three- or four-course lunch, the odds are their evening meal will be no more than a primo and a salad, or a small antipasto and an equally small secondo, or perhaps even just a pizza. Italian cooking grew out of scarcity: Italy is a land long traveled by armies and by want, and its kitchens have learned to adapt, and its diners have too. Moderation is a lesson bred in the Italian bone, just as enjoyment is, and the acceptance of all good things in their season.

PRIMAVERA

· *Spring* ·

pring is more a state of mind than a calendar event. The first morning of the year that one can step outdoors and feel the air around one lighter and fresher, as if a weight has been lifted, a tightness relaxed—that's spring. That stirring of new life comes to each of us individually, without reference to the date of the vernal equinox or the start of daylight savings time. In the film *Amarcord*, Federico Fellini's lyrical remembrance of his childhood in Rimini, spring arrives on the day that a particular kind of tree opens its seedpods and fills the air with swirling cottony puffs, like dandelion clocks. For cooks, spring may be heralded by something more prosaic—the return of the shad, or the arrival of the first local asparagus—but for cooks and consumers alike, for prosers and for poets, the arrival of spring is always a special time.

That first feeling of spring lasts longer in our mental meteorology than it does in real weather, most years. Few lives today are closely enough tied to the land to keep us aware of the slow awakening of nature that starts deep in the ground and proceeds steadily despite apparent setbacks of raw cold, chill winds, sleet, and freezing rains. But the promise of spring we feel in the air of a rare, mild March day sustains us through the recurring assaults of the next two months. Over the years, memory edits out the ugliness and the chill, leaving a montage of images and scents and associations that become our true, personal experience of spring, as willowy and graceful as a Botticelli goddess.

For the two of us, writing this book about the seasons in Italy, spring evokes many memories, some as simple as the sharp, unforgettable taste of the first, minuscule, tart-sweet wild strawberries of the year, others more complex, such as . . .

- Emerging from a nightmare drive through the Passo del Bracco in the coastal mountains of Liguria—blinding rain, dense fog, tortuous switchbacks, mud and rock slides, sheer drop-offs with no guardrails—into a narrow, nameless valley with the sun dazzling rain diamonds off the budding tree branches; the carefully terraced hills wearing a smooth pelt of palest green under a latticework of newly sprouted grapevines; irises blooming in every cranny of the low stone walls edging the road; and in the sky, rainbows shimmering in the fast-dissolving mists—an Emerald City of Oz.

- Cutting short a stay in our normally beloved Tuscany, after too many days of lowering gray clouds and bitter winds blowing down the damp stone walls of fortified medieval hill towns; running north, up into the Apennines and then down into the broad plains and, at last, warm sunshine in Bologna; delighting in that city's broad avenues, blessedly flat after the vertiginous towns of Tuscany, alive with lightly clad citizens out for the afternoon *passeggiata;* joining them ourselves and happening on the public gardens, where the resolutely communist city government was sponsoring a *mostra di bastardoni* (a mutt show) as a rejoinder to the prestigious national dog show opening that day down in aristocratic, frigid Siena.

- Reading, with the ingrained skepticism of New Yorkers, from Waverley Root's *The Food of Italy*: "If you should be lucky enough to find yourself in the province of Modena between April 10 and 20, leave the Emilian Way at Castelfranco and strike southward to Vignola. . . . You will pass through a sea of rosy cherry blossoms extending in every direction as far as you can see." It was April 12, we were en route to Modena, and the autostrada exit was just ahead. Prepared to be underwhelmed, we turned off—and found ourselves, astonished, in the very fantasyland of the book's description: mile after mile of country road so billowing with flowering cherry trees, you had to laugh from the pure joy of the sight. When we stopped the car to take pictures, the scent swirled around us and the only sound we could hear was the buzzing of bees.

For us, April in Paris has nothing on April in Venice—say, on a fair spring Saturday, walking from Piazza San Marco along the Fondamenta dei Schiavoni and the inner edge of the lagoon far enough to be out of the main tourist crush, sitting outdoors at a table under a white umbrella, eating *mollecche* (tiny soft-shell crabs) and drinking a pitcher of local Sauvignon blanc or Friulian Tocai, watching the sun sparkling on the waves from passing gondolas and motorboats. On such a day, in such a setting, the food doesn't even have to be sublime (good thing, since sublimity is as uncommon in the waterside restaurants of Venice as in those of Coney Island)—the essence of the season transforms whatever is on your plate and in your glass.

Those mollecche, however, were pretty sublime. They're a local specialty, taken from the lagoon for only a brief period in spring, when they measure no more than 1½ inches across the shell. When you enter a restaurant, you may see them inconspicuously displayed among the other, larger denizens of the lagoon—crustaceans like spider crabs and mantis shrimps, *seppie* and squid—and you can be forgiven if you think you're looking at nothing more than a large bowl of fiddler crabs, probably the pets or playthings of the restaurant's children. Mollecche are always batter-fried, served in large mounds, and eaten in one or two bites, like Cajun popcorn. We've been told time and again that they are in season only twenty days out of the whole year, but we've encountered them so often on early- and late-season visits to Venice—unlike the punctual cherry blossoms of Vignola—that we've come to suspect some gastronomical romancing on the subject of these tiny creatures. One of the first principles earnest foreign travelers in Italy need to grasp is the universal force of an adage that Italians use to ease the sting of brute fact: *Se non è vero, è ben trovato*—which means something like "Even if it isn't true, it's a nice idea."

But there's nothing untrue about the Italian passion for foods in their season. Unlike the United States—where we can now get fresh raspberries nine months of the year and hardly ever eat them because they're juiceless sugary jujubes 98 percent of the time—Italy revels in the passing pleasures of briefly available feasts. On a wine writers' trip to the Piedmont one year, just around Easter, the hosts of every meal for a week proudly set before us the region's traditional Easter specialty, *capretto*—kid. Twice a day, for lunch and dinner, the delicious but extraordinarily rich meat appeared, grilled, spit-roasted, baked, or braised. By the end, Diane was sure she was growing a beard and Tom could feel his feet turning into cloven hoofs. The Italians on the trip adored every minute of it.

Every food purveyor in Italy, from market stalls to three-star restaurants, takes equal pride in offering *primizie*, the season's first new vegetables. They come in honored procession from asparagus to zucchini, through peas, fava beans, haricot beans, spinach, carrots, and all the rest. These are not the rock-hard, unborn baby vegetables with which the no-longer-nouvelle cuisine assiduously decorated dinner plates: in Italy, primizie are meltingly tender, bursting with rarefied flavors—flavors you haven't tasted since this time last year. So you feast on them as often as you can, in as many ways as you can contrive, until the reawakened craving is satisfied and the palate turns eagerly to the next new thing. In Rome, in May, restaurant staff will hardly let you order a meal that doesn't include a dish of *puntarelli*—pale, curling shoots of a variety of chicory, crisped in ice water, drained, and served with an anchovy-laden vinaigrette.

An equal passion exists throughout Italy in spring for *insalata campagnola*—weed salad, we affectionately call it. A mixed green salad of the earliest shoots of wild greens (of which dandelion is about the only familiar species), tender and remarkably flavorful, seasoned with the lightest touches of salt, extra-virgin olive oil, and lemon, this is probably the best salad of the year, and it epitomizes perfectly both the Italian passion for green, growing things in their season and the reasons for it. In the countryside, every restaurant has its own special mixture of piquant leaves, plucked wild from the nearby fields. Driving through Italy, you'll see people of all ages, off in the distance and right beside the road, rooting out bunches of their favorite early greens. Once, after being detoured off the autostrada for the fifth time with no indication of any work being done on the sections of road we weren't allowed on, we came to the conclusion that the superhighways are periodically closed to allow the locals to clamber along the embankments picking salads.

The same passion animates the Italian appetite for spring's greatest green, asparagus. Italian preferences run decidedly in favor of the thinnest stalks, with the almost grasslike wild asparagus stealing all the attention when it makes its brief appearance in the market. When it comes to white asparagus, however, Italian taste reverses itself, and the great, fat, white asparagus of Bassano becomes practically an object of adoration. How much of that is due to its flavor, which *is* delicious, and how much to its undeniably obscene appearance, which affords endless opportunity for ribald remarks, is something that Italians and tourists decide according to their own priorities.

By the arrival of asparagus and insalata campagnola, rather than by the thermometer or the calendar, Italy knows spring has come at last. Italians pay little attention to the thermometer, or any other mechanical device, anyway—which is why in many parts of Italy devices such as traffic lights and even lane markers remain (in practice if not in law) advisory. During our first trip to Rome, we became mired in a large group of tourists at the edge of the Piazza Venezia's roiling sea of traffic, waiting docilely for the traffic light to change in our favor. Behind us a small, impatient, distinguished-looking, grandfatherly Italian muttered continuously in a stage sotto voce: "It's stupid and sheeplike to let a machine tell you what to do."

There is a national faith in a natural order—a proposition somewhat suspect on close analysis and from which Italians happily retreat whenever it fails, as when spring weather is bad, to more reliable ritual order, which to the long-inured Italian mind is second nature anyhow. So for all practical purposes, spring begins on Easter, whenever Easter happens to fall, and spring dining begins with the Easter feast—endless variations on *torta pasqualina*, early peas, the tiniest artichokes, spit-roasted milk-fed lambs and kids of a tininess and a tenderness and a savor to be remembered all year round. Lent is over, winter is over, the lean times are past: life begins again.

Leggerezza is the Italian word for that lightness of spirit that comes after the frozen weight of a long winter has at last lifted. Leggerezza appears with the mildness of the air, the ability to spend more time outdoors, the fresh new flavors available to the palate after a long diet of root vegetables and thick stews. All is crisp and juicy again, charged with "the force that through the green fuse drives the flower." The dishes that appear on our tables now should be similarly light and delicate, preparations that joyfully renew our acquaintance with each returning food. This season of new energy is a good time to entertain friends, experiment with new dishes, shake the kinks out of long-unused culinary muscles. We chose the recipes that follow to illustrate the leggerezza of spring—with occasional allowance for its relapses into surly winter.

ANTIPASTI

Throughout the year in Italy, antipasti come in innumerable guises. Seasonal specialties there certainly are, but equally relished are the year-round favorites that most Italians can happily eat five days out of seven, twelve months out of twelve.

Prosciutto, for instance, must be the most popular antipasto anywhere in Italy, any time of year. Following close behind are innumerable other types of cured meats: salame, mortadella, bresaola, culatella, sopressata, capicolla, finocchiana . . . and on and on and on. A plate with a few slices of these, perhaps some pickled vegetables *sott'olio* or *sott'aceto*, a piece of bruschetta (country bread toasted in the oven, rubbed with garlic, and topped with olive oil)—these signify the start of millions of good Italian meals in every season.

Among the seasonal specialties, vegetables offer the greatest scope for the antipasto maker's art. Italian cooks play infinite variations on the theme of fresh greens of the season—asparagus, artichokes, spinach, freshly dug onions. The recipes in this section showcase a few techniques: vegetables cooked alone, in combination with other vegetables or meat/fish/eggs/cheeses, as fillings for several different kinds of pastries—including one Eastertide extravaganza—and as topping for a savory country bread. We also offer a preparation of sea scallops that, while not strictly seasonal, definitely sings on the palate like the first beautiful day of spring.

These dishes are not (we feel it incumbent on us to repeat) what a "typical" Italian family would have for antipasto at an everyday meal. They're considerably more elaborate and more time-consuming for the cook than laying out a few slices of salame and some olives and bread. On the other hand, nobody says you have to make our recipes exclusively for antipasto. The courses of an Italian meal are, as we've remarked, extremely flexible; even in quite fancy restaurants in Italy, nobody would blink an eye if you chose to make an entire meal on one or more antipasto selections. Many of these dishes work beautifully on their own as brunch, lunch, supper, or buffet items. So taste our recipes on your mind's tongue and use them in the way that best pleases you.

ASPARAGUS AND PROSCIUTTO ROLLS

Asparagi fritti al prosciutto

FOR 4 SERVINGS:

*T*his simple combination of ingredients yields a collection of quite rich and elegant little bundles, all golden in their egg-and-flour crusts. You can make the rolls up in advance, but coat and sauté them *al momento,* which is to say just before serving.

In Italy, this dish would ideally be made with the fat, white asparagus of Bassano, which are prized for their soft texture and lush flavor. It's still delightful with green asparagus, even with thin ones: just pair up two in each prosciutto-wrapped package. In addition to being delicious in itself, this preparation has the advantage of being quite amenable to wine, which can sometimes be a problem with asparagus dishes.

Here's a useful trick to know about trimming asparagus without losing any of the tender stem or leaving on any of the tough, stringy base: Don't cut, snap. Hold a spear close to the bottom and begin exerting pressure with your fingers to bend it. Move gradually toward the tip, continuing the pressure. The spear will snap cleanly right at the point where the tender part begins.

A light, acidic white, such as a Frascati or Verdicchio or Pinot grigio. For more important occasions, an Arneis (Ceretto's Blangé, for instance) or a Sauvignon (Abbazzia di Rosazzo, Borgo Conventi, Gradnik, Jermann, or Puiatti).

16 thick spears asparagus (about 1¼ pounds), washed and trimmed	*2 eggs, beaten together*
	Flour for dredging
Salt	*1 tablespoon olive oil*
6 tablespoons butter	*16 small slices prosciutto (about 6 ounces)*

Bring a kettle of water to a boil. Lay out the asparagus spears in a pan, pour on boiling water to cover generously and add ½ teaspoon salt. Adjust heat to maintain a simmer and cook uncovered until the spears are barely tender, about 10 minutes (less time if the spears are thin). In a small pan, melt 3 tablespoons of the butter. Drizzle it over the asparagus.

Put the beaten eggs on one plate and flour for dredging on another. In a skillet, heat the remaining butter with the olive oil. Wrap each asparagus spear in a slice of prosciutto. Roll the bundles in the flour, dip them in the egg, and sauté until golden, about 2 minutes a side. Drain on paper towels and serve at once. ■

Carciofi
About Artichokes

Considered aesthetically, artichokes are as unlikely a gustatory object as oysters. Who would eat an overgrown thistle? Yet we do, and Italians more than most of us. They have made the artichoke a delicacy and a staple, with a repertoire of recipe roles from supporting ingredient to culinary star performer.

According to Waverley Root, artichokes probably originated in Sicily. They were important in Saracen-influenced cooking in the Middle Ages, and spread north through the Kingdom of Naples and on up the peninsula. Another of Italy's gastronomical gifts to the world, they were introduced to the French court by Catherine de' Medici in the sixteenth century, where they were promptly deemed to be aphrodisiac and declared improper for feminine consumption. Catherine's own passion for them was one of the many scandals of that lady's reign as queen of France.

Today, the characteristic tall thistle leaves of a row of artichoke plants are one of the commonest sights in kitchen gardens throughout Italy, and they are cultivated on a large scale in the south. If you happen to be driving to the archaeological site of Paestum, south of Naples, along local highways rather than the autostrada, you first catch sight of the pure, Ionic symmetries of the millennia-old temples rising like a mirage on the horizon behind acre upon acre of artichoke fields.

The varieties of artichokes grown in Italy are different from ours. There, they don't look so much like prickly softballs, but are more elongated, teardrop- or tulip-shaped, like the flower buds that they are. All the varieties are tenderer than ours, to the point that when young and fresh they can be eaten raw in their entirety. Don't try that with an American globe artichoke unless some of your recent ancestors were goats! On the other hand, one of the common Italian varieties protects its tender flesh with spines—claws, actually—of a size to put the prickliest American 'choke to shame. But there's also a spineless variety called *mammola*, which means violet; whether so named to suggest the tender spring flower or to describe the color of the foliage, we don't know.

One of the reliable pleasures of street markets all over Italy is the artichoke sellers. Great sheaves of freshly cut, yard-long leafy stalks are brought in, often on handcarts. The artichokes are cut off as they're sold, and there's always a peasant grandmother or grandfather sitting on a stool off to one side, imperturbably trimming some down and dropping them in buckets of water laced with lemons, to sell ready-prepared. One day, we timed an ancient farm woman who was using a knife that looked suitable for sticking pigs: from stalk to bucket, each artichoke took about 30 seconds.

Artichokes are eaten in every conceivable way in Italy. Rome boasts the two most famous artichoke preparations: *carciofi alla giudia* are large artichokes deep-fried in olive oil in a way that opens them out into elegant bronze chrysanthemums, and *carciofi alla romana* are whole artichokes braised in olive oil, garlic, and wild mint. The latter are cooked and served standing on their heads, complete with graceful (and tasty) long stems. Pasta sauces made from sliced artichokes, oil, and garlic are also common and delicious. (Our previous cookbook, *La Tavola Italiana,* has recipes for both deep-fried and braised artichokes in the Roman manner, as well as a *penne con carciofi* as made in one of Rome's oldest trattorias, La Campana.)

Farther south in Italy, large artichokes, trimmed only enough to sit flat, are often baked, with or without a stuffing. Served hot, cold, or anywhere in between, they are eaten with the fingers, one or more diners plucking off a few leaves at a time and pulling them over the teeth to scrape off the succulent flesh. Italian children have as much fun with artichokes prepared this way as American kids do with corn on the cob, and Italian adults are only a short way behind them in enjoyment. Smaller artichokes, or the pared-down hearts of larger ones, are combined with other vegetables in sautés or stuffings. And everywhere, artichoke hearts are pickled in vinegar or preserved in oil for eating in or as antipasti. (We offer a number of these preparations in *La Tavola Italiana* also.)

It's easy to see how artichokes became a staple of peasant cooking. The unexpected fleshiness of these easily grown thistle flowers takes on all the richness of meat in any preparation with oil. Additionally, cooking artichokes with oil makes them much more accommodating to wine than they are when simply steamed or boiled and served with a vinegar-based dressing.

Two difficulties in reproducing carciofi recipes in America are the amount of whittling down our leathery artichokes require before they are completely edible and the length of time they are usually off the stem before they reach our stores. (Fortunately, the first disadvantage tends to at least partially cancel out the second.) Paring artichokes also leaves a nearly indelible brown stain on the fingers, but we've developed a neat way to avoid that. You simply buy at a drugstore or medical supply store—or beg from an obliging family physician—a few disposable examination gloves. You can also use the plastic gloves supplied with home hair coloring kits, but medical gloves fit snugly for more ease in handling a knife, and they're tough enough to reuse over and over. Of course, your doctor may look at you oddly when you first make the request; but ours finally decided it was only to be expected from such food-crazy people, and he now laughingly obliges whenever we need a fresh supply.

The good thing about artichokes in America is the fact that, in addition to the large globes, it's becoming increasingly common in springtime to get tiny ones—eight, twelve, or even fifteen to the pound. These require a lot less trimming to get down to full edibility, and there's proportionately less waste as well. Because of that convenience, we specify small artichokes in all the recipes in this book; large ones can always be substituted. For that matter, if you're pressed for time or your market has only ancient, wizened artichokes the day you need some for a dish, we wouldn't be utterly horrified if you used frozen artichoke hearts. It's a vegetable that stands up well to freezing. A 9-ounce package of frozen hearts is the equivalent of 1¼ to 1½ pounds of small whole artichokes.

To prepare tiny artichokes for cooking: Have ready a bowl of cold water acidulated with lemon juice. (Quantities needn't be precise: the juice of one lemon for each one to two quarts of water is a general guide.) Take an artichoke and cut off its stem. Bend back and snap off the hard, green outer leaves, continuing until you reach the soft, pale yellow or green interior cone. Slice off about the upper third of this. With a vegetable parer, peel the base of the artichoke down to the white flesh. Drop the finished artichoke in the acidulated water until ready to use. Drain on paper towels and, if they are not to be kept whole, slice the artichokes vertically to the width desired. (If your artichokes were largeish—say, only eight to the pound—a wise precaution is to halve them and check on the size of the fuzzy choke. If it's not soft and inconspicuous, dig it out with a paring knife.)

To prepare large artichokes for cooking: If you live next door to an artichoke field and can have as many as you want, you can follow the exact procedure described above for tiny artichokes. However, you lose a lot of flesh from the discarded leaves that way. Here's the technique for preserving all the edible parts: Pull off any small, vestigial leaves near the stem. (Cut off the stem or not, depending on your recipe. If you do, remember that the stem is extremely tasty. Just peel it and add it to the pot.) Starting from the base of the artichoke and working around the circle of the leaves' natural growth, take a leaf and bend it in half backward, using the thumb of your other hand to brace the leaf base. Then pull down toward the stem until the upper half and some of the tough outer part of the lower half of the leaf snaps off.

This technique may take a while to get the feel of, but it is easier to do than to describe. The idea is to strip off the tough outer part of the leaf, leaving a ragged but tender base. Continue until you reach the inner, softer leaves.

Cut off the top third of the leaf cone. Open out the center of the artichoke so you can see down to the heart. Pull off the thin, cellophanelike leaves at the center and use a teaspoon to scrape out the fuzzy choke, taking care not to gouge into the tender bottom. Peel all the hard green parts off the artichoke bottom with a vegetable parer, rubbing the exposed parts, if you like, with a cut lemon to keep them from darkening. Then drop the artichoke into a bowl of acidulated water until ready to use.

One other interesting characteristic of the artichoke is its reputed digestive properties. Italians believe this so firmly that they consume large quantities of an *amaro* (a bitter digestive liqueur) made from artichokes, called Cynar. There must be some truth to the claim, because artichokes contain an enzyme that will curdle milk. A type of rennet derived from artichokes is widely used in cheese making. Perhaps this is why artichokes are often difficult to match with wine—though, as we remarked before, cooking them with olive oil seems to go a long way toward nullifying those wine-antagonistic qualities.

ARTICHOKES STUFFED WITH TUNA

Carciofini ripieni all'abruzzese

FOR 4 SERVINGS:

A white wine of medium body,
such as Lacryma Christi
bianco, or Greco di Tufo, or
even Tocai.

*I*f you've read the preceding essay on artichokes, we hope you'll agree they're a wonderful vegetable, though sometimes a bother to work with. Their flavor rewards, however, always justify any effort they require, and this tasty country recipe is a case in point. Carefully shaped artichokes are stuffed with a mixture of tuna, capers, parsley, and anchovies and then braised in olive oil and a little water to yield a dish that is at once mild and robust, completely edible (if you've trimmed them properly), and very congenial to wine, with which artichokes (like asparagus) often fight.

Select young, fleshy specimens and proceed fearlessly to follow the directions for trimming them. The first time you do it, the process will probably drive you crazy, so allow yourself plenty of time. It's not difficult, but—as with so many techniques in cookery—there is a certain amount of unavoidable apprentice time you have to put in, until you suddenly find that you now do easily a procedure that used to take you forever.

Use only dark-meat tuna packed in olive oil; anything else will result in a blander, less interesting dish. And take note: this is one of those chameleon antipasti that can serve equally well as a luncheon or light supper dish in its own right.

8 medium artichokes, about ¼
    pound apiece
Juice of 1 lemon, stirred into a
    bowl of cold water
One 6½-ounce can imported
    Italian tuna, packed in olive oil
8 anchovy fillets, chopped

2 tablespoons capers, drained and
    rinsed
1 tablespoon finely chopped
    flat-leaf Italian parsley
1 clove garlic
2 to 3 tablespoons olive oil

Prepare the artichokes as directed on page 22, leaving enough leaf wall on them to enclose the stuffing later. Drop them into the acidulated water and leave them there until ready to use. (This is one case in which it's desirable to have them absorb a little water.)

In a small bowl, mix together the tuna and any oil from the can, the anchovies, capers, and parsley. Put the garlic clove through a press and add it to the mixture (or pulse everything in a food processor). Remove the artichokes from the water and stand them upside down to drain. Fill their central cavities with the tuna stuffing.

Oil a heavy-bottomed casserole just large enough to hold the artichokes snugly. Set them in it and drizzle the olive oil over them and onto the bottom of the pan. If the artichokes have not absorbed much water from their soaking, add a tablespoon or two of water. Cover the casserole tightly and set over medium heat. Cook 45 minutes, or until the artichokes are tender. Check the pan from time to time; if all the water has evaporated and the 'chokes are frying, add a few teaspoons of water.

When they are done, lift the artichokes out onto a serving dish. If any water is left in the pot, boil it down rapidly until only flavored oil is left. Pour it over the artichokes and serve, allowing two artichokes to a portion. ∎

STOVE-TOP ARTICHOKE TART

Pizza 're carcioffole

FOR 6 SERVINGS:

A hearty white or young, soft red. Corvo bianco or rosso, Lacryma Christi bianco, Avellanio, Montepulciano d'Abruzzo—all will taste fine.

*T*his is a pizza only in the most generic sense. It's actually a covered pastry tart "baked" in a heavy cast-iron pan on top of the stove—an ingenious technique indigenous to the south of Italy, where "oven" used to mean a free-standing stone structure, fired by wood. An oven was not within the means of every peasant family; and if you did have one, the process of heating it was far too elaborate to use for cooking a single small dish. Sometimes you took your dish to the baker, who would let you use his oven after the day's bread was done. Otherwise, you made do with such heat sources as you had.

The dough for this kind of tart is very simple—clearly the invention of poverty and necessity. Some comments on working with it follow this recipe. Many different fillings can be used. Here, the combination of artichoke, cheese, and salami produces an aromatic and mouth-filling result. This dish is a real hunger satisfier—and it's also very useful as a recycler of leftover bits of cheese or salami. Try your own variants with young pecorino or provolone or Asiago instead of Swiss; use ends of salami or soppressata or even scraps of prosciutto or capocollo for the meat.

FOR THE PASTRY:

2 cups all-purpose flour

½ teaspoon salt

2 tablespoons olive oil

FOR THE FILLING:

3 eggs

Salt

Freshly ground black pepper

1 to 1¼ pounds small artichokes, prepared as directed on page 22

and sliced ¼ to ½ inch thick

3½ ounces Swiss cheese, grated

2 ounces salami, minced

1 to 2 tablespoons olive oil

Mix the flour, ½ teaspoon salt, and 2 tablespoons olive oil in a bowl. Gradually stir in about ½ cup cold water, until the mixture comes together into a soft dough. Knead the dough for a moment, wrap it in waxed paper, and put it in the refrigerator for at least 30 minutes.

In a large bowl, beat the eggs; season lightly with salt and generously with pepper. Mix in the artichokes, cheese, and salami.

Take the dough from the refrigerator and divide it into two slightly unequal pieces. On a lightly floured work surface, roll the smaller piece into a 10-inch circle and the larger into an 11-inch circle, each about ⅛ inch thick. Oil a well-seasoned 9-inch cast-iron skillet with the remaining olive oil and fit the larger dough circle into it. (See next page for details.) Spread the artichoke mixture evenly over the dough. Set the second circle of dough on top, pressing the edges of the two circles together to seal them. Fold and crimp the edges against the rim of the skillet, then gently loosen them from the pan to discourage sticking.

Set the skillet over medium-high heat for 2 minutes, then lower heat to very low and cook the tart 15 minutes. Invert a plate on top of the skillet, grip plate and skillet firmly at either side (using potholders!), and flip them. Replace the skillet on the stove and film the bottom with a little more oil if necessary. Slide the tart off the plate and back into the skillet. Continue cooking another 15 minutes on the other side.

When the tart is done, the crust should be crisp and lightly browned. Slide the tart onto a plate and let it cool 15 minutes before serving. Any leftovers will still be good the next day, but after that they begin to go downhill. ■

About Stove-top Tart Dough

If you're an old hand at pastry making, the amount of dough these stove-top tart recipes produce may not seem like enough for the size of tart we describe. In fact, it's ample: you'll have extra if you treat it right. The dough has to be rolled very thin, and it's elastic enough to get there. Just go slowly. Roll it, and if it sullenly pulls back, let it rest a few minutes, then continue. Pick it up and stretch it over the backs of your hands like strudel or pizza dough. It's not one of those delicate pastries that toughen if you handle them too much. On the contrary: if you don't get it thin enough, the resulting pastry will be coarse and dull.

Roll out both pieces of dough before fitting the bottom one into the pan, so you can take your time and get the dough as thin as possible. Pick it up and hold it up to a light and you'll see the thick parts, where a little working with your fingers will loosen it up and let it stretch more.

When you put the first round of dough in the oiled pan, it will try to slink down, but just hook it over the rim and pinch it with your fingers if necessary to keep it in place. Firm the filling down evenly, and then lay the second round of dough snugly over it. Push and pull it around until there's enough at the edges to pinch top and bottom dough together firmly. Then take a little knife and cut off all but ¼ inch of the joined rims. Flatten them against the side of the pan and fold them over once, just to be sure of a good seal. Then run your hand under the tart and loosen all around. Pat it back in shape in the pan and put it on the heat.

Incidentally, the pastry rarely browns evenly. Splotchiness is one of its rustic charms.

STOVE-TOP ONION TART

Pizza 're cepodde

FOR 6 SERVINGS:

lease see the comments on stove-top tarts on page 26. This recipe adds to the basic dough a sprightly grating of lemon rind, which contrasts nicely with the lush sweetness of the onion filling. If you don't have sweet mild onions, like Bermudas or Vidalias, put the peeled onion rings in a bowl of ice water in the refrigerator for a few hours to draw out some of their bite. Like its companion artichoke tart, this one makes a good supper dish: precede it with a few slices of salami and accompany it with a salad, and you've got a complete light meal. It's also good the next day—if any survives that long.

A dry white with good fruit and good acidity, such as a Sauvignon blanc, or more simply, a Verdicchio or Soave.

FOR THE PASTRY:

2 cups all-purpose flour

½ teaspoon salt

1 teaspoon grated lemon rind

2 tablespoons olive oil

FOR THE FILLING:

1 pound mild sweet onions, thinly sliced

3 tablespoons olive oil

1 egg

2 tablespoons freshly grated parmigiano

¼ teaspoon salt

Freshly ground black pepper

Start by making the pastry:

Put the flour, salt, lemon rind, and olive oil into the bowl of an electric mixer and mix well. With the machine running, add about ½ cup cold water by tablespoonfuls, until the mixture comes together into a soft dough. Knead the dough for a moment, wrap it in waxed paper, and put it in the refrigerator for at least 30 minutes.

Then sauté the onions:

(Drain the onions if they have been in ice water and dry them in a clean dish towel.) In a large skillet, heat the olive oil. Add the onions and sauté over medium heat, turning often, until they are soft and lightly golden—about 15 minutes. This can be done an hour or two in advance.

Make the tart:

Take the dough out of the refrigerator ½ hour before ready to use. In a small bowl, beat the egg with the cheese, salt, and a generous grinding of pepper. Divide the dough into two slightly unequal pieces. On a lightly floured work surface, roll the smaller piece into a 10-inch circle and the larger into an 11-inch circle, each about ⅛ inch thick.

Oil a well-seasoned 9-inch cast-iron skillet and fit the larger dough circle into it. (See page 28 for details.) Spread the sautéed onions over the surface of the dough and pour on the egg-cheese mixture. Set the second circle of dough on top, pressing the edges of the two circles together to seal them. Fold and crimp the edges against the rim of the skillet, then gently loosen them from the pan to discourage sticking.

Set the skillet over medium-high heat for 2 minutes, then lower heat to very low and cook the tart 10 minutes. Invert a plate on top of the skillet, grip plate and skillet firmly at either side (using potholders), and flip them. Replace the skillet on the stove and film the bottom with a little more oil if necessary. Slide the tart off the plate and back into the skillet. Continue cooking another 10 minutes on the other side.

When the tart is done, the crust should be crisp and lightly browned. Slide the tart onto a plate and let it cool at least 15 minutes before serving. It's good warm or at room temperature. ■

PARMESAN CHEESE FLAN

Flan al parmigiano

FOR 6 TO 8 SERVINGS:

T his is a sort-of-quiche, sort-of-tart, filled with a rich cheese custard. Its mild yet rich and savory flavor is assertive enough to stand up to a decent red wine. As an antipasto, one flan is ample for eight because of its richness. With all its cream, eggs, and cheese, this is not a dish for those who are nervous about cholesterol—though, as science has finally, if grudgingly, come to admit, red wine does wonders in ameliorating the potential harm.

In contrast to the sturdy dough used in the stove-top tarts earlier in this section, the dough for this flan is a fragile pasta frolla, its uncooked stickiness requiring a delicate touch. See page 108 for some observations about handling pasta frolla.

Any not-too-austere red wine will match well here—Barbera, Castel del Monte, young Chianti, Dolcetto, Etna rosso, Lacryma Christi rosso, Montepulciano d'Abruzzo, Valpolicella: these are only some of the possibilities.

FOR THE PASTRY:

2¼ cups all-purpose flour

¼ teaspoon salt

12 tablespoons (1½ sticks) chilled

unsalted butter, cut in small
pieces

1 egg yolk

FOR THE FILLING:

1 cup heavy cream

1 cup milk

4 tablespoons butter

½ teaspoon salt

Freshly grated nutmeg

Freshly ground black pepper

⅓ cup all-purpose flour

3 eggs and the extra white from the
pastry

5 ounces parmigiano, freshly
grated (about 1⅔ cups)

To make the pastry shell:

In a large bowl, combine the flour and salt. Add the butter and work it with a pastry blender, two knives, or your fingers to make a coarse meal. In a small bowl, beat the egg yolk with 5 tablespoons cold water. Make a well in the center of the flour mixture, pour in the egg, and mix gradually into a dough. Use another tablespoon of water if necessary. As soon as the dough holds together, stop handling it. Wrap it in waxed paper and chill in the refrigerator for 30 minutes.

Preheat the oven to 400°F. Remove the dough from the refrigerator and roll it between sheets of waxed paper into a circle ⅛ inch thick. Delicately peel off the paper and fit the dough into a 9½-inch tart pan, building up the edges about ½ inch above the rim of the pan. Prick the dough in several places with a fork.

Butter a piece of aluminum foil and fit it over the dough. Fill the pan with pie weights or dried beans and bake 15 minutes. Remove the weights and foil, prick the pastry again, and bake 7 minutes more. Cool the pastry shell on a rack but don't unmold it.

To make the filling and bake:
In a nonreactive pot, combine the cream and milk. Add the butter, salt, a grating of nutmeg, and a few grindings of pepper, and bring the mixture to a simmer. Off heat, sift on the flour a little at a time and beat vigorously with a spoon or whisk to obtain a smooth cream. Transfer the cream to a large bowl and stir briefly to cool it.

One at a time, separate the eggs and beat the yolks into the cream. Then beat in the cheese. In another bowl, beat the egg whites until they form soft peaks. Fold them into the cream mixture.

Preheat the oven to 400°F. Fill the pastry shell with the cream mixture and set it in the oven. Bake 1 hour, or until the filling has set. Start checking after 30 minutes, and if the surface is browning too fast, lay a piece of foil over it. When a knife blade inserted into the middle of the filling comes out clean, the flan is done. Remove it from the oven, let it cool on a rack, and serve either while still somewhat warm or at room temperature. ■

EASTER TART

Torta pasqualina

FOR 6 TO 8 SERVINGS:

Another savory tart, covered this time, and using multiple layers of thin, flaky pastry. Essentially, torta pasqualina is an elaborate Eastertime version of the everyday *pizza rustica*, a hearty country tart of ricotta and various meats (salami, prosciutto, etc). The whole eggs cooked within the Easter tart invoke the traditional symbolism of rebirth—a motif also represented by the fresh greens in the filling—while its overall richness signals the long-awaited return of hearty eating after the rigors of the Lenten fast.

The version we give here is from Genoa, and it's a showpiece: each carefully cut wedge should show a vivid cross section of thin pastry, green stuffing, and bull's-eyes of egg white, with or without yolk. Working with the pastry for this dish is a bit complicated, but it's not at all difficult—and the use of frozen phyllo or strudel dough (a shortcut now employed all over Italy) dramatically reduces the labor involved.

Y

A superior white wine is called for here. Try Pomino bianco, Fiano di Avellino, Pinot bianco, or an excellent Tocai (e.g., Livio Felluga, Puiatti, or Russiz Superiore).

1 pound greens, any combination of Swiss chard, escarole, spinach, or beet tops
Salt
7 eggs, in all
1 teaspoon dried marjoram
5 tablespoons freshly grated parmigiano

1 pound ricotta
½ cup olive oil, approximately
1 package (1 pound) phyllo or strudel pastry leaves
2 tablespoons butter
Freshly ground black pepper

Trim and wash the greens. Put them in a large pot with only the water adhering to the leaves. Add ½ teaspoon salt, cover, and cook until tender, 7 to 10 minutes. Drain the greens in a colander and spray with cold water to cool. Squeeze them by the handful to remove most of their liquid, then chop them fine.

In a large bowl, beat together 3 of the eggs. Beat in the marjoram, 4 tablespoons of the parmigiano, and 1 teaspoon salt. Add the chopped greens and mix thoroughly, then add the ricotta and mix again.

Preheat the oven to 375°F. Put the olive oil in a small bowl. Using a pastry brush (or your fingers), oil the bottom and sides of an 8-inch springform pan. Unwrap the phyllo pastry leaves. As they are extremely fragile and dry out fast, keep them covered with a damp towel except for the pieces you're working with at the moment.

Take a whole pastry leaf (approximately 13 by 17 inches) and line the oiled pan with it, letting the excess hang over the edge. Lightly brush the entire leaf with oil. Place 3 more leaves in the pan in the same manner, oiling each one.

Count out 10 more leaves, lay them one on top of another, cut them in half and stack them again. Using an 8-inch cake pan or a circle of paper as a guide, cut out 20 circles of pastry. One at a time, layer 10 circles in the bottom of the pan, brushing the top of each one with oil.

Spread the greens-and-ricotta filling on top of the pastry. Make 4 deep hollows in the filling and put ¼ tablespoon butter in each. Break an egg into each hollow, being careful to keep the yolks intact. Sprinkle the eggs with salt, pepper, and the remaining parmigiano.

Gently layer 10 more circles of pastry on top of the filling, brushing each with oil as before. Cut the remaining tablespoon of butter into 6 to 8 bits and lay them around the edge of the pan. Gather up the overlapping pastry from the bottom layers and fold it in, enclosing the butter. Brush the top of the pie with oil.

Place the springform pan in a shallow baking dish and set it in the oven. Bake 1½ hours. If the top becomes too brown toward the end of the baking, cover it loosely with foil. Remove the torta pasqualina from the oven to a rack and let it cool in its pan before unmolding. Serve at room temperature. ∎

PLAIN SCHIACCIATA

Schiacciata

*S*chiacciata is the Tuscan and Umbrian name for a flattish
bread that is known throughout most of Italy as focaccia. There are
many variations on the basic dough—in some parts of the south
they use potatoes in it—and endless elaborations of its toppings,
since it's a terrific medium for all sorts of flavors. But don't let that
make you overlook the fact that the basic bread is also perfectly nice
by itself.

Because it is so easy to work with and bakes so quickly, schiacciata is a year-round dish, with different toppings or fillings mark-
ing the progress of the seasons. It doesn't need to be baked directly
on the stone like a pizza, though you can do that if you have a pizza
stone. If you use a pan, a metal one with separate rim and bottom
is handy for unmolding. Schiacciata can be eaten warm from the
oven or at room temperature. It keeps well, freezes well, reheats
well, and will partner any wine—altogether a satisfactory animal.
Here is the basic recipe.

FOR THE BASIC SCHIACCIATA:

1 teaspoon active dry yeast (¹⁄₂
*   envelope)*

2 cups all-purpose flour,
*   approximately*

¹⁄₂ teaspoon salt

1 egg

¹⁄₂ cup milk, at room temperature

1 tablespoon olive oil

FOR A SIMPLE TOPPING:

1 tablespoon olive oil

¹⁄₂ teaspoon crushed rosemary leaves

Start by making the yeast sponge:
In a small bowl, dissolve the yeast in 2 tablespoons warm water
(125°F) and stir in 1 tablespoon flour. Cover the bowl with plastic
wrap and let it sit in a warm room for 1 hour or longer. (The sponge
can be kept for up to 24 hours in the refrigerator. Bring it back to
room temperature before proceeding.)

Prepare the simple topping:
In a small pan, heat the olive oil with the rosemary until it begins to sizzle. Set aside.

Then make the dough:
Put 1¾ cups flour and the salt into a large mixing bowl. Break the egg into a measuring cup and add enough milk to equal ⅔ cup. Beat the egg and milk together briefly and add it to the mixing bowl, together with the yeast sponge. Mix thoroughly, adding a little more flour if necessary, to make a soft dough—just this side of sticky. Add any filling ingredients at this point. Knead 8 minutes by hand, 3 in a heavy-duty mixer with a dough hook.

Oil a 10-inch round metal pan with the tablespoon olive oil. With your hands, push and press the dough into it until it covers the entire pan more or less evenly, to a thickness of about ¼ inch. (Wet your hands if necessary to keep the dough from sticking to them.) Cover the pan with a towel and let it sit in a warm place 30 minutes, to let the dough relax and rise slightly. Meanwhile, preheat the oven to 425°F.

Spread any topping ingredients over the dough, set the pan in the oven, and bake 20 minutes, or until the surface is golden. Remove the schiacciata from its pan and let it cool on a rack before serving. ■

ONION SCHIACCIATA

Schiacciata alla campagnola

FOR ONE 10-INCH LOAF:

*M*ade with the earliest, sweetest spring onions, this version of schiacciata fills the kitchen with a wonderful aroma as it bakes, and its taste fully lives up to its advance notice. It's pretty, too, as the topping onions crisp and darken. If you don't have spring onions, older ones work well too.

Y

If the schiacciata is to be served by itself, accompany it with a light, dry white wine such as Soave, Orvieto, or Frascati. If it is accompanying other dishes, choose your wine according to them.

*All the ingredients for basic
   schiacciata (page 35)*
4 tablespoons olive oil

4 cups thinly sliced onions
Salt
Freshly ground black pepper

Start the sponge for the schiacciata as directed in the basic recipe. While it is working, prepare the onions:

Heat the oil in a broad sauté pan and add the onions. Sauté slowly over moderate heat 20 minutes, or until soft but not browned. Salt and pepper them to taste and let them cool.

Proceed with the schiacciata dough as directed in the basic recipe, kneading into it half the prepared onions. After the dough has had its 30-minute rest, spread the remaining onions over the top and bake as directed. ■

SCALLOPS VENETIAN STYLE

Capesanti in padella alla veneziana

FOR 4 SERVINGS:

In Venice, where the seafood can be dismal or sublime but never so-so, this dish is among the loveliest to see or to taste. Usually it's made with large sea scallops with their crimson roe attached, and its flavor is matchless. It's still very good, however, if all you can get are the regular, trimmed scallops, as long as they are very fresh. If you are lucky enough to obtain scallops with roe, they sometimes also have bits of connective tissue that you should remove before proceeding with the recipe. Like the best of Italian fish cookery, this is essentially a simple preparation that does the minimal amount necessary to enhance the natural flavor of good raw materials. Its only secret is to use (in addition to the freshest possible shellfish) the very best sweet butter you can find.

A dry white wine, with lots of acidity and a reasonably complex flavor, will match best with this exquisite dish. Try a fine Sauvignon from Friuli (Borgo Conventi, for instance, or Jermann, or Puiatti), a cru Soave (from Anselmi, Bolla, Masi, or Pieropan) or a cru Verdicchio.

5 tablespoons unsalted butter	*¼ cup dry white wine*
4 tablespoons minced onion	*4 slices firm-textured white bread,*
1 pound sea scallops, with roe if	*toasted and quartered on the*
available, cut crosswise into	*diagonal into triangles*
thirds	*1 lemon, quartered*

In a large nonreactive skillet, melt 3 tablespoons of the butter. Add the onion and sauté over low heat until soft but not brown, about 3 minutes. Raise heat to medium, add the scallops, and cook, stirring constantly (and carefully, so as not to break open the roe), 1 minute. Add the wine and ¼ cup water. Reduce heat to low, cover, and cook until the scallops are just barely opaque, about 2 minutes.

Using a slotted spoon, remove the scallops to a warm bowl and cover with foil to keep them warm. Over high heat, rapidly boil down the liquid in the pan until it is reduced to a thick syrup. Off heat, stir in the remaining butter to make a creamy sauce.

Distribute the scallops among four warmed plates, pour on the sauce, garnish with toast triangles and lemon quarters, and serve at once. ■

PRIMI

The typical spring primi—somehow "first courses," though literally correct, just doesn't translate the Italian—naturally enough continue the theme of early greens. Light, brothy soups—minestre (all soups are minestre, but not all minestre are soups)—are made of peas and the first and smallest fava beans, or pasta and artichokes, or lettuces and young Savoy cabbage and beet greens or Swiss chard. Among the dishes using *pasta all'uovo* (the fresh-made, egg-and-flour pastas), a seasonal lasagna, rich with meat and cheese, is lightened with interleavings of spinach. The same spinach, paired with artichoke hearts, shows up in an elaborate Abruzzese *timballo* of *crespelle,* the Italian version of crêpes. Among the *paste asciutte* (the dry, usually commercially made, eggless pastas), there is an improbably delicious combination of asparagus tips poached in the lightest of tomato sauces that turns spaghetti into a seasonal feast. And from Venice comes what may be the most thoroughly characteristic dish of the whole time of year: *risi e bisi,* which some mundane souls have described as a wet risotto, but which more appreciative palates and less tinny ears have labeled pure ambrosia, the very essence of spring.

CHEESE DUMPLINGS IN BROTH

Passatelli in brodo

FOR 4 SERVINGS:

*S*imple pleasures are unfailing; the wisdom of Italian kitchen lore comes back again and again to that basic note. One of the best proofs of it is this simple soup, so widespread in Italy and so varied-yet-constant that it hardly qualifies as a recipe at all. Yet its pleasures remain: the comforting flavor of a good broth, the moist, cheese-sweetness of the fluffy little dumplings (*spaetzle*, in German), the nourishment and genial warmth of the simple combination. *Passatelli* literally means "little passed things," and that's exactly what they are—a mélange of parmigiano, bread crumbs, parsley, and egg, passed through a food mill into boiling broth, where they both take and give flavor while magically clarifying the liquid.

It's very easy to make a tasty, usable broth out of kitchen scraps—bits of chicken especially, odd trimmings of meat, a few bones, a carrot and an onion or a leek—and keep a few pints or quarts of it in your freezer for just such uses as this. See About Broth on page 42.

Basic to this preparation is that Italian kitchen tool of a thousand uses, the food mill. If you don't have a food mill, you can get a similar effect by forcing the passatelli mixture through the holes of a colander, but that's a lot of work. Better by far to make the small investment in a food mill with three different-sized blades. It will last your lifetime, and you'll use it constantly for tomatoes and tomato sauces.

Anything except a sweet wine or a big, austere red.

1 cup freshly grated parmigiano	Freshly ground black pepper
½ cup fine dry bread crumbs	Freshly grated nutmeg
2 tablespoons minced flat-leaf Italian parsley	2 eggs
	6 cups broth

In a bowl, combine the parmigiano, bread crumbs, parsley, a generous quantity of black pepper, and a pinch of nutmeg. Break in the eggs and mix everything into a soft paste. If the mixture appears a little stiff, add a few drops of water.

In a large pot, bring the broth to a boil. Set a food mill fitted with the coarse blade over the pot and mill in the passatelli mixture. Stir once, cover, and simmer over low heat 2 minutes. Off heat, let the soup sit undisturbed for 2 minutes more before serving. ■

About Broth

Broth is a major ingredient not just in winter soups but in many of the recipes of this book and of Italian cooking in general. An Italian kitchen without *brodo* couldn't long survive, at any time of the year.

A long-simmered homemade broth to which a whole, mature chicken (complete with head and feet) has given its life and all its liquid essences is one of the most glorious of simple foods. Ladle some over a bowl of fresh egg noodles, and you have the Platonic Ideal of "chicken noodle soup." (This is, incidentally, a dish that—though it never appears on restaurant menus—any restaurant in Italy will gladly prepare for you on a day when you're feeling under the weather. Most waiters enjoy the opportunity to make a show of their delicate sympathy for the unsettled state of your stomach.)

Not everybody has the time or patience to make that kind of broth at home, though. Even Italians have discovered the convenience of bouillon cubes. Printed recipes calling for brodo often append the phrase *anche di dadi*, a concession that it's okay to use broth made from cubes. That said, it's necessary to add that we find almost all European brands of bouillon cubes superior to standard American brands. U.S. manufacturers don't seem to realize that the product is supposed to taste of something other than salt and dehydrated vegetables. Knorr's double-size cubes, which come in chicken, beef, and fish flavors, are among the best we've found here.

But really, we enjoy making our own brodo, especially on a raw, bone-chilling winter day, when our very largest pot, simmering for hours on the stove, perfumes and humidifies the entire house. It's also a minor point of housewifely (and husbandly) pride to be able to make something so good and versatile out of "nothing." You can, of course, buy meaty bones from the butcher or dedicate a whole chicken to broth. But you won't need to incur any expense at all if you just keep a bag in your freezer for poultry trimmings—necks, backs, wing tips, gizzards—to which you can add a few beef or veal bones and scraps, either raw or cooked. (For lightness, the preponderance should be fowl, not flesh. And it's best to avoid pork and lamb bones, which give too pronounced a flavor of their own to the broth.) There's a lot of nourishment that can be recycled from materials that are ordinarily just thrown away. When the bag gets too bulky for its freezer space, it's time for a broth-making.

You'll also need a few vegetables to lighten the meat essences. The basic *odori* of celery, carrot, and onion are the main requirements, but you can add almost anything else you find kicking around in the refrigerator—vegetables that are too few or old or tired to eat, such as wilted lettuce leaves, celery tops, wrinkled mushrooms, limp green beans, one forgotten plum tomato. Everything contributes its mite to the broth, and then you don't have to feel guilty about wasting food.

Here is a basic technique for a generous supply of brodo, on the assumption that you won't often want to invest the time it takes to make small amounts. Freeze it in plastic containers to keep it for months. (If you don't want to tie up so many containers, freeze a few, then run warm water quickly over each container and pop out the cube of frozen broth. Store these "giant *dadi*" nude in heavy plastic bags.)

Quantities given will yield anywhere from 6 to 10 quarts, depending on how much water you start with and how long you let it cook. If storage space is a problem, continue cooking the broth uncovered after straining until it's very concentrated, then remember to dilute it with water before using. The opening step of browning the bones and vegetables in the oven produces a darker-colored, richer-flavored brodo, but it's purely optional. And please regard the quantities and timing given as Italian drivers regard stop signs and lane markings—as only advisory.

5 to 6 pounds bones (chiefly chicken, plus a few beef or veal with a bit of meat left on)	1 to 2 tomatoes, canned or fresh (optional)
2 stalks celery, cut in large pieces	Fresh herbs if available—a handful of parsley, a few sprigs of thyme or oregano
2 carrots, cut in large pieces	1 tablespoon salt
1 cup onions (or leeks or scallions), cut in large pieces	3 to 4 black peppercorns or freshly ground black pepper

If you want a fuller-bodied broth:

Preheat oven to 375° to 400°F. In a large roasting pan, spread out the bones, celery, carrots, and onion. Set this in the oven for 1 to 2 hours, until the bones and vegetables are well browned. Transfer the contents of the roasting pan to a large (10 to 12 quart) pot. Pour a little water into the roasting pan, set it over low heat and scrape any browned bits off the bottom. Pour that water over the bones and vegetables, along with enough additional water to cover them by at least 4 inches. Add the tomatoes, herbs, salt and pepper, and cook as directed below.

If you want a lighter-bodied broth:

Put all the ingredients into a large (10 to 12 quart) pot. Add enough cold water to cover everything by at least 4 inches. Bring the liquid to a boil, skimming off any heavy scum that rises from the bones. (Often there won't be enough to bother about.) Reduce heat to maintain a gentle simmer and cook covered about 4 hours.

Off heat, pour the broth in batches through a large sieve into another pot. Discard the bones, and press hard on the vegetables and meat pieces remaining in the sieve to extract all their liquids before discarding them. Defat the broth if you wish (or leave the fat to seal the surface when refrigerated). Taste for seasoning and add more salt if necessary, or boil the liquid down somewhat if the flavor seems too thin. Store the broth in the refrigerator, where it will keep for about a week, or freeze it.

PEA AND FAVA BEAN SOUP

Minestra di piselli e fave

FOR 4 SERVINGS:

Italians wax rhapsodic over fava beans. They look forward to the first favas of the spring the way some people wait for the first raspberries or the annual shad run, and when the baskets of long, fleshy green pods finally arrive they fall upon them with all the glee and appetite of particularly pagan lions for particularly pious Christians. Those first, sweet favas of spring aren't even cooked: they're eaten raw, right out of the pod, either alone or with little chunks of pecorino cheese. Americans would probably revere the fava just as much if we could get them as fresh. Unfortunately, all too often the favas we encounter in commerce here have been far too long off the vine: limp, detumescent green wands rather than crisp sticks, and the beans inside all starch rather than sugar.

For this recipe, seek out the freshest pods and the smallest beans you can find, and don't worry that the broth gets a little gray-looking and the peas and the beans lose a little brightness: persist, because the flavor is worth it. This is down-home food, simple and comforting.

A good, acidic, dry white wine: Verdicchio, Soave, Bianco di Toscana, Pinot grigio—anything not too complex or attention-grabbing.

3 tablespoons olive oil	4 ounces imported Italian short
⅔ cup chopped onion	pasta—e.g., ditali or shells
1½ cups shelled fresh peas (1 to	1 teaspoon salt
1½ pounds in the pod)	Freshly ground black pepper
1½ cups shelled fresh favas (about	2 tablespoons butter, softened
1½ pounds in the pod)	6 tablespoons freshly grated
6 cups broth	parmigiano

In a large heavy-bottomed pot, heat the olive oil. Add the onion and sauté over low heat 5 minutes. Add the peas and favas and sauté, stirring, 2 minutes.

Meanwhile, in another pot, bring the broth to a boil. When the peas and beans are well imbued with the oil, stir in the broth. Bring the soup to a boil, reduce it to a simmer, cover tightly, and cook 30 minutes.

Stir in the pasta, return to a simmer, and cook until the pasta is slightly softer than al dente, about 15 minutes. Off the heat, stir in the salt, black pepper to taste, the softened butter, and the parmigiano. Serve at once, passing more cheese at the table if you like. ■

CREAMY ASPARAGUS SOUP, MILANESE STYLE

Crema di asparagi alla milanese

FOR 6 TO 8 SERVINGS:

Y

None really recommended with this dish, but a soft, dry white is your best bet—an Orvieto, for instance, or perhaps a Riesling renano.

*I*f the mention of Milan makes you think of fashion and elegance, this soup won't contradict your impression. And if the mention of Milan makes you think of rich food and hearty eating, this soup won't contradict your impression either. This is a very special dish, sweet and succulent and very different on the palate from an ordinary "cream of" soup. It absolutely wants freshly made croutons to provide textural contrast.

Notice, by the way, that the food mill we urged you to purchase for the passatelli recipe will come into use again here to extract the last drops of goodness from the asparagus stems.

4 cups milk

4 cups broth

8 tablespoons butter, in all

⅓ cup all-purpose flour

2 pounds asparagus spears, bases
  trimmed, tips reserved, and
  stems cut into 2-inch pieces

Salt

2 egg yolks

½ cup heavy cream, at room
  temperature

2 tablespoons freshly grated
  parmigiano

2 cups croutons, made from
  day-old crustless bread, lightly
  toasted

In a large pot, mix the milk and broth and bring them to a simmer.

In another large, heavy-bottomed pot, melt half the butter. Add the flour and cook 2 minutes over low heat, stirring frequently. Gradually add the milk-broth mixture, stirring vigorously after each addition to obtain a smooth cream. When all the liquid is added and the cream comes to a boil, add the asparagus stem pieces. Adjust heat to maintain a simmer and cook 1 hour, uncovered, stirring often.

Meanwhile, in a medium pot, bring a small quantity of salted water to a boil. Add the asparagus tips and cook until they are tender, about 5 minutes. Drain and set aside until ready to use.

Pass the entire contents of the soup pot through a food mill, return it to the pot, and set over low heat. Warm a soup tureen. Put the egg yolks, cream, parmigiano, and remaining butter in the tureen and whisk them together. When the soup comes to a simmer, gradually pour it into the tureen, whisking constantly. Float the asparagus tips on top and serve at once. Pass a plate of croutons at the table. ■

SICILIAN PASTA AND ARTICHOKE SOUP

Pasta e carciofi alla siciliana

FOR 4 SERVINGS:

Artichokes with everything is a spring motif. There may seem to be an awful lot of them in this recipe, but they balance out beautifully with the other ingredients after an hour of cooking, which transmutes all the individual flavors into something greater than the sum of the parts. The pecorino romano cheese at the end also has a lot to do with the ultimate marriage of flavors. Unlike many recipes calling for salt pork, this one isn't as good if bacon is substituted, so do take the trouble to get salt pork. A chunk of it will keep for months in the freezer.

2 tablespoons olive oil

4 ounces salt pork, blanched in
   boiling water 2 minutes and
   chopped fine

½ cup finely chopped onion

½ cup finely chopped celery

2 cloves garlic, finely chopped

2 tablespoons finely chopped
   flat-leaf Italian parsley

1 cup drained canned Italian-style
   plum tomatoes, chopped

Freshly ground black pepper

2½ pounds small artichokes,
   prepared as directed on page 22,
   cut into wedges ¼ to ½
   inch thick

Salt

6 ounces imported Italian pasta
   corta—e.g., small shells, ditalini

1 cup freshly grated pecorino
   romano

In a casserole, warm the olive oil and add the salt pork, onion, celery, garlic, and parsley, and sauté 4 to 5 minutes, until the fat is partially rendered and the vegetables are just beginning to color. Add the tomatoes and a generous quantity of black pepper, and cook 2 minutes. Add the artichokes, stir to coat them with the seasonings, and cook 3 minutes.

Add 6 cups cold water. Bring to a boil, reduce to a simmer, cover, and cook 1 hour.

Add ½ teaspoon salt, or more to taste. Add the pasta and cook until it is tender, about 15 minutes. Turn off heat and let the soup sit 15 minutes.

Just before serving, stir in ½ cup of the pecorino and a generous quantity of black pepper. At the table, pass additional pecorino and the pepper mill. ∎

LIGURIAN VEGETABLE SOUP

Zuppa di verdura all'agliata

FOR 5 TO 6 SERVINGS:

*T*his soup comes from the Italian Riviera in Liguria and reflects that region's love of green vegetables and strong herbal flavors. The dish has an intense vegetable sweetness and a richness that is almost meaty, despite the fact that the only meat in it is whatever flavored the broth. The late addition of the *agliata*—the mince of garlic and parsley—keeps the blend light and bright.

A hearty white, such as Breganze or Pomino, or a soft red such as Dolcetto or Valpolicella.

Don't omit the bread and grated parmigiano at the end: they're essential to the full effect. (When an Italian soup is called a zuppa rather than a minestra, it means there must be bread in the bottom of the bowl.) On the other hand, the list of leafy greens is not ironclad: you can use Swiss chard, for instance, instead of beet greens, or dandelion leaves instead of romaine lettuce, and so on, as long as you end up with about 3 cups' worth (loosely packed).

Despite the long list of ingredients, this is not an all-day, minestrone-type soup. Total cooking time is just about 45 minutes—long enough to soften the vegetables but brief enough to keep their flavors distinct. The recipe makes a generous amount of soup, but you will eat lots of it. If there are any leftovers, they are delicious reheated, especially with the addition of a thin slice of onion and a dollop of extra-virgin olive oil.

4 tablespoons olive oil

½ cup chopped onion

¾ pound Savoy cabbage (½ head), shredded

3 large leaves romaine lettuce, shredded

6 large leaves beet greens, shredded

2 stalks celery, sliced ¼ inch thick

2 carrots, sliced ¼ inch thick

3 small boiling potatoes (½ pound), peeled and cut in ½-inch dice

¾ pound fresh peas (1 cup shelled)

1 large tomato, peeled, seeded, and chopped

½ teaspoon salt

Freshly ground black pepper

4 cups broth

2 cloves garlic, chopped together with 3 tablespoons flat-leaf Italian parsley

5 to 6 slices day-old country-style bread, lightly toasted

Freshly grated parmigiano

In a very large pot, warm the olive oil. Add the onion and sauté 2 minutes. Add the cabbage, lettuce, beet greens, celery, carrots, potatoes, peas, and tomato. Stir together and add the salt and a generous quantity of black pepper. Sauté gently 8 to 10 minutes, stirring often, until the greens are well wilted.

Add the broth. Bring to a boil, reduce to a simmer, cover, and cook 20 minutes. Stir in the garlic and parsley and cook 10 minutes more.

Put a slice of bread in the bottom of each soup bowl. Ladle in the soup and serve at once, passing the parmigiano at the table. ■

About Pasta

If anyone needs reasons to eat more pasta, they're easy enough to find. Pasta has at last come into its own in this country. On every side, from every conceivable source—doctors and dieticians and food page editors, athletes and models and unbearably cute kids on TV—you can hear paeans to its praise: Pasta is healthy, it's nutritious, it's inexpensive, it's satisfying, it's versatile, it's simple to prepare, it's fun to eat, and—lest we forget—it always tastes good. After taking many years of abuse for not feeding their families healthily, Italian-American grandmothers everywhere can at last say "I told you so" to the batteries of nutritional experts who used to denounce pasta as merely starch.

Pasta's redeemed reputation brings several attendant boons for macaroniacs. For one thing, first-rate imported pastas are now widely available—and while we two are willing to do our part to help the U.S. economy, we've got to say that anyone who has tasted the imports will find going back to domestic brands a real letdown. Compared to the imported pastas of De Cecco, Del Verde, or Gerardo di Nola, for instance, most domestic pasta cooks up to mushy pap. In commercially made dry pasta, the price differential between domestics and imports reflects a real difference in value.

Unfortunately, the same thing can't be said—in our opinion—of the commercial fresh-egg pastas sold in supermarket refrigerator cases and in gourmet stores. There, the value-for-dollar equation breaks down. A pound of fresh pasta costs anywhere up to $7; that's for—at most—30¢ worth of eggs and 25¢ worth of flour. The markup just doesn't compute. It's worse than what restaurants do to wine (which is another story, and don't get us started on that, please!). Of course, everyone has his or her own calculation for the "time is money" equation, so for you perhaps it's worth it to buy fresh-egg pasta rather than make it. But not for us.

We're going to give you a recipe for making fresh pasta, but only the basic proportions of the ingredients, not detailed instructions about technique. This is not to be coy, but simply because everyone who makes pasta (except for purists of the deepest dye and a few masochists) makes it with some kind of machine. So you either have a pasta machine already, or you don't. If you do have one, the manufacturer's instruction booklet will give you the best technique for your machine, and you've probably already mastered that, and maybe even gone on to develop a technique of your own. If you don't have a pasta machine, then what you need is not a long explanation of how to use the different machines, but something to induce you to go out and buy one. That we can give you—if the promise of an endless supply of *pasta all'uovo*, tender and firm, delicate and flavorful, all ready to be slathered with butter and parmigiano, or fresh tomato and basil, or a meaty *ragù alla napoletana* isn't motivation enough.

The major inducement ought to be that pasta making with even the simplest machine is easy and quick. If you've seen photos of an Olympic-class pasta maker like Giuliano Bugialli swirling a nine-yard-long, cellophane-thin sheet of pasta in circles over his head like a banner bearer at the Palio, you may justifiably feel that such skill is beyond you. Relax: it's beyond most people—and it's also not necessary.

Close to twenty-five years ago, we bought our first pasta machine, from Manganaro's, a long-established Italian food store in what was then New York's Hell's Kitchen. For $25 we got a gleaming chrome Imperia, shaped like an eight-inch-tall T with a hand crank. One wing of the T was the rollers, which look like an old-fashioned washing machine's wringer. The other wing of the T was a pair of cutters, narrow and wide, which look as if they could double quite efficiently as paper shredders, should we ever need to dispose of state secrets. That was it, plus the handle, which you moved from roller to cutters as needed, and a simple clamp for holding the machine on your work surface. Minimal moving parts, no electricity, no circuits.

In the years since then, that machine has seen hard use, but it has never once been out of commission and has never needed washing (you just brush off the flour after each use). The Imperia remains our favorite pasta maker, even though our passion for pasta has led us to acquire others—like the *chitarra* we bought in L'Aquila, high in the mountains of Abruzzi. We had to go to the wood-carvers' stalls in the street market to find one. Stores didn't sell them—too old-fashioned, too low-tech: a wooden frame with wires stretched across it that looks something like a clumsy mountain zither, which is why it's called a chitarra, "guitar." You're supposed to roll out a sheet of dough by hand to the desired thinness, then lay it over the wires and roll again. Strands of pasta like square spaghetti fall down between the wires. We cheat, however, and roll out our pasta on our trusty Imperia before cutting it on the chitarra. Saves a lot of labor—and that's exactly what a pasta machine is for.

Our Imperia didn't even come with instructions back when we bought it, before the American pasta boom. The manufacturer's assumption obviously was that anyone who wanted a pasta maker would already understand how to use it. The only exhortation, printed on the box flap—in Italian—was to never, never wash the machine. (See? Bet you thought we were just lazy and unsanitary!)

At first, we were so excited by the ease of making pasta and by the incredible goodness of our product that we went slightly crazy. We indulged in half-day marathons of pasta making, sustained by a cloud of euphoria and flour dust. We tried for the longest continuous sheet, the longest single strand. Guests slept behind curtains of drying pasta, draped over poles in the spare bedroom. We had to buy special boxes to hold it.

All this was intensely gratifying, but it was also a lot of work. Eventually we evolved our own principle of what's now being acclaimed as the secret of Japanese manufacturing success: just-in-time production. We didn't have to work all day to make a two weeks' or month's supply. The idea, after all, was *fresh* pasta. Making just what we needed for a single meal as we needed it turned out to be no trouble at all. By now, putting together a couple of eggs' worth of pasta for a weeknight dinner is such a matter of habit that we don't even need to plan ahead for it—any more than for mashed potatoes. It takes just about the same time and effort as peeling, cooking, and mashing potatoes. (Of course, if you make mashed potatoes from a packet, there's no use our talking to you.)

Aside from our trusty $25 Imperia and our chitarra (which cost us all of 15,000 lire, or about $12 in 1989), we have a cabinetful of other pasta-related toys: a hand-cranked Neapolitan extrusion-type spaghetti maker that looks like a small brass meat grinder; massive, high-tech Kitchen-Aid and Cuisinart pasta attachments; several ravioli forms; and one or two other machines that have drifted so deep into the closet they haven't been seen (or missed) for years. We stick with the Imperia because it performs two of the three basic pasta-making operations—rolling the dough thin and cutting it—as well as or better than even the most powerful electric models. That leaves only one other operation to perform: kneading the dough. Diane actually enjoys kneading dough by hand, especially when she can displace some job-related aggressions onto an inanimate object. Tom, being of a more equable temperament, prefers to mix and knead pasta dough in our Kitchen-Aid heavy-duty mixer.

That's all there is to pasta making: mixing, kneading, rolling, cutting. This is not a mysterious craft requiring years of apprenticeship to a Zen pasta master. Common sense and a clean kitchen counter are the major requirements. After that, you can make pasta as you like with the equipment you like.

And do it alone or with others, as they used to say in the confessional. Making pasta can be a social activity or a solitary one, contemplative even. If you're the kind of person who takes satisfaction in baking your own bread, you'll probably want to master the skill of rolling pasta paper-thin by hand. You may even enjoy weighing the merits of the Marcella Hazan system (hands curled around the rolling pin as you stretch the dough) versus the Bugialli system (palms flat, moving the rolling pin pretty much as log-rolling lumberjacks use their feet). After all, you never know when you may find yourself in a beach house or mountain cabin with nothing but a bag of flour, a rolling pin, and an insatiable hunger for pasta.

To make 1 pound of fresh pasta, as called for in most of the recipes in this book:

2 cups all-purpose flour

3 eggs

¼ teaspoon salt (or to taste)

1 teaspoon olive oil (omit if you're
  a purist)

1 tablespoon or more water
  (depending on the dryness of
  your flour, the size of your eggs,
  and the humidity of the day)

In a large bowl, combine all of the ingredients and knead by hand 10 minutes, or however long your machine's instructions say, until you've achieved a firm, smooth, unsticky dough. Set aside, covered—we just bury ours in the flour bin—for ½ hour to relax the gluten and make the dough easier to roll. Then roll it out to the desired thinness and cut and shape it according to your needs and equipment.

If those directions are too bare-bones for you, check the instructions that came with your pasta machine, or take a look at *La Tavola Italiana*, where we give more information about pasta and pasta making as well as a number of—if we say so ourselves—great pasta recipes.

FRESH EGG NOODLES WITH MASCARPONE

Trenette al mascarpone

FOR 4 SERVINGS:

T his wonderfully elegant, wonderfully flavorful, and wonderfully simple dish is like the most transcendent fettuccine Alfredo
you ever dreamed of—a fettuccine Alfredo refined to its platonic
essence of delicate pasta imbued with indecent amounts of butter.

    Mascarpone is a rich, satiny, cream cheese—but to say only that
is like calling a white truffle a nice fungus. In this simple, sinfully
rich recipe, the mascarpone behaves like butter, with an intriguing
flavor added. The thinly cut noodles absorb mascarpone the way a
sponge takes up water, and you'll do the same to the noodles. This
dish cries out for a last-minute crackling of fresh black pepper:
don't deny its last request.

A soft, fruity red wine such as Dolcetto or Barbera.

¾ pound mascarpone, at room	*1 recipe (1 pound fresh) trenette*
temperature	*(page 54)*
Salt	*Freshly ground black pepper*

In a small bowl, beat the mascarpone with ¾ teaspoon salt to soften
it. If the cheese is too cold to work, beat in 1 to 2 tablespoons hot
water.

    Put half the mascarpone into a serving bowl. In a large pot,
bring 4 quarts of water to a boil and add 1 tablespoon salt. Drop the
trenette in and cook until al dente, about 2 minutes. Drain the
pasta, transfer it to the serving bowl, and toss until it absorbs all the
mascarpone. Add the remaining mascarpone and a generous quantity of black pepper. Toss well again and serve at once, passing the
pepper mill at the table. ■

LASAGNA WITH SPINACH AND MEAT SAUCE

Lasagna pasticciata con spinaci

FOR 6 TO 8 SERVINGS:

A fruity and acidic red wine with a bit of structure and complexity of its own—a Chianti Classico perhaps, or a Barbera from the Alba region.

This lasagna would be a fine pasta course for an important dinner party. The interplay of the beef, chicken liver, pancetta, and woods mushrooms in the sauce, the classic ricotta-and-spinach filling, and the freshly made lasagna noodles amounts to a rich and quite sophisticated mélange of flavors.

This is not a difficult recipe, though like all lasagnas it is time-consuming. The meat sauce can be prepared and the spinach cooked and drained a day ahead of time. After that, the assembly and cooking are relatively straightforward. The final dish shouldn't be swimming in sauce, but appetizingly moist throughout. If you've made up the components in advance, they may be a bit dry—in which case, simply cover the baking dish for all but the last few minutes of cooking.

FOR THE MEAT SAUCE:

½ ounce dried porcini
2 tablespoons olive oil
2 ounces pancetta, chopped
3 tablespoons chopped onion
½ pound ground round of beef

Salt
Freshly ground black pepper
2 ounces chicken livers, cleaned and minced
2 tablespoons tomato paste

FOR THE SPINACH FILLING:

1½ pounds fresh spinach
Salt
1 cup ricotta

1 egg
Freshly grated nutmeg

FOR THE LASAGNA:

1 recipe pasta all'uovo, made with 2 eggs (see page 54)

1½ tablespoons butter
1 cup freshly grated parmigiano

To prepare the meat sauce:

Put the porcini in a bowl and pour 1 cup boiling water over them. Let them sit 30 minutes, then drain them, reserving the water. Rinse the porcini pieces thoroughly, chop them fine, and rinse again to remove all traces of grit. Line a sieve with a dampened paper towel and strain the porcini liquid into a small bowl.

In a large nonreactive skillet, heat the olive oil. Add the pancetta and onion and sauté over low heat 3 minutes. Raise heat to medium, crumble in the ground beef, and add ¼ teaspoon salt and a sprinkling of black pepper. Sauté 3 minutes more, stirring to break up the meat. Add the chicken livers and the porcini.

In a measuring cup, combine ½ cup of the porcini soaking liquid and ½ cup hot water. Dissolve the tomato paste in this liquid and add it to the skillet. Bring to a simmer, cover the skillet, and cook 1 hour, stirring occasionally and regulating the heat to maintain a gentle simmer.

To prepare the spinach filling:

Wash the spinach carefully and place it in a large pot with only the water adhering to the leaves. Sprinkle lightly with salt, cover, and turn heat to high. As soon as the spinach wilts, reduce heat to medium and cook 5 minutes. Drain the spinach in a colander and spray with cold water to cool. Squeeze it by the handful to remove most of its liquid, and then chop it fine. Put the spinach into a bowl, loosen it with a fork, and add the ricotta, the egg, ¼ teaspoon salt, and several gratings of nutmeg. Mix well.

To prepare the lasagna:

In a large pot, bring 4 quarts water to a boil and add 1 tablespoon salt. Fill a large bowl with ice water. Lay out several clean dish towels on a work surface.

Divide the pasta into 4 pieces and roll them out to the thinnest setting on the pasta machine. Cut them into approximately 5-inch squares, to make about 28 pieces. Spread the pieces on a floured surface so they don't stick together while waiting to be cooked.

Drop the pasta squares a few at a time into the boiling water and cook 1 minute. Drain them with a slotted spoon, dip them into the bowl of ice water to stop the cooking, and lay them out on the dish towels while you cook the rest.

Assembly and baking:

Preheat the oven to 400°F. Butter a 10- by 14-inch baking dish with ½ tablespoon of the butter. Cover the bottom of the dish with a layer of pasta squares. (Use about a quarter of them.) Spread ¼ of the spinach-ricotta mixture over the surface. Sprinkle on ¼ of the parmigiano, then spoon on ¼ of the meat sauce. Make three more layers in the same way, ending with the parmigiano and meat sauce. Finally, dot the top with the remaining tablespoon of butter.

Set the dish in the oven (covered, if it looks a bit dry) and bake 15 minutes, or until you see that the sauce on top is bubbling hot. Remove the dish from the oven and let the lasagna sit for 10 minutes before serving. ■

ENRAGED PENNE

Penne all'arrabbiata

FOR 4 SERVINGS:

This dish needs a red wine with plenty of acidity and some tannin. Chianti Classico is ideal, and Barbera is also good. Good too are young Taurasi, Aglianico del Vulture, or Nebbiolo.

his has been for years one of the most fashionable pasta dishes in Rome. Penne, of course, are a short, tubular pasta; *all'ar-rabbiata* doesn't, in this culinary context, really mean rabid or enraged but fiery, and not temperamentally but from the influence of the peperoncini rossi (little hot red peppers) in the sauce. (For a description of these peppers, see page 223 in the Fall section.)

Many versions of this dish exist, some of them refined to the point of (we feel) namby-pambiness, and some so forceful as to verge on inedibility. This recipe approximates the version we've enjoyed time after time in Roman neighborhood trattorias. The lard called for here, by the way, makes a real difference, as does the finishing of the pasta in the sauce. Note that the sauce itself needs no salt, and that pecorino romano is really the only cheese for this dish: parmigiano is too sweet.

2 tablespoons lard
½ cup chopped onion
2 large cloves garlic, minced
3 ounces pancetta, diced
2 cups drained canned
   Italian-style plum tomatoes,
   chopped

2 dried peperoncini rossi
Salt
1 pound imported Italian
   penne
½ cup freshly grated pecorino
   romano, approximately

In a broad sauté pan, melt the lard. Add the onion and garlic and cook over moderate heat until soft, about 5 minutes. Add the pancetta and continue to cook about 3 minutes more. Then stir in the tomatoes and the peperoncini. Cook 10 to 15 minutes, stirring occasionally, until the tomatoes give up their liquid and the sauce thickens. Remove the peperoncini.

In a large pot, bring 4 quarts water to a boil and add 1 table-spoon salt. Add the penne and cook until just short of al dente. Drain the penne quickly so that they remain a little moist and add them to the pan with the sauce, along with 4 tablespoons of the pecorino. Stir everything together for about a minute, then transfer to a heated serving bowl and serve at once. Pass more pecorino at the table. ■

SPAGHETTI WITH ASPARAGUS TIPS

Spaghetti con punti d'asparagi

FOR 4 SERVINGS:

A dry, acidic white wine will work best with the strong acidity of this dish. Try a Verdicchio, a Frascati, or a Pinot grigio from Alto Adige or Friuli.

*A*n unusual recipe, a charming and fresh-flavored sauce with the uncommon combination of asparagus and tomato—and it has the virtue of taking no time at all to make. On the downside, it extravagantly uses only the tips of 2 pounds of asparagus to serve four. If you don't have your own asparagus bed (or greengrocery store), you may want to save this dish for the height of asparagus season. Of course, you can cheat a little by using the tips and part of the tender stems of only 1 pound of asparagus. Using only the tips is really more a matter of aesthetics than of flavor.

3 tablespoons olive oil
1½ to 2 cups thin asparagus tips
   (tips of about 2 pounds of
   asparagus)
1½ to 2 cups drained canned

Italian-style plum tomatoes,
   chopped
Salt
Freshly ground black pepper
1 pound imported Italian spaghetti

In a large nonreactive skillet, warm the olive oil. Add the asparagus tips and toss over medium heat 1 minute, just to coat them with the oil. Add the tomatoes, ½ teaspoon salt, and a generous quantity of black pepper. Bring the sauce to a simmer, reduce heat, cover, and cook gently until the tips are tender, 12 to 15 minutes, depending on the thickness of the asparagus. Set aside until ready to use.

In a large pot, bring 4 quarts water to a boil and add 1 tablespoon salt. Add the spaghetti and cook until al dente. Meanwhile, reheat the sauce. Drain the pasta, transfer it to a warmed serving bowl, toss with the sauce, and serve at once. ∎

SPAGHETTI WITH MUSHROOMS AND CHICKEN LIVERS

Spaghetti con fegatini

FOR 4 SERVINGS:

This is a very traditional southern Italian dish. Some years ago, a version of it became popular in America under the alias of "Spaghetti Caruso." The dish is still great, with strong, distinctive flavors—perhaps a bit heavy for some tastes these days, but tenors don't eat like birds. Don't omit the extra cheese and pepper at table: they are important last-minute ingredients, not just grace notes.

A medium- to full-bodied red wine of some character— Aglianico, Il Falcone, Regaleali, or Taurasi would all work splendidly, and the great Caruso would have approved of them all.

¼ cup olive oil

¼ cup finely chopped onion

1 teaspoon finely chopped rosemary
  leaves

½ pound chicken livers, cleaned
  and cut in ½-inch pieces

¼ to ½ pound mushrooms,
  cleaned and sliced ¼ inch thick

Salt

Freshly ground black pepper

2 cups drained canned
  Italian-style plum tomatoes,
  chopped

1 pound imported Italian spaghetti

4 tablespoons unsalted butter, cut
  in several pieces

1 cup freshly grated parmigiano,
  approximately

In a large nonreactive skillet, heat the olive oil. Add the onion and rosemary and sauté over low heat 2 to 3 minutes, until the onion is wilted. Raise heat to medium-high, add the chicken livers, and cook 3 to 4 minutes, stirring frequently, until they firm a bit and lose their raw red color.

Add the mushrooms and continue cooking 1 minute, stirring to coat them with the oil. Sprinkle on ½ teaspoon salt and black pepper to taste, lower heat to medium-low, and cook uncovered 5 minutes, stirring once or twice.

Add the tomatoes, stir well, bring to a simmer, cover, and cook 30 minutes. Taste for salt and pepper. Set aside until ready to use.

In a large pot, bring 4 quarts water to a boil and add 1 tablespoon salt. Add the spaghetti and cook until al dente. While the pasta is cooking, reheat the sauce and warm a large serving bowl. Drain the pasta, transfer it to the serving bowl, add the butter, and toss until it is all absorbed. Toss again with ¼ cup of the parmigiano, and then with the chicken-liver sauce, and serve at once. Pass the remaining parmigiano and the pepper mill at the table. ∎

LINGUINE WITH FLOUNDER SAUCE

Linguine alla sogliola

FOR 4 SERVINGS:

This dish flatters, and is flattered by, most dry Italian white wines, but it especially likes Greco di Tufo.

A marvelous dish that gets maximum mileage out of a few simple ingredients. A half-pound of flounder (in Italy it would be sole from the Adriatic), a cup and a half of tomatoes, and a handful of vegetables produce a nubbly, delicate sauce with a gentle but pervasive fresh fish flavor—and in less time than it takes to boil water and cook the linguine, making this an ideal recipe for one of those late-spring days that offer a foretaste of the heat of summer.

Make no substitutions for the fish but stick with the freshest Atlantic winter flounder—unless you are willing to spend a fortune for real Adriatic or Dover sole. What passes for sole on this side of the Atlantic (lemon sole or gray sole) will make a coarser and disappointing dish. You could, however, add a peperoncino rosso to the sauce if you like things lively.

½ pound Atlantic winter flounder
   fillets
4 tablespoons olive oil
3 tablespoons minced onion
3 tablespoons minced celery
1½ tablespoons minced flat-leaf
   Italian parsley
½ teaspoon minced garlic

1½ cups drained canned
   Italian-style plum tomatoes,
   pureed
Salt
Freshly ground black pepper
2 tablespoons dry white wine
1 pound imported Italian linguine

Rinse the flounder fillets and feel them carefully for bones. Divide them along their median line, then cut them crosswise into strips about ¼ inch wide.

In a nonreactive skillet, heat the olive oil. Add the onion, celery, parsley, and garlic, and sauté 5 minutes. Add the tomatoes, sprinkle with salt and pepper, stir, bring to a simmer, cover, and cook 10 minutes. Stir in the wine and set aside until ready to use.

In a large pot, bring 4 or 5 quarts water to a boil and add 1 tablespoon salt. Add the linguine and cook until al dente. While the pasta is cooking, bring the tomato sauce back to a simmer. Add the pieces of flounder and a light sprinkling of salt; stir, cover, and cook 5 minutes. Drain the pasta, transfer it to a heated bowl, toss with the flounder sauce and a sprinkling of black pepper, and serve at once. ■

RICE AND PEAS

Risi e bisi

FOR 4 SERVINGS:

Try a good Friulian Tocai, preferably one from the Collio or Colli Orientale regions.

"ice and peas" doesn't roll off the tongue the same way "risi e bisi" does, but as long as you get the freshest possible peas, it will roll onto the palate every bit as pleasantly. If there is any such thing as the Venetian national dish, this is it. Every spring it is ceremonially served at the festivities commemorating the ritual wedding of the doge, the ruler of the whilom Republic of Venice, to the sea that supplied its (and his) wealth. Despite all that panoply, it's an easily prepared dish. If your peas aren't fresh off the vine this morning, you might want to add a pinch of sugar to the pot. The finished dish should be wet—lightly soupy, not as thick as a risotto.

6 cups broth

4 tablespoons unsalted butter

2 tablespoons olive oil

¼ cup chopped onion

½ cup chopped flat-leaf Italian
  parsley

2 ounces pancetta, chopped

2 pounds fresh peas, shelled,
  rinsed, and drained

1 cup Arborio rice

1 teaspoon salt

Freshly ground black pepper

3 tablespoons freshly grated
  parmigiano

In a large pot, bring the broth to a simmer and keep it hot.

In a large flameproof casserole, melt 2 tablespoons of the butter along with the olive oil. Add the onion, parsley, and pancetta, and sauté over moderate heat until the fat is rendered from the pancetta and the onion is soft but not browned, about 3 minutes.

Add the peas to the casserole and simmer for a minute, stirring to coat them with the seasonings, then add ½ cup of the broth. Adjust the heat to maintain a steady simmer and cook until the peas are almost tender, 20 to 30 minutes, stirring often and adding broth, ¼ cup at a time, as necessary to keep the peas moist. At no point should the peas be awash in liquid. The process will use 1½ to 2 cups of broth in all.

When the peas are nearly done, add the remaining broth, raise heat, and bring to a boil. Stir in the rice. Reduce heat again to maintain a steady simmer and cook uncovered, stirring occasionally, until the rice is just tender, about 20 minutes.

Add the salt, a generous quantity of black pepper, the remaining 2 tablespoons of butter, and all the parmigiano. Stir well, simmer for 2 minutes more, and serve. ■

RISOTTO WITH SPRING GREENS

Risotto con verdura

FOR 4 TO 6 SERVINGS:

The technique of the preceding risi e bisi is an exception to the way Italian cooks usually handle rice, which is exemplified by this recipe. The short-grained rice that makes the best risotto is first sautéed in seasoned butter or oil, not immersed in boiling liquid from the start. The liquid—broth to start, water after the rice has taken as much flavor as the cook wants to give it—is added gradually, so that the rice absorbs each addition more or less completely as it cooks uncovered. Frequent stirring keeps the rice from sticking to the pan and lets the cook accurately gauge the need for more broth as well as the developing texture of the dish.

Novice risotto makers may find that technique demanding, but as you grow accustomed to it, it becomes comfortable and indeed pleasurable—you and your rice are working happily together and communicating closely with each other. A heavy-bottomed pan is needed to keep the rice from burning in case you let it go a bit too

Risottos can stand up to full-bodied white wines. Try a Tocai, Pomino bianco, Vintage Tunina, or Torre di Giano Riserva.

long without an infusion of liquid. The broader the pan—hence the more surface exposed to heat—the quicker the risotto cooks.

You can make a tasty risotto with almost anything—meat, fish, vegetables. This risotto with greens is a good way to use some of spring's bumper crop of tender spinach, beet and turnip tops, chard, early kale, dandelion, *mizuna,* mustard greens—even full-flavored lettuces. Simply wash any combination of greens, put them in a large pot with only the water that adheres to the leaves, cook over low heat just until they wilt, drain, squeeze to remove excess liquid, and chop. To end up with 1½ cups of blanched greens, you'll need to start with what seems like half a bushel—enough to fill your largest pasta cooking pot.

6 tablespoons butter

½ cup chopped onion

1½ cups blanched, squeezed, and chopped mixed greens (see headnote)

Salt

4 cups broth, approximately

1½ cups Arborio rice

¼ cup freshly grated parmigiano

In a large, heavy-bottomed pot, melt 3 tablespoons of the butter. Add the onion and sauté over low heat, 2 to 3 minutes, until soft. Add the greens, stirring to loosen, and coat them with the butter. Sprinkle generously with salt and sauté 2 to 3 minutes.

Meanwhile, in another pot, bring the broth to a simmer and keep it hot.

Add the rice to the greens and mix well. Sauté 1 to 2 minutes. Reduce heat to medium-low and add ½ cup of the simmering broth. Stirring often, cook until the rice has almost fully absorbed the liquid. Continue stirring and adding ½ cups of the simmering broth at intervals for 15 to 20 minutes more, or until the rice is tender but still firm to the bite. If you run out of broth before the rice is done, use hot water.

When the rice is tender and has absorbed almost all its liquid, turn off heat, stir in the remaining butter and all the parmigiano, taste for salt, and serve. ■

TIMBALE OF CRÊPES WITH SPRING VEGETABLES

Timballo di crespelle al verde

FOR 6 TO 8 SERVINGS:

*I*n the Abruzzi, where this recipe originates, it's a specialty dish for wedding dinners. Its style reflects both the intrinsic importance of the nuptial feast and the typical lusty, peasanty flavors of Abruzzese cooking. To be honest, it's a fair amount of work to make from scratch, so we won't reproach you if you resort to frozen artichoke hearts and even frozen spinach (the best quality you can get, of course). We ask only that you try it with all fresh ingredients just one time, to see the difference.

You can make the crêpes a day or so in advance. You need exactly 10 of them the size of your timballo dish (we recommend a 9-cup charlotte mold with a 6- to 7-inch diameter). Thus, since you'll have about 16 ounces of batter, you'll use a ¼-cup measure to dip out the batter for each crêpe, and you'll fill it about ¾ full. (Try the math for yourself: it works out pretty exactly.)

An assertive white wine such as Torre di Giano, Pinot bianco, or Tocai.

FOR THE CRESPELLE:

4 large eggs

½ cup all-purpose flour

2 to 3 tablespoons olive oil

FOR THE FILLING AND ASSEMBLY:

2½ tablespoons butter

3 tablespoons olive oil

2 to 3 small chicken livers (2 ounces), cleaned and cut in 2 to 3 pieces each

9 ounces ground round

¾ pound fresh spinach, washed and cooked in just the amount of water that adheres to the leaves

(or one 9-ounce package frozen spinach, defrosted)

1¼ to 1½ pounds tiny artichokes, prepared as directed on page 22 (or one 9-ounce package frozen artichoke hearts), cut in ⅛-inch wedges

1 tablespoon chopped flat-leaf Italian parsley

2 eggs	Salt
3 tablespoons milk	5 to 6 ounces mozzarella, cut in
3 to 4 tablespoons freshly grated	⅛-inch slices
parmigiano	

To make the crespelle:

Put the eggs and flour into the jar of an electric blender. Add ½ cup cold water and blend on high speed until the batter is perfectly smooth. Heat a cast-iron crêpe pan to very hot. Brush the surface lightly with the olive oil, pour in a scant ¼ cup batter, and tilt the pan to spread it into an even circle. Lower heat and cook until light golden on the bottom, then turn and cook the other side. Transfer the finished crêpe to a plate and make nine more in the same way, brushing the pan with oil between crêpes. These can be made up a day or two in advance and kept wrapped in plastic in the refrigerator.

To make the filling:

In a skillet, melt 1 tablespoon of the butter with 1 tablespoon of the olive oil. Add the chicken livers and sauté 5 to 6 minutes. Remove them to a chopping board and chop them fine. Add the ground beef to the skillet and sauté 4 to 5 minutes, until it loses its raw red color. Mix the chopped livers with the beef and set the meats aside.

In another skillet, melt the remaining 1½ tablespoons butter. Squeeze the spinach nearly dry, chop it, add it to the skillet, and sauté 3 to 4 minutes. Remove it to a dish. Heat the remaining 2 tablespoons oil in the same skillet, add the artichokes, and sauté 6 to 8 minutes. Stir in the parsley and remove the artichokes to another dish.

In a small bowl, beat the eggs with the milk.

Assembly and baking:

Generously butter an 8- to 9-cup round mold, such as a charlotte mold. Read through all the following instructions before beginning, to get a feeling for the procedure.

- Lay one crêpe in the bottom of the mold and spread over it ⅓ the ground meats, 1 tablespoon milk-egg mixture, 1 teaspoon parmigiano, and a sprinkling of salt.

- Set a second crêpe on top, press down gently to firm the first layer of filling, and make a layer of ½ the spinach, 1 tablespoon milk-egg mixture, 1 teaspoon parmigiano, and a sprinkling of salt.
- A third crêpe, more gentle pressure, and a layer of ½ the artichokes, 1 to 2 tablespoons milk-egg mixture, 1 teaspoon parmigiano, and a sprinkling of salt.
- A fourth crêpe, pressure, and a layer of ½ the mozzarella, 1 tablespoon milk-egg mixture, 1 teaspoon parmigiano, and a sprinkling of salt.

Repeat the above steps with crêpes five through eight. Make one final filling layer using the final third of the ground meats. Lay on the last crêpe, moisten it with the remainder of the egg-milk mixture, and sprinkle on a final teaspoon of parmigiano. The assembled dish can be covered and set aside in a cool place (not the refrigerator) for 1 hour or more.

When ready to cook, preheat the oven to 475°F. Set the dish in the oven and bake uncovered 30 minutes. Check after 20 minutes, and if the top crêpe is getting too brown, lay a piece of aluminum foil over it. Remove the timballo from the oven and let it settle for 20 to 30 minutes.

To unmold, run a thin knife blade around the inside of the mold to release any adhering crêpes, place a plate over the top of the mold, clamp the plate and mold together, and invert them. You should feel the timballo settling onto the plate. If it doesn't, rap the two dishes (still clamped together) sharply on a countertop. Lift off the mold carefully and gently realign any slippage in the layers. Slice and serve. ∎

SECONDI

Throughout Italy the characteristic spring meats are milk-fed lambs, kids, and suckling pigs, all of a youth next to impossible to obtain in the United States without special arrangements with a farmer or a butcher. Our recipe for a whole roasted baby lamb—an adaptation of a standard Roman technique—calls for a 20-pounder, which by American market standards is ridiculously tiny, and by Italian palatal standards already too large and on the way to coarseness. Italians do not greatly admire blood meats: their consumption of steak, for instance, is limited to occasional indulgences in *bistecca fiorentina* (a thick T-bone steak from the prized Chianina breed of cattle); and Italian lamb chops tend not to be rare, double-thick clubs taken from well-grown animals but thin, utterly lean medallions of delicate meat attached to a wand of bone, taken from a very young lamb. In Roman trattorias in spring, *abbacchio* and *capretto* and *maialino*—lamb and kid and suckling pig—all run to about the same size: a hindquarter or forequarter of each makes a generous serving for one person. All are prepared in the manner of the recipe we give here, often with differing herbs: lambs tend to get mint, suckling pigs rosemary, and kids marjoram.

Because such small whole beasts are so difficult to obtain here, we've given only the one recipe for them, and offer instead some easy braises of more familiar (and more adult) meats, including a number of preparations for various cuts of lamb. A few of the meats we call for may seem exotic, but they are both popular and ubiquitous in Italian menus and markets. Farm-bred quails and veal sweetbreads in particular, though in this country they tend to be the exclusive property of the higher-priced palaces of gastronomic pretention, are in Italy staples of middle-class tables and the most modest restaurants. At our very first dinner together in Italy (longer ago now than either of us cares to think about), in a no-nonsense Roman trattoria, Diane was delighted to find *due quaglie* unremarkedly listed in a long column of mimeographed secondi that ran from grilled scamorza (a firm cheese, somewhat akin to provolone) through the familiar cutlets and their cousins and on to more mysterious innard meats. Two tiny roasted quails cost—if our notes can be believed—$1.50. That trattoria, La Capricciosa, is still doing business, with a still enormous and varied menu, and still at remarkably reasonable prices. You can still get due quaglie there any day of the week.

GOLDEN BRAISED CHICKEN

Pollo in potacchio all'anconetana

FOR 4 SERVINGS:

*T*his extremely simple recipe develops a rich, creamy sauce with a lovely golden color. Ancona, where this recipe hails from, is an Adriatic Coast city in the Marches, and *potacchio* is a name you'll find on many dishes of the region. It refers to the sauce ingredients—one of Italy's many the-whole-is-greater-than-the-sum-of-its-parts blends of tomato, white wine, oil, garlic, rosemary, and (usually) parsley. Cooks in that region prepare just about every variety of meat *in potacchio,* and you'll see why when you taste this dish. As Diane's father is wont to remark, "The sole of an old shoe would taste good if you cooked it that way."

The basic trick of this dish is one that is common to many Italian braises: never drown the chicken, but keep it simmering in a very small quantity of liquid. This at once extracts flavors from the bird, concentrates the sauce, and allows the chicken to draw flavor from the cooking liquid without being dried out by it, as many boiled chickens and meats often are. It's similar to the risotto technique, which achieves a similar creamy texture and concentrated flavor by adding frequent small quantities of liquid to keep the dish moist but not soaking. It's a bit more labor-intensive than other methods—you have to check the pot from time to time to make sure the dish isn't drying out and frying—but the results in flavor and texture are worth the effort.

A soft, fruity red wine will taste just fine with this dish. Try a young Chianti from around Siena, or a Dolcetto, a Valpolicella, or a Montepulciano d'Abruzzo.

¼ *cup olive oil*

½ *cup sliced onion*

2 *cloves garlic, lightly crushed*

One 3-pound chicken, cut up

Salt

Freshly ground black pepper

1 *teaspoon tomato paste dissolved in* ½ *cup white wine*

1 *teaspoon rosemary leaves*

In a broad casserole, heat the olive oil, add the onions and garlic and sauté over medium heat about 5 minutes, until the onions are beginning to soften.

Rinse the chicken pieces, pat them dry, and add them to the pan. Salt lightly and pepper generously. Sauté the chicken pieces 5 minutes, turn, salt and pepper the other sides, and sauté another 5 minutes.

Raise heat to medium-high and add the tomato paste dissolved in wine. Bring to a boil and boil briskly a few moments, scraping up any browned bits in the pan. Cover the pan, turn the heat to low, and cook about 1 hour. Check the dish every 15 minutes, turning the chicken pieces and adding a few tablespoons of hot water as the liquid reduces. (Don't let the sauce ever get down to clear fat; keep adding water to maintain the creamy texture.) After the chicken has cooked 30 minutes, add the rosemary.

When the chicken is tender, remove it to a serving dish and keep warm. Defat the pan thoroughly. There will be only a small amount of liquid left. Add enough hot water to make about 1 cup liquid in all, and boil it briskly for 1 to 2 minutes, stirring and scraping up browned bits. Pour the sauce over the chicken and serve at once. ■

ROASTED QUAILS

Quaglie al forno

FOR 4 SERVINGS:

*Q*uails are as common on Italian menus and tables as steaks are in the United States, and most Italian treatments of them are quite simple and straightforward, as is this example. (Another appears in the Summer section. For an exception that proves this rule, see the Fall section.) The only trick to cooking quails lies in providing a layer of fat to keep them from drying out. You can use fresh fatback or blanched salt pork or even mild bacon (blanch it too if it's heavily salted or smoked) instead of the pancetta recommended here. You can remove the crisped fat from the quails before serving if you wish, though the sweetness of the pancetta adds a nice flavor element to the ensemble. This simple technique results in glistening brown, plump birds, a treat for the eye as well as the palate.

A white wine with acidity and a distinctive flavor of its own—a Gavi, perhaps, or an Arneis, or even a Fiano di Avellino.

8 quails, about 4 ounces apiece	3 sage leaves
8 thin slices pancetta, about 4 ounces in all	Salt
	Freshly ground black pepper
3 tablespoons butter	1/3 cup dry white wine

Rinse the quails and pat them dry with paper towels. Lay a round of pancetta over the breast and thighs of each bird and tie them securely with kitchen string.

Preheat oven to 400°F. In an ovenproof casserole just large enough to hold the quails, melt the butter. Add the sage, then the quails. Brown them over medium heat 3 to 4 minutes on each side. Salt and pepper them lightly, pour on the wine, and scrape up the browned bits from the bottom of the pan.

Set the casserole in the oven and roast 20 to 25 minutes, or until the quails are tender, turning them once. Remove the strings and serve in a warmed dish. ■

GENOVESE STUFFED BREAST OF VEAL

Cima ripiena alla genovese

FOR 6 TO 8 SERVINGS:

You can let your imagination range here. Cima will partner happily with all but the biggest, most aggressive red wines. As the main course of a dinner, choose a Barbera or a young, non-riserva Taurasi. For a cold buffet, a light red such as young Chianti or Dolcetto. For an antipasto, a light, dry white wine such as Soave or Galestro or Corvo.

Breast of veal is stuffed in many different cultures, and the ingredients used for the stuffing usually epitomize a culinary style. Some versions disappoint us because the veal itself is barely noticeable—it's just a neutral shell to encase a savory pudding. That's not the case with this traditional Ligurian dish: despite the lushness of the stuffing, the veal is very definitely a presence. (Incidentally, if you can't lay your hands on just a few pods of fresh peas, it would be acceptable to substitute frozen. One needn't be absolutely fanatic about what is largely a color accent.)

Cima takes a bit of time to make, though most of it is downtime for the cook: two hours at the simmer and then a few more hours to cool and firm it for slicing. You'll need a big, deep pot to simmer the stuffed breast in, which will create a largish quantity of nicely flavored broth. This is usually filtered (because some egg inevitably escapes from the stuffing and clots in the liquid) and served as a soup with pastina, though you could also use passatelli (see page 41), which are good with any broth.

Thin slices of cima also make excellent antipasti. In Genoa, leftovers are sliced, dipped in egg and bread crumbs, and sautéed in butter, like veal cutlets.

1½ ounces dried porcini

¼ cup fresh small green peas

3 tablespoons butter

¼ pound boneless veal (e.g., trimmings from the breast), cut in 1-inch chunks

¾ pound sweetbreads, trimmed and cut in 1-inch chunks

3 tablespoons freshly grated parmigiano

½ teaspoon marjoram

4 eggs, beaten

½ teaspoon salt

Freshly ground black pepper

One 3-pound boneless breast of veal with a pocket cut in it

1 clove garlic, halved

1 carrot, halved

1 stalk celery, halved

1 small onion, halved

Put the dried mushrooms in a bowl and pour 1 cup boiling water over them. Let sit for 30 minutes, then drain them, reserving the water. While the mushrooms are soaking, drop the peas into a small pot of boiling water and blanch them 5 minutes, then drain and set aside.

Rinse the mushroom pieces thoroughly, chop them coarsely, and rinse again to remove all traces of grit. Line a sieve with a dampened paper towel and strain the mushroom-soaking liquid into a small bowl.

In a small frying pan, melt the butter and add the veal and sweetbread pieces. Sauté over medium heat 5 minutes, stirring often. Scrape the entire contents of the pan into a food processor. Add the mushrooms and pulse until everything has a coarsely ground texture. Put the meat mixture into a large bowl and add the peas, cheese, marjoram, eggs, salt, and a generous quantity of freshly ground black pepper. Mix well. This will be a soft, moist mixture.

Open the pocket in the veal breast and rub its interior all over with the cut side of the garlic clove. (Save the garlic clove to put in the broth.) Fill the opening with the stuffing mixture. It should be no more than two thirds full. If there is too much stuffing, try to enlarge the pocket a little, or don't use all the stuffing. Sew the opening closed with a darning needle and heavy-duty thread.

Put 3 quarts cold water in a 6- to 8-quart pot. Add the carrot, celery, onion, reserved garlic clove, and the strained mushroom soaking water. Bring to a full boil and slide in the veal breast. Reduce to a simmer, cover, and cook 2 hours, skimming frequently. As soon as the meat begins to swell up, prick it deeply with a skewer in several places to keep it from bursting.

At the end of the 2 hours, remove the veal breast from the pan and set it on a platter. Cover it with a board or another platter and set a heavy weight on top (a couple of large cans of tomatoes, for instance), and let it cool completely. Slice and serve. ■

VEAL CHOPS IN RED WINE

Costolette di vitello in vino rosso

FOR 4 SERVINGS:

A full-bodied red wine with lots of flavor of its own and a judicious amount of tannin—Chianti Classico or Taurasi (even riserva bottles), Vino Nobile or Carmignano, Nebbiolo or Cabernet from Trentino–Alto Adige or the Veneto.

ere we encounter one of the rare large meat portions in Italian cookery. This recipe provides a showcase for large, handsome loin veal chops—and we do mean large: they should be about ½ pound apiece. They need long, gentle cooking to keep them tender, but since they can be cooked completely in advance and reheated at the last moment, this dish can fit very comfortably into the framework of a busy dinner party.

The prosciutto fat makes this a very rich dish indeed. With a different fat it's still good, but not as striking in flavor, so it's worth whatever trouble you have to go to to beg, borrow, or steal an ounce of pure white prosciutto fat. Once upon a time butchers and *salumeria* staff gave it away when they trimmed prosciutti, but now most sell it if they will part with it at all (they've gotten almost as stingy with prosciutto bones). Helpful hint: every prosciutto has a heel, which is not of much use for slicing, and can usually be bought at a reasonable price. Trim it up yourself, separating rind, flesh, and fat for different culinary purposes (beans, tortellini, and veal chops in red wine, respectively).

Because of its richness and unctuosity, these chops like a slightly bitter green alongside: the spinach dish on page 100, or escarole cooked the same way, for instance.

1 ounce prosciutto fat	*Salt*
½ teaspoon rosemary leaves	*Freshly ground black pepper*
1 clove garlic	*¼ cup dry red wine*
1 tablespoon olive oil	*1½ cups broth, approximately*
4 thick loin veal chops, 2 pounds in all	*1 tablespoon tomato paste*

Chop the prosciutto fat, rosemary, and garlic together. Put the mixture into a large nonreactive skillet along with the olive oil and sauté over moderate heat 2 minutes, until the fat is rendered.

Pat the chops dry with paper towels, put them in the skillet, and brown them well on both sides. Sprinkle them with salt and pepper, and pour the wine over them. Turn heat to high and boil rapidly until the wine is reduced by half, scraping up any browned bits that cling to the bottom of the pan.

While the wine is reducing, bring the broth to a simmer in a small pot. In a cup, dissolve the tomato paste in 2 tablespoons of the broth. Stir the dissolved paste into the veal chop pan. Lower heat to medium and cook the chops 2 minutes, turning them once or twice to coat them with the tomato liquid, then stir in 1 cup of the broth, cover, and cook the chops 1½ hours, adjusting the heat as necessary to maintain a gentle simmer. Turn the chops from time to time, and add small amounts of broth if necessary to keep the sauce from drying out. At the end of the cooking time, the chops should be meltingly tender, with just enough velvety sauce left in the pan to moisten the chops for serving. ■

BRAISED VEAL WITH SPRING ONIONS

Spezzatino di vitello con cipolle

FOR 4 TO 5 SERVINGS:

*S*omewhat similar in its just-wet-enough-not-to-fry cooking technique to the *pollo in potacchio* on page 71, this recipe too produces a golden sauce, all nubbly and sweet from the carrots and the onions. At the end, the veal should be meltingly tender.

In Italy, some versions of this dish so celebrate those sweet, early spring onions that the veal becomes only an excuse or vehicle for them. That gives real onion fanciers license to raise the quantity of whole onions almost *ad libitum*—though we have found that using more onions than veal (by weight) gets to be a bit much.

1 tablespoon butter	Salt
3 tablespoons olive oil	¼ cup dry white wine
½ cup chopped onion	1 tablespoon tomato paste
1 carrot, chopped	½ cup broth
1 stalk celery, chopped	1 pound small spring onions (or
2 sage leaves	pearl onions), peeled and
2 bay leaves	trimmed close to the base of the
2 ounces pancetta, diced	stem
2 pounds boneless stewing veal	

In a nonreactive casserole, melt the butter in the oil. Add the onion, carrot, celery, and sage and bay leaves. Sauté the vegetables over low heat 5 minutes, stirring occasionally. Add the pancetta and sauté 5 more minutes.

Raise heat to medium-high, push the vegetables to the side of the pan, add the veal, and brown the meat on all sides, about 5 minutes. Salt lightly, pour in the wine, and mix all together well. Reduce heat to low and cook 5 minutes. Dissolve the tomato paste in 2 to 3 tablespoons warm water and add it to the meat along with the broth. Cover tightly and simmer 1 hour, stirring occasionally and adding 1 to 2 tablespoons water if the sauce reduces so much that the meat is frying.

Add the onions to the casserole and cook another 30 minutes, or until the meat and onions are perfectly tender. Either serve at once or set aside and reheat when ready. ∎

HOME-STYLE BEEF STEW

Spezzatino di bue alla casalinga

FOR 4 TO 5 SERVINGS:

The name may make this sound like a winter dish, but the bright, light flavor says *primavera* very clearly. Not as wet in its conclusion as a stew is usually thought of as being, but wetter in the cooking than a braise usually is. Gentle cooking melts the beef into juicy flavorfulness and creates a small quantity of subtle, succulent gravy—terrific on mashed potatoes (or freshly made egg noodles, if you're not having a primo).

Cooking times will vary with the cut of meat you're using, so it's best to leave lots of time. If the beef is done too soon, it can always be turned off and reheated when needed. Time considerations aside, for the richest flavor in this kind of cooking, we prefer to use eye of chuck.

This dish will take as good a red wine as you care to give it, so you can dress it up or down to suit the occasion and the company. A simple Barbera will be fine for a family dinner; or a Barbaresco or Barolo (either one 5 to 7 years old) will make an impressive show on a more elegant occasion.

3 tablespoons olive oil	1 clove garlic, finely chopped
2½ pounds boneless stewing beef, e.g., eye of chuck, cut in 2-inch chunks	2 tablespoons finely chopped flat-leaf Italian parsley
Salt	¼ teaspoon thyme or marjoram
Freshly ground black pepper	1 bay leaf
¼ cup dry red wine	1 cup drained canned Italian-style plum tomatoes, chopped
½ cup thinly sliced onion	2 cups broth, approximately
½ cup thinly sliced celery	

In a casserole, heat the olive oil. Pat the pieces of meat dry with paper towels and brown them on all sides over medium-high heat (in two batches, if necessary). Salt and pepper the meat, then pour in the red wine, raise heat to high, and cook briskly, stirring, 1 to 2 minutes. Remove the meat to a plate. If there is any wine left in the casserole, continue cooking over high heat until it is completely evaporated.

Turn heat to low, add the onion and celery to the casserole, and sauté 5 minutes. Add the garlic, parsley, thyme or marjoram, bay leaf, and tomatoes, stir, and sauté 1 minute. Return the meat to the pan, mix everything together well, and bring to a simmer. Add 1 cup of the broth; when it comes to a simmer, cover the pan and cook gently 1 to 1½ hours, until the beef is tender, stirring from time to time. Add more broth as necessary if the stew seems to be drying out. Taste the sauce for salt before serving. ■

ROASTED EASTER LAMB

Agnello di Pasqua al forno

FOR 12 TO 16 SERVINGS:

*W*hole roasted lamb is a traditional Easter feast throughout the center and south of Italy, rivaled in popularity and deliciousness only by roasted kid in the north.

In Italy, they commonly use milk-fed lambs of 10 pounds and under, but we can rarely get them that small in this country. A 20-pound lamb (about 17 pounds cooking weight, without the head, which is often omitted here though seldom in Italy) will fill the largest roasting pan and will feed twelve to sixteen people. You can have the butcher cut it in half (either lengthwise or across the middle) and make two superb dinners from it if you don't mind spoiling the presentation. This is so wonderfully festive a dish, however, that it makes more sense—and is certainly more fun—to simply invite as many people as your dinner table will hold, roast the whole beast, and eat sumptuous leftovers (if there are any) for a few days.

Most butchers will special-order lambs at Eastertime. Those in

The delicacy of baby lamb doesn't handle huge red wines as well as more mature lamb does, so choose red wines marked by complexity rather than power: Chianti Classico Riserva, Carmignano Riserva, Vino Nobile, Taurasi Riserva, or Aglianico Riserva, even one of the barrique-aged or Nebbiolo-blended Barberas.

Italian or Greek neighborhoods may stock them routinely. In theory at least, small whole lambs should be available all spring long. Just be specific about what you mean by "small": different butchers have different notions of that word as it applies to whole animals, and lambs and suckling pigs tend unavoidably to get larger and larger as spring progresses.

The only trick to this dish, other than patience during its slow cooking, is the seasoned oil with which the lamb is anointed. The oil needs to be steeped in garlic, bay leaf, and mint for several hours (or overnight). The mint is a very Roman touch; altogether, the cooking aromas will drive you crazy.

½ cup olive oil

3 to 4 cloves garlic, lightly crushed

1 bay leaf

2 tablespoons chopped fresh mint

1 20-pound lamb

Salt

Freshly ground black pepper

2 cups broth (optional)

Preparing the seasoned oil:

In a small pan over gentle heat, warm the olive oil together with the garlic, bay leaf, and mint for 10 minutes. Off heat, let it stand several hours (or overnight), then strain into a small bowl.

Preparing the lamb:

Preheat the oven to 400°F. Open the lamb's body cavity, sprinkle it with salt and pepper, and rub it with some of the seasoned olive oil. Truss the lamb with kitchen string so that it fits into a roasting pan. Salt and pepper the exterior of the lamb and rub more of the olive oil over it.

Roasting:

Put the lamb in the oven and immediately lower the heat to 350°F. Roast about 3½ hours in all. For the first 2 hours, baste every 20 minutes with the remaining seasoned oil, and when that runs out, with broth or water and the pan drippings. During the last hour, without basting, the lamb will turn a rich brown color and develop a crisp, crackling skin.

Remove the lamb from the oven and let it sit 20 minutes before carving and serving. ∎

BREAST OF LAMB, HUNTER'S STYLE

Agnello alla cacciatora

FOR 4 SERVINGS:

Y

Match this dish with a simple, hearty red wine, such as Montepulciano d'Abruzzo, Corvo, Salice Salentino, or Lacryma Christi.

*W*hoever the hunter was who first thought up this recipe, he was clearly a better cook than marksman—unless he'd declared an open season on his neighbors' flocks of sheep. This delicious peasant dish from Puglia is absurdly easy to prepare: you simply stir all the ingredients together and bake them. The tomato and the onion melt into a lovely dense sauce, and the potato just glories in it, as do the tender little lamb riblets.

Breast of lamb is sold in long sheets that look like farmer-style spareribs, usually weighing 1 to 1½ pounds. You'll need two of them to serve four. If lamb breast is not available, you can substitute 2 pounds of boneless lamb shoulder cut into 1½-inch cubes, in which case bake about 15 minutes longer than called for here.

2½ pounds lamb breast, cut in
  individual riblets
1¼ cups drained canned
  Italian-style plum tomatoes,
  roughly chopped
8 small boiling potatoes (about 1
  pound), peeled and halved

1 cup sliced onion
4 tablespoons olive oil
1 teaspoon dried oregano
1 teaspoon salt
Freshly ground black
  pepper

Preheat the oven to 350°F. Put the pieces of lamb, tomatoes, and potatoes into an ovenproof casserole large enough to hold everything snugly in one layer. Add all the remaining ingredients and stir well. Cover and bake 1 hour, giving everything a stir every 15 minutes or so. Serve directly from the casserole. ■

BRAISED LAMB, ABRUZZI STYLE

Agnello in umido all'abruzzese

FOR 4 SERVINGS:

Another one-pot meal, another tasty amalgam of lamb and tomato, served this time over a bed of homemade egg noodles. (In the Abruzzi, they would customarily be large, broad, toothsome *lasagnette*.) This is down-home food, but subtle: the lamb—a boneless shoulder, stuffed with garlic and rosemary—and the tomatoes mollify each other's assertiveness, and the dried red peppers impart a pleasing warmth to the sauce. Honest country cooking at its best.

Ⴖ

Middle-range red wines, from Montepulciano d'Abruzzo on up to Chianti Classico. The key factor in the wine you want with this dish, aside from redness, should be acidity.

2 pounds boneless shoulder or leg
   of lamb, in one piece
4 cloves garlic—2 slivered and 2
   minced
1 teaspoon rosemary leaves
4 tablespoons olive oil
Salt
2 dried peperoncini rossi
6 ounces thickly sliced pancetta,
   blanched 1 minute, drained, and
   patted dry
½ cup dry white wine

2 cups drained canned
   Italian-style plum tomatoes,
   chopped
2 tablespoons chopped flat-leaf
   Italian parsley
1 teaspoon oregano
½ pound fresh fettucelle or other
   wide egg noodle
2 tablespoons butter
2 tablespoons freshly grated
   parmigiano

Slice the meat nearly in half, open it like a book, and fill the interior with the slivered garlic and the rosemary. Close the meat up and tie it securely with kitchen string.

In a casserole, heat the olive oil and brown the meat on all sides over medium-high heat. Sprinkle it with salt and add the peperoncini and pancetta. Add the wine and cook briskly until it is evaporated.

Add the tomatoes, parsley, minced garlic, and oregano. Stir all together well and bring to a simmer. Cover and simmer 1½ hours, or until the lamb is tender. Turn the meat and stir the sauce occasionally during the cooking. After the first hour, check the liquid level and continue cooking either covered or uncovered as necessary to thicken the sauce. Remove the peperoncini.

When the lamb is ready, cook the pasta in a large quantity of boiling salted water. Drain it, transfer to a deep serving platter, and toss it with the butter and parmigiano. Remove the strings from the lamb, set it in the middle of the pasta, and pour all the sauce and the pancetta around it onto the pasta. Serve at once. ∎

CASSEROLE ROAST OF LAMB STUFFED WITH PEAS AND MUSHROOMS

Rollato d'agnello alla ragusana

FOR 8 SERVINGS:

♀

A fine red wine is in order here—Gattinara, Barbaresco, Barolo, a fine Tuscan red such as Brunello, or an Aglianico, Taurasi, or Duca Enrico from farther south.

A wonderful presentation for an important spring dinner. Making the stuffing and sewing it into the lamb requires some effort and attention, but the cooking itself is effortless. If, like us, you're fanatic about cooking lamb rare or at least rosy-pink, you may balk at this recipe on first reading. Please have faith. When it comes to lamb, Italian cooks know what they're doing. Treated this way, the meat becomes brown and almost fork-tender but retains all its flavor. It needs no basting, but generates its own charming, light brown sauce. The stuffing, very soft and wet initially, cooks up firm and absolutely delicious. You can't argue with results like that.

Because the stuffing is so soft at first, you must sew all the openings of the meat completely closed. (Think of the dish as a tastier version of haggis.) If you can possibly get a lamb's liver, by all means use that rather than calf's liver: it's what is normally used in Italy. And if you're not worried about being politically correct in terms of peas, frozen (shh!) will do.

1 ounce dried porcini (or substitute ¾ pound fresh white mushrooms)

¾ cup shelled fresh peas—½ to ¾ pound in the pod

2 cups cubes of day-old country-style bread

3 tablespoons olive oil

½ cup chopped onion

¼ pound prosciutto, chopped

¼ pound calf's liver, cut in ½-inch pieces

1 cup freshly grated pecorino romano

1 egg

Salt

Freshly ground black pepper

1 boned leg of lamb, 6 to 6½ pounds

2 tablespoons butter

Preparing the stuffing:

Put the dried porcini in a bowl and pour 1 cup boiling water over them. Let sit for 30 minutes, then drain them, reserving the water. Rinse the porcini pieces thoroughly, chop them coarsely, and rinse again to remove all traces of grit. Line a sieve with a dampened paper towel and strain the soaking liquid into a small bowl. (If using fresh mushrooms, simply wash and coarsely chop them.)

Drop the peas into boiling salted water and blanch them 5 minutes. Drain and set aside. Put the bread cubes into a bowl and pour the porcini liquid over them, turning and pressing them so they absorb it fully. (If porcini weren't used, soak the bread in hot water.)

In a large skillet, heat the olive oil. Sauté the onion over medium-low heat 5 to 10 minutes, until they are just beginning to brown. Add the mushrooms, prosciutto, liver, and peas. Sauté 10 minutes, stirring occasionally. Transfer this mixture to a large bowl and let it cool somewhat. Squeeze the bread fairly dry and add it to the bowl, along with the cheese, egg, ¼ teaspoon salt, and a generous quantity of black pepper. Mix well.

Stuffing and cooking the lamb:

Preheat the oven to 350°F. Spread the lamb out on a work surface. If there are any tears in the meat, patch them with small pieces cut from the ends. Salt and pepper the entire surface lightly. Mound the stuffing on one half of the lamb. Fold the other half over the top and sew all the edges together with a darning needle and heavy-duty thread.

Choose a covered casserole large and deep enough to contain the stuffed lamb. Oil the bottom generously and set the lamb in it. Salt and pepper the lamb lightly, and dot it with the butter. Cover and roast in the oven for 2 hours.

Transfer the meat to a carving board. Defat the liquid in the casserole and boil it down if necessary to make a thinnish sauce. Remove all the thread from the lamb, then slice and arrange it on a platter, moistening the slices with the sauce. ■

PORK STEWED WITH OLIVES

Spezzatino di maiale con olive

FOR 4 TO 5 SERVINGS:

An honest, not very complicated red wine is best. Try a Montepulciano d'Abruzzo, Lacryma Christi, Corvo, simple Barbera, or non-Classico Chianti.

A simple and tasty dish that simmers along quietly while you are busying yourself with other cooking or other chores. The meat turns an attractive pinkish-red and gets quite tender, the sauce thickens nicely, and the whole ensemble tastes pleasingly rich for such humble ingredients. The olives go in only shortly before the dish finishes cooking, but they add the little touch that lifts this homely recipe out of the ordinary. Preferences will divide over whether green or black are better, but there is no question that canned are the worst: avoid them at all cost.

Accompany the stew with gnocchi (page 253 in the Fall section) or potatoes mashed with parmigiano (page 300 in the Fall section) if you are not having a primo.

2 pounds boneless pork, cut in
   2-inch chunks
Salt
Freshly ground black pepper
Flour for dredging
3 tablespoons olive oil
2 cloves garlic, crushed

4 to 5 sage leaves
1 cup drained canned Italian-style
   plum tomatoes, pureed through a
   food mill
1 cup broth
½ pound black or green olives (or
   both)

In a casserole, heat the olive oil with the garlic and sage. Pat the pork chunks dry with paper towels, sprinkle them with salt and pepper, and dust them lightly with flour. Brown them in the casserole over medium-high heat.

Add the tomatoes and broth to the casserole, cover, and cook gently until the meat is very tender, about 1½ hours. While the meat is cooking, pit the olives and blanch them 2 minutes in boiling water, then drain well. Add them to the casserole 15 minutes before the dish is done. ■

BAKED PORK CHOPS

Braciole di maiale al forno

FOR 4 SERVINGS:

This recipe couldn't be simpler or more delicious. The chops come out of the oven crisp yet still tender, moist, and well-flavored from the *battutino*—the herb mixture—you've rubbed them with. There's only one little trick to remember: trim all the visible fat off the chops before you do anything else to them. Otherwise they'll soon be awash in it in their pan, which may toughen them as they then "fry" in the oven.

Needless to say, fresh herbs work much better with this recipe than dry ones. Here's a little trick you might try with herbs, in case you don't know it already: while they are in season and plentiful, freeze small packets of them for use all year round. Sage and basil in particular respond very well to this and both preserve much more of their fresh flavor and delicacy frozen than they do dried.

1 teaspoon olive oil	*Freshly ground black pepper*
4 loin pork chops (about 1½	*6 sage leaves*
pounds), cut ¾ inch thick and	*1 teaspoon rosemary leaves*
trimmed of all fat	*1 clove garlic*
Salt	*½ cup dry white wine*

Preheat the oven to 375°F. Oil a baking dish just large enough to hold the chops in one layer.

Pound the chops with a meat pounder to flatten them to ½ inch or less. Salt and pepper them lightly. Finely chop together the sage, rosemary, and garlic. Spread this mixture on both sides of the chops and rub it in with your hands. Put the chops in the baking dish and add the white wine and enough water to barely cover. Put the dish in the oven and bake uncovered 1 to 1¼ hours, until the chops are tender. ■

FRICASSEED SWEETBREADS

Animelle in fricassea

FOR 4 SERVINGS:

The ingredient list here might seem to indicate that this is a very rich dish, but in fact it isn't: the lemon keeps it light and bright, even delicate in flavor—just as sweetbreads ought to be. Anyone who thinks that sweetbreads must be a lot of work to prepare is in for a pleasant surprise here and with Italian modes of dealing with sweetbreads generally. This recipe takes about half an hour from start to delicious finish: no long blanching, no pressing, no lengthy cooking—just very fresh and straightforward flavor, minimally interfered with. The results are tasty enough that we have been tempted (and once or twice actually succumbed) to dressing them up by serving them in a vol-au-vent shell, but while the sweetbreads will play up to that kind of dinner theater, they certainly don't need it: they're just fine as they are.

Vis-à-vis the membrane that we instruct you below to remove from the blanched sweetbreads: you needn't be fanatical about getting it all off. It's mostly a cosmetic step anyhow, because it's entirely edible.

We like an elegant white wine with this dish: anything from (in the north) a fine Friulian Sauvignon to (in the south) Fiano di Avellino or Regaleali bianco.

2 veal sweetbreads, about 1¼ pounds	*Freshly ground black pepper*
4 tablespoons unsalted butter	*1 egg yolk*
¼ cup finely chopped onion	*Juice of ½ lemon*
Salt	*1 tablespoon broth*

Fill a large pot with 2 to 3 quarts water and bring it to a boil. Drop in the sweetbreads, turn off the heat, and let sit 1 minute. Drain the sweetbreads, pat them dry, and pull off any bits of gristle and thin, translucent membrane. Cut them into pieces 1 to 1½ inches across.

In a broad sauté pan, melt the butter and sauté the onion over low heat 4 to 5 minutes. Add the sweetbreads and salt and pepper to taste. Cook 15 minutes, stirring often. Meanwhile, in a small bowl, beat the egg yolk with the lemon juice and broth.

When the sweetbreads are done, transfer them to a serving dish and keep warm. Pour the egg-lemon mixture into the pan and stir constantly over low heat, without letting the liquid boil, until the sauce just thickens. Dress the sweetbreads with the sauce and serve at once. ∎

SWEETBREADS WITH PROSCIUTTO

Animelle al prosciutto

FOR 4 SERVINGS:

*T*his excellent recipe affords another dramatic example of the simplicity of Italian techniques with sweetbreads and the savoriness of the product of those techniques. Here, the sweetbreads are blanched very briefly before being cut up—largely to make them easier to trim. Once again, it's not necessary to be a perfectionist about the trimming: the membrane isn't pretty but it has no flavor of its own, and so won't harm the dish any way except cosmetically.

Thereafter the sweetbreads are braised in the classic Italian manner of adding only a little liquid at a time so as to concentrate flavor rather than disperse it. The whole process takes about a half hour from start to finish. The resulting dish is rich without being at all cloying. The delicate flavor of the sweetbreads harmonizes intriguingly with the slight smokiness lent by the prosciutto—a wonderful palatal counterpoint.

1 teaspoon lemon juice

1 1/2 pounds veal sweetbreads

1 1/2 cups broth

2 tablespoons butter

1/2 cup finely chopped onion

2 ounces prosciutto, cut in
   matchsticks

Salt

Freshly ground black pepper

Bring 2 quarts water to a boil, add the lemon juice, and drop in the sweetbreads. Boil them 2 minutes, then drain and refresh them in cold water. Pat them dry, remove any bits of tube, fat, or heavy membrane, and cut them into bite-sized pieces.

In a small pot, bring the broth to a simmer. In a broad sauté pan, melt the butter and sauté the onion and prosciutto for 5 minutes. Raise heat to medium and add the sweetbread pieces. Salt and pepper them lightly and sauté 1 minute, stirring to coat them with the seasonings. Add 1/2 cup of the broth, cover the pan, and cook over low heat 5 minutes. Add another 1/2 cup broth, stir, and cook 5 minutes more, then add the remaining broth and cook a final 5 minutes. Serve at once on a warmed serving dish. ∎

BRAISED KID WITH CELERY AND POTATOES

Capretto in umido con verdure

FOR 4 TO 5 SERVINGS:

Kid is not an exotic meat in Italy, where it appears regularly every spring in butcher shops, on restaurant menus, and on home tables. While whole kid remains a rarity everywhere in America, smaller cuts of the meat are becoming more common, especially in markets with a Mexican or Caribbean clientele. It's a meat worth searching out for its unique flavor, which is something like veal with a gamey edge.

If you're curious enough to try—and you must be a palatal adventurer, or else why would you be reading this book?—here's a tasty, very down-home way of preparing it that won't alienate more squeamish souls. The celery helps tone down the slight gaminess of the meat but leaves intact its essential character. You'll notice once again the Italian trick of adding only the minimal necessary liquid to keep the pot simmering along quietly: Italian cookery distinctly prefers adding a small amount of liquid at the end to make a sauce rather than boiling down a large amount of liquid throughout. The result—in our opinion and on our palates—is almost always a lighter, cleaner-tasting dish than one gets the other way around.

A medium-bodied red wine of some character and a lot of fruit. A Rosso di Montalcino would work well, and so would a young Nebbiolo.

2½ pounds kid, cut in 2-inch pieces	Freshly ground black pepper
¼ cup olive oil	¼ cup white wine
½ to ¾ cup coarsely chopped onion	2 cups broth, approximately
1 clove garlic	1½ pounds potatoes, peeled and cut in 2-inch pieces
Salt	¾ pound celery, cut in 2-inch pieces

Rinse the pieces of kid and pat them dry with paper towels. In a heavy-bottomed casserole, heat the olive oil. Sauté the onion and garlic for 2 to 3 minutes over medium heat, until the onion begins to wilt. Add the meat and brown it on all sides. Sprinkle with salt and pepper.

Raise heat to high, add the wine, and boil, stirring, until it is almost evaporated. Add 1 cup of the broth. Cover and cook gently, stirring occasionally and adding more broth if the meat seems to be drying out, for 30 minutes.

Add the potatoes and celery and continue cooking, stirring and adding broth as necessary, another 30 to 45 minutes, or until the meat and vegetables are tender. Taste for salt and pepper before serving. ■

CONTORNI

Greens, greens, greens, and more greens, and usually served as simply as possible so as not to interfere with their natural freshness and flavor: that's the real story of spring vegetables in Italy.

Recipes are almost superfluous: the tiniest peas, cooked—steamed, probably—the day they are picked, before their sugars can start turning into starches; young, tender leaves of spinach, carefully washed to remove all the grit and then in effect "melted" in just the water that clings to them. As the seasons progress, sweet, young beet leaves, the first Swiss chard, dandelions, even sometimes lettuces will be treated exactly as the first spinach is. All such vegetables are served hot from the stove or at room temperature.

Asparagus of course we've already encountered in spring antipasto and primo recipes. They're equally abundant as contorni. One memorable dish we were served in Piedmont was a salad of mixed wild and "tame" asparagus dressed simply with olive oil. The straw-thin spears of wild asparagus apparently grow quite freely in the Italian countryside, and are searched for and gathered just as assiduously as insalata campagnola greens are. In the countryside around Treviso once, we were served a homemade after-dinner amaro flavored with wild asparagus, a spear of which was placed in each glassful. The local name for them was *pungitori,* and pungent indeed the concoction was.

On restaurant menus in Italy, the first and finest spring vegetables are usually listed as *primizie* and priced at a premium. Also, since—as mentioned in our antipasto introduction—there's a great interchangeability between vegetables-as-contorni and vegetables-as-antipasti, any attractive vegetable you see on a restaurant display table ought to be readily given you for either role in your meal.

ASPARAGUS WITH HAZELNUT BUTTER

Asparagi al parmigiano

FOR 4 SERVINGS:

If the asparagus are
accompanying your secondo,
choose the wine recommended
for that. If you are serving
them on their own, they'll taste
fine with almost any light, dry
white wine—Pinot grigio or
Soave are excellent choices—or
with a light acidic red such as
Valpolicella or young Chianti
or simple Barbera.

The first asparagus of the spring are glorious all by themselves, the second almost as good. By the fifth or sixth time, you're probably ready to consider gilding the lily—which is what this recipe is, an elegant way to dress up simple boiled asparagus.

This recipe has two primary virtues: the combination of browned butter and Parmesan cheese flavors with asparagus is wonderful in itself, and it also makes the asparagus much more amenable to wine, even to red wine, which is very useful for those of us who don't want to give up either pleasure.

If you need to keep asparagus for a day or so before cooking it, the best way we've found to keep it fresh and crisp is to treat the spears like the flower stalks that they are: put the whole bunch on your cutting board and with a heavy knife cut a slice off the bottoms of the spears; put the bunch in a pitcher or vase containing an inch of water. This treatment even refreshes limp asparagus. Just be sure to store them in the refrigerator, lest they start opening a bouquet of flowers!

*1½ pounds fresh asparagus,
washed and trimmed (see
technique on page 19)*

*½ teaspoon salt
3 tablespoons unsalted butter
¼ cup freshly grated parmigiano*

Bring a kettle of water to a boil. Lay the trimmed asparagus in a skillet, pour in the boiling water, and add the salt. Boil slowly, uncovered, about 10 minutes (more or less for thicker or thinner spears), until just tender.

Meanwhile, melt the butter in a small pan and heat it until it turns a rich hazelnut color. Drain the asparagus and arrange it on a hot serving plate. Drizzle the butter over it carefully, leaving behind the blackened butter solids. Sprinkle the parmigiano over all and serve immediately. ■

CARROTS WITH FENNEL

Carote al finocchio

FOR 4 SERVINGS:

The combination of crushed fennel seed and red wine vinegar makes this quite an assertive dish. While it is tasty any time of the year with any but the largest, old storage carrots, it's a special treat when made with the earliest, sweet young carrots of the spring. Exact cooking times will vary, depending on the size and age of your carrots, but the dish can be done completely in advance and reheated when wanted.

Y

Follow the wine recommendation for your secondo.

3 tablespoons olive oil

1 pound young carrots, peeled and sliced in ¼-inch rounds

2 teaspoons fennel seeds, lightly crushed

Salt

Freshly ground black pepper

½ cup red wine vinegar

In a heavy-bottomed, medium-sized pot, heat the olive oil. Add the carrots and sauté over medium heat 3 minutes, stirring often. Add the crushed fennel and a sprinkling of salt and pepper and sauté 3 minutes more.

Mix the vinegar with 1 cup hot water. Add half this liquid to the carrots, cover the pan tightly, turn heat to low, and cook 10 to 15 minutes, until the carrots have absorbed all the liquid. Add the remaining liquid and continue cooking, covered, until the carrots are tender—20 to 40 minutes. If all the liquid is absorbed before they are done, add hot water, a few tablespoons at a time.

Transfer the carrots to a heated dish for serving. ■

FENNEL BRAISED WITH HAM

Finocchi al prosciutto

FOR 4 SERVINGS:

Follow the wine recommendation for your secondo.

Bulb fennel is an underappreciated vegetable in America. Italians prize it and fit it into a meal wherever they can—raw as antipasto, cooked alone as a contorno, cooked with various meats and fishes as secondo, cooked with pasta or rice as a primo or raw again as a palate cleanser after the secondo and before cheese. This combination of ham and fennel creates a very savory synergy and makes a fine accompaniment to grilled meats or sausages and simple roast fowl. The leftovers—when there are any—are tasty by themselves and delicious chopped up and made into croquettes.

One caution: be careful about the amount of salt you use during the cooking, since both the ham and the cheese bring salt to the recipe. It's much safer to add more at the end rather than ruin the dish by starting with too much.

4 tablespoons butter

2 tablespoons chopped onion

1½ pounds bulb fennel, trimmed, washed, and cut into pieces about 1 by 2 inches

4 ounces cooked ham, cut in short julienne strips

1 cup broth

Salt

2 tablespoons grated parmigiano

In a nonreactive skillet, melt the butter and sauté the onion 1 to 2 minutes. Add the fennel and ham, mixing to separate the ham strips and coat the fennel with them and the butter. Cook, stirring occasionally, 10 minutes.

In a small pot, bring the broth to a simmer. Salt the fennel lightly, add the broth, cover, and cook 10 minutes, or until the fennel is fork-tender. Remove the lid, raise heat to high, and boil off any remaining liquid. When it is almost entirely evaporated, stir in the cheese and cook 1 minute more. Taste again for salt and serve at once in a heated dish. ∎

PEAS BRAISED WITH TOMATO

Piselli alla napoletana

FOR 4 SERVINGS:

*S*omeone should write an ode to the pea, the green pearl of spring. When you can get them fresh from the vine, tiny and sweet, there isn't a vegetable in the kingdom that can compare with them. When peas are like that, the temptation is to eat them raw, right out of the pod. All too often, however, peas are large and long off the vine by the time they make it to market, even in spring, so here's a recipe for dealing with any that you suspect of a tendency to mealiness or starchiness. This treatment will really brighten them up. A pot with a tight-fitting cover is essential to prevent them from drying out and burning.

Follow the wine recommendation for your secondo.

2½ tablespoons olive oil	1½ teaspoons tomato paste
4 tablespoons chopped onion	dissolved in ⅔ cup water
2½ pounds fresh peas (about 2½ cups shelled)	¼ teaspoon salt

In a heavy-bottomed, nonreactive pot, heat the olive oil and sauté the onion 2 to 3 minutes over medium heat. Add the peas and cook, stirring, 2 minutes. Stir in the diluted tomato paste and bring to a boil. Add the salt, reduce heat to very low, cover tightly, and cook 25 to 30 minutes, or until the peas are perfectly tender, stirring from time to time.

If there is a little liquid left by the time the peas are done, raise the heat to high and boil rapidly, uncovered. (Should there happen to be quite a lot of liquid left—cooking is not an exact science!—remove the peas with a slotted spoon to a heated dish and keep them warm while you boil the liquid down.) When the liquid is only a syrupy glaze, pour it over the peas and serve at once. ∎

PEAS WITH ONION, SAGE, AND SALAMI

Piselli alla rustica

FOR 6 SERVINGS:

This lovely country dish is capable of infinite modification: Add more broth and it's a minestra; add grated cheese and it's a light secondo; leave it as it is and you've got the savoriest of contorni to serve alongside a chicken or a veal scallop. Recipes like this one reflect both the directness and the genius of Italian cookery: it's as versatile and adaptable as commedia dell'arte, and not at all unlike it in playfulness and spirit.

If you're having the dish by itself, choose a simple, dry, white wine—Soave or Frascati or Pinot grigio, for instance. Otherwise, follow the wine recommendation for your secondo.

6 tablespoons unsalted butter

½ cup chopped onion

1½ tablespoons all-purpose flour

2½ cups broth

4 ounces Genoa salami, cut in
   ¼-inch dice

3 to 4 chopped sage leaves

3 cups fresh peas (about 3 pounds
   in the pods)

Salt

In a casserole, melt the butter and sauté the onion 5 minutes, or until softened but not browned. Sprinkle with the flour and cook, stirring constantly, 2 minutes over very low heat so the flour does not brown. Add 1 cup broth, the salami, and chopped sage, and cook gently 2 minutes, stirring occasionally.

Add the peas to the casserole along with ¼ teaspoon salt. Stir thoroughly to coat the peas with the seasonings. Then add enough of the remaining broth to just cover the peas. Bring to a boil, reduce to a simmer, cover, and cook gently 20 minutes, or until the peas are tender. Taste for salt and serve at once in a heated dish. ■

SAUTÉED WHITE TURNIPS

Rape saltate in padella

FOR 4 SERVINGS:

 *I*n Italian neighborhoods in America, rape is most often a short name for broccoli rape—a vegetable that looks like skinny broccoli shoots with very small, tight broccoli-like blossoms buried amid a lot of leaves. That green vegetable is not, however, what we call broccoli but rather the flowering stalk and leaves of a member of the turnip family. And the generic word for turnip in Italian is *rape*.

This recipe is for the first young white turnips of spring. They lend themselves surprisingly well to a garlic-pancetta-parsley flavoring, which adds a great deal of interest to the sometimes bland turnip flesh. The turnip greens can be used exactly like spinach in the next recipe.

Choose according to your secondo.

Salt

2 pounds small white turnips, peeled and sliced in ¼-inch rounds

3 tablespoons olive oil

2 ounces pancetta, cut in matchsticks

1 clove garlic, halved

1 tablespoon chopped flat-leaf Italian parsley

Bring a pot of salted water to a boil. Drop in the turnips, and after the water returns to a boil, cook uncovered 4 minutes. Drain the turnips in a colander and spray them with water to stop the cooking.

In a skillet, heat the olive oil. Add the pancetta and garlic and sauté over low heat 5 minutes, stirring occasionally. Press the garlic pieces against the side of the pan with the back of a fork and remove them. Add the turnip slices and turn them to coat all sides with the oil and seasonings. Sauté 10 minutes, or until the turnips are soft, turning them from time to time. Just before serving, stir in the parsley. ■

SPINACH WITH OLIVE OIL AND LEMON

Spinaci all'olio e limone

FOR 4 SERVINGS:

♉

*Follow the wine
recommendation for your
secondo.*

*I*n spring, in Italy, when the menu simply says *verdura*, nine
times out of ten the greens in question are spinach, and nine times
out of ten the spinach in question is prepared as described below.
Many Italians prefer their spinach even simpler, and so omit either
the lemon juice or the olive oil—most often the olive oil, in which
case the spinach may be described as *all'agro*. Often the spinach
will appear accompanied by cruets of oil and vinegar and a small
dish of lemon quarters. And most of the time, the spinach won't be
hot but room temperature, or tepid at most. (Italians believe that
Americans eat their food too hot and that, in some mysterious way,
that is bad for us. Given all the innate wisdom that Western medi-
cine has recently been finding in "the Mediterranean diet," we two
are not prepared to fight this Italian prejudice.)

The only difficult thing about this recipe may be washing the
spinach. Those fine curly leaves can harbor an inordinate amount
of sand, which doesn't improve the flavor. So leave lots of time to
pass each and every leaf under a stream of cold water, or slosh them
vigorously in a basin of same, or (our recommendation) both. And
don't be dismayed when the bushel of leaves that took you half an
hour to wash comes down to a few handfuls of cooked green.

3 pounds fresh spinach   *1 lemon, quartered*
Salt   *4 tablespoons extra-virgin olive oil*

Carefully wash the spinach and put it in a large pot with just the
water that adheres to the leaves. Salt lightly. Cover and cook 5 to
8 minutes, or until the spinach is completely wilted.

Drain in a colander, let cool, and squeeze lightly. Separate the
strands of spinach and arrange on a serving plate. Garnish with the
lemon quarters, drizzle on the olive oil, and serve. ∎

ZUCCHINI AND SPRING ONIONS WITH BALSAMIC VINEGAR

Zucchini e cipolle saltati

FOR 4 SERVINGS:

This recipe makes a very pretty, interestingly chunky dish, elegant enough for company—especially if they are what Italians call *buone forchette* (good eaters)—but simple enough for family. It can be made even simpler by parboiling the zucchini and onions in advance, leaving only the sautéing for dinnertime.

Be sure to use a good, aromatic balsamic vinegar: it contributes hugely to the success of the dish. Leftovers, if there are any, make excellent frittata or can even be used as pizza toppings.

Y

Follow the wine recommendation for your secondo.

Salt
1 pound tender young zucchini, halved lengthwise and cut in 2-inch pieces
1 pound spring onions, peeled, trimmed close to the base of the stem, and halved or quartered to yield pieces no more than 1 inch thick
2 tablespoons olive oil
2 teaspoons chopped fresh mint
1½ teaspoons balsamic vinegar
Freshly ground black pepper

Bring a large pot of salted water to a boil. Drop in the zucchini and boil uncovered 3 minutes. Lift them out with a slotted spoon, spray them with cold water to stop the cooking, and set aside. Drop the onions into the same water and boil 3 minutes. Drain and spray them as well.

In a large skillet, heat the olive oil. Add the zucchini, onions, and mint, and stir to coat the vegetables with the oil. Sauté over medium-high heat, stirring frequently, 5 minutes. Sprinkle the vegetables with the balsamic vinegar and salt and pepper to taste. Sauté, stirring, 1 minute more. Serve at once in a heated dish. ∎

DOLCI

Spring desserts in Italy are a misnomer: we should say it in the singular, spring dessert—i.e., strawberries. They are a national passion, far more than in this country, where their almost year-round availability and often pallid flavor tends to dull our enthusiasm for them. Loved as the domestic berries are in Italy, the most prized of all are the tiny, tart wild strawberries—*fragoline del bosco*—which appear in profusion in markets and on menus during their brief season. If you are lucky enough to be traveling in Italy when they are available, be sure to try them *con gelato* (with custard-cream ice cream): this is a combination of simple and decadent delight.

We offer recipes for strawberries plain, in a tart, and as a dessert sauce that's good over any number of plain cakes or ice cream. While we've saved our ice-cream recipes for the summer section of this book, we wouldn't try to prevent you from crossing the line and checking them out in late-spring high strawberry season. The blueberry ice cream recipe will adapt very nicely to strawberries.

In every region of Italy, there are special cakes and pastries associated with Easter. Our all-time favorite is the elaborate *pastiera napoletana,* a recipe for which appears in *La Tavola Italiana.* For this book we've selected a simple one, an orange-scented sweet yeast bread called a *piccillato di Pasqua.* And we present a few not-strictly-seasonal favorites that seem to capture the characteristic *leggerezza* of an Italian spring.

STRAWBERRIES WITH LEMON AND SUGAR

Fragole al limone

FOR 4 SERVINGS:

*T*his artless and delicious dish amounts to the Italian national spring dessert. Dressing strawberries with lemon juice is an old Italian trick. The acidity brightens the fruit's own flavor without making the dish actually lemony. A little minced lemon peel provides additional zest, metaphorically and literally. And you can of course cut back the amount of sugar if the berries are extremely sweet. In Sicily, that land of abundant orange trees, orange juice and zest frequently replace the lemon—a different but equally pleasing combination.

In preparing strawberries, you should rinse them before hulling, to prevent water's seeping into their central cavities. And never let them sit in water, because they're absorbent. You don't want to dilute their luscious juice.

With a dessert as simple and charming as this, Italians would rarely intrude a dessert wine, though they might well follow it with one. If you wish a wine with this dish, either finish the last of your dinner wine—you'll be surprised how good a dry wine tastes with these berries—or have an Asti Spumante or (if you can find one on these shores) a Recioto di Soave.

1 teaspoon grated lemon peel
Juice of 1 lemon
2 tablespoons sugar

1 quart strawberries, washed, hulled, and halved or quartered if large

Combine the lemon peel, lemon juice, and sugar in a serving bowl and stir to dissolve the sugar. Add the strawberries, toss with the seasonings, and serve. ■

STRAWBERRY SAUCE

Salsa di fragole

FOR 2 CUPS SAUCE:

Choose according to what the sauce accompanies.

A versatile condiment or dressing, absolutely easy to make, and wonderful over a plain cake or ice cream, or with whatever else strikes your fancy. If you like very sweet sauces, you can increase the amount of sugar, but we prefer to let the fruit flavor dominate. The bit of dry white Italian vermouth—and it must be Italian: French vermouth has a completely different character—gives the sauce a touch of sophistication.

1 pint strawberries, washed, hulled, and dried
5 tablespoons granulated sugar
2 tablespoons dry white Italian vermouth

Puree the berries in a blender or food processor. Add the sugar and vermouth and process well, so the sugar dissolves. Chill at least 1 hour before using. ■

ZABAGLIONE WITH VIN SANTO

Zabaglione al Vin Santo

FOR 4 TO 6 SERVINGS:

Z abaglione is now made with regional variations all over Italy. This version speaks with a Tuscan accent: Vin Santo, though made in other parts of Central Italy, is a specialty of Tuscany. It's a somewhat sherrylike dessert wine of intriguing character and a range of styles running from nearly dry to medium sweet. Good makers that export to the United States are Antinori, Avignonesi, Brolio, and Barbi. If Vin Santo is not available, you can make zabaglione the same way using Marsala or Madeira or even sweet sherry: needless to say, the better the wine, the better the zabaglione will be. Any zabaglione enjoys keeping company with a few crisp almond biscotti.

None needed, but if you want one, make it the same Vin Santo.

For a more elaborate spring dessert, serve this zabaglione, either just made and still warm or made ahead and chilled, over sliced strawberries that have been muddled with a little sugar and a spoonful of the same Vin Santo.

5 egg yolks	½ cup Vin Santo
5 tablespoons granulated sugar	

Put the egg yolks and sugar into a round-bottomed copper zabaglione pan (or the top of a double boiler). With a wire whisk or portable electric mixer, beat until they become pale yellow, thick, and creamy.

Suspend the pan over a pot (or the bottom of the double boiler) containing several inches of boiling water. Regulate the heat so the water maintains a low boil. Beat the Vin Santo into the eggs and continue beating until it foams, swells, and rises into a smooth custardy mound—about 3 to 4 minutes.

Scoop the zabaglione into dessert dishes and serve at once, while still warm. ∎

NEAPOLITAN CHOCOLATE MOUSSE

Coviglie al cioccolato

FOR 4 TO 6 SERVINGS:

Asti Spumante will do
beautifully here.

*T*his richly chocolate-flavored, silken-textured quasi-custard comes near to being foolproof, since it contains no egg and therefore presents no danger of curdling. It goes nicely with a crisp cookie. You can top it with additional whipped cream if you like.

3 tablespoons all-purpose flour

¾ cup sugar

3 tablespoons plus 1 teaspoon
  unsweetened cocoa

2 cups milk

2 tablespoons butter, cut in pieces

1 cup heavy cream

In a medium pot, mix the flour, sugar, and cocoa thoroughly. Gradually add the milk, stirring vigorously with a wire whisk to prevent lumps. (If any develop, put the mixture through a strainer before proceeding.)

Set the pot over medium heat and stir constantly until the mixture thickens somewhat and comes to a boil. (This may take up to 10 minutes, depending on the temperature of the milk and the size of the pot.) It won't become more than a thick pouring consistency. Turn off the heat, add the butter and stir until it is absorbed.

Transfer the mixture to a bowl and let it cool completely, stirring from time to time to prevent a skin from forming on the surface. It will thicken as it cools. Then put the bowl in the refrigerator to chill thoroughly and thicken further.

Just before serving time, whip the cream and delicately fold it into the chocolate mixture. Transfer to individual custard cups and serve at once. ∎

ZEPPOLE

Zeppole

FOR ABOUT TWENTY 2-INCH PUFFS:

*Z*eppole are zeppelins are dirigibles are balloons are lighter than air—at least when they are made right. Most Italian-Americans know a version of these tasty fried pastries in the form of Zeppole di San Giuseppe, a Neapolitan speciality for Saint Joseph's feast day: ring-shaped crullers with centers full of pastry cream and preserved cherries. What we offer here is the plain version, which is perfectly tasty in itself and much easier to make—so much so, in fact, that it has become a staple of Italian-American street fairs.

The best zeppole we ever tasted came from an itinerant street vendor (imagine being itinerant with a cauldron of boiling oil!) one beautiful May Sunday in Venice. Shoals of strollers—Venetians and *personaggi internazionali* alike—were drawn by the irresistible scent (like fish following a line of chum!) to a spot on the wharf where a perspiring countryman stood, alternately dropping gobs of dough into his pot and lifting out puffed, golden zeppole light as clouds. We eagerly returned to the spot the next day, hoping for more, but he was gone. Nor did he appear the following Sunday, or any day after, during our subsequent visits. We always look for him, though. The man was a zeppole genius.

None needed, but Asti is fine.

2 tablespoons butter	*Confectioners' sugar*
Pinch salt	*Cinnamon (optional)*
1 cup all-purpose flour	*Vegetable oil for deep-frying*
3 whole eggs plus 1 yolk	

Put the butter and salt into a saucepan with 1 cup water. Bring to a boil and boil until the butter dissolves. Off heat, dump in the flour all at once and stir rapidly to mix. Return the pan to medium-high heat and cook, stirring until the mixture is smooth and begins to coat the bottom and sides of the pan.

Remove the pan from the heat and, one at a time, add the eggs and the extra yolk, stirring briskly after each addition until all the egg is absorbed. Let the mixture cool to room temperature. Meanwhile, put about ½ cup confectioners' sugar and a sprinkle of cinnamon, if desired, into a small brown paper bag.

In a deep pot or kettle, heat the oil to 375°F. Using two teaspoons, drop in nuggets of dough about the size of a small walnut. Fry a few at a time (depending on the quantity of oil you are using), for 5 to 6 minutes each.

As they cook, the zeppole will first rise to the surface, then turn themselves over when their bottom halves are golden brown, and finally rupture slightly and puff further as the interior dough expands. Remove them from the frying oil when they are golden brown, firm, and hollow inside. (Check one from the first batch, and if the interior is at all soggy, cook the rest longer.)

Drain the zeppole briefly on paper towels, then toss them in the bag with the confectioners' sugar. Serve at once. ∎

About Pasta Frolla

Pastry making as an Italian art is right up there next to fresco painting, marble sculpture, and bel canto opera. It's also a highly specialized form of baking: by and large, pastry shops in Italy don't sell bread, and vice versa. What we two are most drawn to in pastry shop displays, especially in Milan where we feel they reach their apogee, are the intricate mixed-fruit tarts patterned like mosaics and gleaming like jewel boxes. These fabulous confections illustrate the Italian art of making extreme beauty out of simple things: a clear glaze, fresh fruits, a very little pastry cream, and a crust of either flaky pastry (*millefoglie* in Italian) or the humble *pasta frolla*. Paradise enow.

Pasta frolla is the workhorse of Italian pastry dough, with innumerable applications in desserts and savory pastries. It's a rich mixture of butter, flour, and sugar (even if the pastry is to encase a non-sweet filling), and it uses no water to bind the ingredients. The necessary liquid comes only from egg—and that, in one of the mysterious processes of food chemistry, is what makes the pastry crust both so fragile and toothsome when baked and so maddening to prepare.

The word *frolla* is usually translated as tender, but it also means weak or feeble, which are the epithets more likely to come to mind when you've rolled out a beautifully smooth, firm-looking sheet of dough, pick it up to fit it into your tart pan, and it immediately tears apart in your hands into five or six pieces. Nor does your frustration end there. Following a logical problem-solving process, you'll gather up the dough pieces, recombine them with additional flour, and roll again until there's enough surface tension to keep the sheet intact for handling. Makes sense; but if you do that, you find—when you go to serve the finished pastry—that the additional flour and kneading has turned your frail, tender dough into an impenetrable shell of concrete.

Why are we telling you this discouraging tale in a cookbook aimed at inducing you to make pasta frolla recipes? Several reasons. First, because pasta frolla making is one of the few techniques in the whole Italian culinary repertoire that isn't ridiculously easy; so if we admit that here, we hope you'll believe us when we tell you about things that *are* easy. Second, because we don't approve of recipe instructions that make things sound routine when in practice they're fraught with risk; it's not fair of an author to send you trustingly into a procedure that makes you feel like a bumbling idiot when you can't do it as effortlessly as the recipe implies. Third, because pasta frolla is distinctive and delicious and well worth learning to master, even if it never becomes as plain sailing for you as a simple American piecrust. And fourth, because we've learned a few tricks for dealing with the intransigence of pasta frolla, and if we didn't tell you why we recommend these steps, you might feel the whole process is just too bothersome to attempt.

If you read through the instructions below and still feel the process is too bothersome to attempt, you might try instead the pasta frolla we used in our recipes for apple and jam tarts in *La Tavola Italiana*. That's a slightly uncanonical variation of the dough that uses milk instead of egg as the moistener. While not totally unheard-of in Italy, that recipe makes a somewhat less authentic and less luxuriant crust. It is, however, appreciably easier to work with, and you can substitute it for any pasta frolla called for in this or any other cookbook.

Assuming you're game to try the classic version, here is such wisdom as we've acquired on the subject of making pasta frolla. First, in mixing the dough, two things are to be avoided: too much heat from your hands, which prematurely melts the butter, and too much handling, which activates the gluten of the flour. (It's just the opposite of bread and pasta making, where you *want* to develop the gluten to make the dough springy and elastic.) Experience has taught us not to prepare this pastry in our heavy-duty Kitchen-Aid: it's too easy to overheat and overhandle it. Because it's so slightly blended, the dough needs time in the refrigerator to "cure" before it can be rolled. So it's best to make it up well in advance. It will keep a day or so under refrigeration and can also be frozen for a few weeks.

FOR MAKING A SINGLE 9½-INCH PASTRY CRUST:

1 cup all-purpose flour, plus more
  for work surfaces
3 tablespoons sugar
Pinch salt

½ teaspoon grated lemon rind
6 tablespoons butter, cut into 12
  pieces
1 egg

In a medium-size bowl, mix together the flour, sugar, salt, and lemon rind. Blend the butter into the dry ingredients until the whole has reached the consistency of coarse flaky meal. Techniques for this blending vary. If you're very deft and (literally) cool-handed, you can use your fingers in a quick pinch-and-smear motion. A safer way is to work with two dinner knives or flat spatulas: use them one in each hand, in opposition to each other, to cut the butter into smaller and smaller flour-covered pieces. A wire pastry blender, wielded like an old-fashioned potato masher, works very well too.

Push the meal to the sides of the bowl and crack the egg into the central well. Mix the egg with a fork to mix the yolk and white and then continue mixing, gradually working in the dry ingredients from the walls of the well. Soon you'll have a shaggy mass of dough, which probably won't want to take up all the dry ingredients. Persuade it gently, pressing the dry flakes into the mass of dough with the fork, but don't knead it vigorously.

Pick up the ball of dough and set it on a sheet of waxed paper. Gather up any dry bits remaining in the bowl and press them lightly onto the dough with your hands. Don't worry if the bits just sit there, or even if they fall off. Wrap the dough tightly in the waxed paper and put it in the refrigerator to chill for at least 1 hour. (Alternatively, you can put it in the freezer for 20 minutes.) If the dough is not to be used within two days, freeze it. If you're in a terrific hurry and don't mind a slightly uneven crust, you can use the dough without chilling. Just press it into the baking dish like modeling clay. But do it quickly, or the heat of your hands will do its bad stuff to the butter.

Shaping and baking:

You can bake an empty pasta frolla shell wholly or partially in advance. The trick, as we've indicated, is getting the round of rolled dough into the mold without tearing. Our solution is to roll it between sheets of waxed paper, which has the double advantage of keeping the rather sticky dough from taking up too much flour and of keeping it intact for the transfer to the pan. But peeling the sticky dough off the sheet of waxed paper can also be a bit tricky, so please read the instructions before trying this. Of course, if you're one of those rare persons to whom pastry making comes as easily as breathing, pay no attention to these earnest strictures and follow your enviable instincts!

Preheat the oven to 375°F. Flatten the dough somewhat with your hands or the rolling pin and flour it generously on both sides. Position it on a large sheet of floured waxed paper and place another sheet of waxed paper on top. Quickly roll the dough between the sheets of paper into a circle ⅛ inch thick and about 12 inches in diameter.

Carefully peel off the upper sheet of waxed paper. (If you've warmed the dough too much in the rolling, it'll try to stick to the paper. In that case, use a spatula or knife blade to persuade the paper away from the dough.) Flour the surface of the dough and put the paper loosely back on it. Turn the dough upside down, peel off the other sheet of paper, and flour that surface as well. Position a 9½-inch round pan upside down over the dough. Slide your hand under the bottom sheet of waxed paper and flip the dough and pan over. Remove the paper and fit the dough snugly against the sides of the pan. Trim off the excess, leaving a rim of dough slightly higher than the pan's sides, because it will shrink a bit in the baking.

To bake unfilled:

Butter a sheet of foil and place it on the dough, buttered side down. Fill the foil with dried beans or pie weights and set it in the oven. For a fully baked crust, bake 25 minutes, then remove foil and weights and prick the bottom of the pastry all over with a fork. Return the pan to the oven for 5 to 10 minutes more, or until the pastry is golden and beginning to pull away from the edges of the pan. For a partially baked shell, give it 15 minutes with the weights and 10 minutes without. Cool the pastry shell on a rack before unmolding and filling it.

To bake filled:
Follow instructions in the specific recipe you're using.

STRAWBERRY TART

Crostata di fragole

FOR 6 TO 8 SERVINGS:

Y

Vin Santo or a good Passito—perhaps one of the fine ones from Pantelleria.

Most strawberry tarts are fairly elaborate affairs, with the berries arrayed on a bed of pastry cream or fruit preserves. They can be quite lovely, but on a day when you've succumbed to a tempting box of berries and have nothing but pastry dough on hand, you can make a perfectly satisfying tart with just those two essentials. Even the egg wash is optional—it makes for a prettier tart, but it doesn't affect the flavor.

1 recipe pasta frolla dough (page 110)

1 pint fresh strawberries, washed, hulled, and quartered

3 tablespoons granulated sugar

1 egg (optional)

Preheat the oven to 350°F. Roll the dough as directed in the basic recipe into a circle ⅛ inch thick and about 12 inches in diameter, and line a 9½-inch round pan. Trim off excess dough and gather it into a ball.

Place the strawberries snugly in the pastry shell in a circular pattern. Sprinkle the sugar over them.

Roll the small ball of extra dough to a thickness of ⅛ inch, cut it in strips ¾ inch wide, and use them to make a lattice over the strawberries. Beat the egg in a bowl with 1 tablespoon of water and paint the surface of the lattice and the edges of the tart. Wait a moment and paint again. Put the tart in the oven and bake 40 minutes. Cool on a rack before serving. ■

EASTER SWEET BREAD

Piccillato di Pasqua

FOR 1 LARGE LOAF:

*N*ot a panettone, though it is related, piccillato di Pasqua amounts to a pleasant, sweet, yeast bread scented with orange. We like it best as a breakfast bread or midday snack. Toasting it brings up its orange aromas marvelously. It can be baked as a round or a ring: our choice is a Bundt pan.

An interesting technique in this recipe is that of kneading the dough thoroughly once before adding the sugar and then kneading it again. The sugar radically alters the texture of the dough and softens it remarkably. It rises long and slowly, so unless you have a full day available for playing in the kitchen (a favorite form of

Almost any still, sweet wine will serve—Vin Santo, Passito, Moscato, Recioto.

recreation for the two of us), you may want to start it in the evening, let the shaped loaf rise in the refrigerator overnight, and bake the next day.

3 envelopes active dry yeast	*½ teaspoon salt*
2⅓ cups all-purpose flour	*Grated peel of 1 orange*
3 eggs, beaten	*Grated peel of 1 lemon*
2 tablespoons softened butter	*½ cup sugar*

In a small bowl, dissolve the yeast in 5 tablespoons water. Add 2 tablespoons flour and mix to make a thinnish batter. Cover tightly with plastic wrap and let sit 1 hour.

Put the remaining flour into a large bowl. Add the eggs, butter, salt, orange and lemon peel, and yeast starter. Mix into a dough and knead well—8 minutes by hand or 3 in a heavy-duty mixer with a dough hook. Then add the sugar and knead again 5 minutes by hand or 2 by machine.

Butter a 9-inch ring pan with a 1½ quart-capacity. Turn the dough out onto a floured surface and shape it into a roll about 18 inches long and 2½ inches in diameter. Coil the dough into the pan, sealing and smoothing the joined ends. Cover it with a towel and let it rise until doubled in bulk—3 to 4 hours in a warm place, or overnight in the refrigerator.

Preheat the oven to 400°F. Put the loaf in the oven for 15 minutes, then turn heat down to 350°F. Bake 40 to 60 minutes longer, until the piccillato is nicely browned and tests done. Let it cool completely in its pan. Unmold to slice and serve. ■

RICOTTA AND ALMOND TORTE

Pizza dolce

FOR 6 TO 8 SERVINGS:

The pretty daffodil-yellow surface of this pie conceals a cheesecake in a crust, and a very tasty one at that. It's not overly sweet, and many people may be inclined to add a bit more sugar to the filling. Consult your own taste here. This particular pastry crust is a variety of pasta frolla, slightly different from our basic version but with all the touchiness of its kind. See pages 108–12 for handling tricks.

Almost any still, sweet wine—Vin Santo, Passito, Moscato, Recioto.

FOR THE DOUGH:

2¼ cups all-purpose flour

½ cup sugar

Pinch salt

Grated rind of ½ lemon

8 tablespoons butter, cut into
  several pieces

2 egg yolks

FOR THE FILLING:

12 ounces ricotta

¾ cup confectioners' sugar

Pinch cinnamon

⅛ teaspoon vanilla extract

3½ ounces (about ⅔ cup)

chopped candied citron and
  orange peel

3½ ounces (⅔ cup) blanched
  almonds, coarsely chopped

FOR THE BAKING:

Butter and flour for the baking
  dish

1 egg yolk

To make the pastry, blend the flour, sugar, salt, and lemon rind in a mixing bowl. Cut in the butter until the mixture reaches an oatmeal consistency. In a smaller bowl, beat the egg yolks together with ¼ cup cold water. Add them to the dry ingredients and mix to obtain a smooth dough. Gather it into a ball, wrap in waxed paper, and let rest in the refrigerator 1 hour.

When ready to bake, preheat the oven to 350°F. Butter and flour a 9-inch pie dish. Put the ricotta in a bowl with the confectioners' sugar, cinnamon, and vanilla and beat until smooth. Stir in the candied fruits and the nuts.

Remove the dough from the refrigerator and divide it in two slightly unequal pieces. Roll the larger piece as directed on page 111 to a 12-inch circle and line the pie dish with it. Fill the dish with the ricotta mixture and spread it evenly. Roll the remaining dough to a 10-inch circle and position it on top of the pie dish. Seal the two crusts and press a decorative rim around the edges.

Beat the egg yolk with 1 teaspoon water and paint the top of the tart with it. Bake 25 to 30 minutes, or until the crust is golden. Cool the tart completely before serving. ■

ESTATE

· Summer ·

n everyone's imaginary Italy, it's always summertime, always a lazy, dazzling afternoon on a sun-bleached piazza, with passersby moving slowly in the heat, their outlines half-dissolved in the glare of the sunlight, cafe umbrellas making little pools of cool darkness within which one can sit and spoon a *granita*, sip a chilled mineral water, and watch a 6-inch-long sliver of jade flick its tail and stalk flies on a church wall.

The moment is endless, timeless, in an odd way primitive: the lizard, the fly, the stone wall that is now a church but might as well be—might once have been—a temple of Jupiter or the Great Mother or an even earlier god. As you sit in your little shade you come to understand that what endures, in that great Mediterranean light, is stone. Stone survives. And Italy, you see with the insight of the sun-blind, the light-bedazzled, *is* stone, the stone spine of the Apennines that lifts the whole long land out of the sea, the stone that Vesuvius and Etna periodically digest and regurgitate to cover the stones that humans erect to shelter in. The softest, richest wines flow from that cruel volcanic soil. Every tender fruit of summer is wrenched grudgingly from hard stone; every peach at its heart conceals the stone from which it began. Every pleasure, every beauty, every moment, comes at last to stone.

That's why, for us, summer in Italy isn't beaches, as you might expect in a country with so much coastline. Not that Italian beaches aren't beautiful or that we haven't enjoyed them. The Mediterranean can be a blue of heartbreaking clarity, the Adriatic as warm and comforting as your own bathtub. The beaches themselves—where the sheer stone cliffs don't plunge straight down to the surf—range from the finest white sand to the roughest cobble. Even the people on Italian beaches are interesting to look at, with their craggy, definitely-not-Midwestern faces and their preposterously small

bathing suits. For Americans like us, of a certain age and breadth, Italian beaches are very comforting: no one, no matter how unfashionably shaped and fleshed, feels any self-consciousness about sunning, swimming, or strolling in minimal bikinis. In Italy, even nature can surprise: once, on a beach at the foot of the Amalfi peninsula, we discovered that much of the "sand" we were walking on was made up of tiny, colorfully glazed ceramic chips—the accumulation of who knows how many years of rejects and breakage from the pottery kilns of nearby Vietri, ground down by the waves but still bearing the artisans' designs. Even rejected and discarded, stone endures.

That's why for us summer in Italy is ruins: pink snapdragons blooming atop austere Ionic columns at Paestum, lizards basking on cyclopean stones outside Agrigento, asphodel and valerian softening the harsh geometries of Ostia Antica and Pompeii, tall wild celery stalks forming green exclamation points against the hill line at nearly vanished Selinunte, wild mint perfuming the air of the Forum and the Palatine—and over them all, in a sky cloudless and shimmering with heat, swallows and swifts wheeling and diving in endless search-and-consume missions.

Italy's ruins are not the haunted, dark cellars of more northern imaginings: Mediterranean ghosts do their best work in daylight—indeed, in a daylight so sharp that it first intensifies and then nullifies all color, until you can see past the edges of your seeing to the thousands of eyes looking back at you from the past and future of those crumbling, changeless stones.

We felt that very clearly one blazing hot summer day among the tumbled marble and granite of Aquileia, an important Roman town in the north of Italy that fell to Attila a millennium and a half ago, never to rise again. Its refugees abandoned the fire-scarred stones of their city to seek shelter in the marshes of a lagoon some leagues away, and incidentally thereby to found Venice. As we wandered among Aquileia's few remaining columns and wall footings, for whose possession now only nettles and creepers contended, we could understand the logic of turning for safety from land to water. The ancients counted only four elements—earth, air, fire, water—but in fact they counted on a fifth: stone. If fire can bring down the stones you raise on land, then the element of water must be your home, and you will learn the art that makes Venice unique among cities: you will learn to make stones walk upon the water.

So in summer, in Italy, we become ruin haunters. We've descended into subterranean Etruscan burial houses in Perugia, Cerveteri, Tarquinia, Orvieto, Volterra, and Bolsena. We've followed yellow *segnale turistico* signs down roads that dwindled from two lanes to one to dirt to nothing, to find ourselves staring at a shrubby mound that might, if we imagined hard enough, conceal or be a very small tomb. We've retraced Aeneas's steps to the underworld, as Virgil describes them: stared into the shining crater lake of Avernus (finding it true, as Virgil observed, that birds don't seem to fly over it or frequent its shores), smelled the sulfur of the Phlegrean fields and paced the long stone corridor that leads into the Sybil's cave at Cumae (a strange, otherworldly experience). These and many other ancient remains we've looked at with the same sense of awe, the same awareness of permanence and transience, in that same merciless bright sunshine that hides no crack or seam. And they, no doubt, have looked back at us with equal wonder, as we executed our inevitable turn from aesthetic rapture or philosophic reverie to hunger pangs, and unpacked our picnic lunch.

Prosaic as it may seem, amid all those intimations of mortality, time, and eternity, you can't beat a good ruin as a place to picnic. Even the Roman Forum and the Palatine grow quiet as noon approaches. At the more remote sites, you may well have the place entirely to yourself. If you've been a wise traveler, you stopped at a convenient street market and provided yourself with a little wine and acqua minerale, a roll or a small loaf of bread, a chunk of cheese (perhaps the local *caciotta*), some prosciutto or mortadella, a bursting-ripe tomato or two, and a luscious peach or pear for dessert. It's hard to overstate the pleasures of so elemental a lunch, eaten in the shade of ancient umbrella pines on the slopes of the Palatine Hill, with small yellow butterflies dipping lazily by; or sitting in the poppy-dotted knee-high grass of the walled meadow behind the beautiful church of San Biagio in Montepulciano, looking out over the valley to the farther hill, contoured by lines of tall Tuscan cypresses.

Outdoor dining is one of the great pleasures of summer for tourists and Italians alike. The right meal in the right place can be the loveliest memory of a whole trip or a whole year. Nothing in Rome is quite like a summer dinner at Piperno, in the heart of the old Jewish ghetto. Tables are set out on the minuscule Piazza Cenci, across from the looming walls (stone endures!) of the Cenci palace, which looks grim enough to have indeed seen the bloody deeds Shelley ascribes to it. As daylight begins to fail, squadrons of twittering swifts wheel overhead and disappear into their roosts in the eaves, and their place in the twilight is taken by bats, mothing noiselessly through the arc of the streetlights. The moment is magical, with a strange serenity that even the inevitable next automobile horn doesn't break.

Nature's aerial dinner theater at Piperno plays to full houses every warm summer evening. Other outdoor eating experiences are more personal, more private. We celebrated our twentieth wedding anniversary at a lunch on the whitewashed, bougainvillea-splashed terrace of the restaurant Le Rondine in the fishing village of Peschici, at the tip of the Gargano peninsula. (Le Rondine is literally built into a sea grotto. If you dine inside, you sit next to thick glass portals, through which you can watch the Adriatic surf crashing into the cave around and beneath you.) The centerpiece of the meal was a special *zuppa di pesce,* which we had to order the previous day so the chef could go down to the fishing boats in the morning and purchase the particular mix of spiny and scaly sea creatures essential to it. As a first course we'd ordered spaghetti *alle vongole*—rarely missing any opportunity to taste those wonderful tiny clams. The day was glorious, the view from the terrace was of a perfection usually encountered only in cigarette advertisements, and both the pasta and the zuppa di pesce were *da morire* (a gustatory phrase as much used in Italy as its English equivalent, "to die for"). We lazily finished our second bottle of Locorotondo, the local white wine, congratulating ourselves on having so splendidly, so stylishly, so sophisticatedly celebrated our anniversary. Only then did our charming and efficient waiter inform us, most tactfully, that *normalmente* one never eats that pasta dish before a zuppa di pesce because both are so rich; but when we'd asked for it he could see it was a special occasion for us, so . . . We overtipped him outrageously. (After lunch we explored the tiny harbor and jetty, and on returning, ran into our waiter—minus his white jacket and plus a fishing pole—heading out to entertain himself for the hour before the dinner service.)

One last memory: hot July in Rome, and a sweaty morning of frustration spent trying to deal with the *ufficio postale* (always an ordeal in Italy). We walked off most of our annoyance and walked up an appetite, which comes easily in Rome. We fetched up at Trattoria La Maddelena, with its three postage-stamp-sized outdoor tables set out on the postcard-sized piazza of the same name. It was nearly lunchtime. We sat. We had a little red wine and a little bread, and we began to feel better. We had started on an ordinary-looking lasagna, which was tasting better with each bite, when a dusty-looking elderly man in shabby clothing appeared. Without a word, without even looking at us, he plucked a bay leaf from one of the restaurant's potted shrubs, raised it to his lips, and began to make music with it. He played what must have been the simplest and most ancient folk melodies, melodies that perhaps every schoolchild in Italy knew but that we had never heard before. He played them hauntingly, touchingly, and then stood silent with such dignity that we were embarrassed in offering him the money he so obviously needed. He accepted it and bowed with even greater dignity, played one more brief monody on the bay leaf, bowed again, and then, still without having said a word, withdrew. Magic. We've returned often to that tiny piazza at midday in hopes of seeing and hearing him again, but the spirit of the place has never again materialized him for us.

How do you reproduce such moments in a meal, in America? You don't, obviously. The point of all such stories is the uniqueness of the moment, the specialness of the place. Reproduction is a franchise operation, and that is not an Italian speciality. What you can do—and we're trying to give you the wherewithal for—is create your own special times and places and flavors. Using the best produce of summer—red, ripe tomatoes; firm, fresh zucchini; freshly caught fish and shellfish—you can recreate the simplicity and honesty and pure flavor of Italian foods. Do that, and the magic will come of itself.

ANTIPASTI

Summer is the season when antipasti can steal all the attention from the other courses of a meal and become the whole show in themselves. Warm weather makes dining picnic-style, on "a little of this and a little of that," an attractive alternative to a heavier, more formal meal. We have friends who give a much anticipated annual party they call an Antipastis- simo, which features an elaborate buffet of antipasto dishes that serves not only for the entire evening's nourishment, but for much of its animated conversation.

In Italy, we've never met a restaurant waiter who wasn't instantly sympathetic to a request for *assaggini*—very small tastes—of any number of dishes from the antipasto table. Depending on the degree of formality obtaining, you may be invited to serve yourself, in which case the agony of choice can be considerable. One of our favorite casual places in the south of Italy is Rugantino, at the seaside in Salerno. On one visit, we made an inventory of its three-table antipasto display. According to our (oil and tomato stained) notes, it contained:

- Three kinds of zucchini—batter-fried and tomato-sauced, *in saor*, and *a scapece*.
- Three kinds of eggplant—*rollatini* (thinly sliced and fried, wrapped around a spicy meat filling, and baked with a little tomato sauce); small halves baked with olive oil, capers, oregano, and a touch of tomato; and *a scapece*.
- Mushrooms marinated with tons of garlic.
- Marinated carrots.
- Batter-fried cauliflowerets.
- Fleshy, sweet red peppers, halved, rubbed with olive oil, and baked.
- Skinny, slightly hot green peppers, oiled and baked whole.
- *Scarolina* (a bitter green) sautéed with olive oil, garlic, capers, and golden raisins.
- Five kinds of olives in a variety of colors and spicings.
- Three kinds of *frittate*—zucchini, eggplant, and peppers (more or less).
- Marinated fresh anchovies.
- Several different assortments of shellfish, raw and cooked—including many that don't

exist in American waters, with names like *cigale* (crickets), *datteri* (dates), and *tartufi* (truffles) *di mare*.

• *Ovaline di bufala*—tiny balls of buffalo-milk mozzarella.

Not on display because of the heat, but available if you asked, were prosciutto, salame, and other cured meats. Any of these items you were welcome to have—in any quantity—before, with, or after any other dish on the table or on the menu. You can see why we liked Rugantino.

(Another of the restaurant's charms was a habit of serving pasta from huge bowls wheeled around the room on carts. If you craned your neck and evinced interest when a table near you was being served, you were likely to be given an *assaggino* of the dish, just to reward your appreciation. So great did our appreciation tend to be that, one evening, rolling contentedly back to our car parked on the shorefront, we failed to notice that its windshield wipers were missing. We only discovered it the next morning, driving into a rain shower.)

The antipasto recipes in this section contain some vegetable dishes comparable to those we enjoyed at Rugantino. (The Summer Contorno section contains others.) We've added a simple *crostino* recipe that requires no cooking and a simple schiacciata. Finally, we offer three of our favorite shellfish antipasti.

CAPRI SALAD

Insalata caprese

PER SERVING:

Capri may have first claim to this quintessential summer-time salad, but it's an all-Italian favorite now, often appearing under the simple name of *pomodoro e mozzarella* (tomatoes and mozzarella). It's glorious when made with top-of-the-season, vine-ripened,

A dry, crisp white wine is best
with this dish: anything from
a good Soave or Pinot grigio to
a Corvo bianco or Lacryma
Christi bianco will serve well.

never-refrigerated tomatoes; just-plucked basil leaves; and freshly made artisan mozzarella. With lesser ingredients, it's less transcendent but never less than good. Despite the name *insalata*, this dish is always an antipasto, never appearing as a contorno or salad course.

One 6-ounce ripe tomato	2 tablespoons extra-virgin olive oil
4 ounces mozzarella	Salt
1 tablespoon chopped fresh basil	Freshly ground black pepper

Wash, dry, and core the tomato. Cut it into ¼-inch slices. Cut the mozzarella into an equal number of slices and pat them dry with paper towels.

Arrange the tomato and mozzarella slices alternately on a serving plate. Sprinkle them with the chopped basil and drizzle on the olive oil. Add salt and pepper to taste. ∎

About Mozzarella

Of all the wildly different cheeses human ingenuity has produced, none is more surprising than mozzarella. It's a cheese most of us take totally for granted—the obligatory white puddle on a million pizzas, the familiar melting veil on lasagna. You can find it sealed in armor-plate plastic at any supermarket, or lounging nude in pools of water in every good Italian delicatessen or specialty shop. Americans enjoy mozzarella unthinkingly, and rarely pause to wonder at its sheer improbability—the unlikelihood of someone's having stumbled by accident upon the precise sequence of manipulations it takes to turn milk into mozzarella.

We had the chance to observe the process some years ago when visiting friends in Bari whose family owns a *caseificio* (cheese store) that specializes in mozzarella and its allies—scamorza, manteca, and burrata. We asked for a behind-the-scenes tour.

On the day of our visit, we were greeted by eight or nine of the Ludovico *cugini* (cousins) of all ages, curious to see these *americani* who were curious about their work. After elaborate introductions and exchange of compliments in the retail shop (partially for the edification of all the customers there waiting for the next tray of newly made mozzarella to emerge), we were conducted to the back of the building, into a scene of warm, wet, noisy activity. Mozzarella is not one of those cheeses that develop slowly in peace and solitude, reclining on straw mats in cool, airy cellars. The making of mozzarella takes hours, not weeks, and it involves vigorous handling at every stage.

First we saw milk—unpasteurized and straight from the cow—put into 50-gallon stainless steel vats and mixed with rennet to coagulate it. It takes half an hour for the curds to congeal, separate, and float on the whey. Each bucket-sized mass of spongy curds was lifted out, drained, and slid onto a table, where one of the cugini, wielding a huge, curved two-handed blade like a bandsaw, began cutting down through it, heaping the slices in front of him. As soon as a good-sized pile had accumulated, it was dumped into a wooden tub big enough for a week's washing and covered with hot salted water. Another cugino—one with extremely powerful arms—took up a hefty wooden paddle and began rhythmically stirring the curds in the water. After about ten minutes of continual stirring, the curds coalesced into elastic smoothness, a texture quite like that of the melted mozzarella on a freshly baked pizza. (This is a tricky step, we were told, because either too much or too little manipulation will equally ruin the cheese.) The craftsman checked the texture by lifting some out every so often and smearing it out on a tabletop with the heel of his hand.

When the cheese felt right, he used the paddle to lever the whole mass—about 25 pounds' worth—into a vat of cooler water, where other cugini continually stretched and smoothed it. (All this involves much slopping of water onto the floor and onto any interested observers, we can attest.) Finally, when it had reached the precisely right consistency, many hands dipped in to pull up sections of it, which promptly elongated into continuous elastic ropes, and shape them into individual cheeses.

This happened quick as lightning. Squeezed through the hands, balls of infant mozzarella rose like little balloons and were twisted off. Those to be sold immediately were left spherical and put in trays of cold salted water to set briefly. Those to be aged into scamorza were tied in pairs like saddlebags and given a nasal protuberance—the classic gourd shape. Some sections of each mozzarella "rope" were simply tied into little knots about 2 inches long, to be sold for serving on an antipasto plate. Others were molded around succulent lumps of sweet butter, to be chilled to firmness and eaten in slices with country ham and bread. In the morning we spent at that mozzarella works, every stage of the process was occurring simultaneously and at top speed. It was as good as a circus—if rather wetter. We must have seen the birth of about 200 pounds of cheeses—not counting the kilo or two we ourselves sampled while observing!

Wonderful as that Bari mozzarella was, it isn't the kind most prized in Italy— the increasingly scarce *mozzarella di bufala,* made from the milk of a sort of water buffalo. Buffalo mozzarella is made largely in the area around Naples, and it has a clear, sweet flavor and springy texture that is subtly different from cow's-milk mozzarella. Some of it is exported to America (at premium prices, of course). If you try it, eat it just as is, with a drizzle of extra-virgin olive oil and a crackling of black pepper. At most, use it in insalata caprese. For cooking, rely on freshly made domestic mozzarella if possible, which is still head and shoulders above the commercial packaged brands.

Fresh domestic mozzarella varies very much from location to location. That's because the flavor of the cheese depends on the quality of the milk used and what the cow who donated it had recently been eating. Artisan makers choose their milk carefully, so it's worth shopping around to find a store whose mozzarella has some character. The cheeses hold well in the freezer for several weeks, though Italians would be shocked to hear us say so: in Italy, you buy and eat your mozzarella on the day it's made, and not a day later.

MARINATED ZUCCHINI WITH MINT

Zucchini a scapece

FOR 4 SERVINGS:

Neapolitans especially adore the frying-then-marinating technique known as *a scapece*, using it mainly for small fish (as in the Spanish *escabeche*), eggplant, and best of all zucchini. In a classic book, *La Cucina Napoletana*, J. C. Francesconi calls this preparation *"sommamente appetitosi e ghiotti. Un . . . piatto per descrivere il quale, non sarebbe di troppo il lirismo di un poeta."* Freely translated, "supremely appetizing and delicious. A . . . dish that, to describe, needs the lyricism of a poet."

Lyrical poets aside, scapece seems to be one of the techniques that Italians picked up during the years the Spanish house of Aragon ruled Naples, though some food historians argue that the process can be traced all the way back to Roman cookery. The key to achieving a supremely appetizing dish is to use olive oil for frying the zucchini. The only other problem is self-control: it's a temptation to eat the finished zucchini right away, but they improve markedly with a day's keeping, so make this recipe the day before you plan to serve it.

A dry, crisp white wine: a good Soave or Pinot grigio, on the light end, or a Corvo bianco or Lacryma Christi bianco, for a slightly fuller-bodied choice.

1½ pounds zucchini, scrubbed and sliced in ½- to ¾-inch rounds or ovals	1½ tablespoons chopped fresh mint leaves
2 teaspoons salt	Freshly ground black pepper
2 cups olive oil	¼ cup wine vinegar
	1 clove garlic, halved

In a colander, toss the zucchini rounds with the salt and set the colander in the sink for 1 hour to let the zucchini exude moisture. Then rinse, drain, and pat them dry with paper towels, pressing moderately hard to extract more liquid.

In a 9-inch cast-iron skillet, pour the olive oil to a depth of about ½ inch and heat it to 350°F. Fry the zucchini pieces in small batches until golden, about 1 minute to each side. Allow the oil to come back up to temperature between batches.

Drain the zucchini on paper towels and, when all are fried, transfer them to a salad bowl. Reserve the cooking oil. Add the chopped mint and a generous quantity of black pepper and toss to distribute the seasonings.

Put the vinegar, the garlic, and ¼ cup water in a small pot. Bring to a boil and simmer 5 minutes. Pour the boiling liquid over the zucchini and toss them again. Add 2 tablespoons of the zucchini frying oil and toss once more. Cover the bowl tightly and let the zucchini sit in a cool place (not the refrigerator) for 24 hours before using. They'll stay "supremely appetizing" for several days. ∎

About Frying in Olive Oil

Doubtless you're going to be surprised, possibly dismayed, by the number of recipes in this book that involve frying. All good Americans have been conditioned to cringe at the idea of fried foods: after all the dire warnings about cholesterol and lipids and the war in our bloodstream between good HDLs and bad LDLs, the very mention of frying prompts us to make a hex sign to ward off evil and to look around for a sharp stake to drive through the heart of the fryer.

Even if we can get past our health fears, Americans have been brainwashed into thinking of fried foods—especially (shudder!) *deep*-fried foods—as greasy and heavy. Therefore, anyone so degenerate, or so self-indulgent, as to be unable to kick the filthy habit entirely is urged at least to fry with "healthful" corn and peanut oils, which, we're told, have the extra advantage of giving no flavor of their own to the foods that pass through them.

From a cook's point of view (and, we would assume, that of anyone with working taste buds), that last has always been a very dubious advantage: if a process doesn't do anything to improve the taste of a food, why bother? The fact is, of course, that frying does wonders for the flavors and textures of many foods. That's why it remains so popular despite all the assurances that our hearts will clog up and fall out if we don't stop it. With science's recent rediscovery of the health-giving properties of olive oil, some of our exaggerated fears of "oily" foods may begin to dissipate. Perhaps now the time is at last right to reintroduce the pleasures of *frying* in olive oil.

New worlds will open to you once you try it, we promise! Frying in olive oil improves the taste of everything. Now, granted, maybe we two have been as palate-washed by our time in Italy as Americans are brainwashed by nutritional science—but to us, what olive oil does to foods is worth every calorie and every gram of monounsaturation it may involve. We have a music-loving friend whose criterion for buying any new record album or CD is that, the first time he hears it, it has to change his life. That's what learning to fry in olive oil will do for you.

Disabuse yourself of stereotypes. Well-fried food is not greasy or heavy: in fact, properly fried food usually creates a palatal impression of lightness and purity, as if the food's natural flavor had been heightened, not obscured. The olive oil component of the flavor is like the harmony line that makes the melody more interesting. And foods cooked in olive oil are not unhealthy unless they're all you ever eat—but you could say the same thing of water. In the Italian diet, fried foods are balanced out by fresh fruits and vegetables, by pasta and rice and wine. Some fat is essential for human nutrition, and olive oil is one of the best there is.

A more reasonable reluctance about frying is based on the belief that it's messy and troublesome—splatter on the stove, tendency to smoke, smells lingering in the curtains. Let us reassure you.

First of all, troublesome. Not really. Everything gets easier with practice. Like pasta making, frying comes to seem not at all onerous once you've done it a few times. Then you don't have to consciously *decide* everything—what pot to use, how much oil to pour in, where to put the paper towels for draining. You just do things the same way you did them before, and you hardly have to think about it at all.

Second, don't be intimidated by the "deep" in deep-frying. It's only relative. Frying doesn't require great vats of boiling oil. On the contrary, unless you're working with volume like a McDonald's franchise, all you need is enough oil to float the foods you're cooking: an inch or so in a moderate-sized cast-iron skillet. In properly heated oil, most foods turn golden in a minute or two, so you want to fry only a few pieces at a time so you can attend to turning and removing them.

A cast-iron skillet is ideal because it holds heat extremely well (and the oil keeps the skillet beautifully seasoned for subsequent sautéing). Oil temperature can drop

40 or 50 degrees with the addition of raw food, and you want to prevent that as much as possible—which is another reason to fry in small batches. Another way to prevent excessive temperature drop is to use a much larger volume of oil, but that's when you get into the perils of boiling vats. Also, olive oil is expensive—so, all in all, a little is better than a lot. Most of our recipes call for 2 cups of oil in an 8-inch pan, which is an extremely manageable setup.

Third: to solve the problem of smoking oil, use a frying thermometer. Just remember to keep an eye on it. Another (more costly) possibility is an electric frypan. But be aware that they're usually quite large and will need far more oil. Then you'll be tempted to try frying too many items at once because of the large surface area. And *that* will drop the oil temperature. And unlike a stove burner that you can turn up to high, the electric frypan takes its own good time to return the oil to frying temperature, while your food sits there soaking up warm oil. Another high-tech solution is the DeLonghi rotary fryer, which not only doesn't smoke but eliminates the lingering scent of frying even from poorly ventilated (e.g., New York apartment) kitchens. Its drawback is that you can't see how your *fritti* are progressing as you can with an open pan. Really, minimal gadgetry is best for successful deep-frying—a heavy skillet, a thermometer, and flexible gas heat.

So let's say you're now willing to fry. What kind of olive oil should you use? We don't recommend extra-virgin, unless you own an olive grove. Plain old pure olive oil is fine. Buy in quantity and it isn't so expensive. A gallon tin of olive oil in your pantry will give you a warm, provided-for feeling—and if you use our recipes a lot, that gallon will get used. Don't be tempted by the "light" olive oil some Italian makers are pushing—it's been lightened to flavorlessness. If your grocer has what seems like astonishingly bargain-priced olive oil, it's probably pomace oil—that is, oil that was pressed from the solids left over after the higher-quality oil is extracted. Pomace oil isn't contemptible (after all, grappa is a pomace brandy—pomace from grapes, not olives, of course—and we yield to none in our passion for grappa). We've had reasonable results with pomace oil, but it has a coarser flavor and isn't as great a savings as it seems, because it breaks down sooner under repeated heatings, so you can't reuse it as often.

Used olive oil can and should be filtered for several (though not infinite) reuses. A coffee filter works very well but takes a very long time; a paper towel is quicker but not as thorough. Stored in the refrigerator, olive oil can be used several times for frying. Your nose will tell you when it's time to stop!

Relatively few of our recipes in this book have frying as their exclusive cooking process, as the stuffed zucchini blossoms immediately following do. In most, as in the preceding zucchini a scapece, the frying is a preliminary step, followed by some further treatment. This is handy in summertime, since you can do the frying early, in the cool of the day. Or—as the canny peasants who originated most of these recipes undoubtedly did—you can fry up enough of whatever vegetable is involved to have some of it straight out of the pan, as a contorno, and use the rest in the composed dish the next day.

BATTER-FRIED ZUCCHINI BLOSSOMS

Fiori fritti

FOR 4 SERVINGS:

*I*f the idea of eating flowers strikes you as strange, one taste of this dish will make you a convert. This is not the kind of exoticism that adds violets or nasturtiums to a green salad in the name of novelty. Zucchini flowers make delicately flavored natural casings for savory fillings.

Farmers' markets and specialty grocers in our city carry zucchini blossoms regularly in the summer months, but the best source of them is your own (or a neighbor's) garden. Pick the blossoms just before they're ready to open. A brief botanical inspection will show you that zucchini plants produce both male and female flowers. The female ones grow on fat, fleshy stems that develop into the actual squashes. Male flowers grow on skinny stems that never become zucchini. Early in the season, take males, so as not to spoil the subsequent crop. In the height of the summer, when the plants are

Any of the white suggested for the two previous recipes, or, for a more important occasion, a Pomino bianco or Greco di Tufo or Tocai.

pumping out more zucchini than you can eat, you can practice population control by taking the female ones. The 1- or 2-inch squashes attached to female blossoms eat well in this recipe.

The *pastella* used here is a quick, simple batter that can be used for frying small fish, squid rings, thinly cut vegetables, almost anything that will cook up quickly. It gives a thin crisp crust that doesn't compete with the flavor of the food it encases, much like a Japanese tempura batter (which, however, contains egg, as this does not). Since the ingredients for pastella are so few and the preparation so fast—unlike more elaborate batters that sometimes have to sit for a period of time before they can be used—it's easy to make up more if you find you're running out before all the food is fried. By the same token, if the food you're coating is very moist and the first few fried items come out with a thinner crust than you like, it's easy to just beat a little more flour into the remaining batter.

12 zucchini blossoms, about 3 inches long

2 to 3 slices prosciutto, cut in 12 strips 2 inches by ½ inch

2 ounces mozzarella, cut in 12 strips less than 1 inch thick

2 cups olive oil

FOR THE BATTER:

1 cup water

¾ cup all-purpose flour

⅛ teaspoon salt

1 teaspoon olive oil

Put the water in a broad shallow bowl. Gradually add the flour, beating well with a whisk or fork, to make a smooth batter. Stir in the salt and the olive oil. Use at once.

Rinse the zucchini flowers, pat them dry with paper towels, and cut off the (male) stems close to the flower base. Wrap a piece of prosciutto around each piece of mozzarella.

Partially open the petals of a flower (check the interior for insects, while you're at it) and insert a piece of wrapped mozzarella. Close the petals around the filling, twisting them together like a paper sack if necessary. Stuff the remaining flowers in the same way.

In a 9-inch cast-iron skillet pour olive oil to a depth of about ½ inch. Heat it to 350°F. Have the pastella batter handy in a bowl.

Dip one stuffed flower into the batter and coat it thoroughly. Pick it up by the petal tips (so the stuffing can't slide out), hold it for a moment over the bowl to drip off excess batter, and slide it into the hot oil.

Proceed with the remaining flowers, coating and frying a few at a time to keep the oil from cooling down. Fry the flowers about 2 minutes on each side, or until golden. When done, drain them on paper towels and keep warm while you fry the rest. Serve at once. ■

SMALL ZUCCHINI OMELETS

Frittatine ai zucchini

FOR 4 SERVINGS:

*A*s a shrewd eye will see, this recipe is basically a way to use leftover sautéed zucchini. However, these little omelets are tasty enough to justify cooking up some zucchini on purpose for them. They're especially nice in a mixed antipasto plate, with each person getting one *frittatina* along with other items. Our recipe makes eight frittatine—two each for four people—on the assumption that it will be the only antipasto served. Need we add that the omelets also make very nice luncheon dishes?

A dry, medium-bodied white such as Pinot bianco or Tocai; or a soft, light red such as a Bardolino or Valpolicella, Castel del Monte or Etna rosso.

6 tablespoons olive oil, in all

¼ cup minced onion

1½ pounds small zucchini, scrubbed and sliced ⅛ inch thick

Salt

Freshly ground black pepper

1 to 2 tablespoons chopped fresh basil

8 eggs

Freshly grated nutmeg

1 cup freshly grated parmigiano

In a large frying pan, warm 3 tablespoons olive oil. Add the zucchini and onion and cook over low heat, stirring occasionally, 20 to 30 minutes, or until the vegetables are very soft. Sprinkle lightly with salt and pepper, stir in the chopped basil, and set aside to cool somewhat.

For each frittatina, proceed as follows:
Beat 1 egg in a small bowl with ¼ teaspoon salt, a sprinkle of pepper, a sprinkle of nutmeg, and 2 tablespoons parmigiano. Stir in ¼ cup of the zucchini mixture.

In a 6-inch cast-iron skillet or crêpe pan, heat 2 teaspoons olive oil. Put the egg mixture into the pan, spreading it evenly. Cook over medium heat about 5 minutes, loosening the sides and bottom of the omelet with a spatula and shaking the pan occasionally, so its contents slide as a unit. When the bottom is firm and golden brown, flip the frittatina with a spatula and cook 3 to 4 minutes on the other side, or until the egg is fully cooked and the second side is golden.

Keep the finished frittatine warm while making the rest. Serve warm or at room temperature. ∎

EGGPLANT PARMESAN

Parmigiana di melanzane

FOR 6 TO 8 SERVINGS:

This dish of eggplant Parmesan is very different from the heavily sauced, very cheesy ones customarily served in Italian-American restaurants. Which is not to say that either is uncanonical: *la parmigiana*, as Neapolitans will proudly tell you, is *several* of the glories of Neapolitan cuisine.

This is an ancient version, characterized by a tomato sauce made without any oil or fat, egg mixed with part of the sauce, and vast quantities of fresh basil. It produces a shallow dish, only three layers of eggplant deep; not overly saucy but extremely rich. Its flavor evokes a quieter, more rustic Italy than that of the more ebullient Neapolitan stereotype.

Preparing and frying eggplant is time-consuming, so we've given a large recipe on the grounds that if you're going to go to any trouble in hot weather, you'll want to have a lot of people around to admire your results. The sauce can be done a day in advance, the eggplant preparation some hours in advance. Also, the entire dish needs some time to rest after baking. If the weather is cool enough to leave it unrefrigerated, the dish is even better the second day.

A simple, flavorful red wine—Lacryma Christi rosso, Castel del Monte, Montepulciano d'Abruzzo, Corvo, Valpolicella, or even a young Chianti.

FOR THE TOMATO SAUCE:

2 pounds ripe plum tomatoes

2 tablespoons chopped onion

3 to 4 whole basil leaves

¼ teaspoon salt

FOR THE DISH ITSELF:

Salt

3½ to 4 pounds eggplant, peeled and cut lengthwise in ⅛-inch slices

2 cups olive oil

2 eggs

8 tablespoons freshly grated parmigiano

½ to ¾ cup finely chopped basil

¾ pound mozzarella cut in fat matchsticks

To make the sauce:

Wash and halve the tomatoes. Squeeze them lightly over the sink to remove the seeds and some of their water, and put them in a pot with the onion and basil. Cover and cook over medium heat 5 minutes, or until the tomatoes have softened.

Remove the solids with a slotted spoon, leaving behind the watery juices. Discard the juices and wash the pot if any tomato skins have stuck to it. Put the solids through a food mill back into the pot and cook 10 to 15 minutes over low heat, until the sauce is quite thick. Stir in the salt. Set the sauce aside until ready to use.

To prepare the eggplant:

Salt the eggplant slices lightly and stand them in a colander in the sink for 30 minutes to 1 hour, so they will exude their bitter juices. Dry them on a cloth or paper towels, pressing moderately hard to remove more liquid.

In a 9-inch cast-iron skillet, pour olive oil to a depth of ½ inch and heat it to 350°F. Fry the eggplant slices a few at a time until lightly golden, about 1 minute to a side. Drain on paper towels.

To assemble and bake the dish:

Preheat the oven to 375°F. In a small bowl, beat the eggs with a pinch of salt and ½ cup tomato sauce. Take a 10- by 14-inch baking dish and spread 2 to 3 tablespoons of plain (unegged) tomato sauce on the bottom.

Make a layer of one third of the eggplant slices, overlapping them as necessary. Sprinkle on 2 tablespoons of grated parmigiano, then one third of the chopped basil. Spread on 2 to 3 tablespoons of the egg-tomato sauce mixture and 1 tablespoon of the plain sauce. Top with half the mozzarella.

Make a second layer exactly the same as the first. Then make a third layer of eggplant, 2 tablespoons parmigiano, all the remaining basil, all the remaining egg sauce, and 2 to 3 tablespoons plain sauce. Top with the last 2 tablespoons of parmigiano.

Cover the dish with aluminum foil, set it in the oven, and bake 30 minutes. Remove the foil, raise the oven temperature to 400°F, and bake another 5 to 10 minutes, until the dish is bubbling and its surface is lightly browned. Let cool at least 20 minutes before serving. Serve warm or at room temperature. ■

TUNA AND WHITE BEAN CANAPÉS

Crostini di fagioli e tonno

FOR 4 SERVINGS:

*A*s far as we know, we invented this ancient Italian dish by hybridizing the ingredients of one classic Tuscan antipasto (tuna and white cannellini beans) with the technique of another (*crostini*, or toast triangles spread with a variety of savory pastes). The combination is lovely—but it depends absolutely on the quality of the ingredients. You must use imported dark-meat tuna packed in olive oil. Different brands of canned beans vary in flavorfulness, too. If the beans don't taste like anything on their own, they won't have anything to contribute to the dish. The chopped onions are also an essential part of the dish's appeal, both for texture and flavor.

You can make up the spread in advance, but don't assemble the crostini until just before serving. Three per person are enough for a small antipasto, or combine them with other kinds of crostini (chicken liver pâté is the most common Tuscan type) or other antipasti (our zucchini frittatine, for instance) to make mixed antipasto plates. These crostini are also quite nice as party canapés, and people often can't guess what the ingredients are.

Absolutely no problem, since these pleasant little mouthfuls will get along with any wine of any color, still or sparkling— as long as it's dry.

½ cup drained canned white cannellini beans

4 tablespoons imported Italian tuna packed in olive oil (half of a 6½-ounce can)

½ to ¾ cup finely chopped mild, sweet onion

Twelve 3-inch rounds or triangles of crustless bread

Freshly ground black pepper

Rinse the beans in a sieve under running water to remove their canning liquid, and drain them well.

Put the beans, tuna, and ¼ cup onion into a blender or food processor and blend into a smooth paste. If it appears dry, add a little olive oil from the tuna can. Taste for salt.

Toast the bread slices and spread the tuna-bean paste over

them. Top with the remaining chopped onions and serve. Alternatively, put the onions into a small serving bowl and pass them with the crostini, so diners can top each crostino with additional onion to taste. A crackling of freshly ground black pepper is nice, too. ■

TOMATO SCHIACCIATA

Schiacciata al pomodoro

FOR ONE 10-INCH ROUND LOAF:

Y

This schiacciata will match with any simple, dry wine, red or white.

This is as simple and savory a flavored bread as can be imagined, especially nice for a picnic. The relatively small amount of tomato sauce is absorbed by the bread, leaving a pretty, red-gold surface. It doesn't at all resemble a pizza manqué. Like most schiacciatas, this one keeps well a day or so and can be reheated. If you do reheat it, try freshening its flavor by sprinkling on a little grated mozzarella or young asiago before you pop it in the oven—just enough to create a thin veil of melting cheese. It still won't seem like a poor man's pizza.

*All the ingredients for basic
  schiacciata (page 35)*
⅔ cup light tomato sauce, e.g.,

*Quick Summer Tomato Sauce
on page 156*

Prepare a plain schiacciata dough as directed in the basic recipe. After it has had its 30-minute rest, spread the tomato sauce over the top of the dough, leaving an outside rim clear, and bake as directed. ■

SCALLOPS SAN REMO

Capesanti sanremese

FOR 4 SERVINGS:

*T*his is our re-creation of a lovely dish we were served at a restaurant on the Ligurian coast. For the full effect, you will need some steep cliffs tumbling into an incredibly blue Mediterranean, plus some cooling sea breezes on a sun-washed terrace. In the absence of those, we recommend another glass of chilled white wine and the freshest scallops you can lay your hands on.

Italian dry vermouth gives this dish a distinctive herbal sweetness, so don't substitute a French vermouth: the flavor is completely different. As an alternative to scallops, you could prepare medallions of monkfish or lobster tail in this same way.

A crisp white with some elegance will work best. Try an Arneis or a Gavi, a Fiano or a Sauvignon.

4 tablespoons olive oil

2 tablespoons minced onion

1 small clove garlic, minced

¾ pound sea scallops, cut in ⅓- to ½-inch coins

Salt

Freshly ground black pepper

1 tablespoon chopped flat-leaf Italian parsley

3 tablespoons chopped basil leaves

1 tablespoon chopped skinned plum tomato

¼ cup Cinzano bianco or other dry Italian vermouth

3 to 4 tablespoons fine dry bread crumbs

In a nonreactive skillet, heat the olive oil. Add the onion and garlic and cook over very low heat 10 minutes, until they are soft but not browned. Raise heat slightly, add the scallops, and toss 1 minute, until they are coated with oil and have firmed up somewhat. Sprinkle with salt and pepper. Stir in the parsley, basil, tomato, and vermouth. Poach the scallops gently in this liquid, uncovered, 5 minutes. Lift them out with a slotted spoon into an oiled gratin dish (or 4 individual dishes).

Raise heat to high and reduce the poaching liquid to a thin

syrup. Spoon most of it, including the solids, over the scallops, saving a few tablespoons. The dish can be set aside now until almost serving time.

When ready to serve, preheat the broiler. Sprinkle the bread crumbs over the scallops, moisten them with the remaining pan juices, and set the dish under the broiler for 5 minutes, until heated through and lightly browned. Serve at once. ■

SEAFOOD SALAD

Insalata di mare

FOR 4 SERVINGS:

A crisp, dry white is the natural companion of a dish like this. Pinot grigio, cru Soave, Verdicchio, Sauvignon—all will match very happily here.

All over Italy one gets glorious seafood salads, everwhere different according to what the local waters produce, but everywhere the same in their freshness and delicacy of flavor. Their main charm for Americans is the profusion of tiny, sweet, utterly fresh crustaceans and bivalves they use—the thin-shelled clams that are variously called *arzelle* and *tellini* and *vongole veraci*, 2-inch-long squid and octopi with tentacles coiled into rosettes, miniature razor clams, ordinary mussels and the special ones called *datteri*, sea dates. On this side of the Atlantic, we usually have to make do with larger, coarser marine creatures. The difference—to the eye as well as the palate—is great.

Any time the fish markets have tiny octopi, we buy them for an Italianate seafood salad. They tend to toughen if they're frozen and kept for any length of time, so it's best to use them fresh. For this dish, the octopi need to be tenderized by parboiling, which can be done several hours in advance. In fact, all the cooking should be done well in advance, so that the seafood is at room temperature for the final assembly.

FOR PREPARING THE OCTOPI:

1 pound small octopi (about 12)

1 small carrot, peeled and
    quartered

1 small onion, peeled and
    quartered

½ cup white wine

Salt

Freshly ground black
    pepper

FOR THE SEAFOOD SALAD:

8 tablespoons olive oil

1 clove garlic, halved

½ pound small shrimp, peeled and
    halved lengthwise

Salt

½ cup finely chopped celery

¼ cup finely chopped onion

¼ cup thin strips roasted sweet red
    pepper (see directions on page
    222)

2 tablespoons white wine vinegar

Preparing the octopi:

With a sharp scissors or knife, cut away the tentacles of each
octopus just below the eyes, leaving the eyes attached to the head
sac. Remove (either by squeezing or cutting away with a knife point)
the small, hard beak at the center of each group of tentacles, so that
you are left with a doughnut of tentacles. Rinse these and set them
aside. Take the body of the octopus and try to turn it inside out. If
it cooperates, simply detach and discard everything except the
smooth sac itself. If it doesn't readily turn inside out, remove the
eyes by cutting them away as close to the body sac as possible; then
peel the skin away from the body sac and turn the sac inside out,
discarding everything inside. Rinse thoroughly, turn right side out,
and proceed with the recipe.

    Put 6 cups water in a large pot. Add the carrot, onion, wine, 1½
teaspoons salt, and a pinch of black pepper. Bring to a boil, cover,
and boil briskly 20 minutes. Drop in the octopus bodies and tentacles. Return to a boil, reduce to a simmer, and cook 5 minutes,
uncovered. (If your octopi are larger than called for, cook them a
little longer.) Then drain and cool the octopi. Halve each body and
tentacle section.

Making the salad:

In a large sauté pan, warm 4 tablespoons olive oil. Sauté the halved
garlic 2 to 3 minutes, until lightly golden. Flatten the pieces against
the pan with a fork to press out their juices, then discard them. Add

all the shrimp and the octopus pieces. Sprinkle lightly with salt and sauté, stirring, 5 minutes. Transfer the shrimp and octopus to a plate and let them cool to room temperature.

When ready to serve, put the shrimp and octopus (and any oil left on the plate) into a serving bowl together with the celery, onion, red pepper strips, and additional salt and pepper to taste. Toss with the vinegar and then with the remaining 4 tablespoons olive oil. Serve at once. ■

GRATIN OF MUSSELS

Tegamino di cozze

FOR 4 SERVINGS:

Y

Pinot grigio, cru Soave, Verdicchio, or Sauvignon.

*T*his wonderfully delicate mussel dish tastes its best when made at the seashore, where you can gather your own mussels and know they're absolutely fresh. The dish is a little labor-intensive because you have to open the mussels raw, and—for all that they seem more fragile than clams or oysters—mussels can be every bit as uncooperative. Here's the technique we use:

Let the mussels rest awhile after scrubbing and debearding, since they often gape naturally and you can take advantage of that to get a blade between the shells. If they remain closed tight, pick one up and exert contrary pressures on the two shells—i.e., push the top shell in one direction with your thumb while pushing the bottom shell in the opposite direction with your index finger. This will open a gap into which you can insert a knife point. Cut through the large muscle near the front edge of the shell and pry the mussel open.

It's worth the work, because baking them raw keeps mussels

tender and tasty. If you steam them open, they'll get rubbery. Once the mussels are open, the rest of the dish is a snap. One dozen mussels of the size indicated makes an adequate antipasto portion: for a luncheon dish, figure on two dozen mussels per person. If your mussels are larger, just increase the amount of condiment.

4 dozen mussels (2½ inches long), scrubbed and debearded

4 tablespoons minced garlic

4 tablespoons minced flat-leaf Italian parsley

2 tablespoons fresh lemon juice

1½ teaspoons red wine vinegar

4 tablespoons olive oil

1 to 2 tablespoons fine dry bread crumbs

Preheat the oven to 425°F. Open the mussels, scooping all the flesh into one of the shells and discarding the other. Rinse the mussels under running water and drain them thoroughly. Set them close together in a shallow baking pan, keeping the shells as level as possible so the flavorings won't spill out.

Strew the garlic and parsley over the mussels. In a small jar, combine the lemon juice, vinegar, and olive oil and shake well. Spoon this liquid onto the mussels. Top with a thin veil of bread crumbs.

Put the pan in the oven and bake 10 to 15 minutes, until the liquid is bubbling. Serve at once. (If you like, you can finish the dish under a hot broiler for a minute or two to crisp the top.) ■

PRIMI

The appetite for pasta never wanes, not even in the hottest days of summer. (If our philosophical views on pasta aren't known to you yet, please read About Pasta in the Spring section, page 51.) Therefore, our recipes in this section are preponderantly for pasta.

We start, however, with a few light summer soups that take advantage of the season's abundant produce. Tom always loves a soup, no matter what the weather, and Diane has had to learn to feed the beast if she wants him to keep on uncomplainingly carting home the bushels of gorgeous vegetables she regards as essential kitchen decor at this time of year.

Then on to pasta. The only thing particularly "summery" about our two recipes for fresh egg pasta is the ease and speed with which their excellent sauces are made—but that's not to be scorned if your kitchen isn't air-conditioned, or if you'd rather be spending time outdoors than cooking.

Then we move into recipes for pasta asciutta—dried, eggless commercial pasta. Here those gorgeous vegetables come into their own again. The first two recipes are for *salse crude*—uncooked vegetable sauces made up and left to ripen at room temperature before being used to dress freshly cooked hot pasta. (There are many variations on these tasty liquid salads; we gave three others in *La Tavola Italiana*.) Next, an almost-raw sauce: a 30-second sauté of vast amounts of fresh basil in butter and oil, tossed with rigatoni and two kinds of grated cheese.

After a pause for a discursus on making quick pasta sauces with virtually nothing but summer's best tomatoes, we move into a few quick-cooking tomato-based sauces that feature additional ingredients, then end with a non-tomato classic, pasta with garlic and oil. Again, it's mainly the speed of cooking that caused us to locate this dish in the summer section, for *agli'e olio* is wonderful any time of the year. However, using freshly dug (not dried) garlic makes it even more delicious—so there is an estival justification.

Last of all, we've included one unusual gnocchi recipe. To our minds, the real gnocchi season is fall and winter—gnocchi being based on potatoes, and root vegetables being in general colder-weather crops. But in our part of the world, bluefish is very much of a summer "crop," and this is a recipe for bluefish gnocchi.

LIGHT TOMATO-ZUCCHINI SOUP

Minestra di pomodoro e zucchini

FOR 4 SERVINGS:

his extremely simple, refreshing soup is vibrant with the vegetable flavors of summer—tomatoes, zucchini, and basil. Delightful in itself, it's also amenable to endless variations. After you've tasted the soup plain, your imagination will suggest possibilities: Adding cut-up green peppers along with or instead of some of the zucchini. Throwing in a handful of pasta (and a little more liquid). Adding a few minced clams and their liquor for the last two minutes of cooking for a fast chowder. Laying a slice of garlic-rubbed toast in the bottom of each bowl before serving. Passing a bowl of grated parmigiano at table. We don't recommend trying *all* these things at once, because that would complicate and muffle the strong, clear flavors—but you can earn a reputation as a summer-soup chef simply by playing around with this base recipe.

Choose a simple, dry, light white wine: for example, Verdicchio, Soave, Frascati, Bianco di Custozza.

4 cups broth or water

3 tablespoons olive oil

1 clove garlic, minced

2 tablespoons chopped flat-leaf Italian parsley

1½ pounds small zucchini, scrubbed and cut in ½-inch cubes

Salt

Freshly ground black pepper

1½ pounds ripe plum tomatoes, peeled, seeded, and chopped

½ teaspoon chopped fresh oregano leaves

4 to 5 large leaves fresh basil, chopped

In a small pot, bring the broth to a simmer. In a 5- to 6-quart heavy-bottomed casserole, warm the olive oil, garlic, and parsley. Add the zucchini and cook gently over medium heat, stirring often, 3 minutes. Sprinkle lightly with salt and pepper and cook another 2 minutes.

Add the tomatoes, oregano, and broth to the casserole. Stir, cover, and cook at a steady simmer 30 minutes. About 1 minute before serving, stir in the basil. Taste for salt and serve. ∎

CALABRIAN ONION SOUP

Licurdia

FOR 4 SERVINGS:

A simple white: Verdicchio, Soave, Frascati, Bianco di Custozza.

This is a great soup for summer, when the onions are fresh out of the ground and every farm stand has piles of them. It couldn't be easier to make: if you can boil water, you're well on your way to mastering *licurdia*. For all its simplicity, its flavor is charming—and surprisingly delicate. The long simmering of the onions takes all the sharpness out of them. If you don't have lard around the house (it isn't exactly in demand as a summer cooking medium, but we usually have some tucked away in the freezer if nowhere else), use olive oil. We like to use red onions for this dish, but any other color will do as well. The trick of rubbing the toasted bread with a cut hot pepper (as opposed to the more usual garlic) gives the whole dish a nice gentle zing.

2 pounds freshly dug onions, cleaned and coarsely chopped

4 tablespoons lard

2 teaspoons salt

4 large slices day-old country-style bread

1 fresh hot pepper, green or red, any kind (according to your tolerance for pepper heat)

Freshly grated pecorino romano

In a nonreactive pot put the onions along with 2 quarts cold water, the lard, and the salt. Cover, bring to a boil, and simmer 1 hour.

Toast the bread slices. Cut the hot pepper in half, remove the seeds, and rub the halves over the toasted bread. Put a slice of toast in the bottom of each of four soup bowls. Ladle on the soup and serve. Top each with 1 tablespoon pecorino, or pass a bowl of cheese at the table. ■

TUSCAN BREAD SOUP

Pappa al pomodoro

FOR 4 SERVINGS:

Tuscan cooks have developed a number of excellent soups based primarily on bread. This one is close to the most elemental: a delicious mush of bread, tomatoes, and seasonings. Some say *pappa al pomodoro* isn't really a minestra but invalid food (as in the English "pap"). And so it would be, prepared plain. But add judicious proportions of aromatic vegetables and the dish transforms into innocent ambrosia, and you begin to understand why it's so popular in Italy. You won't believe us if you've never had a good pappa al pomodoro (and there are a lot of ho-hum versions in existence), but try this recipe just once. Please.

If you're making the dish with tomatoes that are highly acidic, you can round them out by dissolving a teaspoon or two of tomato paste in ¼ cup of hot water and adding it along with the broth. For a more elegant presentation, dish the hot soup into ramekins, sprinkle with grated mozzarella, and run them under the broiler just long enough to melt the cheese.

A simple white or a light, soft red, either with a touch of acidity: for example, Verdicchio or Frascati for whites, a young Chianti or a simple Barbera for reds.

3 tablespoons olive oil

¼ cup minced onion

¼ cup minced celery

2 cloves garlic, minced

1½ pounds sweet ripe tomatoes, peeled, seeded, and chopped

6 cups cubes of day-old

country-style bread (about ½ pound), lightly toasted

5 to 6 basil leaves, shredded

½ teaspoon salt

Freshly ground black pepper

2 cups light broth or water

Extra-virgin olive oil

In a deep casserole, warm the olive oil and sauté all the minced vegetables until soft, about 5 minutes. Add the tomatoes, bread, basil, salt, pepper to taste, and broth. Mix well and cook, covered, over a low flame 30 minutes. Stir frequently and break up the bread by mashing it against the bottom of the pan with a fork.

When the bread is fully dissolved and the mixture a uniform mush, the dish is done. Taste for salt and either serve at once or reheat when ready to serve. Top each bowlful with a healthy dollop of extra-virgin olive oil. ∎

FRESH EGG NOODLES WITH PROSCIUTTO

Tagliatelle al prosciutto

FOR 4 SERVINGS:

Y

A good, dry red is called for here: Barbera would be an excellent choice, as would young Taurasi or Aglianico or a Chianti Classico or Chianti Rufina.

*N*ow that Americans can at last get prosciutto di Parma, this straightforward preparation offers a good way to show off its succulence. You can use domestic prosciutto to make this dish: it won't be as sublime as it is with the Parma ham, but it's not shabby with any variety. (See page 339 for a discussion of prosciutto.) The dish takes no time at all to make, and the flavors are so simple and pure they really must have fresh egg pasta.

One potential problem: nobody gives you enough fat on your prosciutto these days. At current prices, that's no wonder, but it's a false economy; you want that fat for its sweetness, whether you're eating the prosciutto as is or cooking with it. If your prosciutto is very lean, use a little more butter in this preparation to compensate.

6 ounces prosciutto, preferably with some fat	*Freshly ground black pepper*
8 tablespoons butter	*1 recipe (1 pound) fresh tagliatelle (see page 54)*
2 tablespoons minced onion	*⅔ cup grated parmigiano*
Salt	

Separate the fat and lean of the prosciutto. Cut the lean into ½-inch squares. Chop the fat coarsely.

In a skillet, melt the butter, add the onion and prosciutto fat, and sauté 5 minutes, until the onion begins to turn golden. Stir in the lean prosciutto squares and sauté 2 to 3 minutes. Off the heat, salt very lightly (or not at all, if the ham is very heavily cured) and pepper generously. With a slotted spoon, remove half the prosciutto squares to a small bowl.

Put 4 to 5 quarts water in a large pot with 1 tablespoon salt. Bring it to a boil, add the tagliatelle, and cook 1 to 2 minutes, until al dente. Drain in a colander but don't shake too thoroughly; leave a little moisture on them.

Transfer the tagliatelle to a heated serving bowl and toss with the prosciutto mixture from the sauté pan (including all the fat). Add the parmigiano and more freshly ground pepper, and toss again. Scatter the reserved prosciutto over the top and serve at once. ■

ABRUZZI-STYLE FETTUCCINE

Fettuccine all'abruzzese

FOR 4 SERVINGS:

*A*nother brilliant less-is-more dish from the peasant repertoire. If you've ever started making a complex pasta sauce, gotten as far as sautéing a *battuto* of aromatic vegetables, and remarked, "That smells good enough to serve over pasta as is!" you'll be gratified to find that that's almost what you do here. For all its simplicity, the dish turns out surprisingly good and even elegant. Once the ingredients are chopped, the cooking takes almost no time

This dish likes soft red wines: Montepulciano d'Abruzzo, Lacryma Christi, Chianti Senese, even Dolcetto.

at all. There's just the smallest amount of sauce, but it clothes the pasta very well, with attractive little flecks of pink and green, and produces a nice onion sweetness on the palate. Don't omit the pepper at the end.

2 tablespoons olive oil

2½ ounces pancetta, finely
  chopped

⅔ cup finely chopped onion

4 basil leaves, chopped

2 tablespoons chopped flat-leaf
  Italian parsley

Salt

Freshly ground black pepper

½ cup broth or water

1 recipe (1 pound) fresh fettuccine
  (see page 54)

⅔ cup (2 ounces) freshly grated
  pecorino romano

In a nonreactive skillet, heat the olive oil, add the pancetta and onion, and sauté over low heat 5 minutes. Add the basil, parsley, a sprinkling of salt, and a generous quantity of pepper. Stir and add ¼ cup broth or water. Cook until the liquid almost evaporates, then set the pan aside while cooking the pasta.

In a large pot, bring 4 quarts water to a boil with 1 tablespoon salt. Add the fettuccine and cook until just al dente, 2 to 3 minutes. As the pasta cooks, reheat the sauce, adding another ¼ cup broth.

Drain the pasta and put it in a warmed serving bowl. Toss with the pecorino and then with the sauce. Grind more pepper over the top and serve at once. ■

CORKSCREW PASTA WITH AN UNCOOKED SAUCE

Fusilli con salsa cruda

FOR 4 SERVINGS:

There are almost as many variants on salsa cruda as there are cooks in Italy. This version has the somewhat unusual addition of roasted bell pepper. It's a nice dish to make if you've already got some roasted peppers around; and if not, it provides a good excuse to roast one and scent the kitchen with its savory fragrance. (Or roast a few on the charcoal grill when you're cooking outdoors one evening, for subsequent use.)

You can make up the sauce in the morning and let it sit in a cool place all day, so its flavors can develop. But if the weather is hot, refrigerate it, because roasted peppers are prone to ferment!

Red or white, as you please, as long as either is dry and light. Frascati, Orvieto, Soave—the classic summer whites—or young Chianti, Valpolicella, Lacryma Christi—the classic summer reds.

1 pound ripe tomatoes, peeled, seeded, and chopped

4 tablespoons minced onion

2 tablespoons chopped flat-leaf Italian parsley

2 tablespoons chopped basil

1/2 cup diced roasted bell pepper (see directions on page 222)

2 tablespoons red wine vinegar

1/2 cup extra-virgin olive oil

1/4 teaspoon salt

Freshly ground black pepper

1 pound imported Italian fusilli

Mix all the ingredients except the fusilli in a serving bowl and let them steep together for at least 3 hours. Before using the sauce, check for salt and pepper, and adjust to taste.

In a large pot, bring 4 to 5 quarts water to a boil with 1 tablespoon salt. Cook the fusilli until al dente. Drain them in a colander, transfer to the sauce bowl, toss well, and serve. ■

SEVEN SAVORS LINGUINE

Linguine ai sette sapori

FOR 4 SERVINGS:

Red or white, as you prefer: Frascati, Orvieto, Soave, for whites; young Chianti, Valpolicella, Lacryma Christi, for reds.

*A*nother version of an uncooked sauce for pasta, this one more delicate than the preceding one but intriguing from the interplay of its seven seasoning ingredients. The celery has a surprising presence, especially if you use the minced leaves, as you ought.

As with all uncooked pasta sauces, it's best to combine the ingredients in the morning and let them sit, preferably unrefrigerated, all day long for the flavors to develop.

2 pounds ripe tomatoes, peeled, seeded, and coarsely chopped

4 tablespoons chopped onion

4 tablespoons chopped celery, with leaves if available

4 tablespoons chopped basil

4 tablespoons chopped flat-leaf Italian parsley

1 clove garlic, halved

½ cup plus 2 tablespoons olive oil

¼ teaspoon chopped oregano

Salt

Freshly ground black pepper

1 pound imported Italian linguine

Put the chopped tomatoes in a sieve set over a large bowl and let them drain 30 minutes. Meanwhile, finely mince together the onion, celery, basil, and parsley.

Select a serving bowl and rub its interior with the cut surfaces of the garlic. Discard the remaining garlic. Add the minced vegetables, tomatoes, olive oil, oregano, ¾ teaspoon salt, and several grindings of pepper. Stir, cover, and let the sauce steep for several hours.

In a large pot, bring 4 quarts water to a boil with 1 tablespoon salt. Add the linguine and cook until it is al dente. Drain it in a colander, transfer it to the bowl containing the sauce, toss well, and serve. ∎

RIGATONI WITH BASIL

Rigatoni al basilico

FOR 4 SERVINGS:

Basil fanciers take note: this dish is the southern Italian answer to *pesto alla genovese*. Just as fragrant and flavorful, it has the advantages of being lighter and far easier to make—so much so that you prepare the sauce while the pasta cooks. Despite the absence of the nut paste on which pesto is based, the effect of this sauce is very similar to pesto, thanks to the presence of olive oil and two cheeses. It has a lovely redolence of basil and a clean, fresh herbal taste in the mouth.

This dish will take either a white or a red wine, but they must be wines of some character and, in the case of the red, not too much tannin. Try a Gavi or Sauvignon for the white, or young Taurasi, Aglianico, Chianti, or Rubesco for the red.

1 pound imported Italian rigatoni	*1 tablespoon finely chopped garlic*
Salt	*6 tablespoons grated parmigiano*
6 tablespoons butter	*6 tablespoons grated pecorino*
6 tablespoons olive oil	*romano*
¾ cup packed minced basil leaves	*Freshly ground black pepper*

In a large pot, bring 4 quarts water to a boil with 1 tablespoon salt. Add the rigatoni and cook until al dente. While the pasta is cooking, melt the butter with the oil in a sauté pan large enough to hold all the pasta when it is cooked. Add the chopped basil and garlic, sauté about 30 seconds, then turn off the heat.

As soon as the pasta is ready, turn on low heat under the sauté pan. Drain the rigatoni and add it to the basil mixture, stirring to coat it well with the herbs. Transfer it to a heated serving bowl, add the two grated cheeses, toss, and serve at once. Pass the pepper mill at the table. ■

About Tomato Sauces

Summer is tomatoes, tomatoes are summer. *Lycopersicon esculentum* (the succulent wolf plum, would you believe?) is the very emblem of the season—the one vegetable-fruit without which it isn't summer, no matter what other blandishments the markets and gardens offer.

As the weather warms, we start to dream about the first real tomato, the first truly vine-ripe, acid-sweet, firm-fleshed tomato, carrying the scent of the plant it ripened on, the tang of the soil it grew in. For months on end, no tomato darkens our doorstep, because we can't bear biting into the flavorless, mealy pink balls that are the only things available. Then at last comes summer, the time of tomato orgy.

Of all the wondrous things you can do with tomatoes, none is finer than turning them into a pasta sauce. The gods of pathways and journeys clearly had a gastronomical inspiration when they dispatched Italian voyagers to China for pasta and to America for tomatoes. Actually, pasta appears to have been made in Italy since Roman times, long before Marco Polo ever thought of wandering eastward, but remember, *se non è vero è ben trovato:* a good story makes a point better than the literal truth. Tomatoes and pasta *are* a marriage made in heaven, and it's only because both are so abundant and so inexpensive that we forget how sublime they really are together.

There are all kinds of tomatoes, of course, and not all work equally well in sauces. Large, juicy slicing tomatoes have too much liquid to be ideal. Tiny cherry tomatoes tend to be too acidic. As far as Italians are concerned, there is only one tomato for sauce, the San Marzano. This is a variety of plum or egg tomato: smallish, firm, slightly elongated, looking as often like small crimson pears as like plums or eggs. These sweet, dense-fleshed fruits make a supreme tomato sauce practically by themselves.

We learned that about San Marzanos on their home ground, in Posillipo, a headland on the Mediterranean coast just north of Naples. There, we were repeatedly served wonderful bowls of pasta dressed with what we took to calling squashed-tomato sauce. The name is descriptive if unflattering: the sauce seemed to be nothing but olive oil in which small halved tomatoes had been mashed and ever so briefly seethed—just long enough to loosen the tomato flesh and tint the oil tomato-red. It was a superb sauce: fresh and lively, satisfying and appetite-creating, all at once. We gave a recipe for a similar sauce (though with proportionately more tomato) as our basic southern sauce in *La Tavola Italiana* (where we also gave two other classic sauces to represent central and northern Italian cooking).

What is worth underlining about that kind of very typical, very delicious sauce is its incredible ease. It cooks in no time at all. That's often a great surprise to Americans, who are more familiar with long-cooked Italian-American sauces. Most native Italian tomato sauces do not need long cooking. Those that do usually have a strong meat presence, and the lengthy cooking is to make the meat and tomato flavors—plus, usually, other seasonings—merge into a different animal, something rich and strange. (In that regard, by the way, let us recommend to anyone who hasn't experienced it the incredible synergy of pork braised in tomato sauce. Sear the pork in a little olive oil first, along with some chopped onion and garlic, and maybe a peperoncino rosso for liveliness; then add the crushed or chopped tomatoes and cook until the pork is meltingly tender. The give-and-take of sweet pork fat and tomato acidity transmutes both ingredients into a higher culinary order of being. We are talking celestially good simple food here.)

Tomato sauces are close to foolproof. Basically, any ripe tomato exposed to the heat of a stove wants to become a sauce. All you have to do is get the excess water out of it. You can do that during the cooking or before. If during—and if you're cooking a large potful of tomatoes—it will take a long time to cook off all the water. Also, the flavor of the tomato will be changed by prolonged heat. It won't be hurt, it'll just lose some of its unmediated tomato freshness and develop a more pungent and concentrated flavor. Most quick sauces are cooked shallow, a single layer of tomatoes in a broad sauté pan, so there's a lot of surface for the water to evaporate from. Cooked that way, tomato sauces take half an hour or less.

The alternative method—getting most of the water out before cooking—is especially good in summer when you don't want the kitchen heated up more than is absolutely necessary. In the recipe below, 5 pounds of plum tomatoes become 2 quarts of sauce after spending a mere 15 minutes on the stove. Granted, some additional time is required to skin and seed the tomatoes, but that's another of those simple, basic techniques that quickly become effortless second nature.

QUICK SUMMER TOMATO SAUCE

FOR ABOUT 2 QUARTS SAUCE:

5 pounds ripe plum tomatoes
½ cup olive oil
1 cup finely chopped onion
1½ teaspoons salt
Freshly ground black pepper

2 to 3 tablespoons chopped flat-leaf
* Italian parsley*
2 to 3 tablespoons chopped fresh
* basil*

Bring a pot of water to a boil. Drop in the tomatoes, a few at a time, for 10 seconds to loosen their skins, then remove them with a slotted spoon. Peel, core, and halve the tomatoes. Holding the tomatoes over the sink, use your fingers to scoop out and discard all their seeds and liquid, leaving only the shells of tomato pulp. Coarsely chop the pulp.

Warm the olive oil in a very large skillet or saucepan (14 inches is ideal). Sauté the onion over low heat 5 minutes, until it is soft and translucent but not browned. Raise heat to medium and add the chopped tomato, salt, and pepper to taste. Bring to a simmer and stir in the parsley and basil. Cook 15 minutes, stirring frequently, until the mixture becomes a nubbly sauce. Taste for salt and adjust to your taste.

Two quarts of sauce will dress a lot of pasta. We give the recipe in that quantity because this is a versatile sauce to have around for all kinds of composed dishes. Aside from being delightful just as it is on any pasta, Quick Summer Tomato Sauce is specified in several of our summer recipes, such as:

- Schiacciata al pomodoro
- Pesce al forno
- Melanzane alla partenopea
- Zucchini alla contadina

You can also substitute it in recipes that involve other quickly cooked tomato sauces.

Quick Summer Tomato Sauce will keep in the refrigerator for several days, or freeze for a month or two (not much longer than that if you want to maintain its light freshness). You can, of course, scale the recipe down and make it with a pound or so of tomatoes for current use.

Two last technical notes on tomatoes before we let you get on with your cooking:

First, several of our recipes call for passing tomatoes through a food mill, with the alternative of pulsing them in a food processor or chopping them by hand. The advantage of using the food mill is that you don't have to peel, core, or seed the tomatoes. The food mill separates the juicy pulp from the skins, seeds, and any tough cores. (What's left in the food mill is in fact pomace—just like what remains after pressing olives for oil or grapes for wine.) If you're not using a food mill, it isn't always essential to peel tomatoes, but some have fairly tough skins. The easiest way to handle that is to drop tomatoes into boiling water for about 10 seconds, then make an incision with the point of a knife, and the skins will slip right off.

Finally—should you be the kind of weak-willed person who can't resist making recipes out of season—you'll need to know how to use canned plum tomatoes in place of the fresh items. Good-quality Italian-style canned plum tomatoes are a perfectly acceptable substitution in all but uncooked tomato sauces. The conversion factor is simple: 1 cup of drained, canned plum tomatoes equals 1 pound of fresh plum tomatoes. And, logically enough, the reverse is true—should you want to make a recipe calling for canned plum tomatoes when you have fresh ones around.

SPAGHETTINI WITH CLAMS AND SHRIMP

Spaghettini ai frutti di mare

FOR 4 SERVINGS:

A fine, dry white wine is called for here: Verdicchio (especially a cru), Greco di Tufo, a cru Soave.

*T*his dish calls for tiny clams, like manilas, which are closest in size and flavor to what you would get in Italy. You need to soak and scrub them well to get the sand out. If your clams are so big the shells would be troublesome in the finished dish, steam them open separately (in minimal water or white wine) and filter and reserve their juice, which you can add to the sauce at the same time that the fish broth goes in.

Fish broth can be made from any fish or shellfish scraps and trimmings—a fish head or frame, shrimp tails and shells, the skinny legs of crabs—boiled briefly with a little onion, carrot, celery, parsley, salt, and pepper. We always keep a small quantity of it on hand in the freezer. Alternatively, you can use bottled clam broth or fish bouillon from cubes: Knorr, for instance, makes a good one. For those of you who fear and loathe the humble anchovy, take note that the anchovy's own taste is not prominent here, but it is necessary for achieving a true, briny flavor: don't omit it.

Above all, don't exceed the brief cooking times for the shrimps and clams: this should bear no resemblance to some Italian-American restaurants' misguided thick red sauces with rubbery fish. It's a light, fresh-tasting, almost brothy dressing with delicate and tender shellfish. Finishing the pasta in the sauce both slightly thickens the sauce and at the same time gets some of the flavoring into instead of just onto the pasta. There's a method to all the madness here.

1 pound tiny clams in their shells	2 small peperoncini rossi
½ pound small shrimp, shelled	2 large cloves garlic, halved
¼ cup olive oil	2 anchovy fillets, rinsed and coarsely chopped

2 pounds ripe plum tomatoes,
  peeled, seeded, and chopped or
  pulsed in a food processor
½ cup fish broth
Freshly ground black pepper

¼ teaspoon oregano
Salt
1 pound imported Italian
  spaghettini

Soak the clams in a basin of cold water so that they will expel any sand. Scrub their shells with a vegetable brush. Rinse and pat dry the shrimp.

In a nonreactive skillet, warm the olive oil with the peperoncini. Add the garlic and sauté until just beginning to turn golden, then press it against the bottom of the pan with a fork and discard it. Either discard the peperoncini at this point, or leave them in to the end, if you like your sauce a bit zingier. (But do remove them at the end, so no unfortunate diner gets all the zing in a single mouthful!) Add the anchovies to the pan and sauté 1 minute or less, until they dissolve. Add the tomatoes, broth, a generous quantity of pepper, and the oregano. Stir well, cover, and simmer 10 minutes. Taste the sauce for salt and set it aside, uncovered, until ready to cook the pasta.

In a large pot, bring 4 or 5 quarts of water to a boil with 1 tablespoon salt. Add the spaghettini and cook until al dente. While the pasta is cooking, bring the sauce back to a simmer. Add the shrimp and clams, stir to coat them with the sauce, cover, and cook 2 minutes, until the clams open. Drain the pasta before it is quite cooked, add it to the sauce, and cook, stirring, 1 minute. Serve immediately. ■

STRUMPET'S SPAGHETTI

Spaghetti alla puttanesca

FOR 4 SERVINGS:

This is a white-wine dish: try
Greco di Tufo or Lacryma
Christi bianco, Regaleali
bianco or Corvo, Verdicchio, or
Vernaccia.

*L*ike the white asparagus of Bassano, this is another X-rated Italian specialty—at least nominally. *Alla puttanesca* means literally "the way the whores do it," which must mean fast and good, because those are certainly two things that this sauce is. If you like olives, you will love this recipe—but be aware that the result you get is only as good as the olives you start with. Unlike most (we think denatured) versions of salsa puttanesca, this is not so much a tomato sauce with olives as an olive sauce with tomatoes. Hence, the flavor changes depending on whether you're using mild olives like Gaetas or strong ones like Moroccan oil-cureds.

You can finish the pasta in the sauce if you like, or if your sauce is looking too thin. You do not use any cheese with this sauce, though some people enjoy adding a sprinkling of crushed red pepper.

1 tablespoon capers, drained and
  rinsed
4 ounces Gaeta or oil-cured black
  olives, pitted
3 tablespoons olive oil
1 clove garlic, halved
1 peperoncino rosso

4 anchovy fillets, chopped
2 pounds ripe plum tomatoes,
  peeled, seeded, and chopped or
  pulsed in a food processor
1 pound imported Italian spaghetti
Salt

Chop the capers and half the olives together to a fine mince. In a nonreactive skillet, heat the olive oil, add the garlic and peperoncino, and sauté over medium heat until the garlic is lightly golden and the peperoncino darkened on both sides, then remove them.

Add the anchovies and sauté, stirring, until they dissolve. Stir in the caper-olive mixture and then the tomatoes and whole olives. Reduce heat to maintain a simmer, cover, and cook 10 minutes, stirring occasionally. Taste for salt (but it probably won't need any).

In a large pot, bring 4 quarts water to a boil with 1 tablespoon salt. Add the spaghetti and cook until al dente. Return the sauce to a simmer. Warm a serving bowl. Drain the spaghetti, place it in the bowl, and toss with the sauce. Serve at once. ■

VERMICELLI WITH GARLIC AND OLIVE OIL

Vermicelli con aglio e olio

FOR 4 SERVINGS:

Properly made, this simple preparation is one of the most exquisite dishes in the whole pasta repertoire. It is the Neapolitan national dish. It's hard for Americans, who (with the exception of Calvin Trillin) rarely get very worked up over food, to realize the passions that *vermecielle agli'e uoglio* (in Neapolitan dialect) can arouse. Here's an example from Enzo Avitabile's *Mangiamo alla Napoletana* (our translation):

The appropriately Neapolitan wine to drink with this dish would be Lacryma Christi; whether red or white depends purely on personal preference.

This is one of the humblest dishes of our cuisine but one impressive for its purity, its savor, and its fragrance. Hearty and warm as an old friend, refined by its natural simplicity, it is a true "gentleman of the old school." There's no Neapolitan alive who doesn't hail its appearance with an explosive joy that is utterly Neapolitan. No banquet of any consequence, no rustic dinner table, no midnight supper, is complete unless it concludes with a taste of these vermicelli. They're the "come back soon" gift offered by the chef, the host, the restaurateur; which you can do no less than accept, to show that you enjoyed the dinner they prepared for you. The recipe is elementary, the simplest. Take care only that the vermicelli remain al dente, or verdi verdi, *as the Neapolitans say. . . . Also, the oil should be abundant so that the vermicelli are* sciuliarielli—*sleek and slippery.*

Americans making the dish usually need to take a little more care than Avitabile indicates. Most have to be coaxed to use the amount of seasoning—garlic and other—that this dish needs to rise above the blandly oily norm too often served here. Fear not and keep peeling those cloves. If you don't feel up to making all the thin slices called for in this recipe, you can chop the garlic not-too-fine and add it all at once to the oil after removing the peperoncini.

One further note on varieties of pasta for this dish. Spaghetti and linguine are most commonly used on this side of the ocean. Neapolitans, as indicated, prefer vermicelli. In our neighborhood stores, capellini (the extremely fine "angel's hair" pasta) seems to have taken over the niche formerly occupied by vermicelli. Whatever shape you use, be aware that the thinner the pasta, the more olive oil it will absorb. For capellini, for instance, increase the quantity of oil by about ½ cup.

Salt	*10 cloves garlic, thinly sliced*
1 pound imported Italian vermicelli	*⅓ cup chopped flat-leaf Italian parsley*
1 cup olive oil	*Freshly ground black pepper*
3 dried peperoncini rossi	

Warm a serving bowl for the pasta. In a large pot, bring 4 to 5 quarts water to a boil. Add 1 tablespoon salt, then the vermicelli.

While the pasta is cooking, heat the olive oil in a skillet. Add the peperoncini and half the garlic, and sauté until the peperoncini darken and the garlic turns lightly golden. Remove and discard them. Add the remaining garlic and sauté until it turns lightly golden. Off the heat, mix in the parsley and 1 teaspoon salt.

When the pasta is al dente, drain it in a colander, leaving it a little moist. Put it into the warmed bowl. Toss with the sauce and a generous quantity of black pepper. Serve at once. ∎

BLUEFISH GNOCCHI

Gnocchi di pesce

FOR ABOUT 8 DOZEN GNOCCHI, SERVING 4 TO 6:

Potato gnocchi are normally a little heavy for summer fare, but fish-flavored gnocchi seem appropriate to the time of year. Moreover, it's a time when we two are always looking for ways to use the bounty from our fisherman relatives and friends, and this recipe works very well.

You can prepare the bluefish in advance, but shape the gnocchi as soon as the potatoes are cooked. (See About Gnocchi on page 253.) Then they can be set aside on a floured tray for a few hours before the final cooking. Unlike plain potato gnocchi, these don't freeze well. Obviously, you can dress them with any tomato sauce you like; we find this bright, basil-scented one a good foil to the richness of the gnocchi.

A fine, dry white wine is called for here: a cru Verdicchio, Greco di Tufo, a cru Soave.

FOR THE BLUEFISH FILLING:

2 tablespoons olive oil

¼ cup finely chopped onion

1 clove garlic

½ bay leaf

¾ pound skinless bluefish fillets, cut in pieces about 2 inches square

Salt

Freshly ground black pepper

¼ cup dry white wine

2 tablespoons chopped flat-leaf Italian parsley

FOR THE GNOCCHI BASE:

1 pound baking potatoes

1 egg yolk

½ teaspoon salt

Freshly grated nutmeg

1 cup all-purpose flour

3 tablespoons olive oil

¼ cup minced onion

*½ cup (loosely packed) chopped
celery leaves*

*2 pounds fresh plum tomatoes,
peeled, seeded, and chopped*

Salt

Freshly ground black pepper

*12 large leaves fresh basil,
shredded*

To make the bluefish filling:

In a nonreactive skillet, heat the olive oil, add the onion, garlic, and bay leaf. Sauté over medium-low heat 3 to 4 minutes. Add the bluefish pieces, raise heat to medium-high, and cook until the fish is just opaque—about 1 minute on each side for pieces ½ inch thick, a bit more for thicker fillets.

Sprinkle the fish with salt and pepper, pour on the wine, and cook uncovered, stirring frequently, 5 to 6 minutes or until the liquid evaporates and the fish flakes easily. Discard the bay leaf.

Chop the fish fine in a food processor or by hand. Add the chopped parsley and mix thoroughly.

To make the gnocchi:

Follow the technique in the basic recipe on page 254, adding the fish mixture to the potatoes before the egg yolk and seasonings.

To make the sauce:

In a nonreactive skillet, heat the oil, add the onion and celery, and sauté over low heat 5 minutes. Add the tomatoes, ½ teaspoon salt, and black pepper to taste. Cook uncovered 15 minutes, or until the tomatoes come together into a sauce. Stir in the basil for the last minute of cooking. Taste for salt.

Finishing the dish:

Cook the gnocchi in a large quantity of boiling water as directed in the basic recipe. Bring the sauce to a simmer. Drain the gnocchi and transfer them to a serving bowl. Dress with the sauce and serve at once.

SECONDI

Our summer secondi recipes continue the theme of light foods, quickly cooked. The emphasis is on fish, poultry, and veal rather than heartier meats, and thin slices or small morsels rather than massive cuts.

Fish is not particularly a summer specialty in Italy, of course. With the Adriatic or the Mediterranean so close to almost anywhere you find yourself in Italy, fresh fish is a year-round pleasure. But the American tradition of summer at the seashore does seem to make fish a seasonal treat. And our tradition of outdoor cooking on a charcoal grill plays to the same notion, for Italians are magnificent grillers of fish. Fin fish of every variety, from tiny soles, mullets, and sardines to large *spigole* (bass), *orate* (bream) and *San Pietro* (John Dory), and many shellfish as well, from seppie and octopi to shrimps and crayfish, find their way onto wood-fired grills up and down the length of the peninsula.

Grilling a fish in the Italian manner needs no recipe, though it does take a nice eye to judge the moment of doneness. Soak your whole, gutted, and scaled fish for an hour or two in a brine bath, pat it dry, brush it with a mixture of olive oil and lemon juice, and lay it on the grill. Cook until the flesh separates easily from the bone—which is easy enough to say but not so easy to judge until you've grilled a lot of fishes. The time depends on the heat of the fire, the distance from fire to fish, and the thickness of the fish. Once in Italy when we complimented a waiter on the masterly way he had boned our grilled fish for us, he explained that it wasn't a case of his skill at all, but rather that of the chef. He went on to deliver a small lecture that impressed us very much. He said that anyone can easily bone a fish that has been cooked the exactly right length of time; but let it be at all under- or overcooked, and no one, no matter how expert, can do it without coming to grief.

The fish recipes in this section aren't so dependent on instinctive knowledge, we're happy to be able to tell you.

In the poultry category, we offer recipes for chicken, quail, and turkey breast. There are also some quickly cooked veal scallop recipes and a wonderful treatment for thinly sliced beefsteaks. Returning to the outdoor grill (or the kitchen broiler if you prefer), there's a recipe for the simplest and best of pork spareribs and one for skewered pork liver rolls. And—since there are some chilly days in every summer—we've included a few longer-cooked dishes you could call braises or stews; one each with chicken, veal, and lamb. What makes them summer dishes are the vegetables that cook along with the meats: tomatoes (of course), zucchini, fresh herbs. They're good enough to reconcile you to an unseasonally cool, rainy day.

BLUEFISH BAKED IN TOMATO SAUCE

Pesce al forno

FOR 4 SERVINGS:

A decent, dry white, with good fruit but not too aggressive in flavor, would be the best choice here: Lacryma Christi bianco, Corvo bianco, Verdicchio, perhaps Vernaccia, certainly a good Soave.

*T*his recipe provides another good reason to have Quick Summer Tomato Sauce around. It's also one of the simplest and tastiest things to do with bluefish or any other oily fish. Lovers of ripe olives may enjoy strewing a dozen or so, pitted and chopped, over the fillets in the baking dish before topping them with the sauce.

1 to 1¼ pounds skinless, boneless bluefish fillets

1 cup Quick Summer Tomato Sauce (page 156), or other simple tomato sauce

Salt

Freshly ground black pepper

1 teaspoon lemon juice

¼ teaspoon chopped fresh oregano

Preheat oven to 350°F. Rinse and dry the bluefish fillets. Oil a bake-and-serve dish just large enough to hold the fillets comfortably. Spread 2 to 3 tablespoons tomato sauce over the bottom, then lay in the fillets. Sprinkle them with salt and pepper, squeeze a few drops of lemon juice on each one, and sprinkle on the oregano.

Top the fish with all the rest of the tomato sauce. Put the dish in the oven and bake 20 minutes (for fillets no more than ¾ inch thick), or until the flesh is opaque throughout and flakes easily. Serve at once. ∎

BAKED BLUEFISH WITH SCALLIONS AND LIME

Pesce azzurro alla scalogna

FOR 4 SERVINGS:

*T*he three greens of the scallions, parsley, and lime peel in this dish make for a very pretty presentation and a lively flavor— overall, a very different effect from that of the preceding bluefish recipe.

In the Veneto, this dish would be made with the small whole fish called *triglie*, a kind of mullet. Because of the bright acidity of the white wine and lime, this is a particularly good way to handle rather oily fish (which triglie are), so we've adapted the recipe to bluefish fillets, which we trim to resemble small whole fish. Sardines and smelts would work well here too. You can make the whole dish up in advance and refrigerate it, leaving only 15 minutes of baking to be done—a not unconscionable amount of time to have the oven on in summer.

A dry and supple white wine with good acidity is called for here. Good choices are Sauvignon, Gavi, Arneis, cru Soave, or top-quality Pinot grigio.

1 to 1¼ pounds bluefish fillets

1 lime

5 tablespoons butter

Flour for dredging

*⅔ cup minced scallion, white and
tender green parts*

1 clove garlic, minced

½ cup dry white wine

Salt

Freshly ground black pepper

*1 tablespoon chopped flat-leaf
Italian parsley*

1 tablespoon fine dry bread crumbs

Preheat the oven to 400°F. Rinse and dry the fillets, carefully removing any small bones. Cut them into 8 long tapering pieces shaped like small fish. Butter a bake-and-serve dish large enough to hold the pieces of fish snugly. Remove the peel from the lime in thin julienne strips.

In a nonreactive skillet, melt 4 tablespoons butter. Flour the fillets and sauté them over medium heat about 3 minutes to a side. Remove them to a plate. Reduce heat to low, add the scallion and garlic, and sauté 5 minutes, until the vegetables are soft. Raise heat to high, add the wine, and boil until reduced by half, about 3 minutes, scraping up browned bits from the bottom of the pan.

Spread half the scallion sauce in the prepared baking dish. Lay the fillets in the dish and sprinkle them with salt and pepper. Cover with the remaining sauce, then squeeze the lime over it. Sprinkle on the julienned lime peel, parsley, and bread crumbs, and dot with the remaining tablespoon of butter.

Bake 15 minutes and serve at once. ∎

SICILIAN-STYLE SWORDFISH STEAKS

Agghiotta di pesce spada

FOR 4 SERVINGS:

*F*ish cookery is a source of joy all over Italy, but when it comes to preparing swordfish, Sicilians have the lock, for both variety and light-handedness. This very pretty dish is a good example of the imaginative techniques they bring to bear on an already flavorful fish—first a flouring and light sautéing to seal in the fish's own juices and flavors, then a brief oven braise that develops its flavors under a blanket of piquant sauce. The sauce itself is trademark southern Italy, if not exclusively Sicily: the combination of garlic, capers, raisins, olives, and tomato speaks the deepest southern Italian dialect.

New potatoes boiled in their jackets are a fine accompaniment to this dish, as is the lightest of green salads.

Try a fine Sicilian white such as Colomba Platino or Donnafugata or Regaleali bianco.

Flour for dredging

4 swordfish steaks cut ¾ inch thick (about 1½ pounds)

⅓ cup olive oil

2 cloves garlic, crushed

½ cup chopped onion

¼ cup chopped celery

2 tablespoons golden raisins, softened in hot water for 10 minutes, and drained

2 tablespoons pignoli

1 tablespoon capers, chopped if not the tiny "nonpareil" size

12 black oil-cured or ripe Gaeta olives, pitted

1 pound fresh plum tomatoes, peeled, seeded, and chopped

Salt

Freshly ground black pepper

2 bay leaves, halved

Preheat the oven to 400°F. Lightly flour the swordfish steaks. In a large nonreactive skillet, heat the olive oil, and sauté the swordfish for 3 minutes on each side, then transfer them to an oiled baking dish just large enough to hold them snugly.

To the oil remaining in the skillet, add the garlic and onion. Sauté 2 to 3 minutes and add the celery, raisins, pignoli, capers, and olives. Cook, stirring, 1 minute, then add the tomatoes. Quickly scrape up any browned bits clinging to the bottom of the pan, cover, and cook the sauce over low heat 10 minutes.

In a small pot, bring 1 cup water to a boil. Salt and pepper the swordfish steaks, lay on the bay leaves, then spread the sauce over them. Pour boiling water carefully into the side of the baking dish (so as not to wash the sauce off the fish) until the steaks are barely covered—about ½ cup of water should be enough. Put the dish in the oven and bake 15 minutes.

Remove the dish from the oven. Put the swordfish steaks and their topping on a heated serving platter and moisten with the liquid remaining in the dish. There should be only a few tablespoons of it left. If there is more, rapidly boil it down to a syrupy consistency and pour it over the fish. Serve at once. ■

POACHED TUNA STEAKS

Tonno lessato

FOR 4 SERVINGS:

Thanks to the proliferation of sushi bars, Americans finally appreciate tuna that doesn't come in a can. Now if we can only learn to imitate the Italian reverence for marrying tuna with olive oil, as this recipe does, we'll be well on our way to discovering the culinary El Dorados that have been hidden behind the fish salad.

Simple and savory, good hot or cold, this basic dish gives each diner the opportunity to finish the "cooking" at table according to his or her own taste: the final additions of lemon juice and pepper and—above all—extra-virgin olive oil aren't just garnishes but the

A dry full-flavored white is called for here: Greco di Tufo, Pomino bianco, Tocai, Sauvignon—all would do well.

completion of the seasoning. The combination of flavors gives you all the nuances that fresh tuna is capable of—and that's a lot.

You also get a nice bonus from this preparation. Strain the solids out of the liquid in which the tuna has poached, and you're left with a light broth that you can save—it freezes perfectly well—and use in any dishes that need a little fish accent.

½ cup chopped celery

½ cup chopped carrot

½ cup chopped onion

1 bay leaf

2 teaspoons salt

1¼ to 1½ pounds tuna steaks, cut
   ¾ inch thick

4 tablespoons chopped flat-leaf
   Italian parsley

2 cloves garlic

1 lemon, quartered

Freshly ground black pepper

Extra-virgin olive oil

In a broad skillet, put the chopped vegetables, bay leaf, salt, and 2 quarts cold water. Cover, bring to a boil, lower heat, and simmer 45 minutes. (This is a good step to do in advance; say, in the morning, before the heat of the day.)

Slide the tuna steaks into the skillet. (If the fish isn't covered by the liquid, add a little boiling water from a kettle.) Adjust heat to maintain a steady simmer and poach the fish 20 minutes. While the fish is cooking, mince the parsley and garlic together.

Drain the tuna steaks and arrange them on a heated serving platter. Sprinkle the parsley-garlic mixture over them, top with the lemon quarters, and serve. At table, pass the pepper mill and olive oil. ■

TUNA STEAKS SAUTÉED WITH OLIVES AND CAPERS

Tonno alla stimpirata

FOR 4 SERVINGS:

A complex, dry white wine is needed with this complex and subtle dish. Fiano di Avellino would be ideal, especially if it were three or four years old. Pomino bianco Il Benfizio would also be excellent, as would Vintage Tunina or Torre di Giano Riserva.

This attractive (to the eye and to the palate) Sicilian recipe turns red-meaty tuna white and delicate-looking, like a thick veal cutlet, while at the same time preserving and even accenting the tuna's own unique flavor. The preparation works equally well with swordfish, shark, monkfish—any fairly assertive, moderately oily fish you wouldn't normally think to sauté. The wine vinegar eliminates all "fishy" flavors, making this a good dish to serve to people who aren't usually fond of fish. The key thing is not to overcook whatever fish you are using: indeed, that's the only real secret of all fish cookery. This tuna should still be quite moist when served: better a little rare at the center than dried out.

4 tuna steaks cut ½ to ¾ inch
  thick, about 1½ pounds
Flour for dredging
8 tablespoons olive oil
⅓ cup thinly sliced onion
⅓ cup thinly sliced celery
Salt

16 to 18 green or black olives,
  pitted and coarsely chopped
2 tablespoons capers, rinsed,
  drained, and chopped if large
Freshly ground black pepper
⅓ cup red or white wine vinegar

Rinse and dry the tuna steaks. Dredge them lightly with flour. In a large nonreactive skillet, heat the oil, and brown the tuna steaks on both sides, about 1 minute to a side, over medium heat. Remove them to a plate and keep warm. Add the onion and celery to the pan, sprinkle lightly with salt, and sauté 3 minutes. Add the olives and capers, stir, and cook 1 minute.

Push the vegetables aside and return the fish to the pan. Sprinkle with salt and pepper and cook 1 minute. Turn, salt and pepper the other side, and cook 1 minute.

Reduce heat to low, add the vinegar, cover, and cook 3 minutes on each side. Serve at once. ∎

SAUTÉ OF CHICKEN, PROCIDA STYLE

Pollo alla procidana

FOR 4 SERVINGS:

*T*his originated as a rabbit dish from the island of Procida, in the Bay of Naples, a place that is famed in local folklore for the purity and deliciousness of its rustic cuisine—and for the size of its rabbit population. The recipe also works extremely well with a young free-range chicken.

Two of the techniques of this recipe are unusual. First, the bird or rabbit is sautéed with garlic and parsley to enhance its flavor, but that by-then-exhausted garlic and parsley are left out of the rest of the cooking, which takes place in another pan. Second, a wine reduction is used to render the pancetta's fat without having to sauté it too hard, which keeps its flavor fresh and vibrant.

There should only be a few spoonfuls of the sauce left at the end of the cooking: this is not a wet dish. If you use rabbit, it will take only a few minutes more cooking time than chicken.

Choose a light, fruity red wine to accompany this dish. Lacryma Christi rosso, from the same area, would be ideal, and Corvo, Dolcetto, Montepulciano d'Abruzzo, or Castel del Monte would also serve well.

3 to 3½ pounds chicken, cut in
   serving pieces
5 tablespoons olive oil
2 cloves garlic, sliced in 3 to 4
   pieces each
3 tablespoons chopped flat-leaf
   Italian parsley

1½ ounces pancetta, diced
1½ cups dry white wine
3 plum tomatoes, peeled and
   roughly chopped
1 peperoncino rosso
Salt
Freshly ground black pepper

Wash and dry the chicken pieces. In a medium-sized skillet, heat 2 tablespoons olive oil with the garlic and 1 tablespoon parsley. Lightly brown the chicken a few pieces at a time, over medium heat. As they are done, transfer them to another pan large enough to hold them in a single layer. Reserve the oil remaining in the pan.

Add the diced pancetta and the wine to the chicken in the second pan and cook over high heat until the wine evaporates, about 10 minutes, turning the chicken pieces once or twice.

Lower heat to medium, add the tomatoes, peperoncino, and the remaining parsley and olive oil. Also add 1 tablespoon of the original sautéing oil (but none of the original parsley or garlic). Salt and pepper the chicken lightly, cover the pan, and cook 20 minutes, or until the chicken is tender, turning the pieces occasionally. Add a few tablespoons of warm water if the sauce appears to be too thick.

Remove the peperoncino before serving. ■

SUMMER STEW OF CHICKEN AND VEGETABLES

Pollo in umido con verdure

FOR 4 SERVINGS:

A basically simple and comforting dish, but with a touch of elegance from the addition of Marsala. You can make this stew richer if you roast and peel the peppers (see technique on page 222) before adding them. For more variety, you can substitute eggplant for half the zucchini; treat it the same way, salting and sautéing. A few mushrooms are nice too; they can be added along with the chicken. In short, this is a very amenable preparation, good for a lazy summer day when you don't want to bother shopping and have some odds and ends of vegetables in the refrigerator. You can also stretch out the preparation steps over the entire day, so that at dinnertime all you have left is the last 10 minutes of cooking the stew with the zucchini.

This dish will take either a red or a white wine. Dry and light are the chief qualifications, so Frascati, Orvieto, Soave, for the whites, and Bardolino, Valpolicella, simple Barbera, young Chianti, for the reds.

4 medium zucchini (1½ to 2
    pounds), scrubbed and cut in
    ½-inch rounds
Salt
6 tablespoons butter
¼ cup sliced onions
1 clove garlic, halved
One 3½-pound chicken, cut up, or
    use chicken parts
Freshly ground black pepper
2 tablespoons chopped flat-leaf
    Italian parsley

½ teaspoon thyme
½ bay leaf
1 cup broth, approximately
    (optional)
1 large or 2 small red or green bell
    peppers, cut in 1-inch pieces
1 ounce prosciutto, cut in julienne
    strips
1 pound plum tomatoes, peeled,
    seeded, and chopped
¼ cup dry Marsala

Toss the zucchini slices in a colander with 1 tablespoon salt and set them in the sink to drain for 30 minutes to 1 hour.

In a large casserole, melt 3 tablespoons butter, and sauté the onion and garlic over low heat 5 minutes. Raise the heat to medium, add the chicken parts, and brown them on all sides. Sprinkle with salt and pepper and add the parsley, thyme, bay leaf, and ½ cup broth or water. Bring to a simmer, cover and cook over low heat 20 minutes, turning the chicken after 10 minutes. Add the peppers, prosciutto, tomatoes, ½ teaspoon salt, and Marsala. Cover and cook 15 minutes.

Rinse the zucchini pieces and pat them dry with paper towels. In a skillet, melt the remaining 3 tablespoons butter and sauté the zucchini 10 minutes, stirring often. Add the zucchini to the chicken casserole, stir, and cook a final 10 minutes. Add a little more broth if the dish appears to be drying out; if it's too liquid, leave the cover off for part of the cooking time. Taste for salt before serving. ∎

QUAILS BRAISED WITH TOMATOES AND ROSEMARY

Quaglie al pomodoro

FOR 4 SERVINGS:

Y

This dish wants an elegant red wine with some character and acidity: e.g., a Chianti Classico Riserva.

*Q*uails are such tasty little morsels that even prepared in very simple ways, they give a festive air to a dinner. And since they cook in next to no time, they enhance any summer cook's reputation as an impromptu gastronomical wizard. Here, a few plum tomatoes and a sprig of rosemary leaves provide all the assistance needed for a covey of quail to pass the taste test with flying colors.

Even more labor-saving—for the diner this time, not the cook—are quails you can buy fully boned. Though they do lack the charm of the tiny bird shape, there's no struggling to pry the succulent flesh off those tiny bird bones.

This recipe generates a rich and even complexly flavored dish out of very few ingredients. The tomatoes don't turn into a sauce so much as a soft garnish, and the pan juices thicken up by themselves. If you don't have fresh rosemary on the stem, tie the leaves up in a cheesecloth bag so you can remove them before serving.

8 quail, ¼ pound apiece	2 to 3 basil leaves
2 tablespoons olive oil	½ teaspoon salt
One 2-inch fresh rosemary sprig	Freshly ground black pepper
1 pound ripe plum tomatoes, peeled, seeded, and cut in eighths	½ cup white wine

Rinse the quails and pat them dry with paper towels. In a nonreactive skillet, heat the olive oil, and add the quails and rosemary. Brown the birds on all sides over medium heat, about 4 minutes.

Add the tomatoes, basil, salt, and a generous quantity of pepper. Stir and cook 1 minute, then add the wine. Raise heat to high, and boil rapidly 1 minute.

When the wine has almost evaporated, add 1 cup water. Cover, reduce heat to low, and cook 30 minutes, or until the quails are very tender. Transfer them to a serving dish, pour on the sauce, and serve. ■

TURKEY FRICASSEE

Tacchino brodettato

FOR 4 SERVINGS:

Y

Try a full-bodied, fruity white wine or a lightish red: Pomino bianco, Pinot bianco, Vintage Tunina, Tocai, for whites, or Dolcetto, Barbera, Chianti Classico, young Taurasi, for reds.

*T*hough boneless turkey breast is an extremely virtuous substance according to today's nutritional worldview, we have to admit we often find it pretty boring. Being fortunate enough not to have to worry unduly about our cholesterol count, we were wickedly pleased to come upon this lush recipe for turkey breast. As a sop to current orthodoxy, we note that the dish makes a great foil for simply cooked fresh garden vegetables.

1½ pounds skinless boneless
   turkey breast, muscles separated,
   cut in 2-inch pieces
Flour for dredging
Salt
Freshly ground black pepper
2 tablespoons butter
⅓ cup finely chopped onion

1½ ounces prosciutto, cut in
   julienne strips
¼ cup white wine
1 tablespoon chopped flat-leaf
   Italian parsley
¼ teaspoon marjoram
1 egg yolk
1½ tablespoons lemon juice

Dredge the turkey pieces with flour, salt, and pepper. In a casserole, melt the butter and brown the turkey pieces in 2 or 3 batches, removing them to a plate when done. Sauté the onion and prosciutto in the remaining butter 1 to 2 minutes, until the onion is slightly softened, then return the turkey pieces to the pan.

Raise heat to high, pour in the wine, and cook until it evaporates, stirring and scraping the bottom of the pan. Add ½ cup water, cover, reduce heat to low, and simmer 1 hour, until the turkey is very tender. Taste the sauce for salt.

Mix together the parsley, marjoram, egg yolk, and lemon juice. Pour this over the turkey, turn heat very low, and stir constantly 1 minute or less, until the sauce just thickens. Serve at once in a heated dish. ■

VEAL SCALLOPS WITH PROSCIUTTO, SAGE, AND WHITE WINE

Saltimbocca alla romana

FOR 4 SERVINGS:

*S*altimbocca hardly needs an introduction: it's an old war-horse in American Italian restaurants, where—alas—it is often overhandled and served with cream sauces and other abominations. It's supposed to leap from pan to mouth *(salt' in bocca)* and in this version, it does—in 5 minutes. As with so many veal dishes, quality counts: the lesser your veal, the lesser the dish.

Try a light, dry red like a Barbera or a young Chianti, or, if you prefer, a full-bodied white such as a Pinot bianco or Pomino bianco.

8 small veal scallops, about 1 pound	3 tablespoons butter
Salt	1 tablespoon cooking oil
Freshly ground black pepper	Flour for dredging
8 sage leaves	3 tablespoons dry white wine
8 small slices prosciutto (about ¼ pound)	¼ lemon

Pound the veal scallops to flatten them. Sprinkle with salt and pepper. Lay 1 sage leaf on each piece of veal and top with 1 slice prosciutto. Pin the two meats together with toothpicks. Lightly flour the veal. In a large skillet, melt the butter with the oil and sauté the veal over medium heat 2 minutes to a side (in two batches, if necessary). Transfer it to a heated dish and remove the toothpicks.

Raise heat under the skillet to high, pour in the wine, quickly stir, and scrape up any browned bits from the bottom of the pan. Pour this sauce over the veal, squeeze the lemon over it, and serve at once. ∎

VEAL SCALLOPS WITH GARLIC BUTTER

Scaloppine con burro d'aglio

FOR 4 SERVINGS:

Ⴘ

A light red, like a Barbera or a young Chianti, or a full-bodied white, like a Pinot bianco or Pomino bianco.

*I*talians use composed butters for quick, interesting garnishes on very simply sautéed thin meats: *bistecchine, scaloppine,* etc.: cuts that in recent years have been appearing on restaurant menus in this country under the collective nom de guerre of paillards. Anchovy butter, Gorgonzola butter, mustard butter, basil butter, are some popular kinds. In this one, boiling the raw garlic tames it and gives a flavor that's very subtle and quite different from the kind of garlic butter you think of as accompanying, say, escargots.

3 large cloves garlic, peeled

4 tablespoons unsalted butter, softened

3 additional tablespoons butter

4 large or 8 small veal scallops (about 1 pound), pounded thin

Salt

Freshly ground pepper

Flour for dredging

Drop the garlic cloves into boiling water and boil 10 minutes. Drain and pat them dry. Mash them into the 4 tablespoons softened butter and blend well.

In a large skillet, melt the remaining butter. Dust the veal scallops with flour and put them in the pan over medium heat. Salt and pepper lightly. Cook very briefly, 1 to 2 minutes to a side. Transfer the scaloppine to a serving dish, top each with a portion of the garlic butter, and serve at once. ■

VEAL WITH ZUCCHINI AND POTATOES

Spezzatino con zucchini e patate

FOR 4 SERVINGS:

This recipe makes a complete one-pot meal. It's one of those mysterious Italian dishes that are more than the sum of their parts, and like so many of those dishes, this one is blunder-proof. As long as you are working with good-quality, fresh meat and vegetables you can alter the proportions according to what you have on hand. Simply adjust the amount of broth too: a dish heavy on zucchini will throw more liquid of its own and need less broth. We like the final product just moist, not soupy, but after you've tried it our way once, adjust it to your own taste.

A simple, hearty red will go best with this family dish. Try Montepulciano d'Abruzzo, Dolcetto, Valpolicella, or young Chianti.

5 tablespoons olive oil

2 cloves garlic

¾ cup chopped celery

¾ cup carrot rounds, sliced ¼ inch thick

¾ cup chopped onion

2 pounds boneless veal, cut in 2-inch pieces

½ cup dry white wine

1½ pounds potatoes, peeled and cut in chunks

1 pound fresh plum tomatoes, peeled, seeded, and chopped

2 cups broth

1 teaspoon salt

Freshly ground black pepper

1½ pounds zucchini, scrubbed and cut in ½-inch rounds

In a large casserole, heat the olive oil over medium heat. Sauté the garlic, celery, carrot, and onion 10 minutes, until soft. Add the veal, raise heat to medium-high, and brown it on all sides. Pour in the wine and cook briskly, stirring, until it evaporates.

Add the potatoes, tomatoes, broth, salt, and a generous quantity of black pepper. Stir all together well. Bring to a boil, reduce to a simmer, cover, and cook 30 minutes. Add the zucchini and cook 30 minutes more, or until the veal is perfectly tender. Watch the liquid level during the cooking time, and add small amounts of broth or water if necessary to keep the dish from drying out. At the end, it should be moist but not soupy. ∎

PIZZAIOLA STEAKS

Bistecche alla pizzaiola

FOR 4 SERVINGS:

Y

Taurasi is the ideal thing to drink here, though other top-quality reds—especially barrique-aged Barberas or Barbera-Nebbiolo blends—will also match quite well. And don't forget Taurasi's cousin, Aglianico del Vulture.

his is a great little dish, totally unlike what usually goes under the name of *pizzaiola* in American Italian restaurants. If you have a hankering for red meat but don't want to wolf down a huge steak, this is your recipe. It's quick as a wink to do, so that even though the meat is pounded very thin, it still stays rosy-rare and is imbued with the flavor of the sauce.

You could use slices of top round instead of the expensive Delmonico cut recommended here, but if you do, be sure to pound it very thoroughly to tenderize the meat, and make it no thicker than ¼ inch. (If you find yourself with a thicker piece, put it in the freezer for 20 minutes to firm the meat a bit, and then butterfly it.) In any event, have all the ingredients prepared before you start the cooking: once the olive oil hits the pan, it's only 20 minutes from stove to plate.

4 tablespoons olive oil

1 clove garlic, peeled and halved

1 peperoncino rosso

4 Delmonico steaks cut ½ inch thick (about 1½ pounds), trimmed of all visible fat, and pounded to a thickness of ⅜ to ¼ inch

Salt

Freshly ground black pepper

1 pound ripe plum tomatoes, peeled, seeded, and chopped (about 1½ cups pulp)

2 teaspoons fresh oregano, chopped

In a large nonreactive skillet, heat the olive oil. Add the garlic and peperoncino and sauté 1 to 2 minutes over medium heat, until the garlic is lightly golden and the peperoncino dark brown. Press the garlic firmly against the bottom of the skillet, then discard it and the peperoncino. When the oil is almost smoking, put the steaks in the pan and brown them quickly on both sides over medium-high heat. Salt and pepper them lightly, transfer them to a plate, and keep them warm.

Reduce heat to medium-low. Add the tomatoes, oregano, ½ teaspoon salt, and several grindings of pepper to the skillet. Stir well, scraping up any browned bits left by the steaks, cover the pan, and simmer 10 minutes.

Return the steaks to the pan along with any juices that have run from them, and turn them to coat with the sauce. Cover and cook 1 minute, then turn the steaks and cook 1 minute more. Transfer them to a serving platter, top with the sauce, and serve at once. ∎

SUMMERTIME LAMB STEW

Abbacchio in umido

FOR 4 SERVINGS:

This comforting, homey dish is one of those recipes that "gourmet cooks" are always surprised at, because "there's nothing in it" except the kind of ingredients that every refrigerator provides; and yet it tastes simply delicious.

As we've probably made clear in our paean to the glories of the tomato, we need regular tomato fixes in summer. Cooking lamb with tomatoes is a particularly Mediterranean habit and a good way to alleviate the sometimes heavy, muttony flavor of a "lamb" that is well past its infancy. The pancetta and olive oil replace the lamb's own lanoliny fats and at the same time combine to develop a pleasingly concentrated and meaty flavor of the sort that one normally associates with much longer-cooked dishes. This cheerful little stew further lightens the lamb with aromatic vegetables and herbs as well as the acidity of the tomatoes. The dish may be completely cooked

A simple, hearty red will go best with this family dish. Try Montepulciano d'Abruzzo, Dolcetto, Valpolicella, or young Chianti.

in advance and reheated: one of its many advantages is that it profits by having some time to develop its flavors.

This stew goes especially well with Ciambotta (page 198). You'll want a lot of good country bread to sop up the succulent juices of the two dishes.

3 to 5 tablespoons olive oil

1½ ounces pancetta, chopped

Flour for dredging

2 pounds boneless lamb
    shoulder, cut in 1½- to 2-inch
    chunks

½ cup chopped onion

½ cup chopped carrot

½ cup chopped celery

1 tablespoon chopped flat-leaf
    Italian parsley

¼ teaspoon chopped fresh
    marjoram leaves

Salt

Freshly ground black pepper

¾ pound ripe plum tomatoes,
    roughly chopped

½ cup broth

In a large flameproof casserole, heat 3 tablespoons olive oil and sauté the pancetta over low heat 2 to 3 minutes, until it begins to render its fat. Raise heat to medium-high, lightly flour the pieces of lamb, and brown them a few at a time, removing them to a plate as they are done. Add another tablespoon or two of oil if necessary.

When all the lamb is browned, add the onion, carrot, celery, parsley, and marjoram to the pan and sauté 5 minutes, or until the vegetables are soft, stirring occasionally. Return the lamb to the pan, mix it with the vegetables, and sprinkle with salt and pepper.

Pass the tomatoes through a food mill directly into the casserole. Add the broth and stir everything together. Bring to a boil, reduce to a simmer, cover, and cook 45 to 50 minutes, or until the lamb is perfectly tender. If there is more than a moderate amount of liquid in the pan when the lamb is ready, raise heat and boil rapidly for a minute or two to reduce it. Serve directly from the casserole. ■

GRILLED SPARERIBS

Costarelle in graticola

FOR 4 SERVINGS:

*I*f you're a charcoal chef and an artist of the grill, this is a dish to do outdoors. The technique is a little odd, but when we first tried it, we found we'd solved a mystery that had been teasing us for a long time: how La Stalla gets its grilled meats so wonderful.

La Stalla is an unassuming restaurant high in the hills behind Assisi. It's hard to find, even when you're standing in the piazza of its address. (The sign by the door is invisible after dark.) Walk into the establishment (named for, and still looking like, the stable that it once was), and it's as if you'd stumbled onto a movie set for *The Three Musketeers*. At any moment, you feel, D'Artagnan will sweep out from behind one of the rough-hewn pillars, buss a serving wench, upset a trestle table, and toss one of Cardinal Richelieu's men onto the meats grilling in one of the 12-foot-wide open-fire hearths.

Those grilled meats are incredibly good. The mystery for us was what had been done to them, because they taste of nothing but themselves—yet no pork, no veal, no chicken, in all our experience, has equaled them. Appealed to for the secret, the restaurant staff of course said there was none: they did nothing to the meats except cook them.

Well, maybe. Maybe everyone in Assisi is born knowing what you do to meats before putting them on the grill, so it doesn't count as "doing anything" to them. In any event, when we ran across the utterly simple technique given below, it was the gold at the end of the rainbow. It yields clear, pure meat flavors, without drying out or charring, and just a hint of the fragrance of garlic. You can prepare the ribs in their "marinade" in the morning and leave them all day in the refrigerator under plastic wrap. (Throw in what's left of the garlic clove.)

One caution: the length of cooking time can vary a great deal with the strength of your fire. In our stove's broiler, the ribs are done after 10 minutes on a side. Outside, they've taken as much as

Choose a fruity and slightly tannic red wine to have with this dish: Nebbiolo perhaps, or Rosso di Montalcino, or young Rubesco.

twice that. Don't let fear of trichinosis make you char these ribs into a cinder: when done they should be no more than medium-brown on the outside (no barbecue sauce to darken them, remember) and still juicy.

3 pounds pork spareribs	*Salt*
1 clove garlic, halved	*Freshly ground black pepper*
¼ cup olive oil	

Two hours in advance:

Cut the spareribs into serving-sized pieces. Pat them dry with paper towels and rub them all over with the cut side of the garlic. Lay them out on a platter or roasting pan. Heat the olive oil to almost smoking. Pour half of it over the spareribs, then turn them and pour on the rest of the oil. Let them sit for 2 hours.

When ready to cook:

Heat a broiler or grill to very hot. Salt and pepper the ribs and set them on the rack as far away from the heat as possible. Cook 10 or more minutes on each side, depending on the heat of your broiler or grill. During the cooking, baste the ribs with any oil remaining on the platter. Serve at once. ■

GRILLED PORK LIVERS WITH BAY LEAF AND FENNEL

Fegatelli alla fiorentina

FOR 4 SERVINGS:

*M*ost Americans probably feed pork livers to their cats, which only goes to show that our pets often live better than we do. Italians tend to get as excited about pork liver as they do about calf's liver. This Tuscan recipe moderates the incredible unctuousness of the pork livers with a coating of bread crumbs flavored with bay leaf and fennel. It's still a very rich dish, however, and doesn't take much to feed four persons.

It's common all over Italy to grill small pieces of pork liver wrapped in caul fat. We give directions for oven-baking here, but these luscious little rolls can also be grilled over a charcoal or wood fire. Caul fat is a very thin, webby membrane around the stomach of pigs and cows; it's commonly used in France to wrap pâtés and terrines and in Italy to wrap small, lean innard meats or birds for roasting or grilling.

Red, by all means, and something Tuscan for sure: Chianti, Chianti Classico, Vino Nobile, Rosso di Montalcino—all will match well with this dish.

1½ teaspoons fennel seeds

2 bay leaves

6 tablespoons fine dry bread crumbs

¼ teaspoon salt

Freshly ground black pepper

6 tablespoons olive oil

½ pound caul fat, soaked for 1 hour in cold water

1 pound pork liver, cut into 16 pieces, about 2 by 1½ inches

Preheat the oven to 425°F. Finely grind the fennel seeds and bay leaves together. Put them in a small bowl along with the bread crumbs, salt, and a generous quantity of pepper. Mix well. Put the olive oil in another small bowl.

Take a piece of the caul fat from the soaking water and carefully spread it out to its fullest extent on a work surface. Cut off a piece 5 to 6 inches square. Take a piece of liver and coat it first with the olive oil, then with the bread crumbs. Place it on an end of the square of caul fat and roll it up, tucking in the ends. Set it aside on a plate.

Cut additional squares of caul fat and prepare the remaining pieces of liver in the same way, coating them first with olive oil and flavored bread crumbs.

Line up 4 liver rolls side by side and impale them with a long flat skewer. Put the remaining rolls on 3 more skewers in the same manner. Set the skewers on a baking dish that is narrower than the skewers are long, so that they form a bridge across the sides of the dish and the meat is suspended over the dish. Bake 30 minutes and serve, one skewer to a person. ∎

CONTORNI

Summer vegetables are myriad, but throughout Italy this is the season of the big four: tomatoes, eggplants, zucchini, and peppers. Alone or together, in simple preparations and in elaborate dishes, they sound the dominant notes of the season.

As we said in the introduction to our antipasto recipes, many of these sturdy and delicious vegetable dishes are crossovers between courses. That makes them perfect for summer's informal dining—buffets, picnics, barbecues. Make up the dish ahead of time, carry it to the festivity, set it out, and let people dip into it when and as deeply as they like.

Many summer vegetable dishes are rich enough to serve on their own as light meals, simply with a loaf of good, crusty bread. On the other hand, for those who can't be satisfied without a major hunk of protein with every meal, these vegetable dishes go beautifully with a simple grilled fish or meat.

To show at their very best, each of these vegetables really repays a little special handling. For most preparations other than sautés, eggplant and zucchini need to be salted to extract some of their liquid. This doesn't have to be an elaborate arrangement of measured salting, careful laying out, weighting down, and timing. Simply cut the vegetable to the size you need, salt it generously, dump it in a colander, and leave it in the sink for anywhere from ½ to 2 hours—whatever suits your convenience.

Tomatoes too sometimes contain enough watery juice to make a cooked dish soggy. The technique described in our recipe for grilled tomatoes works well for many cooked tomato dishes. It's basically the same as the preparation for Quick Summer Tomato Sauce, page 156.

For eggplant, zucchini, and tomatoes alike, the idea is simply to get the water out of the vegetable in order to let other flavorings in. Peppers don't have as much excess water, but the great improvement in flavor from the roasting process used to char pepper skins for easy removal is in part due to the extraction of water.

The ingredient that takes the place of water to make our vegetable dishes so luscious is often olive oil. Whether fried in it or combined with it in another manner, vegetables adore olive oil. It is what gives them the richness and satiety value of meat.

BAKED EGGPLANT STICKS

Melanzane a mannella

FOR 4 SERVINGS:

If served by itself, choose a dry and acidic white wine such as Pinot grigio or Soave or Verdicchio. Otherwise, choose according to your secondo.

*E*ggplant brings out the artist in every chef. A true chameleon among vegetables, it enters with enthusiasm into almost any variety of cooking procedure, emerging from each with a distinctly different, always pleasing, effect. Here, eggplant is cut as for French fried potatoes, quickly fried in olive oil, and then briefly baked with garlic, oregano, and wine vinegar. Clearly another recipe born of the need to use up leftover fried eggplant, this preparation is more than good enough to fry up some eggplant on purpose for. It's also less trouble than it seems: it can be made up in stages, well in advance, and the finished dish should be allowed to cool a bit before serving—so it accords well with whatever other cooking you're doing that day. It's also a good component for a mixed antipasto platter.

2 to 2½ pounds eggplant, unpeeled, cut into sticks ⅜ inch thick and 2 to 3 inches long

2 tablespoons salt

2 cups olive oil

2 small cloves garlic, minced

½ teaspoon chopped fresh oregano

1 teaspoon red or white wine vinegar

Stand the eggplant sticks in a colander, sprinkle them with the salt, and set the colander in the sink for 1 hour to draw out the eggplant's bitter juices. Rinse the eggplant sticks and dry them thoroughly with paper towels.

In a small, heavy skillet, heat the olive oil to 375°F. Fry the eggplant a few at a time until lightly golden, 1 to 2 minutes, and drain on paper towels.

Preheat the oven to 350°F. Lay out half the eggplant sticks evenly in a 7-inch-square baking dish. Top them with half the garlic, half the oregano, and half the vinegar. Lay on the remaining eggplant sticks and the remaining seasonings. Bake 20 minutes. Let the eggplant cool 10 minutes before serving. ∎

NEOPOLITAN-STYLE EGGPLANT

Melanzane alla partenopea

FOR 4 SERVINGS:

*T*he name of this dish refers to the ancient history of Naples, which was originally—circa 600–500 B.C.—Nea Polis, the new city, a Greek colony. Partenopea refers to Athena, the virgin (*parthenos* in Greek) goddess to whom the colony was dedicated.

The original recipe for *melanzane alla partenopea* called for *caciocavallo*, but since that is a difficult cheese to find here, we've worked out a version using very young provolone. In flavor and texture, the dish is similar to a sharpish eggplant parmigiana. It's very pretty, with its little sandwich effect. Though it's quite a production number, each of the steps is quite easy, and they can be executed in stages over the course of the day. Ideally, you'll want cylindrical (as opposed to pear-shaped) eggplants 2½ to 3 inches in diameter, for equal-sized sandwiches.

For serving by itself, choose wines as simple or as elegant as you please, red or white, but they must be fruity: for example, Lacryma Christi or Taurasi or Aglianico for reds, or Lacryma Christi or Greco di Tufo or Pinot bianco for whites; otherwise, follow the wine recommendation for your secondo.

1½ pounds elongated (not bulbous) eggplants, peeled and sliced in ⅓-inch rounds
Salt
2 cups olive oil
1 egg

4 ounces young provolone, grated
⅓ cup simple tomato sauce (e.g., Quick Summer Tomato Sauce on page 156)
1 tablespoon freshly grated parmigiano

Toss the eggplant slices in a colander with 1 tablespoon salt and stand the colander in the sink for 1 hour to draw out the eggplant's bitter juices. Then rinse, drain, and dry with paper towels, pressing moderately hard to extract more juices.

In a deep skillet, heat the olive oil to 375°F. Fry the eggplant in small batches until golden, 1 to 2 minutes to a side. Allow the oil to come back up to temperature between batches. Drain the eggplant on paper towels.

Preheat the oven to 400°F. In a small bowl, make a paste of the egg and provolone. Spread 2 to 3 tablespoons tomato sauce over the bottom of a 9-inch-square baking dish.

Pair off the eggplant rounds, matching sizes as closely as possible. Spread about ½ teaspoon of the egg-cheese mixture on one round of each pair, top with the other round, and lay the resulting sandwiches in the baking dish. Top with the remaining tomato sauce and the parmigiano. Put the dish in the oven and bake 15 minutes. Serve hot, warm, or at room temperature. ■

POTATOES SAUTÉED WITH OREGANO

Patate all'origano

FOR 4 SERVINGS:

Y

Choose according to your secondo.

*A*nother country dish, with simple, pure flavors. This one depends utterly on the freshness of its raw ingredients. With the season's first freshly dug potatoes and fragrant, fresh oregano, the dish is aromatic, tasty, charming; without them, it's plain old pan-fried potatoes. Dried oregano absolutely can't pinch-hit for fresh here, because the herb is barely warmed at the end of the cooking to bring up its aroma. If you have access to freshly dug garlic, use that for this dish too.

1½ pounds new potatoes, peeled and cut in ¼-inch slices	*¼ cup olive oil*
Salt	*2 cloves garlic, 1 whole, 1 minced*
	2 teaspoons chopped fresh oregano

Drop the potatoes into boiling salted water and cook 10 minutes, or until they are slightly less than done. Don't let them begin to fall apart. Drain and set aside.

In a skillet, heat the olive oil and sauté the whole garlic clove until lightly golden, then press and discard it. Add the potatoes, salt them generously, and toss to coat them well with the olive oil. Sauté over medium-high heat, stirring carefully so as not to break up the slices, 5 to 6 minutes or until potatoes are lightly golden. Sprinkle with the minced garlic and oregano. Stir once more thoroughly, then turn off the heat, transfer the potatoes to a heated serving dish, and serve at once. ■

PEPPERS IN A PAN

Peperoni in padella

FOR 4 SERVINGS:

The heaps of red and yellow peppers on display in farm markets toward the end of summer exert a magnetic influence over us. What seems like a modest quantity at the time of purchase turns out to be enough peppers to feed an army when we get them back to our kitchen. Should you suffer from the same affliction, this is a good recipe to know. It's an inspired combination of flavors and extremely simple to make.

Despite the four anchovy filets, the dish is not in the least anchovy-tasting: everything blends harmoniously together. With a loaf of good bread, this recipe makes a meal in itself—and it keeps well for several days.

Because of the high acidity of its ingredients, this dish wants a dry, acidic white wine. Verdicchio or Pinot grigio would be ideal.

6 tablespoons olive oil

1 clove garlic

2 large red and yellow bell peppers
 (1 pound), washed, seeded, and
 cut in ½-inch strips

¾ pound ripe plum tomatoes,
 peeled and halved

1 tablespoon drained capers

4 anchovy fillets, coarsely
 chopped

2 teaspoons chopped fresh
 oregano

⅛ teaspoon salt

In a large nonreactive skillet, heat the olive oil and add the garlic and peppers, and sauté over medium heat 5 minutes, stirring often.

Discard the garlic, raise heat to medium-high, and add the tomatoes, capers, anchovies, oregano, and salt. Cook, uncovered, stirring occasionally and lowering the heat as necessary to maintain a steady simmer, 15 to 20 minutes, or until the peppers are al dente—tender but still firm. Serve hot, warm, or at room temperature. ■

GRILLED TOMATOES

Pomodori gratinati

FOR 4 SERVINGS:

♀

If served by themselves, choose a simple, dry white wine such as Soave or Orvieto or Frascati; otherwise, choose according to your secondo.

Grilled tomatoes are a simple summer classic, but they're not always executed in a way that brings out their best. It's important to get most of the liquid out of tomatoes before cooking, so they don't deliquesce under the influence of heat. This also saves searing your mouth on gouts of boiling-hot tomato juice—an all-too-common summer mishap. To prepare tomatoes for grilling, halve them horizontally and gently squeeze out the seeds and surrounding jellylike pulp (over a sink or bowl), leaving the firm, fleshy shell and ribs intact. To be sure you've gotten all the seeds and jelly, poke a finger into the tomato cavities.

After grilling, let the tomatoes sit for at least 15 minutes before serving: this lets them pull back their juices and gives the flavor a chance to develop.

4 firm, ripe tomatoes, 1¾ to 2 pounds

Salt

4 anchovy fillets, rinsed and drained

1 tablespoon chopped flat-leaf Italian parsley

2 teaspoons rinsed and drained capers

⅔ cup fine dry bread crumbs

Freshly ground black pepper

1 tablespoon olive oil

Halve the tomatoes and remove all the seeds and jellylike pulp, leaving only the firm flesh. Salt the cut surfaces generously and place them facedown on a rack for 30 minutes to 1 hour, to drain off excess liquid.

Preheat the oven to 400°F. Finely chop the anchovies, parsley, and capers together. Mix them in a bowl with the bread crumbs, ¼ teaspoon salt, and several grindings of black pepper.

Oil a baking dish just large enough to hold the tomato halves snugly upright. Blot them dry with paper towels and fill them with the bread-crumb mixture. Arrange them in the dish, drizzle with the olive oil, and bake 30 minutes. Let cool at least 15 minutes before serving. ■

COUNTRY-STYLE ZUCCHINI

Zucchini alla contadina

FOR 4 SERVINGS:

Choose according to your secondo.

*A*ll over Italy, zucchini and many other vegetables—eggplants, peppers, potatoes, green beans—are treated in one version or another of this basic preparation. The only trick is not to overcook the vegetable: the zucchini should not be reduced to mush, but should still have some resiliency.

2 tablespoons olive oil
1½ pounds firm, small zucchini,
  scrubbed, ends trimmed, and cut
  in ⅓-inch rounds
Salt

Freshly ground black pepper
¾ cup simple tomato sauce (e.g.,
  Quick Summer Tomato Sauce
  on page 156)

In a skillet, warm the olive oil, add the zucchini, and sauté 5 minutes, stirring frequently, over medium heat. Salt and pepper them to taste. Add the tomato sauce and mix to coat the zucchini with it. Cover the pan tightly and cook 10 minutes, or until the zucchini are just tender, stirring occasionally. During cooking, add a tablespoon or two of water if necessary to keep the zucchini from drying out—at the end the sauce should be thick and clingy, not soupy. Serve hot, warm, or at room temperature. ∎

ZUCCHINI BELLA NAPOLI

Zucchini alla Bella Napoli

FOR 4 SERVINGS:

$\mathcal{A}$s you might infer from the name, this beautiful-to-look-at, better-to-eat dish holds a special place in the Neapolitan repertoire. It's an elaborate "zucchini lasagna" that would make a satisfying meatless main dish for two or a wonderful accompaniment to simple broiled meats for four.

Though the preparation takes some time, much of it can be done well in advance. The simple sauce, for instance, can be made a day ahead (or use Quick Summer Tomato Sauce, page 156). The zucchini can be fried in the morning, the dish assembled in the afternoon, leaving only the baking for the last minute. Given how prolific zucchini are in summer, you might want to make up a double batch of this recipe and freeze one before baking, to serve on another day.

If serving as a contorno, choose according to your secondo. If serving as an antipasto or secondo on its own, choose a straightforward, fruity red wine such as Lacryma Christi, Corvo, or Dolcetto. It will also accommodate more elegant wines, such as Taurasi, Aglianico del Vulture, or Chianti Classico Riserva.

1½ pounds zucchini, scrubbed and
   sliced lengthwise in ⅛-inch
   boards
Salt
2 cups plus 1½ tablespoons olive
   oil
2 tablespoons chopped onion

¾ pound ripe tomatoes, seeded and
   coarsely chopped
2 to 3 basil leaves
Freshly ground black pepper
Flour for dredging
6 ounces mozzarella, sliced very
   thin

Salting and draining the zucchini:

Stand the zucchini slices on end in a colander and sprinkle them with 1 tablespoon salt. Set the colander in the sink for 1 hour, then dry the zucchini with paper towels, pressing moderately hard to extract more moisture.

Preparing the sauce:

In a nonreactive skillet, heat 1½ tablespoons olive oil. Sauté the onion 2 to 3 minutes, then add the tomatoes and basil. Sprinkle with salt and pepper, cover, and cook gently 30 to 45 minutes. Put the sauce through a food mill and set aside.

Frying the zucchini:
In a heavy skillet, heat the remaining 2 cups olive oil to 375°F. A few at a time, dredge the zucchini slices lightly with flour and tap them to remove the excess. Drop them in the oil and fry until lightly golden, about 1 minute on each side. Drain on paper towels.

Assembling and baking the dish:
Preheat the oven to 350°F. Divide the zucchini slices into four equal portions. Oil a baking dish large enough to hold one portion of the zucchini in a single layer. Alternate layers of ¼ of the zucchini, ¼ of the mozzarella, and ¼ of the tomato sauce. Bake uncovered 20 minutes.

Serve hot, warm, or at room temperature. ∎

SOUTHERN MIXED VEGETABLES

Ciambotta

FOR 4 SERVINGS:

*T*his *ciambotta* is one of the many ways to pronounce, spell, and prepare the ubiquitous southern Italian summer vegetable stew. All are tasty, and all differ slightly from each other in effect. What this particular recipe wants, in essence, is one each of all the high-summer vegetables. We've given quantities by weight, but you should regard them (like the traffic lights on Italian streets) as only advisory.

Leftovers keep well for several days: in fact, some people prefer the dish on the second day. A few slices or pieces of grilled sausage—especially lamb sausage—warmed briefly in with the vegetables turn ciambotta into a very satisfying luncheon or light supper dish. Serve with fresh, crusty bread.

If ciambotta is served by itself, choose a simple, fruity red wine such as Montepulciano d'Abruzzo, Lacryma Christi, or Chianti. If it is being served as a contorno, choose your wine according to the meat or fish.

½ pound eggplant, unpeeled, cut in 1½-inch cubes

Salt

3 tablespoons olive oil

½ pound onions, sliced

½ stalk celery, thinly sliced

2 to 3 leaves fresh basil, chopped

½ pound ripe plum tomatoes, passed through a food mill

¾ pound potatoes, peeled and cut into 1- by 2-inch pieces

½ pound zucchini, cut in ½-inch rounds

¾ pound sweet red or yellow peppers, seeded, halved, and cut in ½-inch-wide strips

Toss the eggplant cubes in a colander with 2 teaspoons salt and let the colander sit in the sink 1 hour to extract the eggplant's bitter juices. Rinse, drain, and dry the eggplant with paper towels, squeezing each piece slightly to extract more liquid.

In a large nonreactive casserole, heat the olive oil and add the onions, celery, and basil. Sauté 5 minutes, or until the vegetables are soft, then stir in the tomatoes. When the dish comes to a simmer, add the eggplant, potatoes, and ½ teaspoon salt. Stir, cover, and simmer 15 minutes. Add the zucchini and peppers, stir, cover, and simmer 15 minutes more, or until all the vegetables are tender.

Taste for salt, transfer the ciambotta to a serving dish, and let it sit 15 minutes before serving. ■

About Salad

Salads of all kinds are ubiquitous in Italy. With any meal later than breakfast, you're offered the option of an *insalata verde* or an *insalata mista*. Those two terms, however, cover a multitude of dishes, and for none of them does there exist anything resembling a single, authoritative recipe. Salad allows every Italian a chance for self-expression, and few indeed are the inartistic souls who flub the opportunity.

There are only a few iron-clad rules. One is to use only the season's freshest, youngest, and best. The other is that you can eat salad either with your secondo—using salad as a contorno, in effect—or after it, but never before it. Earlier in the meal, anything that Americans might call salad Italians would consider an antipasto, and it's certain that it wouldn't be just leaves in a bowl. A good example of this sort of thing is *pinzimonio*, an assortment of raw vegetables (for example, bell peppers, fennel, celery, artichokes) served with a seasoned olive oil dipping sauce. A small pinzimonio, in Italian eyes, is an antipasto; a large one is a lunch by itself or a dinner secondo.

That said, Italians have few other fixed ideas about salad. Most often, *insalata* consists of one predominant variety of lettuce plus one or two other, usually sharper, greens dressed with olive oil and either lemon juice or wine vinegar. That lettuce will never be iceberg; usually it resembles either romaine (despite the Frenchified spelling, the name accurately indicates the green's Roman origin) or the kinds of lettuce we know as Boston or Bibb. The sharper greens will often be a few pale sprigs of *cicoria*—what we call curly endive—or of the heart of escarole. Certain seasonally special greens, especially wild or semiwild ones such as dandelions or the Roman favorite *puntarelle* (the early tender shoots of a kind of pungent chicory), are usually served by themselves and receive special, and specialized, dressings. Puntarelle, for instance, are always dressed with a garlicky olive oil and vinegar melange that has been thickened with a mashed anchovy or two. Rucola—our arugola—and radicchio di Treviso also are usually served in solitary splendor, unaccompanied by any other green, though in newer Italian recipes rucola has begun appearing as a component in elaborate antipasti—as an edible garnish on a plate of carpaccio, for instance. Served uncooked, all these leafy vegetables—even radicchio, despite its red color—qualify as insalata verde, green salad.

A mixed salad—*insalata mista*—can be, and often in summer is, as simple as one kind of lettuce and a tomato, though usually it will consist of two or three greens, some thin slivers of onion, and wedges of tomatoes. Salads of tomatoes alone are, of course, also relished in their season. But even at the height of summer, the tomatoes used for salad are most often half green and quite firm. Somehow or other, these "unripe" Italian tomatoes are as rich and flavorful as our own when fully red and soft to bursting.

Mixed salads can contain more exotic items as well, such as cooked asparagus or cooked beets. The latter, for instance, may appear along with other cooked vegetables (potatoes, onions, carrots, squash) in the winter salad specialty, *insala-tone* (see page 330 in the Winter section). But most of the time, in the Italian calculation of things, such ingredients decidedly move the dish in which they feature into the category of antipasto or even secondo.

A major difference between salads in Italy and salads in the United States is due to the quality of each ingredient and the way it was grown and marketed. For instance, Boston and Bibb lettuces—the kind Italians call *cappuccio*—de-cored and spread open look like a large bull's-eye of buttery yellow surrounded by a narrow circle of jade green. Romaine lettuces in Italy are rarely as large as ours, nor do they come to market with a heavy jacket of large, coarse outer leaves. They average a third smaller than the ones we usually see, with fewer "thickened" outer leaves and with larger pale and tender hearts, and they taste accordingly richer and better.

Not only do the vegetables taste better, but there is also no such animal as Italian dressing—the variety of viscid liquids bottled under that misnomer—to degrade them. Salads in Italy are dressed with generous doses of olive oil (the only variation is whether one uses extra-virgin or a less-expensive grade), wine vinegar (very rarely, balsamic vinegar) or fresh-squeezed lemon juice in quantities usually minute compared to the oil, and salt. A few fresh herbs—notably oregano and basil—may be used in season, but that's just about all that ever goes into "Italian dressing." You don't need a recipe, only a pair of eyes to gauge the amount of condiment going into the salad bowl.

DOLCI

Summer desserts in Italy are a holy trinity: fruit, gelato, and granita. *Granite adoremus:* those cooling, flavored water ices make the world's best thirst quenchers. In the middle of a scorching-hot summer afternoon, life in Italy has few pleasures simpler than sitting in the shade outside a quiet cafe and spooning at a cup of granita *di caffe* or *limone.* Yes, granita is wonderful; but gelato! Gelato is ambrosia. Italian gelato is the best ice cream in the world—bar none, hands down, no arguments please.

Fruit, of course, everybody knows, or so everybody thinks, so we won't afflict you with reminiscences of the glories of Italian fruit; how every donkey driver in every tiny town has access to peaches richer in flavor than our mangoes, or melons of a succulence to eclipse the pampered produce of our gourmet marts. If you've been there, you really do know; and if you haven't, you probably won't believe us.

This is not say that it's impossible to find good fruit in these United States: only that it isn't easy, even in the height of summer. Your best bet is to buy fruit as locally as possible and as near ripeness as possible. If it's truly local it will have been picked ripe and will have far more flavor and character than anything that had to be harvested green in order to be shipped thousands of miles. Never buy fruit on appearance alone: color and symmetry aren't reliable guides to quality. The feel of a fruit in the hand and its scent in the nose will tell you a lot more about it than its pretty face. Pick up a fruit and gently feel it for its actual degree of ripeness, its tautness or its give. Put it right up to your nose and take a good long sniff of it before you buy. If a fruit has no aroma, forget how lovely it may look. Just put it back and pass on. Fruits should smell like themselves, and the more richly they do so, the better they're going to taste. We all of us live so far from nature these days that we've lost track of just which sense it is that guides birds and bears to the berry bush just at the time of perfect ripeness. (With large fruits like melons, be sure to smell the blossom end, not the stem end. That's where ripening starts.)

You might think that anything as commonsensical as all the above wouldn't have to be said, but an extraordinary number of Americans of all generations have lost touch with unprocessed fruits and vegetables. Just last year, in a farmers' market in Manhattan, we overheard the following sad interchange between an elderly couple who were wandering among the baskets of summer produce with wonder and amazement:

HE (wistfully): Don't those green beans look delicious! Couldn't we buy some?
SHE (slightly frightened): Oh no, no! I wouldn't know how to cook them.

Fruit spares you even that potential embarrassment, of course: you don't have to cook it to enjoy it. Once you have your fruit, just eat it with as much elegance as possible, but, above all, eat it with alacrity. A plum in the hand outdoors on a sunny afternoon, juice dripping down your chin and onto the grass, is a paradigm summer treat. At a formal dinner table, "plain" fruit takes on considerable elegance when it's served forth on an attractive plate, to be peeled and sliced with a pearl-handled fruit knife. And if you're not quite that formal, let us recommend the bliss of eating peach slices off the point of a knife after dipping them into your glass of young red wine.

Then there's macedonia, a compote of fruits. The fine Italian hand with this humble dish consists largely in the judicious addition of lemon juice and grated lemon rind (or orange—juice or rind or both), which seem to add brilliancy to any fruit combination. Also, remember the lesson in the name: the Balkan region known as Macedonia has been a meeting place of nations since the dawn of history. Fortunately, fruits can coexist more peacefully than mankind's races. You can't put too many kinds of fruits into a macedonia.

The next step up from the simplicity of eating fresh fruit is to use fruit juices in a granita. And after granita, the other wonderful thing to do with the best of summer's fruits is to make them into ice cream. Both these classes of frozen desserts deserve discussions of their own, so please read on.

About Granita

Granita (plural, *granite*) is water ice, the simplest of frozen desserts. For fruit granite, which are most of the breed, the ingredients are simply fruit juice (or puree), water, and sugar. Not too much sugar, either—the bracing refreshment that's characteristic of a real Italian granita demands a little mouth puckering!

Granita doesn't require churn-freezing, as ice cream does: the only equipment you need is a shallow metal pan and a fork. It does require fairly constant tending during the freezing process, though, to achieve the proper texture and consistency. If you put a fruit syrup into the freezer and just leave it there, its water content tends to rise to the surface and freeze first, leaving a fruit sludge on the bottom. That, as much as the need to prevent the formation of a solid block of ice, is the reason granita needs to be mixed and mashed frequently during the freezing, and that regular mashing is what produces the grainy crystals that granita fanciers seek.

The physics of freezing fruit syrups is actually quite fascinating. Change the proportions of fruit to water to sugar, and you get a completely different sort of result. Though we learned the pleasures of eating granita years ago in Italy, we mastered the tricks of making it only recently, thanks to an American writer, Harold McGee. His excellent book *The Curious Cook* has an entire chapter on the history and "science" of fruit ices, complete with diagrams of ice crystals and tables indicating relative proportions of ingredients for different styles of water and waterless fruit ices. Following McGee, one can make granita out of dozens of fruits, including such uncommon ones as avocados and tomatoes. We ourselves, being more traditional in our granita fancying, tend to rely on the classic Italian flavors, coffee (that is to say, espresso) and citrus fruits.

Granita is best when served as soon as it's made. Left in the freezer, it will compact and try to convince you that the name alludes to granite rock. However, you can make up the syrup well in advance and leave it to chill thoroughly in the refrigerator. Then, 2 hours before you want to serve the granita, start it freezing. A kitchen timer is an essential to remind you of the need to break up the developing crystals every 10 or 15 minutes. If you make a granita in advance, its texture can be refreshed by pulsing it briefly in a food processor or blender—just enough to loosen, not liquefy, it.

ESPRESSO COFFEE ICE

Granita di caffè

FOR 1 GENEROUS QUART:

*G*ranita di caffè, to us, is *the* most Italianate of ices, the glory of a summer afternoon. For this recipe we've indicated an optional whipped-cream topping. We ourselves like this granita straight and strong, but fainter spirits—especially cappuccino drinkers—may find it more pleasing with the cream.

None needed.

2 cups strong espresso

10 tablespoons sugar

1½ cups water, approximately

Freshly whipped cream (optional)

Make the espresso according to your preferred method. While it is hot, dissolve the sugar in it. Add enough cold water to bring the measure up to 4 cups. Chill this liquid very thoroughly in the refrigerator.

Transfer the liquid to one or two shallow metal cake pans and put it in the freezer. Set a kitchen timer for 15 minutes, and when it rings, mash the solidifying mixture with a fork to break up the ice crystals. Repeat after another 15 minutes. Thereafter repeat the mashing process at 10-minute intervals for a total freezing time of 2 hours, or until the granita reaches a uniform texture like dry, crystalline snow. Serve at once, with—if you like—a dab of whipped cream atop each portion.

If the granita is not to be served at once, or if there is some left over after serving, transfer it to a container, cover, and store in the freezer. If it has solidified again by the time you are ready for it, pulse it briefly in a food processor or blender to loosen the texture (but don't let it liquefy). ■

LIME-GRAPEFRUIT WATER ICE

Granita di limone verde e pompelmo

FOR 1 GENEROUS QUART:

Y

None needed.

*I*ntensely flavored, crisp, and palate-cleansing, this citrus combination makes a lovely and rather sophisticated ice. You get alternating effects of the two fruits in each mouthful. Unlike the preceding granita di caffè, we find this one doesn't like whipped cream.

Juice of 5 limes (½ to ⅔ cup)	*8 tablespoons sugar*
Juice of 1 grapefruit (¾ to 1 cup)	

In a bowl, combine the two fruit juices, add the sugar, and stir until it is completely dissolved. Measure the resulting amount of fruit syrup and add enough cold water to bring the liquid to 4 cups. Chill it thoroughly in the refrigerator.

To freeze the granita, follow the instructions for espresso coffee ice, page 205. ■

About Gelato

Americans and Italians are unanimous in their love of ice cream—which is only right for the people who invented it (the Italians) and the people who first started taking the labor out of making it (the hand-cranked dasher was invented in America, in 1846; the first commercial ice-cream manufactory opened in Baltimore just five years later).

The old-fashioned ice-cream parlor is still alive and well in Italy. On any warm afternoon in Rome, any tourists, no matter how befuddled by its maze of ancient streets, can find their way to Giolitti or Palma by walking against the stream of happy strollers with rainbow-colored cones and cups of gelato. Those crowds of contented ice-cream fans usually contain as many Romans as tourists and more adults than kids. We know several old Roman hands whose first act upon arrival, after dropping their bags, is a ritual beeline for Giolitti.

In Italy, ice cream isn't just kid stuff, nor is it simply good street food. Odd as it may sound to Americans, ice cream in Italy is sophisticated: bars serve it, cafes serve it, and designer-suited executives—male or female—are as likely to order a *coppa mista di gelato* for their afternoon pick-me-up as they are to request a caffè or a Campari and soda. We recall one sunny afternoon in Grado, a fascinating little island off Venice's northeastern shore. We had been strolling up the central canal—Grado is like a scaled-down Venice, with its own Canal Grande lined with working fishing boats, ranging in size from skiffs to trawlers—and through the ancient central square, with its red-brick mini-duomo and *palazzo publico*, finally emerging on the far side of the island, facing the Adriatic. The landward side and center of Grado are picturesque, quaint, workaday Italian. The seaside looked like a perfect still shot from one of Fellini's best-composed scenes: dazzling white sand beaches; a placid blue sea; tall, modern resort hotels set back from a spotless esplanade; a few clean lines of railing along the walk; strollers silhouetted against the sky and the calm sea; a few obviously international loungers seated at umbrellaed tables languidly spooning ice cream. We sat down too and shared a *coppa mista* (regular size, not *gigante*), which came as a pyramid of six different flavors, each tastier and more intriguing than the last: great pistachio, real walnut (no maple!), banana, transcendent raspberry, and two others we couldn't even identify but loved anyhow.

The reason for our enthusiasm is simple: Italy makes the best ice cream in the world. And it makes more kinds of it too—ice creams flavored with every conceivable sort of nut, in size from pea- to coco- and in flavor climaxing in a glorious hazel- *(nocciola)*; ice creams lush with every fruit from grape to grapefruit; ice creams redolent of coffee and chocolate and even cheese. Unlikely as it may sound, ricotta ice cream is wonderful.

What makes Italian ice creams so superior are the basic ingredients and the purity of their preparation. Rich cream—not ultrapasteurized into inertness—fresh eggs, the season's finest fruits: those and only those are the ingredients of the best ice creams. No fillers or extenders, no preservatives or emulsifiers. They stay fresh because they are made fresh, every day.

The freshness and the absence of extraneous ingredients you can re-create at home, with the simplest of home ice-cream makers. Electric machines are enormously labor-saving—though there's no more festive way to entertain casual summer guests than by pitching in to make a huge batch of ice cream in a wooden, hand-cranked machine, with everyone taking a turn on the dasher and trying to avoid a soaking from the melting salt-and-ice slurry. Making an ice cream that recalls the richness of Italian gelato isn't quite as easy. Most ice-cream makers come with plenty of recipes, all perfectly calibrated to the machine's capacity. But too many of them, we find, turn out commercial American-style ice cream. We keep trying to re-create the lushness of true Italian gelato, even though we can rarely get the rich, flavorful, truly fresh cream that Italians rely on. The recipes in this section are the nearest we've come to paradise.

ICE CREAM

Gelato di crema

FOR 1 QUART:

⚲

None needed.

*N*ever was literal translation so accurate: ice *cream*. The flavor that Italians call *crema* is a custard cream that beats vanilla hands down. It is often used as a base for other flavors, and the technique employed in making crema is one that can be applied to any number of other flavored ice creams.

The one difficulty sometimes encountered in making crema is curdling of the egg yolks, which is usually due to using an improvised double boiler rather than the real thing. If you must improvise, a round-bottomed copper zabaglione pan over a tall pot works well—but you've still got to regulate the heat very carefully so as not to cook those yolks.

One other thing: if you possibly can, make up the custard base the day before you want the ice cream. The more thoroughly cold the mixture is, the more smoothly and readily it will freeze.

⅔ cup sugar	Pinch salt
4 egg yolks	1 strip lemon peel
1 cup milk, at room temperature	1 cup heavy cream

In a mixing bowl, beat the sugar and egg yolks together until they are pale yellow and very thick. Slowly add the milk, beating gently to avoid a buildup of too much foam. Stir in the salt and the strip of lemon peel.

Transfer the mixture to the top of a double boiler and set it over 1 inch of boiling water in the bottom half. Regulating the heat so the water remains at a low boil, stir continuously with a wooden spoon or hard rubber spatula 8 minutes, until the cream thickens enough to coat the spoon. (Just at the moment of thickening, the surface foam will disappear.)

Immediately remove the custard from the heat and set its pan into a large bowl of cold water. Stir for 1 to 2 minutes to stop the cooking and cool the mixture somewhat. Transfer it to a bowl, cover, and set in the refrigerator to chill thoroughly—from 1 hour to overnight.

When ready to proceed, whip the heavy cream into soft peaks. Remove the lemon peel from the custard and fold in the whipped cream. Transfer the mixture to an ice-cream maker and freeze according to the machine's directions. ■

COFFEE ICE CREAM

Gelato di caffè

FOR 1 QUART:

Ⓨ

None needed.

 his is one of the easiest and most common variants on the basic crema recipe. It yields an intensely coffee-flavored ice cream with absolutely no fuss, thanks to the use of instant espresso. As serious *tifosi* (fanatics) of espresso, we don't use instant for any other purpose. We rely on a restaurant-size espresso machine to brew our own mix of freshly ground, not-too-heavily roasted beans (currently Illycaffe Roma and Vintage Colombian), even for breakfast. However, the richness of the other gelato ingredients makes up for any flavor deficiencies in instant espresso, and the easily dissolving granules obviate the need to boil milk with coffee beans and leave it to steep. So for speed and simplicity, try instant.

⅔ cup sugar

4 egg yolks

1 cup milk, at room temperature

4 tablespoons instant espresso

 granules

1 cup heavy cream

Make the custard cream base from the sugar, egg yolks, and milk as in the recipe on page 208. Dissolve the espresso granules in the custard mixture just before putting it into the refrigerator.

When ready to proceed, whip the heavy cream into soft peaks and fold it into the custard. Transfer the mixture to an ice-cream maker and freeze according to the machine's directions. ∎

BLUEBERRY ICE CREAM

Gelato di mirtille

FOR 1½ QUARTS:

One more variant on the basic custard cream recipe. This technique can be used for any number of fruits or berries. Because of the extra volume added by the fruit, this recipe makes about 1½ quarts. Halve it if you have only a small ice-cream freezer.

None needed.

⅔ cup sugar

4 egg yolks

1 cup milk, at room temperature

Pinch salt

1 strip lemon peel

2 cups fresh blueberries, pureed

1 cup heavy cream

Make the custard cream base from the first five ingredients as in the recipe on page 208. While the custard mixture is chilling, chill the blueberry puree in the refrigerator as well. When ready to proceed, remove the lemon peel from the custard and stir in the blueberry puree. Whip the heavy cream and finish the ice cream as directed on page 209. ∎

PEACH ICE CREAM

Gelato di pesche

FOR 1½ TO 2 QUARTS:

Y
None needed.

Our friend, Italian food expert, and fellow Giolitti gelato fan Al Cirillo coaxed this recipe and technique from the horse's mouth, in the course of a long, earnest, and highly idiomatic conversation with the Giolitti people on one of their rare slow afternoons. We can't vouch for the absolute authenticity of the recipe, but we can verify that it does have the true, undiluted peaches-and-cream taste, and that's good enough for us.

This recipe differs from our basic custard cream recipe; it's even simpler and purer. Again, the fruit-and-cream mixture needs to be very cold before it goes into the dasher, so if possible, start the preparations the day before. If your peaches are less flavorsome than you'd like, you can slice them, toss them with a tablespoon or two of lemon juice, and let them steep for an hour before pureeing. This will brighten the flavor.

You can also make a splendid pineapple ice cream with this recipe, using two cups of fresh pineapple chunks.

1 cup sugar	*1 cup heavy cream, chilled*
1 to 1¼ pound ripe peaches	

In a heavy-bottomed saucepan, mix the sugar with 2 cups water. Stir over medium heat until the sugar dissolves, bring the syrup to a boil, and boil 5 minutes. Cool it completely.

Drop the peaches into boiling water for 10 seconds to loosen their skins, then drain, peel, and pit them. Puree them in a food processor or blender. Measure out 2 cups of puree and stir it into the sugar syrup. Chill the mixture very thoroughly—6 hours minimum.

When ready to proceed, whip the heavy cream into soft peaks and stir it into the fruit mixture. Transfer the mixture to an ice-cream machine and freeze according to the machine's directions. ■

RICOTTA ICE CREAM

Gelato di ricotta

FOR 1 QUART:

This surprising ice cream is much easier to make than custard-based mixtures, but the creaminess of the ricotta gives it much the same palatal effect. We give it in two versions: one the original Italian recipe, and another a "sanitized" version for those who fear salmonella in raw eggs. If you have confidence in your local chickens, we think you'll find the original recipe just a bit better. You can use whole-milk or part-skim ricotta for either one.

None needed.

VERSION 1: WITH EGG

4 egg yolks

½ cup sugar

5 tablespoons brandy

1 pound fresh ricotta

In a large mixing bowl, beat the egg yolks and sugar together until they are pale yellow and creamy. Beat in the brandy, then fold in the ricotta. Chill the mixture very thoroughly. Transfer it to an ice-cream maker and proceed according to the machine's directions.

VERSION 2: WITHOUT EGG

½ cup confectioners' sugar

2 tablespoons Marsala (or
substitute Madeira or sherry)

1 pound part-skim ricotta

½ cup heavy cream

In a large bowl, stir the confectioners' sugar and Marsala together until the sugar dissolves. Push the ricotta through a sieve into the mixture and stir well. Chill thoroughly.

When ready to proceed, whip the cream into soft peaks. Fold it into the ricotta mixture. Transfer to an ice-cream machine and freeze according to machine's directions. ■

AUTUNNO

· *Fall* ·

"Mellow fruitfulness"—the phrase is from Keats—may be accurate as a description of an English autumn, but it's only half right about fall in Italy. Italian autumn is fruitful, to be sure, but there's little mellow about it. Rather, fall in Italy has a violent streak that seems to afford the average citizen considerable satisfaction. The sickle and the scythe, those traditional tools of the harvest, are murderous-looking implements, and both have associations (think of the hammer-and-sickle emblem on its blood-red field; think of Father Time, or Death) that suggest uses other than mowing fields and bringing in the sheaves.

On the farm, this is pig-slaughtering time, the time for preparing salame, coppa, capocollo, culatella, prosciutto, and the numerous local varieties of sausage for their long winter cure. In the market, as in the fields and woodlands, the green harmonies of summer give way to vivid reds, strident yellows, and velvet browns. Vegetable stalls offer a cornucopia of the last full burst of the sun's bounty and the first fruits of autumn: piles of gleaming, purple-black eggplants; gaping, golden slabs of *zucca*, a great, knobby pumpkin-like squash; peppers in barbaric reds and yellows; pears of green and amber-brown; the first brown-suede caps of funghi porcini.

This is also the time of *la selvaggina*—wild food, game—the beginning of the hunting season, when Italians in legions take to the hills and plains with gun in hand and dinner in mind. Market stalls throughout Italy display their trophies whole and in their full pelts of fur or feather. You may see heaps of small birds—everything from the pathetically tiny bodies of sparrows and starlings and thrushes up to quail and exotically plumaged pheasants—arrayed beside the imposing bulk of a wickedly tusked and hooved *cinghiale*, a dark-bristled wild boar, still looking dangerous, even dead and on display. In more mountainous regions, butchers feature chamois; in the plains, hare.

Everywhere, several kinds of deer. And everywhere products of a different kind of hunt: mushrooms in a variety that no American market can equal and few American consumers would dare to eat.

If summer in Italy moves us to an appreciation of the durability of stone, autumn prompts meditations on wood, its variety and permutations, its malleability and adaptability. Not just what people have made of wood, though that is evident in everything from the sturdy rafters and massive roof beams of older Italian houses to the masterfully delicate inlay and marquetry of tables and walls and doors in palaces and churches. No, our special autumn associations with wood are in its myriad natural forms. Fall is the time when fireplaces are swept out and logs and kindling carried in, preparing for the first frosty evening. You mark the season's shift when, in long-established trattorias like La Tana di Noiantri, in Trastevere, the outside tables are suddenly abandoned, and tourists vie with locals for the all-summer-long-scorned, now-suddenly-desirable indoor seats, near the massive fireplace and its reassuring logs.

As the season progresses, the ubiquitous and beautiful umbrella pines and the cypresses show more prominently against the low Italian skyline, as the chestnuts and other hardwoods let fall their summer crop of leaves and nuts. In vineyards, after the harvest, birds glean the last of the grapes from stout, twisted woody vines now only half-covered in scarlet and golden leaves. Soon, too, the gnarled, patient olive trees, their silvery leaves drying slowly to gray, will yield their season's growth of olives, deep green and purple and black. Ancient olive trees spell out the season and carry the message of wood most clearly—half-hollowed shells whose live, bearing branches thrust improbably out from decades-old, even centuries-old, desiccated trunks. There is a durability in wood to match the lastingness of stone, an indomitability and a kind of secular eternity in the long, slow cycles of its changes. Gazing on wood, you think not of the hard eternity that stone suggests but of the softer resiliences of life, of the sea-anchors of home and hearth and harvest.

Fall works its slow transformations on everything. For the wanderer in city or in country, distant objects take on a hazy edge, even though the day is still bright and luminous. The sky, though still the same high, depthless blue of summer, appears vaguely out of focus, as if you were looking at it through a soft filter. Shadows grow longer, the sun sets sooner, the mornings start cool, foggy in the hills, and the nights quickly grow chill. And the change is welcome, like exhaling joyously after long holding your breath. It's as if a country typified even in its own mind as *sole e mare*—sun and sea—has started a long-awaited vacation from both. And not just nature: people too— cooks and diners alike—welcome relief from the hard, Cartesian light of summer. Away from the glare and heat, refreshed, the appetite picks up again, and once more it's cool enough to really cook, to simmer and stew and baste and bake, to make dishes that will perfume the kitchen all day long as they slowly gather flavor and complexity.

Barbaric as the market scene and the season's colors may be, fall's flavors and fall's cooking are paradoxically more subtle and harmonious than summer's. Summer dishes are all sharp thrusts and cool lancets of flavor, angular and bright. Fall's are deeper-toned, rounded and comforting. In the slow alchemy of the cooking fire, animal and vegetable essences merge and mingle and take on new identities compounded of each one's best. For the cook, there is no clearer expression of the season's evanescent and yet permanent values than the sophisticated interplays of flavors and textures produced by autumn's more complex cooking.

For the connoisseur—or for the simple soul who enjoys what life offers—the soft resiliences of autumn, and the comfort that flows from its violence, are represented best in the grape harvest. Fall brings the new vintage, the fresh blood of Bacchus, pouring from the old wood and the old earth for the renewal of human life. Summer's wines are light and white and chilled. Autumn's are red and mouth-filling and warming: complex, harmonious wines to match the subtler nuances and deeper flavors of autumn foods. Nourishing, stimulating wines whose names roll like poetry on the tongue—Barbera and Barolo and Barbaresco, Dolcetto and Amarone, Sangue di Giuda and Lacryma Christi, Chianti and Carmignano, Taurasi and Teroldego. These are the music of autumn, compared to which "the songs of spring"—Keats again—are only children's ditties.

The climax of Italian autumn and the foundation of Italian cooking are one and the same: late autumn's olive harvest. Olives and olive oil are a food and a condiment so basic to Italian cooking as to be pandemic. The second and third pressings of the olives yield the oil that is the commonest cooking medium of the peninsula, but the first, gentle pressing of the fruits releases the green-gold, intensely flavored drops that alone can be designated as extra-virgin olive oil. Drizzle or pour some over a piece of toasted country bread that has been rubbed with a cut garlic clove, and you have a transcendent bruschetta which, with a few slices of prosciutto or salami and a glass of young red wine, makes either a perfect antipasto or a satisfying small meal. Even ordinary olive oil, used to dress or to cook autumn's fruits and vegetables, has two great culinary virtues. First, it unites with them to produce invariably delicious juices and natural sauces that beg to be mopped up with fresh bread. And second, it makes them all, from artichokes to zucchini, more pleasing with wines of all colors than they are by themselves.

It may be true that oil and water don't mix, but oil and bread and wine—the three great harvests of autumn, and another of the Mediterranean's sacramental trinities—certainly do, even as, from time out of mind, the olive tree and the grape vine were intermingled in Mediterranean plantings. Ceres and Bacchus, the goddess of the harvest and the god of wine, are the tutelary deities of the Italian table—in autumn or out of it.

ANTIPASTI

In choosing vegetable antipasti for fall, we're fortunate to have many of the high-summer vegetables still available, in some cases right up to the first frost. Thus, we can continue to play the infinite variations of tomatoes, eggplant, and peppers—enriched now by the addition of sweeter, ripe peppers in their handsome reds and yellows (even purples and browns and oranges and whites, in today's "designer" peppers). Of the two vegetable antipasto dishes here, one is very simple, showcasing the affinity of beets and balsamic vinegar, and the other quite elaborate—the best stuffed peppers we've ever achieved. As in other seasons, many of the vegetables in the Fall Contorni section can also serve as antipasti.

Another cold antipasto here is a combination of prosciutto and pears—one that will take you right into cold weather without much regret for the passing of summer's figs and melons that graced the prosciutto plate.

Another new star in the antipasto firmament at this time of year is mushrooms: an array of subtly spiced new flavors from the forest floor. (See About Mushrooms, page 227, for a discussion of fall woods mushrooms.) They're represented here with two recipes: one a mushroom topping for crostini—Italians' beloved little toast canapes that can appear all year long bearing such toppings as pureed chicken livers, nubbly olive paste, or the merest veil of a melted local cheese. (See our Summer Antipasti for yet another crostini recipe.) Our second mushroom-based antipasto is a savory tart of mushrooms and ham.

The main thrust of our fall antipasti is baked dishes, like the mushroom tart. Cooler weather not only makes oven work a pleasure again, but it sharpens our appetites for heartier tastes of breads and pastries enriched with meats and cheeses. In that category we offer a recipe for *frollini al finocchio*, intriguing little cocktail cookies made with a ham-and-Swiss-cheese-enriched pastry dough, and Gatto Santa Chiara, an unusual Neapolitan potato-based bread studded with ham and mozzarella. Our schiacciata for this season is also a cheese-flavored bread.

Finally, since fall also brings the grain harvest and the new crop of cornmeal for polenta, which can appear in every course of an Italian fall meal, we represent it here with "crostini" made from polenta and topped with a lush spread of Gorgonzola cheese. Please see About Polenta on p. 388 of the Winter section for more on this cold-weather kitchen workhorse.

BEETS WITH BALSAMIC VINEGAR

Carote rosse al balsamico

FOR 4 SERVINGS:

A dry, acidic white (Soave, Verdicchio, Frascati) or a simple, soft red (Montepulciano d'Abruzzo, Rosso Conero, Castel del Monte) will work equally well here.

The combination of sweetness and pungency in this cold vegetable dish gives your palate a rousing shake. This simple preparation makes a fine, invigorating start for a rich dinner.

We like to boil beets in their skins to preserve as much of their flavor as possible. Slipping the skins off cooked beets is a bit messy, but no more so than the slaughterhouse effect you get on your hands when peeling raw beets. Alternatively, you can roast them whole in the oven: this dries them a bit, but marvelously concentrates the flavor. So popular is that technique in Italy that many markets sell large beets (a pound or more apiece) already roasted and peeled—a great convenience, considering how long even quite small beets can take to cook.

For this recipe, the beets need some time to absorb the balsamic vinegar; we suggest 30 minutes. If you've cooked the beets a day in advance and refrigerated them, bring them up to room temperature before dressing them, so they'll absorb more readily.

2 pounds beets, stems trimmed to within 1 inch of the base
Salt

1 to 2 tablespoons balsamic vinegar
3 to 4 scallions, white and tender green parts, chopped

Bring a kettle of water to a boil. Put the beets in a pot and pour in enough boiling water to cover them by 2 inches. Cover and boil until the beets are tender—30 to 60 minutes, depending on size.

Drain the beets and let them cool somewhat. Cut off the root and stem ends of each beet and slip off the skins. Slice them ¼ inch thick and arrange them on a serving plate. Sprinkle with salt and drizzle with balsamic vinegar. Let them sit 30 minutes.

Strew the chopped scallions over the beets just before serving. ■

About Peppers

Nothing in the kitchen says autumn so clearly as the heady aroma of roasted peppers. Ripe red and yellow bell peppers look festively, not to say exuberantly, autumnal—but just spear one on a long meat fork and start charring its skin over a stove burner, and your whole kitchen will be filled with a redolence of fallen leaves and campfires, gleaned fields and hayricks. It's one of those bits of inexpensive magic that Mediterranean cookery in general and Italian in particular seem to specialize in.

We are unashamed idolators of Italian bell peppers. They're so much larger, lustier, craggier, and more individualized than the foursquare commercial American bell. Pepper stalls in the open markets exert a powerful magnetism for us. Every trip we've made to Italy is commemorated by at least a few color slides of gorgeous peppers—voluptuous close-ups of a few glossy bodies, artful "found" arrangements on a counter or against a wall, Busby Berkeley–style ensemble shots of riotous heaps of *capsicum* color and contour.

When we're engaged in these photographic efforts, Italians regard us with amused toleration—just another version of American craziness. They appreciate peppers just as much as we do, but for eating, not for looking at. Bell peppers play a stellar role in Italian cuisine: most prominently in the south, but really the entire length of the peninsula. You'll encounter them raw *in pinzimonio* (a dipping sauce of olive oil, wine vinegar, and lots of salt and pepper presented with a platter of assorted raw vegetables). Pepper strips and stalks of fresh young celery and fennel make a very pleasing pinzimonio combination. Peppers are sautéed or stewed alone or in combination with other vegetables. *Peperonata* is the generic name for the all-purpose sauté of peppers, tomatoes, and onions in much olive oil (and usually a few bay leaves), the proportions of each ingredient varying with the whim of the cook or the contents of the pantry that day. Peppers also find their way into many composed meat dishes, especially those with veal or chicken, with or without the pepper's faithful sidekick, the tomato. And peppers are baked or broiled with a myriad of stuffings—whole peppers encasing a filling, opened halves making a boat for a topping, or any other architectural arrangement you can think of and cause to be.

A rare quality of peppers is their culinary utility both ripe and unripe. (Need it be said that a red or yellow bell pepper is merely the ripe stage of a green bell pepper? Just how far off the farm have Americans gotten?) Different Italian recipes may specify green or red/yellow according to whether the predominant pepper quality desired is acidity or sweetness. However, you can usually interchange green and ripe peppers in a recipe if you realize that the effect will vary.

The simplest preparation of either green or ripe bell peppers, and one that makes them available for any number of uses from eating as is to the elaborate stuffed-pepper recipe that follows, is to roast them directly over an open flame. This chars the shiny, cellophanelike outer skin and lightly cooks and softens the flesh; it also intensifies the flavor a bit. Once seeded and cleaned of the bits of char, a roasted pepper can be dressed with olive oil for an antipasto just as is or draped over a piece of toasted country bread, or incorporated into more elaborate preparations.

In early fall, when ripe peppers are most abundant and inexpensive, it's a wise householder who lays in a stock for keeping. Roasted peppers respond very well to being laid out flat on waxed paper or aluminum foil and frozen. Defrosted, they lose a bit of texture, but the flavor holds up extremely well. In the depths of winter, the taste of one of your own home-roasted peppers can be as nostalgic and haunting as the last honks of geese overhead flying south.

After bells, there are the long, slender, pointed, lighter-green peppers known in America as "Italian frying peppers." More delicately flavored, thinner-walled, and thinner-skinned, these cook faster than bell peppers and never need to have their skins charred off. They're surprisingly good simply rubbed with olive oil, laid out in a baking dish, and roasted until soft, along with whatever meat is in the oven. You can also halve and core them for a natural boat-shaped receptacle for a savory filling. And—not to slight our Italian-American memories of heroic veal-and-pepper or pepper-and-egg sandwiches—they sauté beautifully with a mess of onions.

Another Italian-American favorite, the hot cherry pepper, isn't as often used in Italy itself, either in its plain or pickled form. But tiny green peppers shaped like the "frying peppers" are very common ingredients of *sottaceti* (pickled vegetables) in Italy.

The other ubiquitous pepper in Italian kitchens is the tiny *peperoncino rosso*, the *diavolillo* (little devil), as it is affectionately known. A small (about an inch long), straight, crimson strain of chili pepper, diavolillo is dried in enormous quantities in Italy every fall for use in accenting sauces and oils all through the year.

Any tomato sauce can be brightened by warming a peperoncino in olive oil before the other ingredients go in (and then discarding or retaining it, as your palate prefers). We call for it often in our recipes in this book, but realize that it may not be readily available. The obvious substitute would be the "crushed red pepper flakes" so familiar in pizza parlors throughout the United States. The difficulty is that too often the contents of those plastic cylinders are heavy on seeds, light on actual pepper flesh, and occasionally they're so old and stale as to contribute nothing but raw heat to a dish. A better substitute would be any small dried red chili pepper—remembering, as capsicum lovers know, that chili flavor and fire vary widely.

SPECTACULAR STUFFED PEPPERS

Peperoni imbottiti

FOR 4 SERVINGS:

Lacryma Christi, red or white, would be ideal; or try also Corvo, red or white.

*D*espite the prosaic class they belong to (think of all the limp, tired, cafeteria-style pepper cases filled mostly with bread that pass as economical food in America), these peppers are a Neapolitan *capolavoro*—a real culinary masterpiece. The first time we tried this recipe, adapted from J. C. Francesconi's *Cucina Napoletana*, we were prepared to be underwhelmed. The ingredient list is a roster of the commonest ingredients in the southern Italian peasant pantry, and we couldn't believe anything extraordinary would come of it—certainly not anything worthy of the beatific *Benedetti siano i peperoni imbottiti!* ("Blessed are the stuffed peppers!") with which Francesconi introduces the dish. We were wrong.

As with so much of Italian culinary artistry, it's all in the particular handling of the ingredients. What's done to these stuffed peppers is not at all difficult, though it is labor-intensive and rather time-consuming. But the results are truly spectacular. The finished peppers really need to rest a day to fully develop their flavor, and they'll hold up for a second day without losing too much of it.

Red or yellow peppers are preferable for this recipe; not only for appearance, but because their sweeter, riper flavor makes a richer contribution to the dish. Choose them carefully, however; any blemishes and their walls may rip under either the initial roasting or the baking. It won't hurt the flavor if that happens, but when you're going to this much trouble, you want a handsome dish.

8 small red or yellow bell peppers
  (about 2 pounds)
1½ cups olive oil, approximately
1½ pounds eggplant, peeled and
  cut in ½-inch cubes
2 cloves garlic, 1 halved, 1 chopped

3 tablespoons fine dry bread
  crumbs, made from Italian-style
  bread
2 ounces Gaeta or Sicilian black
  olives, pitted and coarsely
  chopped

1½ tablespoons capers, rinsed, drained, and chopped if large	3 tablespoons chopped flat-leaf Italian parsley
3 ripe plum tomatoes (½ pound), peeled and coarsely chopped	Freshly ground black pepper
	6 small anchovy fillets, coarsely chopped
½ teaspoon dried oregano	Salt

Preparing the peppers:

Turn a gas stove burner to its highest flame. Set a pepper directly onto the grate. As the skin blackens, turn the pepper with tongs until its entire surface is charred. Drop the pepper into a brown paper bag and close the mouth of the bag. Roast the remaining peppers in the same way, and let them sit in the paper bag for at least 5 minutes.

Remove the peppers from the bag and scrape away all the blackened skin with a paring knife, taking care not to pierce the flesh. (You can use a thin stream of running water to help clean away the bits of skin, but sparingly, so the pepper flesh doesn't absorb too much water.) Then carefully carve out the stem end of each pepper and extract all the seeds and whitish membrane.

Preparing the stuffing:

In a medium skillet, put enough olive oil to reach a depth of ¼ inch (1 cup oil for an 8-inch skillet) and heat it to 375°F. Fry the eggplant cubes in batches until golden, about 2 minutes per batch. Drain them on paper towels.

In another, nonreactive skillet, heat 4 tablespoons olive oil and sauté the halved garlic clove over medium heat until lightly golden, then press and discard it. Add the bread crumbs to the pan and stir until they are browned—less than 1 minute. Add the olives, capers, tomatoes, oregano, parsley, and a generous quantity of black pepper. Stir, turn heat very low, and cook 5 minutes. Add the anchovies and the eggplant cubes. Stir once, taste for salt, turn off the heat, and let the filling sit until ready to use.

Stuffing and baking the peppers:

Preheat the oven to 400°F. Oil a baking dish just large enough to hold the peppers snugly. Fill each pepper with a portion of the stuffing and arrange them in the pan. Drizzle a little more olive oil over their surfaces and bake 30 minutes.

Remove the peppers from the baking pan and arrange them on a serving dish. Pour the pan juices around them, cover the dish with foil or plastic wrap, and let the peppers sit overnight—at cool room temperature if possible. If it is necessary to refrigerate them, bring them back to room temperature before serving. ∎

PROSCIUTTO AND PEAR ROLLS

Rotolini di prosciutto e pere

FOR 4 SERVINGS:

Y

A crisp, dry, characterful white is the best match here: Sauvignon, Arneis, Gavi, Pinot grigio—all are good possibilities.

Prosciutto with figs or with melon are classic combinations. We could eat them forever, except that figs and melons are the most seasonal of fruit. Here's a tasty combination of prosciutto with a cool-weather fruit, fall's crisp new pears. Among easily available pears, we like Boscs best in this dish. However, if your local farmers are growing Clapp's Favorites, do try those.

The *robiola* called for below is a very young, not quite creamy cow's milk cheese from the Piedmont. Its delicate, slightly sour flavor beautifully bridges the saltiness of the prosciutto and the sweetness of the pear. The Mauri brand is very reliable and is beginning to appear regularly in Italian specialty stores. It's worth seeking out, because American cream cheese doesn't quite make it in this pleasing recipe. Odd as it may seem, don't stint on the black pepper on the pears—it really pulls the dish together.

4 medium-sized Bosc pears, fully
   ripe
1 tablespoon lemon juice
4 ounces robiola
Salt

1 teaspoon finely minced onion
16 slices prosciutto (6 to 8 ounces,
   depending on size and
   thickness)
Freshly ground black pepper

Peel and core the pears. Divide each one into 8 wedges and drop them into a bowl of cold water acidulated with the lemon juice.

In a bowl, mash the robiola, add a sprinkling of salt and the onion. Beat vigorously with a spoon until the robiola softens to a spreadable consistency. (As an aid to apportioning the spread, divide the mass in half while it's in the bowl, and then in half again. Each quarter of the robiola is the amount to use for 4 prosciutto rolls.)

Lay out a slice of prosciutto and spread it thinly with a portion of the cheese mixture. Take 2 wedges of pear out of the water, pat them dry with paper towels, and lay them together, "head to tail," at one end of the slice of prosciutto. Sprinkle the pears generously with pepper and roll them up in the prosciutto.

Make the remaining rolls in the same way. Arrange them on a serving platter, cover with foil or plastic wrap, and chill in the refrigerator for 30 minutes to firm the cheese before serving. ■

About Mushrooms

For many residents of Italy, the fall is made glorious by mushrooms. Especially in the northeast part of the country, there are restaurants that specialize in mushroom dishes, and autumn is their time to shine. We gourmandized our way through one such splendid lunch some years ago at Da Lino al Solighetto, a classic, airy rustic restaurant near Treviso marked by that combination of innocent enthusiasm and natural courtesy that is the hallmark of the best regional restaurants everywhere. Beneath oak rafters hung with antique copper polenta pots, surrounded by masses of autumn flowers and side tables displaying the season's and the kitchen's abundance, we were served dish after wonderful dish featuring funghi.

We began with a salad of thinly sliced raw *ovoli* (small, brown-capped, white-fleshed mushrooms in the Agaricus family) and slivers of the local prosciutto. We proceeded to a best-of-breed *risotto ai funghi*, with a flavor so intense and an aroma so rich we decided, after serious discussion, that it had to have some white truffle in it—even though that would be gilding the lily with a vengeance. "Of course," the proprietress told us later on. "You always put truffle in risotto ai funghi. They go together." (Easy for her to say, we thought, recalling the price of white truffles in New York.)

The secondo was a tour de force. Before each of us was placed a long oval platter with a hefty strip of polenta down the middle and five different preparations of porcini (the big pore mushrooms identical to the French *cèpe* and the German *Steinpilz*) arrayed around it—large caps grilled, large chunks battered and deep-fried, young buds sautéed with parsley and garlic in the fashion Italians call *trifolati*, thick slices braised, and medium-sized pieces simply sautéed. It was a mycophile's dream of paradise.

You know it's October in Italy when every restaurant north of Rome begins featuring dishes with *finferli*. Finferli are a type of chanterelle, though not the exact same variety as the one used extensively in France and also fairly common in the United States in the fall. To our taste, finferli are even better-tasting than French chanterelles and more versatile. Italians especially like them in combination with shrimp as a pasta sauce. Another wild mushroom especially abundant around October is *chiodini*, the honey mushroom *(Armillaria mellea)*.

Finferli and chiodini are at least identifiable to the botanically curious diner. Other wild mushrooms Italians serve and eat with gusto are more elusive. A few years ago, in a modest trattoria called Jacopone, hard by the bus terminal in the small Umbrian city of Todi, Diane was served a plate of *tagliatelle con funghi del bosco* that was beyond all her experience. The sauce consisted of barely tomatoed olive oil and masses of wonderful mushroom in quite small pieces. She pulled them out for examination, nibbled different bits to determine how many kinds they might be, tried to sort them into different types (feeling like an anthropologist working with potsherds) and finally had to ask her shy young waiter what kinds of mushrooms they were. He professed entire ignorance but promised to try to find out. Disappearing into the kitchen, he returned at length with a slip of paper with these words penciled in by the chef: GRASSELLI BIANCHI—TODI. BIETTE—PERUGIA. NOMI SCIENTIFIC NON SO! That is to say, the waiter explained, one of the mushrooms, gathered right there in Todi, was known locally as *grasselli bianchi;* the other, which came from nearby Perugia, was called *biette.* The chef had no idea what their correct scientific names were. Nor do we, to this day: none of the books we've checked includes those particular local names for any edible mushroom species. Still, it was a fantastic dish and a steal at 7,500 lire (about $6).

Italians in all walks of life are dedicated and knowledgeable amateur mushroom hunters. As the story from Todi shows, the pursuit of the wily *fungo* is also a viable cottage industry in Italy, since restaurants and markets are supplied on a daily basis with fresh wild mushrooms with an efficiency and an economy that so far has been impossible to achieve in the United States. In autumn, the great outdoor markets in the Campo dei Fiori and Piazza Vittorio Emmanuele in Rome and the great covered markets of Genoa and Milan will have stand after stand heaped with funghi fresh and dried—some so amazingly ugly and virulent-looking that even we have not been tempted to try them.

Most of those mushrooms, or their equivalents, do grow in American forests—but of course relatively fewer Americans spend much time in forests or in mushroom hunting, and there's considerable suspicion attached to the idea of eating "toadstools," which means there's little commercial market for them. But we are, happily, beginning to see a few. Funghi porcini, both domestic and imported, are beginning to be available—at very high prices to be sure. (In that respect, it's well worth knowing that the caps of the much more commonly available shiitake, a Japanese mushroom, can be substituted for porcini in most recipes. They are by no means identical, but their textures are similar and there's at least an allusion to the flavor of porcini.) And there has apparently been widespread commercial success in cultivating *cremini,* a variety of mushroom that looks like a dark-capped cousin of our domesticated white meadow mushroom or champignon but has a much deeper and more intense—a wilder—flavor. They grow much bigger, too: the large, opened caps of cremini, sometimes the diameter of dinner plates, are often sold under the name of portobellos. They are excellent for grilling whole: they have a rich, almost meaty flavor that makes it possible to use them as part of a mixed grill or instead of a chop. The smaller, younger cremini are not quite that intense, and will invariably improve a dish calling for ordinary mushrooms—as long as your family or friends like the taste of mushrooms.

When it's simply the essence of mushroom you need for a recipe, rather than the fresh fruiting bodies, you can do very well with dried porcini, which are quite widely available in Italian specialty stores in America. Less than an ounce of dried mushroom, reconstituted in hot water, very carefully cleaned of grit and finely chopped, gives the characteristic porcini depth and resonance to sauces and gravies.

Dried porcini are most commonly sold in fractional-ounce quantities in cellophane envelopes (usually stapled to a cardboard display board). These are usually not as good-quality porcini as those sold in larger packages. Look for large mushroom pieces rather than shards and powder, light brown color rather than almost black, and pieces with some softness and flexibility rather than desiccated chips. Best of all, next time you're in Italy buy a half-kilo or kilo bag—even at the airport on your way home. (You won't have to hide them among your underwear to get them through customs; they're perfectly legal. The USDA doesn't classify dried mushrooms as fruits or vegetables, which *are* prohibited.) Porcini you get in such large bags usually have a high proportion of fine large, light pieces. They'll keep almost forever, and even when old and dry will have better flavor than most you can buy in America.

MUSHROOM CANAPÉS

Crostini ai funghi

FOR 4 SERVINGS:

*D*epending on the meal and service, these versatile hors d'oeuvre can play the rustics or the sophisticates. In Italy, this recipe is done with porcini whenever possible and with other woods mushrooms as available. You can substitute cremini or shiitake caps. The dish is still quite flavorful even when made partially or entirely with ordinary white mushrooms.

3 tablespoons unsalted butter	*½ teaspoon salt*
1½ tablespoons olive oil	*Freshly ground black pepper*
¾ pound firm fresh mushrooms,	*2 tablespoons Marsala*
porcini or cremini if possible,	*1 tablespoon heavy cream*
coarsely chopped	*12 to 16 small round slices of*
1 clove garlic, chopped	*country bread, crusts trimmed*
2 tablespoons chopped flat-leaf	*off*
Italian parsley	

Ᵽ

Still or sparkling, red or white, as inexpensive or as costly as your purse allows or the occasion demands.

In a large sauté pan, melt the butter and oil and add the mushrooms, garlic, and parsley. Sauté over high heat, stirring, 1 to 2 minutes, until the mushrooms take up all the fat.

Reduce heat to low, add the salt and a generous quantity of black pepper. Cook, stirring, until the mushrooms begin to release their juices. Raise heat to medium and cook 5 minutes, stirring occasionally.

With a slotted spoon, transfer the mushrooms to the bowl of a food processor. Raise heat to high and rapidly boil any juices left in the pan until they become a glaze. Add the Marsala and continue cooking, scraping up the browned bits on the bottom of the pan, until the wine is reduced by half.

Puree the mushrooms in a food processor or blender. With the machine running, add the reduced pan juices, then the cream. Taste for salt and pepper. (It should taste slightly oversalted while still warm.) Transfer the mushroom puree to a bowl to cool completely.

When ready to serve, toast the bread rounds, spread them rather thickly with the mushroom puree, and serve at once (before the moisture in the puree softens the toast). ■

HAM AND MUSHROOM TORTE

Torta di funghi e prosciutto

FOR 6 TO 8 SERVINGS:

Try a nice, soft red such as Dolcetto or Merlot or, if you can find one, a Teroldego.

*W*e think of this dish as a gentrified *pizza rustica*, a modernized and sophisticated version of that savory peasant pie filled with assorted cheeses and cured meats. The pastry is not the traditional pasta frolla, but a crisp, short crust that is much easier to work with. For the filling, a béchamel enriched with lots of freshly grated parmigiano is the medium for sautéed mushrooms and sliced ham. Don't be misled by the simplicity of the ingredient list: this is not any sort of ho-hum quiche. By that mysterious Italian kitchen alchemy, the whole comes out greater than the sum of its parts—a delightful harmony of flavors. It's at its best served warm, not hot, but room temperature isn't bad either—and leftovers will keep well for a day, giving someone (usually Tom) a fine little lunch.

FOR THE PASTRY:

1¾ cups all-purpose flour

¼ teaspoon salt

5 tablespoons chilled butter, cut in
   small pieces

1 egg yolk beaten with 5
   tablespoons water

FOR THE FILLING:

4 tablespoons butter

½ pound firm white mushrooms,
   thinly sliced

1 tablespoon all-purpose flour

1 cup milk

Freshly grated nutmeg

3½ ounces freshly grated
   parmigiano (about 1¾ cups)

6 ounces boiled ham, thinly sliced

To prepare the pastry:

Put the flour and salt in a mixing bowl. Rub the butter into the flour with your fingers to obtain a coarse meal. Make a well in the center, pour in the egg yolk–water mixture, and mix with a fork, gradually pulling in the flour until it gathers into a ball. Use your fingers as necessary to incorporate the last of the flour. Wrap the ball of dough in waxed paper and let it rest in the refrigerator while you make the filling.

To prepare the filling:

In a nonreactive skillet, melt 1½ tablespoons butter, add the mushrooms, and sauté over medium heat, stirring often, 5 minutes. Turn heat to high and continue cooking and stirring just long enough to evaporate the cooking liquid. Transfer the mushrooms to a dish and set them aside.

In a small pot, bring the milk to a simmer. In a large pot, melt 2 tablespoons butter and stir in 1 tablespoon flour. Cook over low heat 2 minutes without letting the flour brown. Add the milk 1 to 2 tablespoons at a time, stirring vigorously after each addition, to obtain a smooth, thin sauce. Bring the sauce to a boil and boil slowly, stirring, 3 to 4 minutes, until it thickens slightly. Add nutmeg to taste, then stir in all the parmigiano. Gently fold in the mushrooms.

Assembly and baking:

Preheat the oven to 350°F. Butter a 9-inch tart dish with the remaining butter. Divide the pastry in two slightly unequal pieces. On a floured work surface, roll the larger piece of dough into a circle 11 to 12 inches in diameter and line the tart dish with it. Lay one third of the ham slices over the bottom of the tart. Put in half the mushroom-cheese filling, spreading it evenly.

Make another layer with one third of the ham slices, then add the remaining filling and top with the remaining ham. Roll the remaining piece of dough to make a top crust. Position it over the filling and seal the top and bottom crusts together. Put the tart in the oven and bake about 1 hour, or until the pastry is golden. Let cool 30 minutes before serving. ∎

FENNEL-FLAVORED COCKTAIL COOKIES

Frollini al finocchio

FOR ABOUT SEVENTY 1-INCH ROUNDS:

Y

Any wine you like: frollini love them all.

We fretted about how to translate the name of these toothsome little morsels and finally chose accuracy over style. Whatever they're called, they pack a lot of flavor into a single bite. The dough is easy to assemble and roll, and the results are cheerful and festive-looking. They make good party fare as well as excellent foils for a preprandial glass of wine. Finally, they keep well for a long time stored in a tightly covered tin.

1½ cups all-purpose flour, approximately

⅓ cup minced boiled ham (about 2½ ounces)

⅔ cup grated Swiss cheese (about 2 ounces)

8 tablespoons butter, softened and cut in 8 to 12 pieces

1 tablespoon dry white wine (optional)

1 egg

2 tablespoons fennel seeds

Mix together 1⅓ cups flour, the ham, and Swiss cheese. (A heavy-duty mixer with a flat paddle makes this very easy; otherwise, work the ingredients with a fork or your fingers like pastry.) Add the butter pieces, reserving about 1 tablespoon for buttering the baking pans. Add the wine (if you happen to have an opened bottle; if not, use water) and mix until the dough just holds together. Wrap the dough in waxed paper and refrigerate 30 minutes.

Preheat the oven to 400°F. Butter and flour 2 baking sheets. On a lightly floured work surface, roll the dough to a thickness of ¼ inch. Cut out 1-inch rounds or any desired shapes with a cookie cutter and lay them out on the baking sheets. They can go close together, as they won't spread.

In a small bowl, beat the egg and brush the tops of the frollini with it. Wait a moment and brush again. While this glaze is still wet, put a pinch of fennel seeds on each piece and press them lightly into the surface.

Bake 20 minutes, until the frollini are a light golden brown. Cool them on a rack and store in an airtight tin. ∎

SAINT CLARE'S BREAD

Gatto Santa Chiara

FOR 1 ROUND LOAF:

A classic Neapolitan antipasto bread, subtly but intriguingly flavored with prosciutto and mozzarella. It is named for the ancient convent of Santa Chiara, whose nuns apparently developed the recipe.

Gatto Santa Chiara takes about 5 hours to make all told, but 80 percent of that is pure waiting time—first while a yeast sponge works and then while the dough rises. This is a mannerly dough: it behaves well and is quite willing to mark time in the refrigerator to meet your convenience or speed up if placed in a very warm place.

The bread's rich flavor comes up best while it's still warm from the oven, but leftovers can be born again by toasting. Or try cutting thickish slices, spreading them with a touch of light tomato sauce, and reheating briefly in an oven.

Any light, dry wine, white or red. Lacryma Christi would be ideal.

1 envelope active dry yeast	1 ounce lard, melted and cooled
2 cups all-purpose flour, approximately	1 egg
1 small potato (3 to 4 ounces)	2 ounces cooked ham, diced
1 teaspoon salt	3 ounces mozzarella, diced

In a small bowl, dissolve the yeast in 2 tablespoons warm water and stir in 2 tablespoons flour. Cover the bowl with plastic wrap and set it aside in a warm place for 2 hours, until this sponge bubbles and puffs.

Boil the potato in its jacket in salted water until done. Peel it and pass it through a food mill or potato ricer into a bowl. Add the flour and salt, and beat well. Beat in the melted lard, egg, and the yeast sponge, plus any extra flour necessary to obtain a consistent dough.

If you are using a heavy-duty mixer with a dough hook, knead 2 minutes. By hand, knead 5 minutes. Then add the ham and mozzarella and knead for another 2 minutes by machine, 5 by hand.

Lightly oil a 9-inch pie dish or round baking dish. Pat and press the dough evenly into it. Cover with a towel and set the dough in a warm place to rise until it fills the dish, about 2 hours.

Preheat the oven to 350°F. Bake the bread about 35 minutes, until lightly golden. Remove it from the pan and set it on a rack to cool somewhat before slicing. For best flavor, serve while still warm. ∎

CHEESE SCHIACCIATA

Schiacciata con formaggio

FOR ONE 10-INCH LOAF:

*T*his cheese version of schiacciata bakes to a rich amber-golden color and has a drier texture than some of the other versions given in this book. It just cries out for wine. For picnics (tailgate or otherwise), simple lunches, and informal dining, try splitting a

Any dry wine will match well.

piece horizontally and putting a slice of prosciutto in the middle, or even wrapping a slice of good salami around a wedge. Cheese schiacciata is the most basic form of good eating.

All the ingredients for basic schiacciata (page 35), but reduce the salt to ⅛ teaspoon

2 ounces pecorino romano in all: half grated (¼ cup) and half cut in ¼-inch dice

Prepare the schiacciata as directed in the basic recipe, adding the grated pecorino to the flour and the other ingredients as the dough is mixed. Then knead in the diced pecorino. Let the dough rest 30 minutes and bake as directed. ■

POLENTA CANAPÉS WITH GORGONZOLA

Crostini di polenta con gorgonzola

FOR 4 SERVINGS:

*T*his is a fine savory antipasto and an excellent way to use up leftover polenta. The mildness of the polenta is a perfect foil for a spicy Gorgonzola. If your Gorgonzola is aged and strong, rather than a young *'zola dolce* (remember that heating intensifies the flavor), you may want to raise the proportion of butter. Contrariwise, if you're a rabid blue cheese lover, you may want to lower it! These are among the relatively few Italian antipasti that are best served piping hot.

These crostini will get along well with any wine at all.

1 cup cornmeal	Pinch paprika
2 ounces Gorgonzola dolce	Few drops brandy
2 tablespoons butter, softened	Freshly ground black pepper

Make the polenta as directed on page 390. Pour it onto a dampened marble slab or platter, to a thickness of ⅜ inch. When cool, cut out 8 rounds 2½ inches in diameter.

In a small bowl, mash the Gorgonzola with the butter into a smooth cream. Stir in the paprika, brandy, and—if the Gorgonzola is very mild—freshly ground pepper to taste.

Just before serving time, toast the polenta rounds in a broiler about 2 minutes, until crisp and lightly golden. Remove them to a serving plate. Quickly spread them with the Gorgonzola cream and serve, two to a person. Pass the pepper mill at the table. ∎

PRIMI

After a summer of carefree cooking—pastas with light, quickly cooked or raw sauces, or casual meals without a formal primo at all—it's a positive pleasure to look forward to the more varied and challenging fare of the fall season. Vegetables and fruits from local farms come in almost too fast to keep up with, as if the plants could already sense the killing frosts that lurk behind the gratefully mild evenings and cool mornings. And the cook's instincts respond to that urgency. Let's *do* something in the kitchen!—try new recipes, master a new technique, put up some preserves, throw a dinner party, invite the local Indian tribes to a Thanksgiving feast.

When that harvesttime cooking hunger comes over you, the recipes in this section should give you something to get your teeth into. Here are primi of soup, pasta, rice, polenta, gnocchi, and pizza. You can swell your farm-stand shopping list with eggplant, beans, peppers, zucchini, escarole, mushrooms—and of course tomatoes. As long as the vines produce, we'll seize the tomato season, because once they're gone, it's a long time before the next crop.

Fall is a Janus season: days and nights as close and sticky as summer, then suddenly it's 30 degrees cooler, with half the humidity, and time to put the blankets back on the bed. Just when you start thinking about woolen clothes, Indian summer sneaks back in. And is that baseball or football they're playing on TV? With an eye to those autumnal duplicities, we've presented primo recipes suited to the weather and produce of both summery fall and wintry fall. In that same vein, some call for fresh tomatoes and others for *pelati*—imported canned plum tomatoes. As we've said in About Tomato Sauces, the two are interchangeable in almost any recipe: 1 cup canned equals 1 pound fresh.

Alternatively, you might want to indulge an autumnal cooking yen by putting up some tomatoes of your own, while they're still abundant and your summer's experience has told you which local market sells the sweetest, best-flavored ones. Freezing is the most practical method for most of us, and plum tomatoes take very well to it. Drop a few at a time in boiling water for 10 seconds, slip off the skins, halve them if you like (a wise precaution in years when the crop is bothered by blossom-end rot—a mild pestilence of tomato plants that results in small, hard black spots right in the heart of the tomato but doesn't otherwise hurt the fruit), and freeze them in double plastic bags.

With this system, tomatoes freeze into a single block. Not a problem if you standardize on 1 or 1½ pounds per bag, or whatever quantity you normally need for recipes. However, for greater flexibility, take one additional step: Lay the tomatoes out, not touching each other, on oiled cookie sheets or whatever large platters will fit into your freezer. When they're frozen solid, transfer them to bags. That way, they won't stick together and you'll have a supply of whole or half tomato "ice cubes" to use just like fresh tomatoes—by count, by volume, or by weight.

You'll find a lot of basic "how-to" information in this section, techniques for foods that are typically and essentially Italian. No matter how sophisticated Italian cuisine gets, these sorts of dishes—risotto, polenta, gnocchi, pizza—are, along with pasta, the bedrock on which it rests.

ZUCCHINI EGG-DROP SOUP

Minestra di zucchini e uova

FOR 4 SERVINGS:

A buttery, homey, gentle soup that harks back to the flavors of summer. This pretty, pale, yellow-green minestra amounts to a *stracciatella* with zucchini. Its delicacy makes it a good foil before assertive secondi or after aggressively flavored antipasti. It's also a good way to prepare the palate for mild fish or fowl dishes.

3 tablespoons butter

2 tablespoons olive oil

¼ cup chopped onion

1½ pounds small zucchini, scrubbed and cut in ½-inch cubes

5 cups broth

3 eggs

3 tablespoons freshly grated parmigiano

¼ cup chopped flat-leaf Italian parsley

½ teaspoon salt

Freshly ground black pepper

A light, dry white is your best choice here—a good Soave or Pinot grigio, perhaps even a not too expensive Gavi.

In a large casserole, melt the butter with the olive oil and sauté the onion for 5 minutes. Add the zucchini and cook another 5 minutes, stirring occasionally. In another pot, bring the broth to a boil and add it to the casserole. Stir, cover, and cook gently 30 minutes.

In a bowl, beat the eggs with the parmigiano, parsley, salt, and black pepper to taste. When ready to serve, bring the soup to a rolling boil and pour in the egg mixture in a thin stream while stirring vigorously with a fork or whisk. As soon as the eggs gather, turn off the heat and serve at once. ■

ESCAROLE AND BEAN SOUP

Minestra di fagiole e scarole

FOR 4 TO 5 SERVINGS:

Simply wonderful and wonderfully simple, this hearty country soup delivers pure down-home comfort. Some of our friends think of it as Italian penicillin.

Don't, we beg you, decide that the 6 tablespoons of olive oil in the beginning is excessive. Its interaction with the bean juices is the magic in this soup, as are the extra-virgin olive oil and crushed hot red pepper stirred into the bowls at the table. Think of these not as condiments but as the final steps of the cooking.

This soup is easy to prepare and the final cooking takes only about an hour; but the beans do need to be soaked—either overnight or 1 hour after a 2-minute boiling, as described below (unless you've been able to find fresh cannellini beans, which would certainly be fine)—and then almost fully cooked before they're combined with the other ingredients. These steps can be done a day in advance. If for the final cooking you use a pot without a tight-fitting lid, you'll probably need to add water toward the end, but do so freely to achieve the degree of thickness you like in a soup.

A simple, hearty wine, red or white, with a slight edge to red. Montepulciano d'Abruzzo would be fine; so would Etna rosso or a young Chianti. For a white, try any inexpensive Tuscan white wine.

12 ounces dried white cannellini beans (or fresh, see note above)

6 tablespoons olive oil

2 large fresh or canned Italian-style plum tomatoes

⅓ cup chopped celery

¼ cup chopped onion

Salt

Freshly ground black pepper

¾ pound (1 large head) escarole, washed and coarsely chopped

3 tablespoons chopped flat-leaf Italian parsley

Extra-virgin olive oil

Crushed red pepper flakes

Pick over the beans and rinse them. Put them in a large pot with cold water to cover generously, and bring to a boil. Boil 2 minutes, then turn off the heat and let the beans sit 1 hour in the water. Drain and return them to the pot with 2 quarts fresh cold water. Bring to a boil again, reduce to a simmer, and cook, covered, about 1 hour, or until the beans are almost tender.

Uncover the pot and add the olive oil, tomatoes, celery, onion, 1 teaspoon salt, and a generous quantity of freshly ground black pepper. Stir, cover, and simmer 30 minutes.

While the beans are cooking, bring a large pot of salted water to a boil and drop in the escarole. Stir, cover, and as soon as the water returns to a boil, drain the escarole in a colander. Squeeze some of the water out of the escarole and add the escarole to the bean pot at the end of the 30 minutes. If the beans have absorbed most of their water, add enough more to keep the consistency soupy. Cook 20 minutes more.

Taste for salt. Stir in the parsley and cook 1 to 2 minutes more.

Then turn off the heat and let the soup rest a few minutes before serving. Pass the extra-virgin olive oil and crushed red pepper at the table. ▪

EGG NOODLES ROMAN STYLE

Pappardelle alla romana

FOR 4 TO 5 SERVINGS:

*H*ere is robust fall flavor aplenty. This is a sort of rough-and-ready dish in the Roman offal-butcher tradition. (Roman cooking is noted for its ingenious uses of "variety meats." The folklore explanation is that the people were forced to it because, from time out of mind, the capital's politicians and the Vatican's popes took all the best parts of the animals for themselves.) The broad, wavy-edged pappardelle are most attractive in this dish, but you can substitute fettuccine or even, in a pinch, any short, tubular dried pasta.

A substantial red wine is called for here, such as Barbera, Dolcetto, Chianti, or Lacryma Christi.

½ ounce dried porcini

4 tablespoons butter

8 to 10 ounces chicken gizzards, trimmed and cut in ½-inch pieces

¼ cup dry white wine

2 cups broth, approximately

2 ounces prosciutto fat or pancetta, roughly chopped

¼ cup chopped onion

1 clove garlic

1 cup drained canned Italian-style plum tomatoes, chopped

Salt

Freshly ground black pepper

1 recipe (1 pound) fresh pappardelle or other broad egg noodles (page 54)

¼ cup freshly grated parmigiano, plus more for serving

Put the dried porcini in a bowl and pour 1 cup boiling water over them. Let them sit for 30 minutes, then drain, reserving the water. Rinse the mushroom pieces thoroughly, chop them coarsely, and rinse again to remove all traces of grit. Line a sieve with a dampened paper towel and strain the mushroom-soaking liquid into a small bowl.

In a nonreactive skillet with a lid, melt 2 tablespoons of the butter. Sauté the chicken gizzards 3 minutes, turning occasionally. Pour in the white wine, turn heat to high, and cook, stirring, until the wine evaporates. Add 1 cup broth (or part broth, part mushroom liquid), stir, cover the pan tightly, and simmer the gizzards 1 hour, or until tender. Check the pan frequently and add small amounts of additional broth (or mushroom liquid) as necessary to keep the gizzards from frying.

While the gizzards are simmering, render the prosciutto fat in another nonreactive skillet over medium heat. Add the chopped onion and the whole garlic clove, and sauté 5 minutes. As soon as the garlic turns a light golden color, press it against the bottom of the pan, remove, and discard it. Add the tomatoes and porcini, together with ½ teaspoon salt and a generous quantity of black pepper. Stir, cover, and cook 5 minutes. Set aside until ready to use.

Bring 4 quarts water to a boil with 1 tablespoon salt. Add the pappardelle and cook until al dente. While the pasta is cooking, combine the tomato sauce with the chicken gizzards and their juices, adding a little more broth if necessary for a saucy consistency. Cook 5 minutes.

When the pappardelle are done, drain and transfer them to a heated serving bowl. Toss first with the remaining 2 tablespoons butter and the parmigiano, then with the chicken gizzard sauce. Pass additional parmigiano at the table. ∎

BUCATINI WITH MUSHROOM TOMATO SAUCE

Bucatini con pomodori e funghi

FOR 4 TO 5 SERVINGS:

This classic fall mushroom sauce is glorious when made with porcini or another variety of woods mushrooms, but it's also quite decent just with white mushrooms. Use a branch of fresh rosemary if you have it, so you can retrieve the leaves before serving. If not, chop (if fresh) or crush (if dried) the leaves, which aren't attractive to eat whole. But never buy rosemary already ground: it stales with incredible speed.

This robust sauce wants a not-too-delicate pasta, hence the suggestion for *bucatini*, which are like heavy-gauge, hollow-tube spaghetti. If they're not available, choose a short chunky pasta rather than a long thin one.

A hearty, dry red is optimum: Montepulciano d'Abruzzo, Rosso Conero, Corvo, Lacryma Christi, Dolcetto—all will work well here.

2 tablespoons butter
½ cup thinly sliced onion
1 clove garlic, crushed
¾ teaspoon chopped fresh rosemary
   leaves
¾ pound mushrooms, sliced ¼
   inch thick

1½ cups drained canned
   Italian-style plum tomatoes
Salt
Freshly ground black pepper
1 pound imported Italian
   bucatini

In a nonreactive skillet, melt the butter, and add the onion, garlic, and rosemary. Stir to coat the vegetables with the fat, then cover and cook over low heat 4 to 5 minutes, until the onion softens.

Discard the garlic clove. Add the mushrooms to the pan and cook 2 minutes, stirring. Set a food mill fitted with the medium blade over the pan and mill in the tomatoes. (If you don't have a food mill, pulse the tomatoes briefly in a food processor.) Stir, cover, and cook slowly 45 minutes, stirring occasionally. At the end of the cooking time, add ½ teaspoon salt and a generous quantity of freshly ground pepper.

When the sauce is nearly ready, bring 4 to 5 quarts water to a boil. Add 1 tablespoon salt and then the bucatini. Cook until the pasta is al dente. Drain the pasta in a colander and place it in a warmed serving bowl. Toss with the sauce and serve. ■

MACARONI WITH BAKED TOMATOES

Maccheroni con pomodori al forno

FOR 4 TO 5 SERVINGS:

Y

A white with some force or character—Greco or Pomino, for instance—is your best bet here, though you could also use a mannerly red such as Barbera or young Chianti, especially Chianti Senese.

This is a dish at once simple and extravagent, prosaic and imaginative. Pasta and tomato? Old hat—except when you create the sauce purely by baking sliced tomatoes. That's it: essentially, just tomatoes baked in olive oil, draped over pasta. It makes a pretty presentation and a surprisingly delicate dish, one that really showcases the wheaty taste of good imported pasta.

As we've had occasion to say in connection with other recipes, please don't balk at the seemingly large amount of olive oil called for here. It's the main liquid medium of the sauce. You can, of course, create some additional liquid by using especially juicy tomatoes, but oil tastes better. Plum tomatoes aren't required in this dish, because the baking concentrates the flavor of any variety you use; but this is one of the very few recipes in our entire book in which you can't substitute canned tomatoes.

For a slightly more elaborate dish, top the tomatoes with some shredded basil leaves and thinly sliced onion before baking.

½ cup olive oil

2 pounds ripe tomatoes, sliced ⅜ inch thick

¼ cup chopped flat-leaf Italian parsley

2 to 3 cloves garlic, chopped

Salt

Freshly ground black pepper

1 pound imported Italian pasta corta (ziti, penne, etc.)

Preheat the oven to 350°F. Coat a large roasting pan with a little of the olive oil and spread the tomato slices in it, as nearly in one layer as possible. Sprinkle them with the chopped parsley and garlic, and salt and pepper to taste. Drizzle on the rest of the olive oil. Put the pan in the oven for 30 minutes.

Bring 4 quarts water to a boil with 1 tablespoon salt. Add the pasta and cook until al dente. Drain and transfer to a warmed serving dish. Arrange the entire contents of the roasting pan over the top of the pasta and bring it to the table for the diners to see. (It's a more attractive dish before mixing.) After the presentation, mix the sauce into the pasta and serve it out. ■

COUNTRY WIFE SPAGHETTI

Spaghetti alla ciociara

FOR 4 TO 5 SERVINGS:

*C*iociara means peasant woman in Roman country dialect, equivalent to the more familiar Italian term *contadina*. Any cook anywhere, town or country, should be happy to add this excellent, quick dish to her—or his—repertoire. This is a strikingly harmonious preparation. The tomato almost disappears in the very brief cooking, leaving a juicy sauce of peppers and olives. The pecorino isn't noticeable in itself, either: melted into the pasta and sauce in the pan at the last moment, it blends seamlessly into the whole.

If you happen to have a chitarra among your pasta-making equipment (see page 52 in the Spring section), this is an excellent recipe to use it for. Otherwise, use a good imported spaghetti. And good loose olives, too: they're such an important component of the flavor that trying to use canned olives would be equivalent to playing Mozart on a kazoo.

A simple, fruity red wine is best here. Try Lacryma Christi, Corvo, Montepulciano d'Abruzzo, Dolcetto.

½ cup olive oil
1 cup drained canned Italian-style
    plum tomatoes, coarsely chopped
2 red or green bell peppers,
    washed, seeded, and cut in strips
    2 by ¼ inches
24 Gaeta or oil-cured black olives

(about ¼ pound), pitted and
    halved
Salt
Freshly ground black pepper
1 pound imported Italian spaghetti
2 tablespoons grated pecorino
    romano

In a broad flameproof casserole, warm the olive oil and add the tomatoes, peppers, olives, ½ teaspoon salt, and a generous quantity of black pepper. Stir all together well and simmer uncovered 10 minutes, stirring occasionally. Turn off the heat and set the sauce aside until the pasta is ready.

Bring 4 quarts water to a boil with 1 tablespoon salt. Add the spaghetti and boil until slightly less than al dente. Meanwhile, return the sauce to a simmer. Drain the spaghetti and add it to the casserole. Toss over medium heat 30 seconds, then add the pecorino and toss once more. Serve at once. ■

PALERMO-STYLE ZITI

Ziti con salsa alla palermitana

FOR 4 TO 5 SERVINGS:

*H*ere is yet one more of the infinite variety of lively, zesty sauces that southern Italians make from virtually the same basic ingredients. This Sicilian dish features black olives and tomatoes, like the preceding ciociara sauce, but its effect is quite different. It's a chunky, juicy, spicy sauce, compared to the mellowness of its cousin. We find that people's tastes vary as to the amount of this sauce they like on their pasta, so we dress it rather lightly to begin with and pass additional sauce at table.

A light-bodied and slightly acidic red wine such as a young Chianti or a Barbera is excellent with this sauce, but it also responds well to a fuller, southern-style white, such as Lacryma Christi or Corvo or even Greco di Tufo.

4 tablespoons olive oil

1 clove garlic, halved

4 small anchovy fillets, chopped

20 Gaeta or oil-cured black olives, pitted and halved or roughly chopped

1½ teaspoons capers, chopped if large

Scant ½ teaspoon dried oregano

1½ tablespoons chopped flat-leaf Italian parsley

1 peperoncino rosso

1½ cups drained canned Italian-style plum tomatoes, roughly chopped

Salt

Freshly ground black pepper

1 pound imported Italian ziti

In a saucepan, warm the olive oil, add the pieces of garlic, and sauté over medium heat until they are just golden. Press them against the pan with the back of a fork and then discard them. Add the anchovies, olives, capers, oregano, parsley, and peperoncino. Stir all together and cook over low heat until the anchovies dissolve—about 1 minute.

Add the tomatoes, raise heat to moderate, and cook uncovered 15 minutes, stirring occasionally. Discard the peperoncino, add salt and pepper to taste, and set the sauce aside until ready to use. Reheat it while the pasta is cooking.

Bring 4 quarts water to a boil with 1 tablespoon salt. Add the ziti and cook until al dente. Drain the pasta in a colander, transfer it to a warmed serving bowl, and toss with half the heated sauce. Put the remaining sauce into a bowl and pass it at the table. ∎

SPAGHETTI NORMA

Spaghetti alla Norma

FOR 4 TO 5 SERVINGS:

♀

Why not a fine Sicilian red like Regaleali or, if expense is no object, Enrico IV from Duca di Salaparuta? Failing that, try an Aglianico del Vulture or a Taurasi.

This lovely Sicilian dish was created in honor of the composer Vincenzo Bellini (born in Catania), who wrote the opera *Norma*. Like Bellini's opera, Spaghetti alla Norma is rich and succulent, the whole substantially greater than the sum of its parts.

Preparing and frying the eggplant takes a little time, but it can be done well in advance. Once that's ready, everything moves quickly: 15 minutes to make the tomato sauce (which can also be done in advance), and everything finished in the time it takes the pasta to cook.

To make this dish properly, though, you must have *ricotta salata*. It's a dry, crumbly, slightly sour cheese available in Italian specialty shops. Neither parmigiano nor pecorino romano makes a good substitute for it.

1½ pounds eggplant, peeled and cut in ½-inch slices
Salt
2 cups olive oil, approximately
1½ pounds ripe plum tomatoes, peeled, seeded, and chopped (or pulsed in a food processor)

3 cloves garlic, chopped
6 to 8 fresh basil leaves, chopped
Freshly ground black pepper
1 pound imported Italian spaghetti
2 to 3 ounces ricotta salata, coarsely grated

Preparing the eggplant:

Toss the eggplant slices in a colander with 1 tablespoon salt and stand the colander in the sink for 30 to 60 minutes. Then rinse the eggplant slices, drain, and dry them with paper towels, pressing moderately hard to extract their moisture.

In a medium skillet, pour enough olive oil to reach a depth of ½ inch and heat it to 375°F. Fry the eggplant a few slices at a time, 1 to 2 minutes to a side, until golden. Drain them on paper towels and set aside until ready to use.

Preparing the tomato sauce:

Heat 3 tablespoons olive oil in a flameproof casserole large enough to hold all the pasta eventually. Add the tomatoes, garlic, basil, ¾ teaspoon salt, and a generous quantity of pepper. Cook uncovered over moderate heat 15 minutes, or until the sauce thickens nicely. Set it aside until ready to use.

Finishing the dish:

Bring 4 quarts water to a boil with 1 tablespoon salt. Drop in the spaghetti and cook until slightly less than al dente. While the pasta is cooking, add the eggplant to the sauce and bring it to a simmer.

Drain the spaghetti and transfer it to the casserole with the eggplant and tomato sauce. Sprinkle with the ricotta salata. Mix all together delicately and cook 1 minute. (Don't worry if some of the eggplant slices come apart.) Serve at once. ∎

SAFFRON RISOTTO

Risotto alla milanese

FOR 4 TO 5 SERVINGS:

A big, dry white, such as
Vintage Tunina or Pinot
bianco, or a soft, generous red,
such as Dolcetto or one of the
Lombardy reds that blend
Nebbiolo with other grapes
(Valtellina, Sassella,
Inferno), would match
beautifully with this dish.

*R*isotto alla milanese, along with the Venetian risi e bisi, are the two most famed and best loved dishes in the Italian rice repertoire. This gorgeous golden risotto is also the only member of its class that is not served exclusively as a primo, but also as the indispensable partner to *osso buco* (a recipe for which appears on page 282).

There are many "original and authentic" versions of this risotto, most of which call for the addition of beef marrow. We find that using marrow makes the dish overwhelmingly unctuous, especially for serving with an already rich meat preparation like osso buco. For us, the small amount of dried porcini here adds the resonance of marrow without its heaviness.

A legend dates the creation of risotto alla milanese to the year 1574. An apprentice glassmaker in Milan was nicknamed Zafferano because he insisted on using saffron to enrich all the colors of his stained glass. One day, the master glassmaker teased him about it in front of everyone in the workshop, ending up with, "If you keep on like this, you'll be putting saffron into your risotto!" Shortly afterward, the master's daughter was married to a wealthy merchant of the city. At the bridal banquet, an unexpected dish was brought in: a vast risotto that looked as if it was made out of grains of pure gold—the wedding gift of Zafferano.

1/3 ounce dried porcini	1/4 cup dry white wine
6 cups broth	1 1/2 cups Arborio rice
1/8 teaspoon saffron threads, crushed	1 cup freshly grated parmigiano
4 tablespoons butter	Salt
1/3 cup minced onion	Pepper

Put the dried porcini in a small bowl. Pour boiling water over them to cover generously, let them sit 30 minutes, then drain them, reserving the liquid. Rinse the mushroom pieces carefully, chop them coarsely, and rinse carefully again. Strain the soaking liquid through a paper towel–lined sieve and set it aside.

Bring the broth to a simmer and keep it simmering throughout the cooking. Put ½ cup hot broth into a small bowl, stir in the saffron, and set it aside in a warm place to steep.

In a casserole, melt 2 tablespoons of the butter, add the onion, and sauté until it softens, about 5 minutes. Add the porcini and sauté 1 minute. Raise heat to high, add the wine, and cook until it evaporates. Add the rice, stirring to coat all the grains with the fat. Sauté 1 to 2 minutes. Reduce heat to medium-low and add ½ cup simmering broth. Cook, stirring often, until the rice has almost fully absorbed its liquid, about 5 minutes.

Add the saffron-tinted broth, cook and stir until it is almost all absorbed, 5 to 10 minutes. Continue adding ½ cups simmering broth at intervals for 15 to 20 minutes more, or until the rice is tender but still firm to the bite. If you run out of broth before the rice is done, use the reserved mushroom-soaking liquid—or hot water, if necessary.

When the rice is done and has absorbed almost all its liquid, turn off the heat, stir in the remaining butter, all the parmigiano, and salt and pepper to taste. Serve at once. ∎

About Gnocchi

Gnocchi are wonderful food and deserve to be much better known than they are. "Gnocchi" is a wonderful word, too: though pronounced more or less as *nyucky*, it doesn't seem to carry the pejorative connotations of yuckyness. Must be the ingeniously nonphonetic (to a native speaker of English) spelling. "Gnocchi" is also a plural without a singular: the only Italian use of the singular, *gnocco*, is for a mild insult equivalent to "Dolt!" Presumably, Italians are far too polite to need a locution such as "Pardon me, but I think you just dropped a gnocco into your lap." (Or then again, maybe that's exactly the message carried in the epithet.)

However, let us abandon the language arts and return to the culinary. The basic gnocchi paste is a mixture of potatoes and flour. Since fall brings us a new crop of firm, flavorful potatoes, it's the ideal time to apprentice yourself to the making of this initially demanding and finally forgiving food.

That last remark was meant seriously. Making gnocchi is easy, but like so many other culinary techniques it seems governed by a natural law that demands you get it wrong a few times before you get it right forever. Don't be distressed if your first gnocchi-making experiment results in a pot of library paste; just don't ask anybody to dinner that night.

One important thing to remember is that different potatoes require different amounts of flour. Baking potatoes—e.g., russets—are the best for gnocchi because they are themselves somewhat dry and floury, and consequently blend easily with the flour. Waxy boiling potatoes are the worst: they tend to make a sticky paste rather than a soft, workable dough. But even within a class of potato—say, the ubiquitous "all-purpose" potato of the American supermarket—individual batches vary in moisture content, depending on how long since they've been dug, the conditions under which they've been kept, and so on. You have to learn to adjust the amount of flour to the potatoes you're working with.

Here is a basic recipe for 4 to 5 servings of gnocchi:

1 pound baking potatoes
Salt
1 egg yolk

¾ cup all-purpose flour,
approximately, plus more for the
work surfaces

Boil the potatoes in their jackets in salted water until tender. Drain them and put them back in the pan over a low flame for a few seconds to dry them out somewhat. Then peel them and put them through a food mill or potato ricer into a bowl.

Mix in the egg yolk, ½ teaspoon salt, and flour to make a soft dough. Use as much more flour as necessary to make the dough hold together.

Turn the dough onto a generously floured work surface, knead it briefly, and divide it into 3 or 4 pieces. Take one piece and roll it out lightly with your hands into a rope about ¾ inch in diameter. (If it collapses instead of cooperating, gather it back into a ball and knead in a bit more flour.) Cut it into 1-inch pieces.

Now comes the fun part: shaping the gnocchi:
Take a dinner fork in one hand, as if you were going to eat with it, but turn it sideways so the tines are perpendicular to the countertop. Position a piece of gnocchi dough at the base of the tines and hold it there with the thumb of your other hand.

With a quick flicking motion, roll the dough along the tines of the fork and off them onto the counter. (Think of the motion of striking a match, but put a little spin on the end of it.) It will take a few tries to work out exactly how much pressure to use for a shapely gnocco—one that comes out with a ridged, convex upper surface (from the tines) and a deeply dimpled underside (from your fingertip).

If in your early attempts you press too hard and smear gnocchi paste on the fork, clean and flour it before proceeding. Squashed gnocchi can be patted back into shape, floured, and rolled again. Once you get the feel of it, you can shape gnocchi very quickly—and you should, to keep the heat of your hands from warming and oversoftening the dough. (If you truly can't make them roll and "corrugate" properly, you can give up and simply leave your gnocchi in the form of little nuggets. But they'll be heavier after cooking, and they won't have all the little nooks and crannies to trap the tasty sauce.)

Spread the finished gnocchi on a heavily floured dishtowel (or newspaper in a pinch; newsprint is sterile) until ready to cook. If you leave them longer than ½ hour, check them occasionally and move them around to be sure they aren't sticking to the paper.

Finally, the cooking—which is no challenge at all:
Bring 4 to 5 quarts water to a boil with 1 tablespoon salt. Drop the gnocchi one at a time into the water (so they don't stick together). After 1 or 2 minutes in the water, they'll rise to the surface. Cook them 2 more minutes after that, then drain in a colander.

In Rome, where gnocchi are an institution—every Thursday is gnocchi day in every home and restaurant—they are served with every conceivable sauce. Anything that can dress pasta can adorn gnocchi, and they are delicious with everything from simple tomato sauces to *quattro formaggi*—a dressing of four cheeses melted together, usually Gorgonzola, fontina, ricotta, and parmigiano.

The two recipes that follow are preparations that we find have a particular affinity for gnocchi. See also the Bluefish Gnocchi variant on page 163 of the Summer section.

GNOCCHI GRATINÉED WITH TOMATO AND MOZZARELLA

Gnocchi alla sorrentina

FOR 4 SERVINGS:

Red or white, and as simple or as elegant as your wishes dictate, from a Lacryma Christi (of either color) to a young Taurasi or Greco di Tufo.

This lovely dish combines the delicacy of gnocchi with the verve of a fresh tomato sauce and the sweet-and-sour milk flavor of two cheeses. Here, mozzarella isn't used as a melted topping but is distributed throughout as succulent molten pearls. With a good green salad and a chunk of real bread, we call *gnocchi alla sorrentina* a complete and completely satisfying meal.

When making gnocchi for this dish, keep them a bit firmer and drier than usual. Soft gnocchi tend to semidissolve under the broiler. Any simple meatless tomato sauce will serve, such as the basic sauce from Spaghetti alla Norma on page 250.

¾ cup simple tomato sauce

1 tablespoon olive oil

1 recipe gnocchi (page 254)

½ teaspoon crumbled dried
   oregano

1 ounce grated pecorino romano
   (about ⅓ cup)

7 to 8 ounces mozzarella, cut in
   ½-inch cubes

Freshly ground black pepper

Heat the tomato sauce and keep it warm. Preheat the broiler. Oil the bottom and sides of a large gratin dish.

Make and cook the gnocchi as directed in the basic recipe. Drain them thoroughly and transfer them to the gratin dish. Delicately (so as not to smash the gnocchi), mix in the tomato sauce, oregano, pecorino, and mozzarella. Set the dish in the broiler, as far as possible from the heat, and cook 3 minutes. Serve at once, topping each portion with freshly ground pepper at table. ∎

GNOCCHI WITH LAMB AND PEPPER SAUCE

Gnocchi con ragù di agnello e peperoni

FOR 4 TO 5 SERVINGS:

As we have observed before, cooking lamb in tomato does intriguing things to both ingredients. Here's another example of it, this time an easygoing, slow-simmered mélange of harvest-season flavors. Any cut of lamb will do for this dish: shoulder or trimmings from the front of a leg are ideal. If you don't use the optional peperoncino rosso, the finished dish cries out for a lacing of freshly ground black pepper—and oddly enough, it doesn't really like cheese. This *ragù* also goes very well over any short tubular pasta.

Try a biggish, dry red, such as Chianti Classico Riserva, Vino Nobile, Rubesco, Nebbiolo, or Teroldego.

½ pound boneless lamb, cut in
 ½-inch pieces

Salt

Freshly ground black pepper

4 tablespoons olive oil

2 cloves garlic

2 bay leaves

1 peperoncino rosso (optional)

¼ cup dry white wine

2 large red, yellow, or green bell
 peppers, washed, seeded, and cut
 into strips 2 by ¼ inches

4 ripe plum tomatoes, peeled and
 coarsely chopped (or use canned
 Italian-style tomatoes)

1 recipe gnocchi (page 254)

Sprinkle the lamb with salt and pepper. In a casserole, heat the olive oil with the garlic, bay leaves, and peperoncino. As soon as it is sizzling, add the pieces of lamb and brown them well on all sides (about 5 minutes). Pour in the wine and cook, stirring occasionally, until it evaporates, about 10 minutes.

Remove the peperoncino. Add the peppers and tomatoes and a generous sprinkling of salt. Bring to a simmer, cover, and cook very gently 2 hours. Check from time to time, and if the liquid has evaporated so that the solids are frying in the oil, add a few tablespoons of water (or juice from the tomatoes, if you used canned).

Cook the gnocchi as directed in the basic recipe. Drain and dress them with the sauce, and serve at once. ■

GRATINÉED POLENTA GNOCCHI

Gnocchi di polenta con prosciutto

FOR 4 TO 6 SERVINGS:

*N*ot really gnocchi, but small rounds of a richly flavored polenta, broiled with a topping of melted butter and grated cheese. Cooking this polenta in milk instead of water and then stirring in butter, egg, prosciutto, and parmigiano turn it into a very rich and savory dish indeed. In addition to serving alone as a primo, it's a fine accompaniment for a simple broiled meat.

If you have any reason to fear that your eggs could be harboring salmonella, and therefore need to be cooked more than indicated here, simply add the egg-milk mixture 5 minutes before the polenta is finished. The cooking will kill off any nasty critters.

Y

A big white or a medium-sized red—Pomino, Pinot bianco, Fiano, or Vintage Tunina for the white; and Dolcetto, Rosso di Montalcino, or Carmignano for the red.

1⅓ cups cornmeal

4 cups milk

10 tablespoons butter

Salt

Freshly ground black pepper

Freshly grated nutmeg

2 ounces prosciutto, chopped

2 egg yolks beaten with 1
*   tablespoon milk*

½ cup plus 2 tablespoons freshly
*   grated parmigiano*

Cook the polenta, using milk instead of water, as directed in the basic recipe on page 390. As it cooks, stir in 3 tablespoons butter and a sprinkling of salt, pepper, and nutmeg.

When the polenta is made, take it off the heat and stir in the prosciutto, egg yolk–milk mixture, and 2 tablespoons parmigiano. Spread it on a marble slab as directed in the basic recipe, leveling it to a thickness of ½ inch, and leave it to cool.

When ready to proceed, preheat the broiler. Melt the remaining butter and spread a little of it on the bottom of a gratin dish. Cut the polenta in rounds with a 2-inch cutter and lay them in the dish, overlapping slightly like shingles. (Gather the excess, lightly knead it together, pat out, and cut again.) Sprinkle the remaining parmigiano over them and drizzle on all the melted butter.

Broil 2 minutes, or until the surface of the polenta rounds is crisp and golden. Let the dish sit for a few minutes before serving. ■

About Pizza

Pizza is bread, period. Pizza is also bread, apotheosized, bread metamorphosed into the bearer of the fall's bounty, bread turned into an edible dinner plate.

The word itself indicates how basic to the Mediterranean world that stone-baked disk of dough is: *pizza, pitta, pita*—they're all fundamentally the same, and none of them is far away, in thinness and crispness, from matzoh. There's a major lesson there for all of us who are far distant from our roots, who could never imagine as grade-schoolers how Wonder Bread could ever have been the staff of life.

Those who've eaten pizza in Italy know that on the mainland it is normally a very thin, frequently very crisp, dinner plate–sized disk and that its toppings, while they may be varied, are not laid on with a trowel. In fact, they're probably skimpy by current American standards. Tomato and mozzeralla alone (Margherita) or with anchovy (Napoletana) remain by far the most popular combinations, with *quattro stagioni* (each quadrant of the pizza a different color, for the seasons: tomato for summer, mozzarella for winter, a green herb or vegetable for spring, prosciutto for fall) next in favor, and various versions of *capricciosa* not too far behind (the "caprice" varies with the maker, and may include seafood or olives or eggs, though rarely any meats other than prosciutto).

Being traditionalists at heart (some might say curmudgeons), we've never been able to enter with enthusiasm into the wilder fantasies of "contemporary American" or "Cal-Ital" pizza trends. Our view is, if God had wanted pizzas to be made with tomatillos, beans sprouts, and avocados, She would have arranged to have all those things grow in the environs of Naples.

Whatever the topping, the underlying factor that makes or breaks a pizza is the underlying factor: the bread. Italian flour is different from ours, and so is Italian yeast, and so—alas!—are Italian pizza ovens (theirs are wood-fired). We've experimented extensively to find a dough that, with American ingredients, will give us an authentically Italian flavor and texture. We can't, unfortunately, do anything about the wood-fired oven, but we think we have gotten close on the bread dough.

Here, then, is the latest step in our ongoing search for the perfect Italian pizza dough. It's based on buttermilk, which we find produces a nice thin, crusty, savory dough. However, you can use regular milk, or even water, instead—but then add about ½ teaspoon salt. With buttermilk, salt doesn't seem necessary. You can use bread flour if you have it, though we find it doesn't make much difference in the final product. For a supple, stretchy dough, keep it as soft as possible, using minimal extra flour in the kneading.

FOR 1¾ TO 2 POUNDS DOUGH, ENOUGH FOR FOUR 10- TO 11-INCH PIZZAS ROLLED ¼ INCH THICK:

2 envelopes active dry yeast
1 cup buttermilk, at room
  temperature

3½ to 4 cups unbleached
  all-purpose flour

Dissolve the yeast in ¾ cup very warm (125°F) water. Stir in the buttermilk. Add 3½ cups flour and mix to make a soft dough. Knead 10 minutes by hand or 4 minutes with a heavy-duty mixer with a dough hook, using additional flour as necessary.

Shape the dough into a ball, put it in a clean bowl, cover tightly with plastic wrap, and let it sit in a warm place until double in bulk, about 1 hour. Punch it down, knead it for a moment, reshape it, and let it rise again. If not to be used at once, divide the dough and form it into 4 balls, flour them, wrap loosely in individual plastic bags, and freeze.

We like to make up a double or triple batch of dough at a time and freeze it for later use. However, defrosting yeast doughs need some attention, and not everyone (including us) has the luxury of being at home all day to keep an eye on the dough and use it as soon as it's ready. For those times, we've developed this technique:

The night before you want to make pizza, take a ball of dough out of the freezer and let it sit at room temperature 1 hour. Lightly oil both a plate and the surface of the dough. Set it on the plate inside a plastic bag, tented to keep it from touching the dough. Put this construction in the refrigerator overnight, and leave it there all the next day if you wish. Two hours before you want to eat the pizza, take the plate out of the refrigerator, remove the dough, knead it briefly, and reshape it. Oil the surface again, return it to the plate inside the plastic bag, and let it sit at room temperature until time to use it.

Basic Pizza Equipment

We have a friend who has lived in Italy for several years, off and on. He's a quiet, observant sort of person, a fine amateur photographer. One evening a few years ago, when he and his wife were dining with us in a very "in the neighborhood" pizzeria-trattoria in Rome, he remarked that he'd been noticing a fact for some time, and tonight once again confirmed it: all Italian pizza chefs look crazed.

"Oh, Bruce!" Joan exclaimed, in tones of wifely exasperation. (The cadence was familiar. Diane often finds it necessary to say, "Oh, Tom!" in just those tones, after some outrageous assertion by her own *caro sposo*.) We all craned around in our seats to look at the pizza chef, and we had to admit that this one, at least, certainly looked crazed.

Since that night, we've had many opportunities to test Bruce's hypothesis, and the evidence is building that he's right: pizza chefs in Italy look crazed. Of course, anyone might who had to spend long hours inches away from a raging inferno of superheated brick—with the opening just about at eye level—and who's frequently required to shove an arm into it as far as the shoulder to rearrange burning wood, add more fuel, rake out ashes and insert, shift, and remove an endless succession of pizzas.

Despite those occupational hazards, it's the dream of every amateur pizza maker we know to have a real, free-standing, wood-fired, brick-and-tile, beehive-shaped pizza oven. Ourselves included. (When we win the lottery and retire to a place in the country!) Fortunately, it isn't absolutely essential to making good home pizzas. But you do need some specialized equipment. To wit:

- A stone of some sort for the pizzas to bake on. There are two possible ways of dealing with this: a commercially made pizza stone of a size that fits into your oven (there are several brands, usually available in the kitchenware departments of large department stores); or a number of baking tiles sufficient to line your oven shelf (available in tiling specialty shops and some department stores). Both do the job well, so choose according to aesthetics or availability. Pizza cooked in a pan never has as good a crust as pizza cooked directly on a hot stone.

- A peel; i.e., a wooden paddle for sliding the shaped and garnished disk of dough into the oven. For home use, a short-handled, 12-inch (approximately) diameter peel is handiest. You'll assemble your pizza right on the peel *after* you've generously sprinkled it with cornmeal (which acts like a layer of ball bearings, allowing the dough to slide smoothly off the peel and onto the stone).
- A pizza wheel: a strong, sharp-edged circular blade mounted to rotate at the end of a short, sturdy handle. This is not absolutely necessary, but it is the easiest way to cut a pizza—and besides, it looks very professional.

That's it: you are now a fully equipped *pizzaiuolo,* licensed to invent pizzas according to your own caprice, and to look crazed or not, as you prefer. To get you started, there follow two recipes, one looking backward to the ripenesses of summer, the other looking forward to the heartiness of winter.

Incidentally, you can't have too hot an oven for baking pizza. The faster it goes, the better it'll be. A typical dressed pizza takes 15 minutes to bake at 450°, compared to 8 to 9 minutes at 500°F.

TOMATO PIZZA

Pizza al pomodoro

PER INDIVIDUAL PIZZA:

*N*ot pizza with tomato sauce, but the purest, most un-mediated tomato-and-bread experience. This is a pizza to make at that magical moment in the early fall when tomatoes are still at their peak but the weather has turned cool enough to make an oven-heated kitchen tolerable. Use the best, sweetest, fleshiest tomatoes available, and take care to get most of the water out of them before cooking, so as not to dilute the tomato flavor in the finished pizza. One pizza of the size given makes a modest appetizer for two, a full primo for one.

Simple, not-too-assertive red or white so as not to unbalance the pure aromas and flavors of the pizza. For whites, Soave or Frascati or Orvieto; for reds, Valpolicella or Chianti or Barbera.

1 ripe 7- to 8-ounce tomato, sliced
  ¼ inch thick
Salt
One 7-ounce ball pizza dough (¼
  recipe, page 261)

Cornmeal for the peel
Freshly ground black pepper
¼ teaspoon chopped basil
1 teaspoon olive oil

Half an hour before you are ready to make the pizza, preheat an oven lined with baking tiles to 500°F. Poke the seeds and jellylike pulp out of the tomato slices. Lay the slices out on a rack, salt them lightly on both sides, and leave them to exude liquid until ready to bake the pizza.

Roll the dough into a circle about 10 inches in diameter and ¼ inch thick. Spread cornmeal over a pizza peel and lay the dough on it. Working quickly, overlap the tomato slices all over the dough, leaving a clear rim. Sprinkle with salt, pepper, basil, and olive oil. Slide the pizza into the oven and bake 8 to 9 minutes, or until the crust is lightly browned. ■

MUSHROOM PIZZA

Pizza ai funghi

PER INDIVIDUAL PIZZA:

This splendid, simple recipe is one more wonderful way to use the autumn bounty of woods mushrooms. If oyster mushrooms or shiitake are not available, use cremini or even the common white mushrooms, though they'll produce a less dazzling effect. This isn't a really cheesy pizza; the provolone is just enough to make a nice savory veil over everything. If you're using this as the centerpiece of a lunch or a light supper, it's worth knowing that sliced raw fennel goes oddly well as an accompaniment.

A simple, fruity red wine works best here—Dolcetto, Barbera, Chianti, Lacryma Christi, etc.

1 tablespoon butter

1 tablespoon olive oil

¼ pound oyster, shiitake, or other woods mushrooms

Salt

One 7-ounce ball pizza dough (¼ recipe, page 261)

Cornmeal for the peel

4 tablespoons grated provolone

Freshly ground black pepper

Half an hour before you're ready to make the pizza, preheat an oven lined with baking tiles to 500°F.

In a large skillet, melt the butter and olive oil. Turn heat to high, add the mushrooms, and sauté until all the liquid they give off has evaporated—about 5 minutes. Lower heat to medium, salt the mushrooms lightly, and sauté 2 minutes more.

Roll the dough into a circle about 10 inches in diameter and ¼ inch thick. Spread cornmeal over a pizza peel and lay the dough on it. Working quickly, sprinkle the provolone over the dough, leaving a clear rim, then lay on the mushroom slices. Drizzle on any liquid remaining in the skillet and top with some freshly ground black pepper.

Slide the pizza into the oven and bake 8 to 9 minutes, or until the crust is lightly browned. ■

SECONDI

In Italy as in America, fall brings changes in cooking and dining habits; social changes as well as climatological ones.

Long-cooked dishes, roasted dishes, fancier preparations that require time in the kitchen and some fussing over: all those are of interest again, once summer's heat has passed. Instead of outdoor barbecues with dishes jostling one another companionably on the table all at once, entertaining now means formal dinners, planned and orchestrated for flavor contrasts and counterpoints. Instead of light, chilled white wines, you now want authoritative reds—maybe more than one per meal, to bring out their various excellences. Autumn reopens a complex culinary world, and secondi are often the keystone to designing meals within the wealth of possibilities.

The recipes in this section should offer plenty of material to work with. Prominent among them are game dishes—feathered, for the most part, but also one representative of the furred variety. You'll find preparations here for wild duck, pheasant, quail, guinea hen (a game bird by courtesy of rarity, in America), and hare. Happily, you don't have to be a hunter yourself to enjoy the trophies of the hunt: many of us who cavil at shooting Thumper's cousins have no qualms at all about consuming them. Feather and fur are also represented here more mundanely by chicken and rabbit dishes. Nor have we completely neglected fins and scales.

Veal is another theme here, most prominently in the form of shanks—a cut above the ordinary, in our opinion, and a good value-for-dollar choice for an important dinner, considering the stiff cost of veal. We also offer a veal rollatini recipe that's fine enough, in our opinion, to set before honored guests. And then, for trompe l'oeil effect, a recipe you'll recognize as a very familiar way to handle veal cutlets, except that the central item is an outsize mushroom cap, actually meatier than the meat would be.

But don't think that every recipe here will be too elaborate for anything but weekends and special occasions. Some are extremely simple, like lamb stew and baked pork chops. There's also a splendid, easy tripe dish that might just convert any of your family or friends who believe themselves to dislike tripe. In short, there's something for just about everyone here, from novice cook to accomplished hosts and party givers.

SARDINES BAKED WITH TOMATO

Sarde all'anconetana

FOR 4 SERVINGS:

resh sardines are not exactly seasonal. They appear sporadically in markets at any time of year—apparently whenever the roving schools of fish wander into the same part of the ocean as the commercial fishing boats. So it's hard to plan a meal around them. But we urge you to snap them up whenever you see them truly fresh in a fishmonger's.

People sometimes say they don't care for sardines because of their strong, oily taste. This preparation, from Ancona on Italy's central Adriatic coast, which has you marinate, bread, and bake the sardines on (not in) a little tomato sauce, gentles down the fish's natural oiliness without camouflaging its excellent flavor. Freshly ground fennel seed is sometimes used instead of rosemary in the marinade; this makes a slightly brighter, spicier dish. In addition to a main course, this can be served at room temperature as an excellent antipasto.

Cleaning sardines is one of the easiest of fish-handling chores. Those who do it often (watch your fishmonger!) can simply grip a large sardine's body in one hand and with the other pull down steadily on the head, which will usually come away from the body, drawing the gills and guts with it. If you're more fastidious or your fish are smaller, take a sharp knife and open the sardine's belly from vent to gills, then turn the fish over and make a cut behind the head down to the backbone, and, finally, firmly and steadily pull head and backbone and entrails away from the flesh. The first time may be messy—another culinary apprenticeship—but by your third sardine you should be doing the job smoothly and efficiently. The result should be two parallel fillets, still joined by the intact skin—a sort of sardine booklet.

A bright, acidic white would serve best here—a good Verdicchio perhaps, or a Sauvignon.

1½ pounds fresh sardines, cleaned
and boned
6 tablespoons olive oil
1 teaspoon chopped rosemary
Salt
Freshly ground black pepper

¼ cup finely chopped onion
2 cups drained canned
Italian-style plum tomatoes,
chopped
1 cup (approximately) fine dry
bread crumbs

In a nonreactive dish, lay out the sardine fillets and sprinkle with 4 tablespoons olive oil, the rosemary, ¼ teaspoon salt, and several grindings of pepper. Turn the fillets to coat with the seasonings and let them marinate 30 minutes.

Preheat the oven to 400°F. In a skillet heat 1 tablespoon olive oil and sauté the onion 3 minutes. Add the tomatoes and salt and pepper to taste. Stir and simmer 10 minutes.

Lightly oil a bake-and-serve dish large enough to hold all the sardines loosely. Spread the tomato sauce over the bottom. Put the bread crumbs in a shallow dish. Take the sardines out of their marinade, coat them in bread crumbs, and lay them in the baking dish. Pour the marinating liquid over them and sprinkle with 2 tablespoons bread crumbs. Bake 20 minutes and serve. ∎

CHICKEN WITH CINNAMON AND CLOVES

Pollo alla canevesana

FOR 4 SERVINGS:

his lightly spice-scented chicken dish is probably very ancient. Its curious combination of "sweet" spices and vinegar recalls the days when northeastern Italy was the hub of the international spice trade, the destination of caravans and galleons whose cargoes may have originated in China or India.

The recipe itself is almost effortless. All you have to do is remember in the morning to set up the chicken pieces for their day-long marination; then you poach them in the same dish, with only their own liquids and those of the marinade. By the time the chicken is done, the liquid has evaporated and the chicken pieces brown in the remaining flavored oil.

The intriguing, complex flavor of this dish needs a wine of equal interest. Tocai would be ideal; a good Chardonnay or Pinot bianco would also serve well, as would Pomino bianco or Fiano di Avellino.

3 pounds cut-up chicken
Salt
Freshly ground black pepper
1½-inch cinnamon stick
4 whole cloves

6 to 7 fresh sage leaves
½ cup thinly sliced onion
¼ cup red or white wine vinegar
½ cup olive oil

Marinating the chicken—9 to 12 hours in advance:
Rinse and dry the pieces of chicken. Lay them out snugly in a casserole with a cover and sprinkle them with salt and pepper. Distribute the cinnamon stick, cloves, sage leaves, and onion among them, then pour in the vinegar and olive oil. Turn the chicken pieces over to coat them with the marinade, then cover, and let the chicken marinate at least 8 hours, turning the pieces from time to time. (If the weather is warm, put the casserole in the refrigerator.)

Cooking the chicken:

Put the casserole on the stove, still covered. Bring it to a simmer, then turn heat low and cook gently 45 minutes, or until the chicken is tender. Adjust heat as necessary to maintain a steady simmer, and turn the chicken pieces occasionally. If the liquid has not all evaporated by the time the chicken is done, raise the heat to boil it off rapidly, and let the chicken brown lightly in the remaining oil. Serve directly from the casserole. ■

BRAISED MALLARD DUCK

Anatra alla romagnola

FOR 3 TO 4 SERVINGS:

Y

This delicious, deeply flavored dish deserves a fine red wine. Ideal would be a Barbaresco from a maker like Ceretto, Conterno, Gaja, Giacosa, Pio Cesare, Prunotto, or Vietti.

A classic autumn entree: after all, what is fall without the rich, pungent flavor of game birds? This preparation is specifically meant for a lean wild duck. (It also works with a Muscovy, but if you try it with a Peking, you'll be drowned in duck fat.) It makes a rich, mahogany-colored sauce, which can be served with the nubbly vegetables intact or strained. Since you don't lose much weight in fat with a wild duck, you can actually serve four persons on a 2-pounder—especially in an Italian-style dinner of multiple smallish courses.

In our experience, game birds are rarely as thoroughly plucked as domestic ones, and mallards in particular seem to be sold with a lot of pinfeathers (and sometimes even the odd flight feather) left on. In preparing this dish, therefore, you should build in some time to go over your bird carefully with a large pair of tweezers and pluck out the hard, unsightly quill bases.

½ ounce imported dried funghi
  porcini
1 teaspoon tomato paste
One 2- to 2½-pound mallard duck,
  quartered
2 tablespoons butter
2 ounces pancetta, diced

½ cup chopped onion
½ cup chopped carrot
½ cup chopped celery
½ cup dry white wine
Salt
Freshly ground black pepper

Put the porcini in a bowl and pour 1 cup boiling water over them. Let them sit for 30 minutes, then drain, reserving the water. Rinse the mushroom pieces carefully, cut up any that are larger than 1 inch, and rinse again to remove all traces of grit. Line a sieve with a dampened paper towel and strain the soaking liquid into a small bowl.

Measure out ½ cup porcini liquid and dissolve the tomato paste in it. Rinse the duck quarters, pat them dry, and go over them carefully for pinfeathers.

In a heavy casserole large enough to hold the duck pieces in one layer, melt the butter and add the pancetta and onion. Sauté over medium heat, stirring occasionally, 3 minutes, then add the duck quarters and brown them on both sides.

Add the carrot, celery, and porcini, stirring to coat them with the butter and pancetta fat. Sauté 1 minute, then raise heat to high, pour in the wine, and cook until it evaporates, stirring and scraping up any browned bits from the bottom of the pan.

Reduce heat to medium, sprinkle the duck with salt and pepper, and stir in the porcini liquid with the dissolved tomato paste. Cover the casserole, adjust the heat to maintain a steady simmer, and cook until the duck is tender, about 1 hour and 20 minutes. During the cooking, stir occasionally and turn the duck pieces several times. If the lid of the casserole is not tightfitting and the sauce reduces too much too fast, add small amounts of the remaining mushroom-soaking liquid as needed.

Transfer the duck pieces to a heated serving dish. Defat the sauce if necessary, strain or puree if desired, pour the sauce over the duck, and serve. ∎

ROAST GUINEA HEN

Faraona al cartoccio

FOR 4 SERVINGS:

Y

To match with this bird's simultaneous delicacy and strength, choose a red wine with power and restraint of its own. Youngish (4- or 5-year-old) Taurasi or top-quality Barbera would be perfect.

*I*n Italy, guinea hen is a regular item in the market most of the year round. In America, it's still exotic, and still rates in most people's minds as a game bird, despite its white flesh and relatively delicate flavor. If you haven't tasted it, guinea hen is well worth getting to know. It can be quite delicious, but because it is very lean, you must take care that its flesh doesn't dry out and toughen in cooking. This recipe's foil-and-parchment technique makes for a beautifully moist bird with a very tender breast, and it has the added advantage of permeating the guinea hen with the wonderful scents of sage, rosemary, and juniper berries.

The preparation itself is a snap, requiring about 20 minutes to set up and 1 hour for roasting, with a bird of the suggested size. If you have a larger one that may need more cooking time, you can plunge an instant-read meat thermometer right through the parchment to check for doneness.

1 to 2 tablespoons softened butter	1 tablespoon grappa or other brandy
1 guinea hen, 2½ pounds	Salt
3 tablespoons olive oil	Freshly ground black pepper
8 to 10 sage leaves	6 thin slices pancetta (about 1
1 teaspoon rosemary leaves	ounce)
2 juniper berries	

Preheat the oven to 375°F. Heavily butter a piece of parchment paper large enough to enclose the guinea hen completely. Cut a piece of aluminum foil slightly larger than the parchment and lay it in a roasting pan. Lay the parchment, buttered side up, on top of the foil.

Rinse the guinea hen and dry it inside and out. In a small saucepan, heat the olive oil, add the sage, rosemary, and juniper berries and sauté 5 minutes. Add the grappa and cook 15 seconds more. Lift out the herbs with a slotted spoon and transfer them to the cavity of the guinea hen. Sprinkle with salt and pepper.

Set the bird on the buttered parchment and, using a brush, paint it all over with the flavored oil remaining in the saucepan. Sprinkle it with salt and pepper. Drizzle any remaining oil on the guinea hen's breast and legs.

Drape the slices of pancetta over the bird, then close the parchment around it and pinch the edges to seal them. Close the aluminum foil and seal it as well. Set the pan in the oven for 30 minutes. Then open the foil (but not the parchment), turn heat down to 350°F, and cook 30 minutes more.

To serve, open the parchment and transfer the bird to a carving board or platter. Remove the foil and parchment from the roasting pan, preserving the pan juices. Defat the juices if you like (but they're mostly good butter and pancetta fat) and use them to dress each serving of guinea hen. ∎

CASSEROLE-ROASTED PHEASANT

Fagiano ai sapori veneziani

FOR 4 SERVINGS:

*T*his is a great dish for a fall feast or an elaborate dinner party. The *sapori veneziani* ("Venetian seasonings," though that city certainly doesn't have a lock on celery, carrot, onion, pancetta, prosciutto, sage, rosemary, and white wine) are assertive and complex enough to make even a farm-raised pheasant taste like wild game. They'll do the same for a guinea hen, which can be substituted in this recipe.

If you are entertaining guests, this recipe can be done entirely in advance: reheat the pieces of bird for 10 minutes with the pureed sauce before serving. Grilled polenta (page 390) would be a good accompaniment.

A robust and slightly complex, dry, red wine is needed here. Try something on the order of a 3- to 5-year-old Nebbiolo or Rosso di Montalcino or Chianti (a good Rufina Chianti would be fine).

1 pheasant, 3 to 3½ pounds, quartered	2 ounces pancetta, cut in thin strips
3 tablespoons olive oil	2 ounces prosciutto, minced
3 tablespoons butter	12 sage leaves
1 stalk celery, chopped	1 teaspoon rosemary leaves
1 carrot, chopped	1 cup dry white wine
½ cup chopped onion	Salt
	Freshly ground black pepper

Rinse the pheasant quarters and pat them dry.

In a casserole large and deep enough to hold the pheasant, heat the olive oil and butter, add the celery, carrot, onion, pancetta, prosciutto, sage, and rosemary, and sauté 5 minutes over medium heat. Remove the vegetables to a plate. Add the pheasant quarters to the casserole and brown them on both sides.

Return the vegetables to the casserole, pour in ½ cup wine, sprinkle with salt and pepper, cover, and cook 20 minutes, stirring occasionally. Then turn the pieces of bird over, pour in the rest of the wine, cover, and cook 20 minutes more, or until the bird is tender.

When cooked, remove the pheasant pieces to a heated serving plate and keep them warm. Defat the sauce and puree it through the fine blade of a food mill, keeping at it until the solids are quite dry and all the juices extracted. Stir the sauce, pour it over the pheasant, and serve at once. ■

BRAISED QUAILS ON A BED OF RISOTTO

Quaglie alla piemontese

FOR 4 SERVINGS:

This is an extravaganza of a dish; "elegant" and "soigné" are the words that come to mind. On its own turf—in the Piedmont's red-wine-and-white-truffle country—it would have a snowfall of fresh white truffle shaved over it at the last moment, which would be paradisal. If you can get hold of and can afford a small fresh truffle, by all means use it here.

Even without truffle, the finished dish is rich and butter-lavish in the extreme, in a manner more reminiscent of the extravagances of Milanese or Bolognese cuisine than of Piedmontese country cooking. Our guess is that this is an urban recipe, an example of the *alta cucina borghese,* and probably therefore originally from Turin, that most Belle Epoque of Italian cities. The addition of Marsala makes for a slight smoky sweetness in the sauce, which blends beautifully with the flavor of the quail.

This is one of those rare Italian dishes (osso buco is another) wherein primo and secondo are served together. As with osso buco, part of the beauty of the presentation is the visual appeal of the whole tiny birds in their nest of risotto. However, if you're willing to sacrifice artistic appearance for greater ease of eating, you could use boned quails.

One final comment: If you're not confident of your ability to get the quails and the rice to finish cooking simultaneously, you can do the birds up entirely in advance and reheat them in their sauce just before serving.

Especially with fresh truffle, a Nebbiolo-based wine would be perfect with this dish. Try a simple Nebbiolo from a very good vintage, or a young Barbaresco, or—best of all—a Gattinara of five or six years of age.

8 quails	Freshly ground black pepper
8 sprigs flat-leaf Italian parsley	½ cup dry Marsala
¼ cup leafy tops of celery	2 cups broth
8 sage leaves	3 tablespoons all-purpose flour
4 basil leaves	2 cups Arborio-style rice
16 tablespoons butter in all	1 cup freshly grated parmigiano
Salt	

Rinse and dry the quails. Tie the herbs into a bundle with string. In a large nonreactive casserole, melt 4 tablespoons butter. Add the herb bundle and the quails. Brown the birds on both sides over medium heat. Salt and pepper them lightly and remove them to a plate. Add the Marsala to the pan, turn heat to medium-high, and boil briskly until the wine evaporates, stirring constantly and scraping up any browned bits. Return the quails to the pan, cover, and cook 10 minutes, turning them once or twice.

While the quails are cooking, bring the broth to a boil in a small pot. In a larger pot, melt 3 tablespoons butter, stir in the flour, and cook, stirring, over very low heat 2 minutes without browning. Add a few tablespoons broth and stir vigorously until it is absorbed. Continue adding the broth a few tablespoons at a time, stirring well after each addition, to make a smooth velouté. Bring this sauce to a simmer and cook 2 minutes, stirring.

Stir this sauce into the quail casserole, mixing it with the cooking liquids, cover, and cook about 25 minutes, or until the quails are tender when pierced with a fork. Turn the birds occasionally and stir the sauce, adding a little more broth or hot water if the sauce gets too thick.

Remove the quails, discard the herb bundle, and strain the sauce. There should be about 1½ cups. If not, either boil it down rapidly or stir in enough hot water to reach that quantity. Return the quails to the sauce and keep them warm (or reheat when ready to serve).

Meanwhile, cook the rice. Bring 4 cups water and 1½ teaspoons salt to a boil in a pan with a tightfitting lid. Stir in the rice, cover, and cook over low heat 20 minutes, or until the rice is al dente. Drain it, return it to the pot, and stir in the parmigiano and the remaining 9 tablespoons butter, cut in several pieces.

Make a bed of the rice on a heated platter, lay the quails on top, pour the sauce over them, and serve. ■

SWEET-AND-SOUR BRAISED RABBIT

Coniglio in agrodolce

FOR 4 SERVINGS:

The preceding recipe came from the French-accented north of Italy; this one hails from the Greek and Arab accented south. The classic Sicilian sweet-and-sour flavors are, in their radically different way, as elegant and as rich as any butter-based dish.

Contrary to the usual interchangeability of rabbit and chicken, we feel this recipe really needs the firmness and density of rabbit flesh (guinea hen might work). While you need to factor in time for 4 hours of marinating, the whole dish can be prepared in advance—up to but not including the addition of the *agrodolce* ingredients. They should go in only 5 minutes before serving, as described below: the longer they're exposed to heat after that, the less *agro* or *dolce* the dish will be.

This dish calls for a biggish, complex, red wine. Try Regaleali's Rosso del Conte, Corvo's Enrico IV, Taurasi, or Aglianico del Vulture.

FOR THE MARINADE:

2 cups dry white wine

½ cup thinly sliced onion

1 tablespoon chopped flat-leaf
   Italian parsley

3 cloves

1 bay leaf

4 whole peppercorns

FOR THE BRAISE:

1 cut-up rabbit, 2½ to 3 pounds

1½ to 2 cups broth

2 tablespoons olive oil

½ cup chopped onion

1½ to 2 ounces pancetta, chopped

Salt

Freshly ground black pepper

FOR THE AGRODOLCE:

1½ tablespoons sugar

⅓ cup red wine vinegar

2 ounces pignoli

2 ounces raisins, plumped in hot
   water and drained

In a nonreactive pot, bring all the marinade ingredients to a boil. Turn off the heat and let them cool to almost room temperature. Meanwhile, lay out the rabbit pieces in a dish just large enough to hold them snugly. Pour the marinade (liquids and solids both) over them, cover tightly, and let marinate 4 to 6 hours, turning the pieces midway through.

Put the entire contents of the marinating dish into a large sieve set over a bowl. Remove the rabbit pieces and pat them dry with paper towels. Press the marinade solids against the sieve with a spoon to extract their juices, then discard the solids.

In a small pot, bring the broth to a simmer.

In a casserole large enough to hold the rabbit, heat the olive oil, add the onion and pancetta, and sauté over low heat 5 minutes. Raise heat to medium and brown the rabbit pieces 2 to 3 minutes on each side. Turn heat to high, pour in about ½ cup marinade, and cook until it evaporates, stirring and scraping up any browned bits from the pan. Continue gradually adding and boiling down the marinade, turning the rabbit pieces once or twice.

When all the marinade has been added and is reduced to a syrup, stir in 1 cup broth. Sprinkle with salt and pepper, reduce heat to maintain a steady simmer, cover, and cook until the rabbit is tender, about 30 minutes. Turn the pieces every 10 minutes and add small amounts of broth if the dish appears to be drying out.

When the meat is tender, remove it from the pan and keep it warm. Reduce the sauce if necessary to a coating consistency. Stir in the sugar, vinegar, pignoli, and raisins. Bring the sauce to a simmer, return the rabbit pieces, and cook 5 more minutes. Serve immediately. ■

About Veal Shanks

Veal is an all-year-round meat in Italy, but different cuts of it have their seasons too. Autumn is the time when center stage belongs to veal shanks, a wonderful and undervalued cut. Particularly succulent and fleshy, veal shanks are nevertheless a bit awkward to deal with because of their size—especially in the case of American calves, which are much larger when slaughtered than are Italian. A whole veal shank is not so much a food as a weapon for a caveman, a formidable club of bone sheathed in pale, delicately flavored flesh that rewards long, slow cooking by melting to an almost sinful tenderness.

Only a sumo wrestler, however, could eat a whole veal shank, and their normal size makes them awkward to divide into equitable dinner portions. If you are lucky enough to find a butcher who sells cut and trimmed pieces, of course, you have no problems at all: just buy what you need or what your appetite tells you you need. If you can't purchase already cut shanks, here's a useful way to deal with the problem.

On a day when whole veal shanks are on sale (all veal is expensive, and the better it is—the closer it comes to being real veal—the more costly it is), buy three large ones, which will tip the scales at 7 to 9 pounds. Have the butcher lop the heavy bone at both ends (don't throw them away: save them for the stock pot) and saw each of the shanks into four 2- to 3-inch pieces, each consisting of a generous wrapping of moist, pink flesh around a bull's-eye of bone and marrow.

What you've got there is osso buco, the "hollow bone" that is so much admired in Italy (though it isn't hollow initially. The central marrow is luscious when cooked and should be spooned out and savored along with the meat). In a multicourse dinner, one such piece is ample for a serving—except for the bottommost slice, which is mostly bone. This can go for seconds to a big eater. So sort your twelve pieces into two roughly equal packages of at least four meaty shanks each. Distribute the remaining pieces between the two packages and freeze them for two generous veal-shank dinners for four.

That may seem like a lot of fuss, but your butcher will do all the real work: all you have to do is sort and wrap—and then, of course, cook and consume. The following two "company" recipes should offer plenty of inducement to do that. And for a more down-home, family veal shank dinner, see page 382.

ROASTED VEAL SHANKS

Stinco di vitello arrosto

FOR 4 SERVINGS:

An elegant and complex red wine is what you want here: a Taurasi or a fine Carmignano or Teroldego would be perfect.

In Italy, where *vitello* is a genuinely young calf, the usual serving of this northern dish is one whole shank per diner. Even with small animals, that calls for large appetites: it's probably the most formidable meat dish you'll encounter in Italy. When the calves are running large, the preference there is still for roasting whole shanks, making a dramatic presentation of them, and then ceremonially carving them, taking slices and nuggets for each diner just as if they were one of the great roasts.

Since neither of those alternatives is very practical for home dining, we've worked out a method of roasting smaller cuts of veal shank that gives you all the flavor of the whole roasted joint *and* the additional pleasure of access to that sublime spoonful of pleasure, the veal marrow, the animal kingdom's answer to the truffle.

This recipe requires about 1½ hours of slow roasting with occasional basting. It's ridiculously simple but the results are quite elegant, and it makes a wonderful pan sauce—the kind of foolproof recipe that makes a kitchen duffer look like a culinary genius. Because of its ease, it's also a good company dish to prepare when you need to fuss a lot over the other parts of the menu.

New-crop potatoes mashed with parmigiano (recipe on page 300)—what Italians refer to lovingly as "la purea"—are a heavenly accompaniment.

4 large meaty pieces of veal shank,
  2 to 2½ inches long (plus any
  extra pieces in the package, if
  you've purchased the shanks as
  suggested on page 279)
¼ cup olive oil
Salt
Freshly ground black pepper
¼ cup finely chopped carrot
¼ cup finely chopped onion
¼ cup finely chopped celery
1 clove garlic, finely chopped
1 tablespoon chopped flat-leaf
  Italian parsley
5 to 6 fresh sages leaves, chopped
1 teaspoon chopped fresh thyme or
  marjoram or ½ teaspoon dried
½ cup dry white wine

Preheat the oven to 350°F. Rinse and dry the pieces of veal shank. Oil a roasting pan with 1 tablespoon olive oil. Lay in the meat, being sure that the sides with the wider marrow opening are face up. Drizzle on the remaining olive oil and sprinkle lightly with salt and pepper. Put the dish in the oven and roast 45 minutes.

Remove the dish from the oven and transfer the meat to a plate. Put all the vegetables and herbs into the baking dish and stir to mix them with the pan juices. Add a sprinkling of salt and pepper. Then lay the pieces of veal shank back in. Pour half the wine over the meat, roast 10 minutes, then pour on the rest of the wine. Roast 30 minutes more, basting twice during that time with the pan juices.

When the shanks are done, remove them to a warmed serving platter. Pass the entire contents of the roasting pan through a food mill and transfer it to a gravy boat. Serve at once. ∎

MILANESE BRAISED VEAL SHANKS

Ossibuchi alla milanese

FOR 4 SERVINGS:

Y

*A Sassella, Inferno, or other
Valtellina red would be the
regionally appropriate wine to
serve with this, but other
medium-bodied reds would also
work: Merlot, for instance, or
Venegazzu, or Teroldego, even
Chianti Classico Riserva.*

*O*ssibuchi is the plural of osso buco: *oss' buss'* in most dialects. This is a simple, clean-flavored version of this very traditional dish, with a good bright flavor from the final garnish of *gremolata*, the mince of garlic, parsley, and lemon rind that is its equally traditional dressing.

An interesting trick in this recipe is the removal of the sautéed onions, after pressing them to extract all their juices. It provides all the onion flavor without the danger of burnt onion bits in the final presentation. The left-behind onions themselves can be recycled onto a steak sandwich or an onion focaccia or pizza.

The almost-compulsory accompaniment to this dish is *risotto alla milanese*. Our recipe is on page 252.

4 tablespoons butter	Freshly ground black pepper
½ cup thinly sliced onion	½ cup dry white wine
4 large meaty pieces veal shank, 2 to 2½ inches long (plus any extra pieces in the package, if you've purchased the shanks as suggested on page 279)	1 tablespoon tomato paste dissolved in ½ cup water
	1 large clove garlic, minced
	1 tablespoon minced flat-leaf Italian parsley
Flour for dredging	Grated peel of ½ lemon
Salt	

In a large casserole, melt the butter, add the sliced onion, and sauté over medium-low heat until it is soft and just beginning to color, 8 to 10 minutes. Using a slotted spoon, transfer the onion to a strainer set over the casserole and press with the back of the spoon to extract the onion juices. Discard the onion or save it for another use (see headnote).

Dry the veal pieces with paper towels. Flour them lightly and brown them over medium heat in the onion-flavored butter. Salt and pepper the meat, raise heat to medium-high, and pour in half the wine. After a moment, turn the pieces of veal over and salt and pepper the other sides. Pour on the rest of the wine when the first half has evaporated.

When all the wine has evaporated, arrange the veal pieces so that the wide marrow opening is up. Pour on the diluted tomato paste, cover, and cook at low heat about 1½ hours, or until the veal is tender. During that time, move the pieces around to prevent them from sticking and baste them occasionally with their cooking juices, using a bulb baster. (Don't turn them over, or the marrow will run out.) If the sauce seems to be reducing too much, add 1 to 2 tablespoons warm water—but the veal will probably exude plenty of its own juices.

While the veal is cooking, chop together the garlic, parsley, and lemon peel to make a gremolata. Five minutes before serving, stir the gremolata into the casserole. Serve the osso buco with or over risotto alla milanese. ∎

VEAL ROLLS FILLED WITH PORK, MUSHROOMS, AND PARMIGIANO

Involtini all'abruzzese

FOR 4 SERVINGS:

*T*his recipe offers the traditional hearty flavors of the Abruzzo in an unusually elegant presentation. The veal scallops account for the elegance, the touch of hot red pepper the rusticity. The rolls can be prepared in advance and refrigerated until ready to cook. Experimentalists will find that this filling also makes a very tasty dish of cannelloni.

4 tablespoons olive oil

¼ pound mushrooms, chopped

1 small clove garlic, minced

1 tablespoon chopped flat-leaf
   Italian parsley

Salt

Freshly ground black pepper

1 cup broth, approximately

¼ pound ground pork

¼ cup grated parmigiano

1 egg

⅛ teaspoon crushed hot red pepper

4 large veal scallops about 6 inches
   square (about 1½ pounds)

⅔ cup drained canned
   Italian-style plum tomatoes,
   roughly chopped

To make the filling:

In a small skillet, heat 2 tablespoons of the olive oil over medium-high heat. Add the chopped mushrooms, garlic, and parsley. Stir well, and as soon as they take up all the oil, sprinkle them with salt and pepper, turn heat very low, add ½ cup broth, and cook gently, uncovered, 15 minutes. Add another ¼ cup broth if the liquid evaporates before the end of the cooking time.

In a bowl, combine the ground pork, parmigiano, egg, ¼ teaspoon salt, black pepper to taste, and crushed red pepper. Add the entire contents of the mushroom pan and mix very well.

To prepare the involtini:

Pound the veal slices to flatten them somewhat. Sprinkle them lightly with salt, and spread one quarter of the filling mixture over each one. Roll them up, tucking in the ends, and tie them snugly with kitchen string. Refrigerate if not to be used at once.

To cook the involtini:

In a skillet, heat the remaining 2 tablespoons olive oil. Brown the veal rolls over medium heat. Add the tomatoes and a sprinkling of salt. Cover and cook very gently 1 hour, stirring the sauce and turning the rolls every 15 minutes, and adding a few tablespoons broth if necessary to keep the sauce from drying out. Serve at once. ■

BOLOGNESE MUSHROOM CAPS

Mazze di tamburo alla bolognese

FOR 4 SERVINGS:

The mushrooms of choice for this preparation in Italy, *mazze di tamburo*, are the very large open caps of parasol mushrooms. The Italian name, "drumsticks," is in reference to the early stages of this mushroom, in which a tiny nub of a cap rises on the end of a very tall, straight stalk. At maturity, the cap opens to a size and shape that fully justifies the English name. Since parasol mushrooms are hard to find, we suggest using portobellos, but just about any hefty, flat mushroom cap will do nicely in this dish. The preparation is actually more substantial with mushrooms than it is with meat.

The cutlets can be fully cooked and set up in their baking dish some hours in advance (don't refrigerate them, though), leaving only a brief heating in the oven just before serving.

Wanted here is a medium-bodied (by Italian standards) red wine with some complexity: try a Venegazzu or a Teroldego.

8 portobello mushroom caps about 4 inches in diameter, stems trimmed off	1½ cups fine dry bread crumbs
	1 cup olive oil for frying
Flour for dredging	8 small slices prosciutto (about ¼ pound)
3 eggs, beaten together in a bowl with a pinch of salt	3 ounces fontina, cut in 16 sticks about 4 inches long

Quickly rinse the mushroom caps and drain them briefly, gills down, on paper towels. While they are still damp, dredge them with flour. Dip them in the beaten egg, then in the bread crumbs. Set them on a rack while you prepare the frying oil. (The caps can be prepared to this point in advance and held in the refrigerator until ready to cook.)

In a small heavy skillet, heat the olive oil to 360°F. Put in a few caps at a time, gill side up, and cook until golden, about 2 minutes. Turn them and cook the other side, about 2 minutes more. Drain them on paper towels.

Preheat oven to 400°F. Lightly oil a large gratin dish and arrange the mushroom caps in it. Top each one with a slice of ham and 2 crisscrossed sticks of fontina. Put the dish in the oven and bake 5 minutes, or until the fontina is just melted. Serve at once. ■

ABRUZZESE LAMB STEW

Agnello alla montanara

FOR 4 SERVINGS:

Full-flavored reds with a little tannin work best: for example, Rosso di Montalcino, Nebbiolo, Salice Salentino.

*T*his comfortable peasant dish is as close to effortless as cooking gets: put everything in a pot and cook it for 2 hours, stirring occasionally; serve. It's perfect for the first chilly days of autumn, when it's pleasant to have something simmering on the stove, warming the kitchen, and perfuming the house.

The stew has a nice litle bite from the peperoncino—characteristically Abruzzese—and makes a richly flavorful sauce for itself, which the bread is there to capture. (Polenta would do the job too.) Note that we don't say to dry the pieces of lamb before putting them into the pot. Don't bother to. The meat may exude a lot of pale liquid at first, but the stew needs that moisture to prevent its drying out. It might even need a bit of water added toward the end.

2 tablespoons olive oil

3 pounds lamb stew meat, with
   bone

¾ cup thinly sliced onion

4 to 6 fresh sage leaves

2 tablespoons chopped flat-leaf
   Italian parsley

1 peperoncino rosso

½ teaspoon salt

8 slices day-old country bread

Put all the ingredients except the bread into a heavy-bottomed casserole. Stir, cover, and set over low heat. Cook 2 hours, stirring occasionally.

Toast the bread slices lightly in the oven or broiler. Lay them out on a serving platter. When the lamb is tender, remove it to the platter with a slotted spoon. Defat the sauce, strain it if desired, pour it over the lamb, and serve. ∎

BAKED PORK CHOPS

Braciole di maiale al cartoccio

FOR 4 SERVINGS:

An effortless dish, and a delicious one. Wrapping pork chops in foil keeps all their succulent juices from drying out in the oven, while at the same time the meat takes on a delicate flavor and scent from the herbs that bake along with it. Fresh rosemary really makes a difference here, though the dish will still be good if you have to use dried (if so, use half the quantity indicated).

Choose a good, hearty white, such as Pomino, Pinot bianco, Tocai, or Chardonnay, or a gentle red, such as Barbera or Dolcetto.

4 loin pork chops, 1 to 1¼ inches thick
1 to 2 cloves garlic

1 teaspoon fresh rosemary leaves
2 teaspoons olive oil

Preheat the oven to 375°F. Cut 4 sheets of aluminum foil 12 inches square. Pat the pork chops dry with paper towels and set one in the middle of each square of foil.

Chop the garlic and rosemary together to a fine mince and distribute this evenly over the chops. Drizzle ½ teaspoon of oil on each chop. Close the foil packets tightly, set them on a baking sheet, and put in the oven for 1 hour.

To serve, either remove the chops from the foil, arrange them on a serving dish, and pour the juices from the packets over the chops, or set each foil packet on a dinner plate, open them carefully, and fold back the foil into a boat shape to expose the chop. ■

TRIPE IN GOLDEN FONTINA SAUCE

Trippa alla valdostana

FOR 4 SERVINGS:

ripe suffers from a bad press and a bad image in the Anglo-Saxon world. The word itself has all the wrong connotations, so try to think of it in Italian, where it sounds—and tastes—much better. *Trippa* falls trippingly from the tongue, and this dish, from the half-French province of Val d'Aosta, falls delightfully on the tongue.

This is a lovely, sweet, harmonious concoction, golden-creamy from the cheese in its sauce, fragrant from its basil. A dish to offer people who don't like tripe. The seemingly mammoth quantity of onions melts right in during the long, slow cooking (about 3 hours in all, but with very minimal care).

Be sure to use real Italian fontina, not one of the Scandinavian imitations; the difference in the flavor is enormous. In fact, if you're not familiar with real fontina, take this opportunity to introduce yourself to it: this is one of the world's truly great cheeses.

Serve this dish with boiled potatoes, good bread, and a green salad as a complete meal in itself. And drink lots of wine with it: it loves wine.

The regional choice would be Donnaz, but that's not very widely available in the United States (or in Italy, for that matter). Try instead a good Barbera or a Chianti Classico, a cru Valpolicella or an Aglianico. A reasonably assertive red wine with good acidity is the idea.

4 cups onions, coarsely chopped
   (1½ pounds)

1 carrot, coarsely chopped

1 stalk celery, coarsely chopped

3 to 4 basil leaves

7 tablespoons olive oil

1 cup imported Italian canned
   tomatoes, with their juices,
   coarsely chopped

2 to 2½ pounds tripe, rinsed in
   cold water, drained, and cut in
   pieces ½ inch wide and 2 to 4
   inches long

1 teaspoon salt

Freshly ground black pepper

1 cup broth, approximately

5 tablespoons butter

5 to 6 ounces fontina cheese, grated

In a broad casserole over medium-low heat, sauté the onions, carrot, celery, and basil in the olive oil for 15 minutes, until the vegetables are softened and golden. Add the tomatoes and continue cooking 10 more minutes. Add the tripe, salt, and a generous quantity of pepper. Stir to coat the tripe thoroughly with the vegetables and oil. Bring to a simmer, cover, and cook 2 to 2½ hours, until the tripe is very tender, stirring occasionally. Initially, the tripe will exude a good deal of liquid, but after about an hour it will start absorbing it back. Once it does, check every 15 minutes and add broth, ¼ cup at a time, as necessary. If you run out of broth use water.

When the tripe is fork-tender, stir in the butter and grated fontina. Cook 1 to 2 minutes more, until the cheese dissolves and blends with the cooking liquids into a smooth golden sauce. Serve at once. ∎

STEWED HARE

Lepre in salmi

FOR 6 TO 8 SERVINGS:

⏹

*A dish like this needs a big
and complex red wine:
Amarone would be wonderful,
especially a mature one;
equally fine are mature Barolo
or Barbaresco, Taurasi or
Brunello.*

*A*nother ancient and delicious formal-occasion dish from noble (or at least wealthy bourgeois) kitchens, now prepared largely in restaurants. We first tasted it in Palermo, at the esteemed regional restaurant Charleston. Connoisseurs of French cuisine may notice a great similarity between this recipe and *lièvre St. Hubert.* We would not presume to guess which way the influences ran.

This rich and succulent recipe is, unfortunately, hedged round with negatives, but it's worth the effort of surmounting them. First, hare really means hare: rabbit will not do. Then, the hare has to be tended through at least two days of marinating: it is unquestionably a labor-intensive undertaking. And third, this is not a dish for the squeamish cook, since it requires the animal's blood.

The good news—aside from its flavor, which is nothing but good news—is that you don't have to be a hunter to make the dish, as long as you have a good butcher: game farms nowadays sell dressed-out hares shrink-wrapped in heavy plastic, with the blood in the package. The directions below presume you're dealing with just such a store-bought animal.

FOR THE MARINADE:

½ cup chopped onion

2 chopped shallots

1 clove garlic, chopped

3 tablespoons chopped flat-leaf
  Italian parsley

1 bay leaf

½ teaspoon dried thyme

½ teaspoon salt

6 whole black peppercorns

¼ cup grappa or other brandy

1 cup red wine

FOR THE DISH:

1 hare, about 4½ pounds

½ cup plus 2 tablespoons dry red
  wine

10 tablespoons butter, in all

6 ounces pancetta, chopped

½ pound small white onions

Flour for dredging
½ cup broth

¼ to ½ pound small mushrooms,
cleaned and halved

Two to 4 days in advance:

Unwrap the hare, carefully preserving the blood. Put the blood in a jar, stir in 2 tablespoons red wine, cover, and refrigerate it until the final steps of the dish.

Cut the hare into serving pieces, lay them out in a glass or enameled dish, and add all the marinade ingredients. Cover the dish tightly with plastic wrap or foil and put it in the refrigerator for at least 2 days. If the pieces of hare aren't fully covered by the marinade, turn them once or twice a day.

On cooking day:

Drain the pieces of hare, pat them dry with paper towels, and let them sit on a rack to dry a bit more. Reserve the marinade.

In a heavy-bottomed casserole large enough to hold all the pieces of hare in one layer, melt 8 tablespoons butter. Sauté the pancetta 5 minutes, or until crisp. Remove it to a plate with a slotted spoon.

While the pancetta is sautéing, drop the onions in boiling water and boil 1 minute, uncovered. Drain, run cool water over them, and peel off their skins. Add them to the casserole and sauté until golden and about half cooked (8 to 10 minutes), then remove them to the plate with the pancetta.

Lightly flour the pieces of hare. Brown them on all sides in the casserole, a few pieces at a time, over medium-high heat. When all are done, return them to the casserole and pour in ½ cup red wine and the broth. Cook briskly, turning the pieces once or twice, until the liquid is almost evaporated.

Add all the reserved marinade, including its vegetables. Cover and cook over low heat, turning the pieces of hare every 15 to 20 minutes, until the meat is tender, about 2 hours in all. If the sauce dries out, add a few tablespoons of water.

While the hare is cooking, sauté the mushrooms in the remaining 2 tablespoons butter and set them aside.

When the hare is tender, remove the pieces to a plate. Strain the sauce into a bowl, pressing hard to extract all the juices from the solids, and wash and dry the casserole. Return the hare to the casserole, add the reserved onions and pancetta and the mushrooms. Pour on the strained marinade and simmer about 10 minutes, until the onions are fully cooked. (Again, if the sauce reduces too much, add a few tablespoons water.)

Remove the pieces of hare to a serving dish and keep warm. Off the heat, stir the reserved hare's blood into the sauce, which will thicken it immediately. Continue stirring 1 minute, then pour the sauce over the meat and serve at once. ∎

CONTORNI

In addition to the final flowering of summer's eggplants and peppers, fall brings in a profusion of beans, both green and shell. We've found that American cranberry beans best approximate the characteristics of *borlotti* and the other sorts of fresh shell beans available in Italy, and they can even stand in for fresh cannellini, which are rarely found here. Green beans are green beans, happily, even when they are the large, broad, flattish variety that occasionally appear in American markets under the name of Italian or Roman green beans.

Fall also brings in a new crop of crisp, firm potatoes, for which there are a good many Italian recipes. Especially in the north, Italians eat quite a lot of potatoes, and not all of them are in the form of gnocchi. Since Italian cooking and Italian thinking about diet don't use the concept of "a starch" as a single component in a meal—an idea that has long dominated American menu planning—Italians consequently regard the potato as they do any other vegetable. So they see nothing wrong with a meal that contains both pasta and potatoes. Indeed, sometimes they use pasta and potatoes in combination in the same dish: in Genoa, for instance, a dish of pasta and boiled potatoes dressed with pesto is a regional specialty.

We included one potato recipe among our summer contorni, since the very first new potatoes start that early. Three more are to be found here, and still another among the winter contorni.

You'll also find in this section a few vegetable dishes that make good foils for elaborate secondi—green beans in salsa verde, baked onions, pureed potatoes with parmigiano—and a few others that partner better with simpler grilled or broiled meats—in particular, the eggplant dish, the Calabrese potato salad, and the Tuscan beans. Several can also be used in their own right either as antipasti or as vegetarian secondi—the stewed chick-peas, the baked onions, and the eggplant.

CHICK-PEAS WITH TOMATO AND ONION

Ceci in umido

FOR 4 SERVINGS:

♀
Choose according to your secondo.

*O*utside the Mediterranean cuisines, chick-peas are an underexploited resource. Very mild but distinctively flavored in themselves, chick-peas are splendid vehicles for other flavors and accents. This way of preparing them makes an extremely easy and tasty accompaniment to any simple meat dish. While the soaking and boiling of the chick-peas are time-consuming, those steps can be done well in advance. Then only a few minutes of cooking with tomato and onion serve to *insaporire* the chick-peas quite delightfully. *Insaporire* is a much-used Italian culinary verb meaning roughly "to cook together and trade flavors with"—which is exactly what happens here.

½ pound dried chick-peas
¼ cup olive oil
¼ cup minced onion
2 cloves garlic
1 peperoncino rosso
1 cup fresh or canned plum
tomatoes, passed through a food mill or pulsed in a food processor
1 teaspoon salt
1 to 2 tablespoons chopped flat-leaf Italian parsley

Soak the chick-peas overnight in a large quantity of water. In the morning, drain them, add fresh water to cover them generously, and boil 1½ hours, until they are almost tender. Leave the chick-peas in their liquid until ready to use.

In a nonreactive casserole, heat the olive oil, add the onion, garlic, and peperoncino, and sauté over medium heat 5 minutes. Drain the chick-peas and add them to the casserole. Cook 1 to 2 minutes, stirring often. Add the tomatoes and salt and cook uncovered over high heat 10 to 15 minutes, or until the sauce reduces by two thirds. If the sauce becomes too thick before the chick-peas are fully tender (leaving them in danger of frying), add small quantities of the soaking liquid or plain water.

Remove the peperoncino and garlic, sprinkle with parsley, put into a heated dish, and serve. ∎

ONIONS CASTELLARE

Cipolle alla Castellare

FOR 4 SERVINGS:

*W*e've named this recipe for the Chianti Classico estate where we were first served onions cooked this way. They were so tasty that we found it hard to believe the recipe was so simple. But there it was, and here it is in all its stark deliciousness.

Tuscan red onions are much sweeter and milder than ours, hence the instruction to soak the onions in cold water, which draws out their sharpness. If you substitute large yellow Bermuda onions, you can omit this step. This is a very amenable dish: if the oven is in use for another purpose, it can bake at a lower temperature for a longer time. It can also be done entirely in advance and reheated.

Choose according to your secondo.

4 large red onions, peeled and halved

3 to 4 tablespoons extra-virgin olive oil
Salt

Place the onions in a pan full of cold water and let them soak 2 hours. Let them drain, cut side down, on paper towels for several minutes before proceeding.

Preheat the oven to 400°F. Oil a baking pan just large enough to hold the onion halves snugly, and set them in it, cut side up. Salt them lightly and drizzle 1 teaspoon olive oil on each half, encouraging the oil to penetrate the onion layers rather than run off. Put the dish in the oven and bake 30 minutes.

Drizzle another teaspoon of olive oil over each onion half, return to the oven, and bake 30 minutes more, or until the onions are soft and meltingly tender. Serve hot. ■

TUSCAN-STYLE BEANS

Fagioli alla toscana

FOR 4 SERVINGS:

Choose according to your secondo.

No Italian cookbook can be considered complete without at least one Tuscan recipe for beans: the honor of the Tuscan people, whom other Italians call *mangiafagioli* (bean eaters) demands it.

This is one of the most traditional Tuscan preparations available. The romantic way to cook these beans is in a Chianti flask stripped of its straw, plugged with a wisp of hay, and snuggled into the embers of a fireplace. Less romantic but still an impressive presentation is to use a large wine bottle, set in a water bath and baked in the oven. The trouble with either of these is that you have to shake the beans out of the bottle's neck virtually one at a time, a procedure that usually leads to burnt fingers and short tempers. So we settle for preserving the essential flavorings but cooking the beans in a tightly covered pot on top of the stove.

Any white bean will respond well to this treatment. If you are using dried beans, you'll need about ½ pound. Pick them over, soak them overnight in cold water (or boil them for 2 minutes, then let them steep for 2 hours), then drain them and proceed with the recipe.

2 pounds fresh cranberry beans,
  shelled (about 3 cups)
½ cup olive oil
3 cloves garlic

16 fresh sage leaves
1 peperoncino rosso (optional)
1 teaspoon salt
Freshly ground black pepper

Rinse the beans and put them into a heavy-bottomed pot. Add the oil, garlic, sage, peperoncino, and enough water to cover the beans. Bring to a boil, reduce to a simmer, cover tightly, and cook 45 minutes to 1 hour, until the beans are tender. Stir from time to time to prevent the beans from sticking to the bottom of the pot.

When the beans are done, stir in the salt and add pepper to taste. Discard the sage leaves and peperoncino before serving. ■

GREEN BEANS IN GREEN SAUCE

Fagiolini in salsa verde

FOR 4 SERVINGS:

For anyone who may be familiar with the salsa verde that accompanies boiled meats in Italy: this is not the same animal. This sauce, which is designed to accent the flavor of fresh vegetables rather than the stronger flavors of meats, is considerably lighter and less oily—sprightly even. It cleans and refreshes the palate quite pleasantly, making this dish a good foil to broiled fish or meats, or even secondi with more elaborate, complex flavors.

Y

Choose according to your secondo.

1 pound green beans, washed,
   snapped, and cut in 2-inch
   lengths
Salt
¼ cup chopped flat-leaf Italian
   parsley

1 small clove garlic, minced
1½ tablespoons white wine
   vinegar
2 tablespoons olive oil
Freshly ground black pepper

Bring a large pot of water to a boil. Add the green beans along with 1 teaspoon salt and boil rapidly, uncovered, until the beans are just tender (10 to 15 minutes depending on the age of the beans).

Meanwhile, put the parsley and garlic into a small pot along with the vinegar, olive oil, ¼ teaspoon salt, and a generous quantity of black pepper.

When the beans are done, drain them in a colander and transfer them to a heated serving bowl. Bring the sauce ingredients to a boil, then pour them over the beans. Toss well and serve at once. ∎

EGGPLANT IN EGG-TOMATO SAUCE

Uova con melanzane

FOR 4 SERVINGS:

To accompany this dish by
itself, choose a soft red wine
such as Lacryma Christi or
Dolcetto. Otherwise, choose
according to your secondo.

*W*hich comes first, the egg or the eggplant? Depends on how you look at it. The Italian name for this peasant dish is "eggs with eggplant," but since the eggs lose their distinctive identity in the sauce, we feel the eggplant deserves top billing. The recipe has the look of impoverished-student fare, but it is a very filling and tasty dish nevertheless. And it's pretty too, in a down-home sort of way—chunks of eggplant and tomato popping up like islands in a smooth, pink sea. You can serve it as a main dish on its own, or as an accompaniment to, say, grilled sausages. It also has the virtue of being a very easy dish: it can be done almost completely in advance, right up to the addition of the eggs. The eggplant takes a bit of time and attention early on, but it's well worth it: Serve plenty of good hearty bread with this dish to sop up its tasty juices.

1 ¼ pounds eggplant, peeled and
  cut in 1-inch dice
Salt
¾ cup olive oil
1 pound ripe tomatoes, peeled and
  chopped

Freshly ground black pepper
3 eggs
4 tablespoons grated pecorino
  romano

Toss the eggplant in a colander with 1 tablespoon salt, and stand the colander in the sink for 30 to 60 minutes. Dry the eggplant cubes with cloth or paper towels, squeezing moderately hard to extract their moisture.

In a nonreactive skillet, heat the olive oil to just below the smoking point—375°F. Fry the eggplant in several batches about 3 to 4 minutes, until golden. Drain it on paper towels and set aside until ready to use.

Remove all but 3 tablespoons of oil from the skillet. Add the tomatoes and cook over moderate heat 15 minutes, until they become a rough sauce. Return the eggplant to the skillet, sprinkle with salt and pepper, stir, and heat through.

In a small bowl, beat the eggs and cheese together. Pour them onto the eggplant mixture and cook, stirring, 1 minute, or until the eggs have gathered just enough to make a thick sauce. Serve at once. ■

PARMESAN MASHED POTATOES

Purea al parmigiano

FOR 4 SERVINGS:

Choose according to your
secondo.

This is a terrific way to dress up plain old mashed potatoes. For very special occasions, to really gild the lily, you can beat an egg into the mashed potatoes—and some freshly grated nutmeg if you like it (one of us does; the other doesn't)—put them in a buttered baking dish, sprinkle on some extra parmigiano, and bake them in a hot oven until the top turns golden (or heat them through in the oven and run them briefly under the broiler to achieve the same effect).

We once served potatoes so adorned to a visiting southern Italian wine maker, who was so smitten with their flavor that he insisted we translate the recipe into Italian for him to take home. That seemed to us the highest compliment an Italian recipe of ours could receive.

*1½ pounds all-purpose potatoes,
    peeled and quartered*
*2 cups broth or 1 large beef
    bouillon cube*
Salt

*4 tablespoons freshly grated
    parmigiano*
Freshly ground black pepper
½ cup milk

Put the potatoes in a pot with the broth or bouillon cube and enough water to cover generously. Add 1 teaspoon salt. Bring to a boil, cover, and simmer until the potatoes are done, about 20 minutes.

Drain and mash the potatoes. Beat in the parmigiano, salt and pepper to taste, and then the milk. Serve at once—or gratinée, as indicated in the headnote. ∎

COUNTRY-STYLE SCALLOPED POTATOES

Patate al forno alla contadina

FOR 4 SERVINGS:

℮very cuisine seems to have some variety of scalloped potatoes. The onion-bacon mixture in this dish gives it a nice fillip, and the technique is a little unusual: the seasoned, parboiled potatoes are first baked uncovered and without liquid, then baked again covered and with liquid. The combination produces a very nicely textured dish—al dente potatoes. Cooking time varies because potatoes themselves do, so test them at intervals toward the end of the cooking.

Choose according to your secondo.

Salt

2 pounds potatoes, peeled and
   sliced ¼ inch thick

3 tablespoons olive oil

2 ounces bacon, diced

½ cup thinly sliced onion

2 to 3 tablespoons butter or
   additional olive oil

Freshly ground black pepper

1 cup broth

Preheat the oven to 400°F. Bring 2 to 3 quarts water to a boil with 2 teaspoons salt. Add the potatoes, and when the water returns to a boil, cook 5 minutes, then drain the potatoes in a colander.

In a skillet, heat the olive oil and sauté the bacon and onion over medium-low heat until the onion is translucent and the bacon rendered but not yet crisp, about 5 minutes.

Butter a 2-quart ovenproof casserole. Layer in half the potatoes and sprinkle them lightly with salt and pepper. Spread the bacon-onion mixture evenly over them. Make a second layer of the remaining potatoes, salt and pepper them, and dot with the butter. Put the casserole in the oven uncovered for 10 minutes.

Bring the broth to a simmer. Take the potato dish out of the oven, pour in the broth, and cover it snugly with a lid or aluminum foil. Return it to the oven and bake 20 to 30 minutes more, until the potatoes have absorbed almost all the liquid and are perfectly tender. If you like potatoes crisp on top, turn up the oven heat for the last few minutes of cooking. Serve directly from the casserole. ■

CALABRESE POTATO SALAD

Insalata calabrese

FOR 4 SERVINGS:

This is a pleasant, rustic dish, great for enlivening everyday meals. You can use extra-virgin olive oil for the dressing, but we find it a bit overwhelming in so unassuming a dish. However, the combination of green pepper and potato is better than you'd expect from just tasting the recipe on the mind's tongue. The only trick in making this dish is to peel and dress the potatoes while they're still hot enough to absorb the olive oil. Asbestos fingertips help.

Choose according to your secondo.

4 large baking potatoes (about 2 pounds)
½ cup thinly sliced onion
1 small or ½ large green pepper, seeded and cut in strips about 2 inches long and ⅛ inch thick
½ teaspoon salt
Freshly ground black pepper
½ cup olive oil

Bake the potatoes in their jackets in a stovetop baker or a 400°F oven until they are just done, about 1 hour. Let them cool for a few minutes, then peel and slice them as thinly as you can without their falling apart. Put them into a large salad bowl.

Add all the remaining ingredients. Toss delicately to distribute the oil without breaking up the potatoes. Taste for seasoning and add more salt and pepper if desired. Serve at once. ■

About Cheeses

The formal dinners of fall are ideal occasions for serving a cheese course between the *secondo* and the *dolce,* either to finish the main red wine of the meal or as an excuse to open an even better bottle. For many Europeans (and those with European palates), the cheese tray can be the high point of even the most spectacular meal.

Italians tend to be a bit more restrained about cheese service than the French, for whom the acme of felicity is a restaurant that rolls over to your table two wheeled carts with a selection of forty to fifty cheeses. But that is largely because cheese, like so many other foods, is a very local phenomenon in Italy. If Tuscans, for example, can have a plate with three slices of caciotta made by a local farmer—one cut from a soft young cheese, the second from a firmer, slightly aged cheese, and the last from a wickedly strong, hard, aged specimen—they see no reason to complicate the experience with the addition of "foreign" flavors—even if the foreign cheese comes from a valley fifty kilometers away.

Though individual Italians may be parochial in their cheese preferences, Italy itself is a thoroughly turophilic nation. It makes cheese from the milk of cows, sheep, goats, buffaloes, alone and in combinations. It has even recently enacted a D.O.C. law *(denominazione di origine controllata)* to protect and regulate the quality of its cheeses, just as it did many years ago for its wines. At present, nineteen Italian cheeses have D.O.C.s, and many of them are now available in the United States.

Here is a selected, alphabetical list of Italian cheeses. Because they are living, evolving things, their availability is intermittent in both time and place, and their quality depends a great deal on how well they've been handled. Our list reflects what has been consistently seen lately, in season, in major metropolitan areas on the East Coast.

Asiago. Made in northeastern Italy in large wheels. Semifirm and mellow when young, drier, harder, and more assertive as it matures. Young, it makes an excellent luncheon and after-dinner cheese (it also melts beautifully for crostini); older, it's fine for grating, though a small piece nibbled with a glass of wine is still far from contemptible.

Bel Paese. This is an industrial cheese from Lombardy, invented early in the twentieth century and immediately successful and popular. As industrial cheeses go, Bel Paese stands in the same relation to processed American cheese as fresh white truffles do to canned mushroom slices. A soft cheese, buttery and delicate, delicious by itself or on crackers or with apples and pears. An American version is made in Wisconsin by the Italian firm. It's not bad, but is blander than the import. The easy way to tell them apart is by their wrappings: the import displays a map of Italy, the domestic product a map of North America.

Caciocavallo. A southern cheese, usually gourd-shaped, with a pale, waxy rind. Its flesh is firm and mild to sharp, depending on age. Because these cheeses are very soft when "born," like mozzarella, and are kneaded and molded during their manufacture, they're sometimes given fanciful shapes, like wooden-toy pigs and donkeys. Some caciocavallos are smoked, which gives them a tawny hide and a nice tang.

Caciotta. Made throughout Italy from differing mixes of milks (cow, sheep, goat); usually a medium-sized wheel, semifirm when young; drying and hardening gradually as it ages. It's good to eat at every stage—*fresco, maturo, stagionato*—and each has its partisans, as do the offering regions that produce it. Caciottas from Tuscany and Sardinia are among the most esteemed.

Caprino. A class of young goat cheeses, very fresh and delicate. They come in a variety of shapes, though small rounds and cylinders predominate.

Crescenza. A very soft, often runny, buttery fresh cheese; similar to stracchino (see below), which is a term used for a category of cheeses as well as a general name for any of the members of the class.

Fontina. A semifirm cheese of exquisite flavor, as good for eating in the hand as for cooking (it melts beautifully). Beware of imitation "fontina-type" and "Fontal" cheeses, often from the Scandinavian countries: the real fontina tastes like nothing else and comes only from the tiny northern Italian region of Val d'Aosta.

Gorgonzola. The history of Gorgonzola goes back over a thousand years. The Lombardy town of that name was a traditional stopping and milking place in the annual drive of the dairy herds from their winter pasturage south of Milan to the high Alpine valleys for the summer. The milk was made into cheese at Gorgonzola and then taken to caves in those same valleys for aging. There, natural molds developed into the blue-green veining that gives Gorgonzola its pungency. The best examples have a smooth and moist flesh, lightly to heavily veined depending on age. 'Zola is eaten at every stage, from *dolce* (young and very soft) to *stagionata* or *piccante,* which can be a real test of the true blue cheese fan. At no age is it ever anything less than wondrous with ripe, juicy pears.

Mascarpone. Freshness is crucial to the charm of this extremely rich, almost sweet, cow's milk cheese with a texture like softly whipped butter. It begins to lose its attraction within a few days of exposure to air and refrigeration. It's eaten by itself, or with fruit, or in combination with other cheeses—you may see various "tortes" of mascarpone layered with Gorgonzola and other cheeses—or tossed with and absorbed into fresh egg pasta (see recipe on page 55).

Montasio. From Friuli, this is a zesty table cheese when young and a sharp grating cheese when aged, though even at that age friulani like to gnaw a chunk of it with wine. In Frico (see recipe on page 336), through the alchemy of heat, it becomes a crisp wafer of concentrated cheese flavor. We only wish it were more widely available in this country.

Mozzarella. Please see About Mozzarella on page 124.

Parmigiano. Please see About Parmigiano on page 363.

Pecorino. This name covers a large group of cheeses made from the milk of sheep (*pecora*). The primary ones that come to this country are aged granas intended for grating, usually specimens of pecorino romano. This cheese is by no means a "poor relation" of parmigiano. Certain dishes—usually those of southern origin, where sheep are far more abundant than cattle—absolutely demand the salt pungency of pecorino romano rather than the sweet, almost fruitiness of parmigiano. Although it is also a D.O.C. cheese, we've found a range of quality in American imports and tend to seek out reliable brands like Locatelli Romano. Younger pecorinos can be served on a cheese tray, though they are not for those faint of palate. Pecorino siciliano, an "eating" variety occasionally seen here, has whole peppercorns embedded in it.

Provolone. A firm-fleshed and assertive southern cheese, slightly sweet when young and piquant when older and drier. The young is eaten as a table cheese (you frequently see pieces of it as part of a mixed antipasto in Italian-American restaurants), the older raunchier specimens are used as grated cheese. *Provola* is a name given to a smaller version of provolone.

Ricotta. A very soft, fresh-curd cheese, resembling cottage cheese but with a sweeter taste. Used in all sorts of cooking and also eaten "raw" with fruit or in composed desserts like cannoli. Ricotta can be made at home by mixing a bit of lemon juice into fresh milk and warming it until the curds and whey separate (we gave a recipe in our previous book, *La Tavola Italiana*), but the sad fact is that highly processed American milk makes a dull-tasting ricotta. Some ricotta is left in small baskets to drain, whereupon it makes a soft, crumbly cake not unlike the Greek feta in texture. *Ricotta salata* is a medium-sized round of salted, dried, and firmed ricotta, good for eating by itself or crumbling into salads.

Robiola. Two quite different kinds of cheeses go under the name of robiola. One is a group of fresh, soft, moist cheeses, mostly from the Piedmont, and usually formed in small rounds or squares. Freshness is crucial to these, since the delicate flavor and aroma of young robiola deteriorates rapidly. The other variety, from the same region, is a group of pale to orange-rinded soft-ripening cheeses of more subtle and complex flavor and aroma. They also come in small rounds or bricks, and at their gently runny peak, they stand among the best of Italian cheeses.

Scamorza. A gourd-shaped or spherical southern cheese, in appearance not unlike a caciocavallo (see above), and like it sometimes smoked, sometimes molded into frivolous shapes and tied with string or raffia. Essentially, scamorza is aged mozzarella.

Stracchino. A general name used for a number of very fresh, soft, often even runny cheeses. Though they don't actually ripen, as soft-ripening cheeses do, some can take a little aging. Then their flavor deepens and they begin to resemble soft-ripeners. Crescenza is the best-known variety of the classic stracchino.

Taleggio. A Lombardy cheese, square or rectangular. Its texture and flavor vary at different times of year from very soft and sweetly fresh to firmer and more pungent. An excellent table cheese in either state. Taleggio belongs to the stracchino class of cheeses, most of which are eaten very young and "close to home," but it has greater firmness and staying power, thanks to a month or more of aging that sharpens its flavor, firms it a little, and allows it to travel—but good taleggios still retain a lush velvety softness.

Toma. A whole class of northern semisoft cheeses, many of them soft-ripening. *Tomini* are smaller, fresher versions of all of these—a situation parallel to the two different kinds of robiola. Indeed, some of these cheeses are known indifferently as toma or robiola, depending on where you are in Italy.

Many particular examples of these kinds of cheeses reach the United States bearing regional or brand names as their primary identifying marks, so you may have to scrutinize the label or ask your cheese merchant a few searching questions to discover exactly what kind of cheese you're dealing with. And hope that he or she is knowledgeable enough—and honest enough—to tell you if the cheese is in good condition. Some Italian cheeses look squashed and mauled when they are at their peak of perfection, and others can look perfectly appealing when they're either too young or too old.

Buying Italian cheese in America can be tricky, though the rewards are great. Buying cheese in Italy is all that and more. In About Parmigiano (page 363), we told of one such incident. Another we'll never forget is the time, in Siena, when we inveigled a friend to stop at a chic little shop so we could buy one of the famous caciottas that are the specialty of the city.

Though caciottas are relatively small—about two pounds to a wheel—local people of course never buy an entire cheese at a time. (Should they want that much, they'd go to a farm. We, of course, wanted an uncut one to bring home with us.) Accordingly, the shopgirl asked how much of the caciotta we wanted. Our Italian deserted us as we tried to remember how to say "a whole cheese." We tried various likely seeming phrases. She didn't understand. We tried gestures. She didn't understand. We tried larger, sweeping gestures. She looked aghast: You want to buy *all* the cheeses in the shop? The ridiculousness of it grew on us (though not, unfortunately, on her): There we were, three large giggling persons, standing in this small, elegant shop, trying to act out the concept of wholeness in cheese. We'd probably be there to this day if one of the other patrons hadn't taken pity on us and explained to the young lady that what these *signori* appeared to want was *un formaggio intero*.

If you'd like to set up an Italian cheese tasting, either after the secondo at a dinner party or for an evening devoted primarily to wine and cheese, here are some suggestions that cover most of the range of styles and flavors:

- A wedge of young parmigiano
- A young, fresh toma or robiola
- A well-ripened toma or robiola of the soft-ripening type
- A piece of taleggio
- A piece of fontina
- A piece of Gorgonzola, dolce or piccante

For a cheese course with dinner, as mentioned above, you can either continue drinking the red wine you served with the secondo or try something different. There is no Italian red wine that doesn't like cheese, though some of the lighter wines may be a bit overwhelmed by the stronger cheeses. For a "stand-alone" wine-and-cheese event, you might try a selection from each of our three different size groupings of red wine (see About Wine, page 433), which offers the opportunity to observe the ways the various wines change as they interact with different kinds of cheese.

DOLCI

Oranges and lemons may say the bells of St. Clement's, as the old English folk verse claims, but apples and pears are the song of fall's desserts. We in America are inured, of course, to having apples and pears available year round, and hence thinking of them, along with oranges and lemons, as basically seasonless pantry staples. But in autumn, when they arrive fresh off the local trees (in increasing varieties now that boutique farmers are at last reviving the many strains of apple and pear that were on the point of disappearing because they didn't fit the requisite corporate profile for fruits that would ship 5,000 miles unblemished and keep 5,000 days untasted), we remember what extraordinary foods they are.

Any fine, fresh apple or pear can make a worthy basis for a fall fruit tart, simply sliced thin, layered on a sheet of pasta frolla, liberally garnished with a mixture of sugar and cinnamon (or, as your taste suggests, nutmeg, mace, cloves, cardamom—all the spices of the Indies, which, after all, Italian voyagers were among the first to bring home), and baked in a hot oven.

And now that cool fall weather makes turning on that oven a not unbearable prospect, there is a new range of desserts to get reacquainted with. Baked apples may, to us, seem peculiarly Anglo-Saxon; but Italian home cooks bake apples too, and pears as well. Their artfully simple ways of baking both start out this section. Apples are also represented here in a warm fruit compote—not baked, actually, but flamed like a miniature bonfire of autumn leaves.

Continuing the theme of pears, we present a covered tart of spicy poached pears (pears so poached in wine and spices are not a shabby dessert in themselves) and a heavenly concoction of pears and Gorgonzola. If you haven't yet discovered the sheer ambrosia of an unadorned peeled pear eaten with a dab of unadorned Gorgonzola on each slice, don't even consider the fancier recipe yet. Try the Ur-experience first. Fundamentally canny marketers and bargainers that they are, Italians have a proverb that goes, "Don't ever tell the farmers how well Gorgonzola goes with pears." The synergy of flavors there is enough to make you go out and put a down payment on an orchard and a cow.

To round out the return-to-the-oven revival, we offer two very old regional recipes, one for a delicate cake and the other for a traditional harvest-season rock cookie.

BAKED APPLES

Mele al forno

FOR 4 SERVINGS:

Finish whatever you've been drinking with your secondo.

*T*his is a very simple, family-style preparation, but not quite like the usual American approach to baked apples. The cooking time will vary considerably, depending on the size and kind of apple you're using. We like Staymans and Winesaps best, Greenings next. McIntosh or Rome are not recommended, as they have too strong an urge to turn into applesauce.

Serve the apples hot or warm. If you let them sit too long, their syrup will harden into an impenetrable glaze.

4 large apples	*2 lemon quarters*
⅓ cup sugar	*4 tablespoons apricot jam*
2 teaspoons cinnamon	*1 tablespoon butter*

Preheat the oven to 425°F. Butter a baking dish just large enough to hold the apples snugly.

Peel the apples and remove their cores with a paring knife, cutting from the top and leaving a solid bottom on each apple.

In a small bowl, mix the sugar and cinnamon. Rub the lemon quarters over each apple, including its core cavity, to moisten the surfaces, and then roll the apples around in the cinnamon and sugar, pressing firmly to make the mixture adhere. Set the apples in the baking dish and drop a tablespoon of jam into the cavity of each one. Top with a pat of butter.

Set the pan in the oven and bake until the apples are just tender and the sugar coating is caramelized. Winesaps will take 30 to 45 minutes, depending on size. Greenings will take about 30 minutes. McIntoshes will be done in 20. ∎

AUTUMN APPLES

Mele d'autunno

FOR 4 SERVINGS:

*T*his warm fruit compote seems Halloweeny, possibly because it's flamed. If you don't have grappa for the conflagration, you can use another spirit—rum or brandy—but why wouldn't you have grappa? It's more likely that you won't have *cantucci*, aka *biscotti di Prato* or simply biscotti, the dry, almond-studded zweiback-looking cookies that Tuscans love to dunk in vin santo or espresso. If not, you can use amaretti, the almond macaroons that are widely available in the United States.

One nonpurist note: Italians would never do this, but this dish is heavenly with a scoop of ice cream.

Y

Asti Spumante would be nice, as would a sweet Vin Santo or a Passito.

4 tablespoons butter

4 large Winesap apples, peeled, quartered, cored, cut in ¼-inch slices, and tossed with 2 tablespoons lemon juice

2 ounces clear, unaged grappa

4 tablespoons sugar

4 tablespoons golden raisins, plumped in a small bowl of hot water for 30 minutes and drained

4 tablespoons (2 ounces) pignoli

5 tablespoons cantucci crumbs (about 6 cookies, crushed)

Pinch of ground cinnamon

In a nonreactive skillet, melt the butter, add the apple slices, and sauté 3 to 4 minutes, turning often. Raise heat to high, pour in the grappa, and set it aflame. Tilt the pan back and forth so that all the alcohol burns off.

When the flames die down, sprinkle with the sugar and stir well. Add the raisins, pignoli, and cookies. Sauté, stirring 1 to 2 minutes more. Off the heat, stir in the cinnamon and serve at once. ∎

DOLCI / 311

BAKED PEARS

Pere al forno

FOR 4 SERVINGS:

Y

Finish what you've been drinking with your secondo.

$\mathcal{O}$ne of those genius-of-simplicity dishes. If you're using the oven for something else, your dessert can be baking simultaneously; a lower oven temperature simply means a longer cooking time. We've tried various kinds of pears baked this way, and all seem to come out fine. Devoes, in particular, have a very nice texture baked.

4 *large pears*   6 *to 8 teaspoons sugar*

Preheat the oven to 400°F. Wash and dry the pears and set them upright in individual custard cups. Place the cups on a baking sheet and bake in the oven for 30 minutes, or until a skewer inserted into the pears meets no resistance.

Remove the pears from the oven and delicately peel away their skins, taking care not to mash the tender flesh. Put the sugar on a small plate and roll each pear in it. Place the pears on serving dishes to cool. As the sugar draws out the pear juices, spoon them back over the pears (or let each diner do so when served). Serve warm or at room temperature. ■

SPICED PEAR TART

Timballo di pere

FOR 6 TO 8 SERVINGS:

e discovered this ingenious and wonderfully cooperative pastry crust in an old Piedmontese cookbook, in a recipe that called for the flour to be part *meliga*, a name that our dictionaries said means a type of wild grass. The technique was distinctly odd, but we experimented with all-purpose flour and were pleased with the result. The crust is short and crumbly as a sugar cookie, but tender—not hard, as pasta frolla so easily gets if it escapes from the cook's control. We've since learned that *meliga* is Piedmontese dialect for corn. We tried the recipe a few more times, using combinations of finely ground cornmeal and white flour. They all made reasonable pastry crusts, but we finally preferred our original version, which we give here.

Choose fully ripe pears for this dish, since it isn't necessary for them to hold their shape after poaching. In fact, the filling should bake down almost to a spicy pear jam. Both the fruit and the pastry dough can be prepared a day in advance.

Asti Spumante is lovely with pears.

FOR THE PEAR FILLING:

1½ pounds ripe pears, peeled, quartered, cored, and cut in 1-inch pieces

1½ cups Dolcetto or other full-bodied dry red wine

½ cup sugar

One 2-inch piece cinnamon stick

10 cloves

FOR THE PASTRY:

1½ cups all-purpose flour

½ cup sugar

7 tablespoons butter, melted and cooled to room temperature

2 egg yolks, beaten together with 3 tablespoons water

To prepare the filling:

In a nonreactive pot, combine the pears, wine, sugar, and spices. Cover, bring to a boil, reduce to a simmer, and poach until the pears are translucent and extremely tender, from 30 minutes to 1 hour. If you are doing this step in advance, leave the pears in their syrup until ready to use.

To prepare the pastry:

In a large bowl, stir the flour and sugar with a fork until blended. Make a well in the center and pour in the cooled butter. Gradually mix the flour into the butter. (It will become the consistency of sandy marbles.) Break up the lumps with the fork or your fingers, and when there are none bigger than pea-size left, add the egg-yolk mixture. Mix lightly, first with the fork, then with your fingers, until the dough just holds together. Gather it into a ball, wrap it in waxed paper, and chill in the refrigerator at least 1 hour.

Take it out of the refrigerator 20 minutes before proceeding with the recipe.

To assemble and bake:

Preheat the oven to 400°F. Divide the dough in two uneven balls. Roll the larger one to a thin round about 11 or 12 inches in diameter. Line a 9-inch tart pan with a removable rim. Remove the pears from their poaching liquid with a slotted spoon and spread them over the dough. (You don't have to drain them too carefully, a little of their liquid can go in with them.)

Roll the second sheet of dough to a 10-inch round and position it over the pears. Press the two pastry rounds together at the edges and make a fluted or other decorative edging.

Bake 35 to 40 minutes, until pastry is crisp and lightly golden. Cool the timballo on a rack before disengaging the removable rim and sliding the pan onto a serving plate. ■

POACHED PEARS WITH MASCARPONE AND GORGONZOLA

Pere al mascarpone e gorgonzola

FOR 4 SERVINGS:

*U*nadorned, ripe pears and Gorgonzola constitute one of the greatest desserts in this galaxy. But if you're looking for a more studied and elegant approach to that brilliant flavor combination, this mannerly dish is just the thing.

Part of its appeal is the addition of mascarpone, a fresh, almost sweet Italian cheese that's as lush on the tongue as freshly churned butter. For the Gorgonzola, it's best to seek out the young Gorgonzola *dolce* rather than *piccante* or *stagionata*. The youthful stage of this great blue cheese isn't actually sweet, but it is rather creamy in texture, moist, and still only lightly blue-veined as opposed to the denser, drier, more acrid aged type (which, as one *Monty Python* character says of a mythical Australian table wine, "has a kick on it like an aborigine's armpit"). Of course, you can vary the proportions of the two cheeses according to the virulence of your Gorgonzola and your own taste for the lovely blue mold.

Picolit would be wonderful with this, but alas! it tends to be frighteningly expensive. A dry Vin Santo will also do very well, and so will whatever is left of your dry dinner wine.

4 large firm pears

1 cup dry white wine

⅔ cup sugar

Small piece cinnamon stick

3 cloves

½ cup mascarpone (about 5 ounces)

3 to 4 ounces Gorgonzola, at room temperature

Peel, halve, and core the pears. In a nonreactive pot just large enough to hold them snugly, place them in a single layer. Pour in the wine and enough water to barely cover. Add the sugar, cinnamon, and cloves. Bring to a boil, reduce to a simmer, cover, and poach until the pears are just tender, about 15 minutes.

While the pears are cooking, cream the two cheeses together. With a slotted spoon, remove the pears to a dish. Rapidly boil the poaching liquid until it is reduced to a thin syrup.

Shortly before serving time, put the pear syrup into a flame-proof gratin dish and bring it to a simmer. Lay in the pear halves, cut side up, and warm them 1 to 2 minutes, basting two or three times with the syrup. Put a dollop of the cheese filling in the center of each pear. Cook 30 seconds more, basting once or twice again. Serve hot in the gratin dish, giving each person two pear halves and a portion of syrup. ■

SAND TART

Torta sabbiosa

FOR 6 TO 8 SERVINGS:

Vin Santo is an ideal companion to this delicate cake.

This subtle, extremely delicate cake has an unusual, pleasantly grainy texture that results from its combination of cornmeal and potato starch. It's related to a rich shortcake, but the baking powder and the beaten egg whites keep it light. Proportions are a bit tricky, so we've given critical quantities by both volume (in the usual American measures) and weight. If you have a kitchen scale, this is a good time to use it.

Also, please note the instructions for slicing and serving, or you may run into difficulties: its "sandy" composition makes the cake very crumbly.

18 tablespoons softened butter

1 cup fine white cornmeal (5½ ounces by weight)

1 cup potato starch (5½ ounces by weight)

1 tablespoon baking powder

½ teaspoon salt

1 cup plus 2 tablespoons sugar (7 ounces by weight)

2 eggs, separated

1 tablespoon anisette liqueur

½ teaspoon vanilla extract

Confectioners' sugar

Preheat the oven to 350°F. Butter a 10-inch round baking dish with 1 tablespoon of the butter. Sift together the cornmeal, potato starch, baking powder, and salt.

In an electric mixer, cream the sugar and the remaining butter until light and fluffy. Beat in the egg yolks, anisette, and vanilla. Gradually beat in the dry ingredients to make a dense batter.

In a separate bowl, whip the egg whites until they stand in soft peaks. Fold them into the batter. Transfer the mixture to the buttered baking pan and set it in the oven. Bake 30 to 40 minutes. Test by plunging a toothpick or skewer into the center of the cake. When it comes out clean, the cake is done. Cool the finished cake on a rack, and sprinkle its top with confectioners' sugar before serving.

Because this is such a delicate cake, it must be served directly from its baking pan. Cut it with a very sharp knife and remove the pieces carefully with a cake server. ■

SPICED HONEY-NUT BALLS

Pan pepato

FOR ABOUT 16 BALLS:

Vin Santo.

 $\mathcal{T}$ hree kinds of nuts; citron and raisins and honey; chocolate, nutmeg, and black pepper—this harvesttime specialty of Umbria and Abruzzo is obviously an ancient type of sweet.

The traditional recipe makes bun-sized pieces. Since they're so rich, we've suggested walnut-sized balls, which take well to dipping in a glass of Vin Santo. Watch the time very carefully as they bake, because the bottoms burn easily.

1 ounce raisins	*½ teaspoon freshly ground black*
2 ounces each shelled walnuts,	*pepper*
almonds, and hazelnuts	*½ teaspoon freshly grated nutmeg*
1 ounce citron, finely chopped	*4 tablespoons honey*
1 ounce semisweet chocolate morsels	*½ cup plus 2 tablespoons*
¼ teaspoon salt	*all-purpose flour*

Preheat the oven to 400°F. Put the raisins in a small bowl and add hot water to cover.

Put the walnuts, almonds, and hazelnuts on a baking sheet, keeping the hazelnuts to one side. Toast the nuts in the oven 5 minutes. Remove them and rub the hazelnuts in a rough towel to get off as much of the bitter brown skins as possible.

Chop all three nuts together finely (or pulse them in a food processor). Put them in a large bowl. Drain the raisins, squeeze them lightly, and add them to the bowl, along with the citron, chocolate, salt, pepper, and nutmeg. Mix well.

Mix the honey with 1 tablespoon hot water to loosen its consistency, and add it to the fruit-nut mixture. Sift on the flour and mix well to obtain a dense dough.

Oil or butter a baking sheet. Break off bits of the dough, roll them between floured palms into balls about 2 inches in diameter.

If chocolate bits come to the surface, poke them into the center of the balls (otherwise they'll melt and burn on the baking sheet). Set the balls on the baking sheet, put it in the oven, and immediately turn heat down to 350°F. Bake about 20 to 25 minutes, until the balls are golden brown. Cool on a rack.

After the balls are completely cool, they can be kept for some weeks in a tightly covered tin. ■

INVERNO

· Winter ·

In Italy, winter simplifies at the same time that it complicates. If summer is stone, then winter is light—a steadier, clearer light than the dazzle and glare of summer, a light that lets you see things whole. To see things whole in this long, variegated peninsula is to realize how basic and conservative are the rhythms and patterns that underlie the impassioned exfoliation that is Italian life. Sculpture, painting, music, opera, and all the arts of civilized life—the arts of dress and address, fashion, and style—grow out of the clear-eyed observance of the realities of the eternal cycle that winter clarifies and completes.

Winter in Italy is light also in the sense of understanding. In the cool, silver light of winter, you can see more clearly the slightly melancholy, distinctly conservative core that underlies a country and a national character that at other times can seem all flamboyance and opera buffa. Even the holidays and feasts change character: instead of the national flight to the seashore of Ferragosto and the secular gaiety of the Festa di Noiantri, the winter calendar measures itself across a slow progression of liturgical observances: Advent, Christmas (not at all the secular spending extravaganza it is in America), Epiphany (when La Befana, the winter witch, brings presents to Italian children), and, finally, after Carnevale, the long, lean Lent that leads up to Easter and the start of another cycle.

The hearth, the home, the neighborhood. Local people, local shops, local restaurants. The circle of life draws smaller and closer as the days get colder and the clear winter light surrenders earlier and earlier to the enveloping dark. The warmth of family and friends, the warmth of familiar food, taken in familiar places, at traditional times: these carry one through the cold, the dark, the turning inward that winter enforces.

Even the casual visitor can see the difference. In the countryside, summer's jungle

greens and blazing scarlets and desert umbers have long faded to cool and gentle yellows and browns. The bright, burning sunlight that danced in the air a few months ago has stilled to a silvery light that softens all the colors and structures it reveals. In the cities, Italians of all classes, visible now that the great flood of gaudily dressed tourists has abated, reveal the ageless domestic and work rhythms that persisted all through the pleasure hunt of summer. To the visitor's eye, they materialize as if by magic, a serious, even formal horde, clad in their businesslike dark woolens, as if all over Italy citizens had been waiting for the signal of the first cold evening to metamorphose via their wardrobes. For the traveler, even the cities themselves change their appearance: instead of eye-dazzling, glittering surfaces, they now present themselves as all light and shadow, chiaroscuros and wash tints of gray and silver and ash and charcoal replacing the bold, primary colors of summer.

We experienced the magic of this transformation for the first time in Venice, on a visit that began with bright, lingering sunny days—an Italian Indian summer. One night, suddenly, the weather changed and we awoke to find the brilliant colors of the city's gaudy summer face completely gone. Yesterday, the vast front of Saint Mark's cathedral had been an icon of burning gold. Today, without the floodlighting of sunshine, we could discern its sturdy Romanesque skeleton and the essential simplicity of its design. The same was true of the huge piazza before it—always in summer a formless blur of color, with tourist throngs milling and laughing and photographing, children ricocheting through on foot and bicycle and skateboard, and shoals of pigeons rising from underfoot to wing past your ears, wheel overhead, settle briefly, and bolt into the sky again. Now—the crowds thinned, the pigeons suddenly huddling for warmth in eaves and pediments all around the square—we could see the geometry and the architectural precision that Canaletto and Guardi recorded two centuries ago, still there, now undisguised by all that great concourse of people and motion and color. Soft wisps of mist drifted over the canals, and hints of cottony fog hung over the lagoon, making it look smaller and more intimate, more private. Overnight, the pagan Venetian reds and golds had vanished, to be replaced by a veiled wraith of silver and gray and white, a city just as beautiful as summertime Venice, but more haunting, more meditative: we understood, for the very first time, how and why Venice could have been called La Serenissima.

Naples, Florence, Rome—all seem to change the same way. Rome, in the glare of summer a city of stones and ruins and monuments, under the silver kiss of winter sunlight becomes a city of people—not tourists, but shopkeepers and commuters and office workers, diners and shoppers and loungers, who were there all along but now seem able to reclaim their city for themselves. Even the seemingly most immutable of monuments and stones and ruins reveal themselves in a new light, even if it is just the light of our delayed comprehension. The Forum, for instance, with its flowering shrubs and wild mint, masquerades all summer long as landscape. In winter, we can see it as architecture and—even more telling—as human relics: all around the city small shopkeepers still set out their wares in arcades and *botteghe* exactly like those of the Forum. Winter presents Italy in a humanizing light: it lets you see the country as it is really lived in, see how Italians really cope with their cumbersome thirty centuries of past and their problematic present when the summer mask of *sole e mare* is removed.

Even dining, even food preparation, the recipes and ingredients themselves, show this same seriousness—we almost want to say gravity, remembering that, for the ancient Romans, *gravitas* was the most distinguishing character of a nobleman or -woman. The Italian winter menu is probably the most conservative of all the seasons. Even its cooking techniques are conservative: This is the light-the-oven, set-the-stewpot-on-to-simmer, warm-the-house-with-cooking season. Baked dishes and boiled dishes and braised dishes, pasta and beans and meats: This is the season not only to dine, but to eat to keep out the cold, to consume flesh to preserve flesh.

Lightness and brightness now give way to solidity and substance. What are, at most other times of the year, fairly small meat portions begin to grow both in size and in importance within a meal. Where at other times cooking is mostly quick, to interfere as little as possible with each ingredient's integrity and flavor, now many recipes call for long, slow cooking, to blend and harmonize many flavors into complex unities. Arias give way to choral songs, in cooking as well as life. Summer's tenors and mandolins fall silent before the sonority of winter's Gregorian chant.

Italy's choice of foods in winter is no richer than anybody else's. But what Italian cooks do with their resources remains incomparable. All the familiar old warhorses of the winter kitchen—stews and braises, cabbages and root vegetables—in Italian hands take on a new life and a richer, more satisfying flavor. But in its most complex stews and medleys of ingredients, Italian cooking preserves a paradoxical simplicity.

The most complicated of its flavor combinations resolve themselves into the clearest harmonies.

Nothing shows this better than the pan-Italian winter-favorite dish, *bollito misto*—mixed boiled meats. It often comes as a surprise—it certainly did initially to us—that Italians prize boiled meats. Their purity and directness speak to something in the otherwise baroque and complicated Italian character. The finest restaurants pride themselves on their *carrello di bolliti* and the plates of mixed boiled meats and fowl that issue from the steamy depths of a heavy silver trolley. In our earliest travels in Italy, we were puzzled by the obvious enthusiasm that greeted what we had thought of as rather spartan fare. (The New England boiled dinner is all very well in its way, but not, as Dr. Johnson would have said, a meal to ask a man to.) All it took for our enlightenment was one really bone-biting cold day in Venice, with a wind coming off the Grand Canal fiercer than the Turks at Lepanto. It pushed us right across and out of the Piazza San Marco and up the Calle Paradiso—apt name!—into our soon-to-be-beloved local, Trattoria da Bruno. There we tasted our first-ever bollito misto. Our notes say it contained *cotechino*, beef, chicken, *testina*, and fresh bacon. The next day we would discover that this bollito was, by more ambitious restaurant standards, quite a modest affair, but for us at that moment it was heaven—pure, unmediated flavors moistened and harmonized by an ambrosial, warming, life-sustaining broth of the meats' own making.

The next day found us in Ferrara, lunching at the elegant Ristorante Giovanni da Italia. There we underwent the total bollito experience. In deep comfortable chairs, in a warm and well-upholstered room, insulated from the sleety blasts that howled around and through the massive Castello d'Este that dominates the city center, we began what was not so much the courses of a meal as a course in surviving winter. First, *maltagliati con fagioli*, handmade egg noodles in a bean sauce, the pureed, refined, concentrated souls of hundreds of sun-ripened beans. With that as our primer, we graduated to the bollito, or rather the bolliti: chicken, cotechino, *zampone*, testina, *salama da sugo*, *guanciale*, and beef, accoutered with salsa verde, tiny gherkins, pickled onions, pickled green peppers, and mounds of parmigiano-flavored pureed potatoes. It sounds like an exercise in excess, but it ate effortlessly, each mouthful light and moist, each meat sufficiently different, sufficiently itself, to lure the appetite on from bite to bite even without the help of the acerb and invigorating condiments.

On subsequent travels we've encountered other great incarnations of the bollito misto—notably at the splendid Ristorante Fini in Modena—and many augmentations to its contents—ham, both fresh and cured; tongue, both fresh and smoked; sowbelly;

capon; venerable stewing hens—and one great addition to its condiments, the spicy fruits in mustard syrup called *mostarda di Cremona*. In a land of—usually—small meat portions, bollito misto is an extravaganza of flesh and fat and the plasma they create in cooking together. The sheer amount of meat offered in one course, one meal, the total number of different flavors juxtaposed in a single dish: these defy the logic that animates Italian cookery at any other time of the year.

For Americans, that may not seem a shocking amount of flesh. But in the environment of Italy, among a people so vegetable-loving as Italians normally are, there's something almost primitive, something uncivilized, about eating that much meat. It's old-fashioned. It's atavistic. But in winter, it's right, in a deeply human and moral way. It's downright comforting: it reminds us that dining is art, but eating is life. All those meats are life-sustaining in the most fundamental way, in the way that all food, all eating, is at bottom. Eating a bollito misto is going back to the roots, back to the days before refrigerators and freezers and freeze-drying and canning and chemical preservatives, back to when the only really *fresh* food you could get in the middle of winter was whatever you could kill and skin and cook right away.

That's the sense in which we mean that Italian winter cooking is the most conservative, the most deeply traditional, of the whole Italian repertory. Tasting it, savoring it, relying on it for warmth and comfort, you begin to understand why, in Italy, the waning of winter and the first hopeful intimations of spring are marked not by the first flowers but, according to the liturgical calendar, by Carnevale (the farewell to flesh) and Lent, an orgy of meat-eating followed by forty slow days of penitence and fasting, to cleanse the body and the spirit so they can begin the cycle of life again.

ANTIPASTI

Cold weather calls out for solid, rib-sticking food, even as antipasti. These seem to be the very climate conditions for which *salumi* were invented—the pigs slaughtered, the meat chopped or ground, seasoned, salted, stuffed into casings, hung from rafters to shrink and solidify in the dry cold air. Winter is the time when all that tightly packed energy needs to be transferred back to the maker-turned-consumer, to stoke the internal fires we need to keep out the cold. As few of us today have the facilities to cure our own meats—still less the desire to kill our own pigs—there are no recipes in this section for those delicacies. Fortunately, they are available from good Italian specialty stores, albeit not in the variety and succulence to be found in Italy itself.

Meat is far from all the winter antipasto table has to say for itself, however. In addition, there is—not surprisingly—an intriguing array of bread-based dishes that also do well at keeping out the cold. The recipes here, variously incorporating meats, greens, spices, and new olives, go very nicely alongside a plate of cold meats, and stand up just as well on their own with an aperitivo or glass of wine.

Beyond that, winter antipasti also include a surprisingly large repertory of vegetables, both cooked fresh and pickled. One of the real joys of the season is the return of radicchio, a cold-weather crop and the jewel of the cabbage family. Cauliflower, broccoli, and root vegetables are also prominent at this time of year. But—let's face it—the variety is not as great as at other seasons. Not to make a fetish of using nothing but what local fields produce, even when they're under a blanket of snow and ice, we've included two dishes that call for some green vegetables that are pretty much year-round standards—beans, peppers, zucchini.

MARINATED WINTER VEGETABLES

La rinforzata

FOR 4 TO 5 SERVINGS:

*T*his dish is traditional in Campania for the *feste natalizie*, the feast days that stretch from Christmas to Epiphany. It's called *rinforzata*—the reinforced one—because as it gets eaten up, you "reinforce" it with fresh batches of ingredients and just keep it going all through the holiday visits.

Rinforzata also belongs to the large class of cooked vegetable dishes that are harmoniously joined together in a vinegar-based marinade. Collectively, they are known as *giardiniera,* meaning they utilize the produce of the whole garden, whatever is available at each time of year. It does really take a couple of hours of the ingredients' getting acquainted with each other for the flavor to develop; and it can sit all day without losing its crispness. Thus, it makes a great buffet or picnic dish any time of the year.

One note: The peperoncini called for here are not dried hot red peppers, but a pale-green pickled pepper, 1 to 3 inches in length, with only an occasional hint of hotness. They are usually sold in jars labeled antipasto peppers, salad peppers, or Tuscan peppers. Good ones are also imported from Greece.

And one caveat: Don't use canned olives. They have so little flavor (and the wrong kind at that) that they'll spoil the dish. Any kind of loose olives will do here: Italian Gaetas, Barese, Sicilian; French *picholines* or *niçoise;* oil-cured Moroccans. If pitting the olives is too irksome to you, leave the pits in and just warn your guests.

A light, dry, aperitif-style white would be your best bet: a simple Soave or Orvieto or Pinot grigio, for instance.

1 small cauliflower, about 1½
    pounds before trimming
Salt
Freshly ground black pepper
1 tablespoon white wine vinegar
2 ounces black olives, pitted
2 ounces green olives, pitted
2 ounces cornichons, sliced

2 ounces pickled peperoncini,
    seeded and cut in 1-inch pieces
1 tablespoon capers, drained and
    rinsed
6 anchovy fillets, cut in 1-inch
    pieces
½ cup olive oil, preferably
    extra-virgin

Trim the cauliflower and separate it into large florets. Drop them in 3 to 4 quarts boiling salted water and cook 7 to 8 minutes, until not quite tender. (They'll continue to soften in the marinade.) Drain and spray them with cold water or plunge them into a sink filled with cold water, to stop the cooking.

Further divide the florets into bite-sized pieces and put them in a large bowl. Salt and pepper them lightly, sprinkle on the vinegar, and toss gently with a wooden spoon.

Add the olives, cornichons, peperoncini, capers, and anchovies. Dress with the olive oil and mix thoroughly. Cover the bowl with plastic wrap and let sit at least 3 hours. Before serving, taste and add more salt, pepper, or vinegar if necessary. ∎

RAW VEGETABLES WITH CREAMY GARLIC DIPPING SAUCE

Bagna cauda

FOR 4 SERVINGS:

This is a great, classic Piedmontese specialty. There are two very different versions of the deeply but gently garlic-flavored sauce that is the "hot bath" that gives this dish its dialect name and distinguishes it from ordinary vegetable dips. The commoner version is dark, oily, and tends to separate. This recipe is rarer and finer: it makes a palate-charming puree that is thick, creamy, and consistent.

Do not—repeat, do not—panic at the amount of garlic; the long stewing in milk gentles it down enormously. Less would be insipid. For the surround, you can use any raw vegetables you like (thinly sliced kohlrabi, for instance, is excellent). You can prepare all the vegetables in advance and keep them in ice water, but the sauce should be made just before serving. A chafing-dish flame under the sauce when served is traditional, but not absolutely necessary.

The Piedmontese, who are blessed and spoiled to a degree envied by gastronomes everywhere else in the world, sliver a white truffle into the sauce just before serving.

While this dish is flavorful enough to tolerate a gentle red wine (Dolcetto or Barbera would be the regional choices), we think it responds best to a big white, dry and full-bodied. Try an Arneis, a Pinot bianco from Trentino, a Friulian Tocai, Vintage Tunina, Torre di Giano Riserva, or an older bottle of Fiano di Avellino—the last three especially if you've sprung for that white truffle.

FOR THE SAUCE:

6 ounces garlic cloves (1 to 2
   heads), peeled

1 cup milk

4 small anchovy fillets, chopped

½ cup olive oil

FOR THE VEGETABLES:

1 bell pepper, seeded and cut in
   strips

2 medium carrots, peeled and cut
   in sticks

1 medium zucchini, peeled and cut
   in sticks

4 large firm white mushrooms,
   quartered

1 small head bulb fennel, trimmed
   and cut into spears

1½ cups broccoli flowerets

6 scallions, trimmed

Put the garlic cloves and milk in a small, heavy pan. Bring to a simmer, cover the pan tightly, and cook gently 1 hour, or until the garlic is meltingly tender. Check frequently to be sure the garlic is not sticking and the milk not evaporating.

Transfer the garlic cloves to a blender or food processor with a slotted spoon, reserving the milk. Add the chopped anchovies and puree until smooth. With the machine running, pour in the olive oil in a thin stream.

Transfer the puree to a pot and stir in the garlic cooking milk by tablespoons until the sauce is a good coating consistency (about 4 tablespoons should do it). Simmer the sauce 5 minutes, stirring constantly.

For individual servings, divide the sauce among four small heated bowls. Set each bowl in the middle of a large plate and arrange portions of the prepared vegetables attractively around it. For communal dipping—especially for buffet service, where the bagna cauda may not be eaten immediately—put the sauce into the top of a chafing dish with a flame underneath, and present the vegetables on a single large platter alongside. ∎

WINTER VEGETABLE SALAD

Insalatone

FOR 4 SERVINGS:

*S*ome dishes in the Italian repertory are staggering in their sheer simplicity: their whole genius is in delivering—utterly un-diluted—the purest, freshest flavors of the ingredients that compose them. This is one of those dishes. The bright, delicate flavors of the vegetables really sing under their veil of extra-virgin olive oil.

In fact, this is a dish that shows off to advantage the range of differences in extra-virgin oils—from the typically light-bodied and pale-colored Ligurian ones to the thick, deep green or old-gold Sicilians.

The only art to making *insalatone* is adding things to the cooking pot at the right intervals so all are done at once. It's crucial that the vegetables, which are dressed still hot from the boiling, all be tender but still firm. Mushy is anathema. The vegetables suggested here are basics; add or substitute Belgian endive, leeks, beets (cooked separately, so as not to bleed over the other items), kohlrabi, broccoli, or any you like. The small, flat onions called *cipolline* are particularly good for this dish.

Insalatone could also be a contorno for a simple grilled meat or a light meal in itself. Leftovers make an excellent frittata, or they can be used in a risotto.

A gentle, unobtrusive white wine is the best choice here: a decent Soave or Orvieto or Frascati, or a simple Tuscan white.

Salt

8 small boiling potatoes, peeled but left whole

8 small onions (about ¾ pound), peeled and a cross cut into the root end

¾ pound small carrots, peeled and left whole (or cut up if larger)

¾ pound green beans, ends snapped and left whole

1½ pounds small zucchini (about 1 inch in diameter), cut in 2-inch logs

1 cup extra-virgin olive oil, approximately

2 lemons, quartered

Freshly ground black pepper

Bring a large pot of water to a boil along with 1 tablespoon salt. Put in the potatoes and onions. After they have boiled 5 minutes, add the carrots. After 10 more minutes, add the green beans. After 5 more minutes, the zucchini. Continue cooking about 10 minutes more, until all the vegetables are tender but still crisp.

Drain the vegetables, arrange them on a heated platter, and serve at once. Pass the olive oil, lemon, salt, and pepper at table. The condiments can be applied directly to the vegetables, or you can give each diner a small bowl in which to mix a dressing to his or her taste. ■

BRAISED LENTILS ON BRUSCHETTA

Lenticchie all'umbra

FOR 4 SERVINGS:

A soft, warming red wine goes best with this dish: a young Rubesco, a fine Lacryma Christi, a Dolcetto—any of these would be good.

This recipe is so simple, you wonder how it'll have any flavor at all. We were served it in a country inn near Norcia, to start off a midday meal that had to see us through an afternoon of tramping through winter woodlands to watch a demonstration of black truffle hunting. The dish was ambrosia.

The secret, as we discovered, is that there are lentils and then there are lentils. The prized lentils in Umbria are from Castelluccio, very tiny, with a rosy-brown or golden-brown hue. Naturally, as soon as the truffle hunt was over, we went on our own lentil hunt, to buy a supply of them to take home. (Actually, they're available in the United States now, in specialty stores.) Re-created here, the dish was still ambrosia. However, from experience, we can tell you not to try this dish with the ordinary type of lentils sold in supermarkets. They're too old and bland (though even they can taste good enough when cooked with a lot of other flavorings). Expensive lentils from fancy food stores, it turns out, may well be worth the cost. Try them and see for yourself.

½ pound imported lentils, preferably from Castelluccio	1 teaspoon salt
1 stalk celery, chopped	8 slices country bread
2 cloves garlic	Extra-virgin olive oil
	½ cup chopped mild onion

Pick over the lentils very carefully (they often contain tiny stones). Rinse them in a sieve and put them into a heavy-bottomed pot. Add the celery, 1 clove garlic, and 3½ cups cold water. Cover the pan tightly, bring to a boil, reduce to a simmer, and cook 40 minutes, or until the lentils are tender. If the liquid evaporates too fast during the cooking, add a few tablespoons water. The finished dish should still be lightly soupy. Stir in the salt at the end.

Toast the bread slices and rub them with the remaining garlic clove. Set 2 slices on each plate and drizzle a little olive oil on each slice. Top with ¼ to ½ cup lentils. Pass more olive oil and the chopped onion at table so that diners can dress their lentils to their taste. ■

WARM SALAD OF BELGIAN ENDIVE, MUSHROOMS, AND HAM

Insalata belga saporita

FOR 4 SERVINGS:

T his dish belongs to the modern Italian repertory, which has adopted Belgian endive as a cousin and stand-in for good radicchio di Treviso, which even in Italy isn't always in abundant supply. As Italian cooks have discovered, you can do a number of things with Belgian endive besides eat it raw. One of the most popular Italian treatments bakes it with pancetta and milk and cheese, much like scalloped potatoes: that makes a hefty dish that's almost a meal in itself.

Our present recipe is for a kind of warm salad, served in individual gratin dishes—*molto moderno*. The sweetness of the pancetta (Italians really like the contrast of the bitter bite of the endive and the meat-sweetness of pancetta) is very important to the overall effect, so you can't really substitute even well-blanched bacon here.

This dish definitely takes red wine. A Dolcetto or Barbera works well, and a Chianti Classico is an even better match for its subtleties and complexities.

2 tablespoons lemon juice

6 small heads Belgian endive,
leaves separated, larger ones cut
in 2 to 3 pieces

3 tablespoons olive oil

2 ounces pancetta, cut in
matchsticks

4 ounces boiled ham, cut in 1-inch
squares

2 tablespoons minced onion

¼ pound mushrooms, thinly
sliced

Salt

Freshly ground black pepper

1 to 2 tablespoons chopped flat-leaf
Italian parsley

Bring 2 quarts of water to a boil with the lemon juice. Drop in the endive leaves and boil 2 minutes. Drain them, spray or dip briefly in cold water to stop the cooking, and spread them on paper towels to dry.

In a pan, warm the olive oil and add the pancetta, ham, and minced onion. Sauté over medium heat 1 minute, stirring often. Add the mushrooms and cook, stirring, 3 to 4 minutes more. Sprinkle with salt and pepper to taste, and continue cooking until all the mushroom liquid is evaporated. Add the endive leaves and cook, stirring, 2 more minutes.

Transfer the mixture to four small gratin dishes, sprinkle with the chopped parsley, and serve at once. ■

GRILLED RADICCHIO WITH SCAMORZA

Radicchio con scamorza

FOR 4 SERVINGS:

This appetizing combination of smoky-lush cheese and savory-bitter green (well, it's a red, really, but the family is definitely green) makes a surprisingly sophisticated dish, for all its simplicity of preparation. You really must use the elongated heads of radicchio di Treviso here; the round-headed Verona variety is just too cabbagy. In trimming radicchio for cooking, leave on a bit of the core—just enough to hold the frond of leaves together. Diners can cut it away on their plates. If radicchio is not available, you can substitute Belgian endive, which, while not an exact fit, at least approximates the quality of radicchio di Treviso.

Scamorza is a southern Italian cheese, similar to young provolone in texture and flavor, though a bit milder and less tangy. It appears both "raw" and cooked in many southern antipasti. Grilled scamorza is popular in Rome as a light secondo. Like mozzarella, it is often smoked, and the smoked version gives a special accent to this currently fashionable antipasto.

A soft red wine is ideal here: Lacryma Christi, Dolcetto, a simple Barbera, a Chianti Senese.

3 tablespoons olive oil	*Salt*
2 large heads radicchio di Treviso, washed, trimmed, and halved lengthwise	*Freshly ground black pepper*
	4 ounces smoked scamorza or smoked mozzarella

Preheat the oven to 350°F. In a skillet, heat 2 tablespoons of the olive oil. Add the radicchio halves and, handling them gently, sauté 3 to 4 minutes on each side, until the leaves are wilted and browned. Salt and pepper them lightly.

Oil a bake-and-serve dish with the remaining olive oil, and arrange the radicchio on it. Slice the scamorza ¼ inch thick and distribute it over the radicchio. Bake 10 minutes, or until the cheese is melted and bubbling. Serve at once. ∎

FRICO

Frico

FOR 4 SERVINGS:

Y

Like most simple cheese dishes, frico responds well to any dry wine, white or red. Barbera or Chianti Classico would be fine all-purpose choices.

heese in general is one of the miracles of nature's own food chemistry, and this dish is a particular example of it. *Montasio* is a semisoft cheese from Friuli and the Veneto that is now, happily, in pretty regular supply in this country. When thin slices of it are laid on a hot grill, they first melt and then firm into golden wafers with especially delicious crisp lacy edges. The mild, nutty flavor of the cheese is intensified by the cooking.

Frico is best eaten piping hot, but the wafers can be cooked in advance and reheated, and they are not at all unpleasant even at room temperature. They are, as you might expect, great with aperitifs.

For the benefit of the curious: we've tried this technique with other cheeses (young Asiago, for instance, which is a close relative of Montasio), and it doesn't work as well. Other cheeses tend to get brown rather than golden, lumpen rather than lacy, and they also tend to stick tenaciously to the griddle. Our advice is to stay with Montasio for this particular crunchy effect.

½ pound Montasio cheese, sliced
⅛ to ¹⁄₁₆ inch thick

Heat a nonstick frying pan or a very well-seasoned griddle to very hot. Lay on a slice of cheese and cook over medium heat 2 to 3 minutes, until the bottom is firm and bright golden brown. Turn it and cook the other side until golden, about 1 minute. Set it briefly on a paper towel to blot up the excess butterfat.

Once you have the timing down and see how much the cheese spreads out as it melts (it shouldn't be much), cook the rest in batches, according to the capacity of your pan or griddle. If they are not to be served immediately, spread them on a baking sheet to reheat for about 10 minutes in a 350°F oven. ∎

SCHIACCIATA WITH GREENS

Schiacciata con verdura

FOR ONE 10-INCH ROUND LOAF:

*T*his hearty flat bread is as good and flavorful with escarole as it is with the broccoli rape suggested here, and it's a great way to use leftovers of either. It makes a very pretty dish too, with the white of pignoli and the black of raisins dotted among the green of the vegetable and the gold of the bread.

This schiacciata takes about 5 minutes longer to cook than the others in this book, especially if the greens are very moist. Leftovers reheat well the next day; if you like, they can be gussied up with a thin veil of mozzarella or a sprinkling of grated parmigiano.

Try a reasonably acidic, dry white, such as a good Pinot grigio or a cru Soave or perhaps even a Gavi.

All the ingredients for basic schiacciata (page 35 in the Spring section)
1 tablespoon raisins

1 cup cooked broccoli rape (page 402), chopped
1 tablespoon pignoli
1 tablespoon olive oil (optional)

Prepare a plain schiacciata dough as directed in the basic recipe. While the dough is having its 30-minute rest in the baking pan, soak the raisins in hot water to soften them. Preheat the oven to 425°F.

When ready to bake, spread the cooked greens over the surface of the dough. Drain the raisins and gently squeeze the water out of them. Strew them and the pignoli over the top of the greens. Bake the schiacciata 25 minutes, or until the outer rim of the dough is lightly browned. Serve hot or warm.

If desired (especially if the greens were fairly dry), drizzle a tablespoon of olive oil over the surface of the schiacciata before serving. ∎

SCHIACCIATA WITH PROSCIUTTO

Schiacciata al prosciutto

FOR ONE 10-INCH LOAF:

Just about any at all, as long as it's dry.

A quick and simple preparation, like all schiacciatas, this one makes an excellent substitute for the elaborate prosciutto breads or pork breads featured by some Italian specialty bakers. Serve it alongside other antipasto dishes (especially vegetable), or by itself with aperitivi.

Once upon a time, butchers and deli men would give away the odd bits of meat from the knuckle end of the prosciutto, just as they used not to charge for the bone or rind or trimmed fat. Now, alas! all merchants have become cannier or less free-spirited. Nevertheless, they usually sell—or can be persuaded to sell—all those "by-products" of the prosciutto at a reduced price.

All the ingredients for basic schiacciata (page 35)

¼ cup minced prosciutto
Freshly ground black pepper

Prepare a plain schiacciata dough as directed in the basic recipe, kneading in the prosciutto and 5 to 6 generous grindings of black pepper. Let the dough rest 30 minutes while you preheat the oven to 425°F. Bake as directed in the basic recipe. ∎

About Prosciutto

Prosciutto is the king of Italian cured meats. But prosciutto is not a single food. There are so many local varieties of this succulent, air-cured ham that a moderately mobile traveler in Italy can order prosciutto for days in succession and never eat the same thing twice. And not a bad fate, that would be.

The word "prosciutto" simply means ham. When used alone it usually refers to an air-cured (not smoked or brined) ham. Strictly speaking, however, this is prosciutto *crudo* (raw) as opposed to prosciutto *cotto*, which is cooked ham. Like the Bayonne ham of France, the Serrano of Spain, the Westphalian of Germany, good Italian prosciutto is costly. But it is so lush and satisfying—simultaneously full-flavored and delicate, sweet and salty, forceful and silken—that it's well worth the expense. As the characters in Li'l Abner used to say of their pig Salome, the Hammus Alabamus, prosciutto is "the ham what am."

Prosciutto is made throughout Italy in various styles. The two most prized are the prosciutto of San Daniele, from Friuli, in northeastern Italy, and the prosciutto of Parma, where the pigs whose hams are destined to become prosciutto are fed on a special diet including whey from Parmesan cheese. For more than twenty years, Americans who wanted to taste these Italian hams could do so only in Italy, because the United States barred the importation of all European pork products. Recently, prosciutto di Parma won an exemption and is now available here, alongside the many domestic brands that stay-at-home prosciutto lovers have had to settle for. (When that happened, many people were surprised to learn that the prosciutto they'd been enjoying for years, from makers with thoroughly Italian names, was actually made in the United States or Canada.) Imported prosciutto di Parma is vastly superior to domestic varieties. It's generally moister, less salty, and more subtly flavored. It also tends to be substantially more expensive, which puts it definitely in the range of luxury foods. However, a little prosciutto goes a long way: two ounces per person is a generous antipasto portion.

Whether you buy domestic or Italian prosciutto, some care is required in shopping. Once a prosciutto is cut open, it's susceptible to drying out, which concentrates the saltiness and makes for a leathery texture. You should look carefully at the ham that your butcher or deli counter person proposes to slice for you, and if it's dry-looking and brownish-red rather than moist and rosy pink, don't buy it. Prosciutto should be sliced paper-thin, and when the slices are laid out on paper, they should be spaced well enough to separate easily—there's nothing worse than spending all that money and then finding the slices so stuck together that you wind up with shreds on your plate. Finally, each prosciutto slice should have a rim of creamy fat left on: the fat is definitely to be eaten and enjoyed.

BLACK PEPPER BISCUITS

Taralli col pepe

FOR 24 BISCUITS:

Y

Any at all, as long as it's dry.

*T*aralli come close to qualifying as the Italian Ritz cracker. They're found everywhere, in many varieties and many flavors. Most of them—and this one is no exception—seem at first quite chewy and a bit dry to the American palate, but you acquire the taste for them very quickly. Also, because of those characteristics, taralli go very well with aperitivi of all sorts, as well as with salami and prosciutto and most other cured pork products. For an interesting change of pace, serve these peppery nuggets alongside a meat antipasto instead of regular bread.

Between the time needed for the yeast to work and the long baking in a very low oven, these taralli take about 4 hours from start to finish. But you can make them up whenever you have some free time. They keep well in a tightly covered tin, and to some palates they actually improve as they dry and harden with age.

½ envelope active dry yeast
2¼ cups all-purpose flour,
  in all
½ teaspoon salt

¾ teaspoon freshly ground black
  pepper
1 tablespoon fennel seeds
1 egg

In a small bowl, dissolve the yeast in 3 tablespoons warm water. Add ⅓ cup flour and knead briefly into a smooth ball. Place this sponge in a bowl, cover with plastic wrap, and let it rise until double in bulk, about 1 hour.

Put the remaining flour, the salt, pepper, and fennel seeds in a large mixing bowl. Add the sponge and about ¾ cup warm water, and mix to make a dough. Knead 10 minutes. Transfer the dough to a clean bowl, cover, and let rise again 1 hour.

Grease a baking sheet and flour a work surface. Divide the dough in half and set one half aside, covered with a towel. Take the other half of the dough, knead it briefly, and divide it into 12 pieces. Roll each piece under your hands into 7-inch lengths about ½ inch in diameter. Bend them into rings or loops and pinch the ends closed. Place each finished piece on the baking sheet, leaving a small space between them. (They don't spread much in the baking.) Shape the remaining half of the dough in the same way. Cover the taralli with a towel and let them sit 30 minutes.

Preheat the oven to 225°F. In a small bowl, beat the egg with 1 tablespoon water and brush the taralli with this egg glaze. Wait a moment and brush them a second time. Put the pan in the oven and bake 1 hour.

Cool the taralli on a rack and transfer them to a tin, where they'll keep for several weeks. ∎

PRIMI

Winter's primi are as you would expect them to be: robust, satisfying, warming. Soups star, especially in combination with legumes, which are the winter vegetables par excellence. Beans in all their splendid variety, usually in happy and healthy alliance with pasta, appear in minestra after minestra, most of them variants on a single rich theme: broth-beans-pasta-cheese-olive oil. Doesn't it just start your taste buds tingling? Another splendid thing about winter soups is their resiliency. Most of them are as good or better the second day, even the third day—which makes leftovers a treat and gives you lots of flexibility to cook when you have the time and eat when you're ready.

When they're not keeping company with beans, the pastas are happily snuggling down with the deep-flavored, long-cooked meat sauces that most of us know through their descendants in Italian-American cooking. Here is where we will encounter the whole family of ragùs, the rich sauces that even more than others in the Italian repertory call out for cheese and red wine.

Finally, winter's rice and polenta dishes provide the deepest bass notes of an already profound chorus, with rich, complex flavors and surprisingly sophisticated sauces, whether made from a single, mellow-flavored vegetable like bulb fennel or from a medley of tasty ingredients, like *risotto alla sbiraglia* or the "antique Roman manner" of serving polenta. For those still unfamiliar with the range of possibilities inherent in rice and cornmeal, winter's risotto and polenta recipes hold quite a few surprises.

All these dishes, of course, are moving our palates rather markedly in the direction of the big red wines, bringing us closer to some of the true glories of Italian viniculture, the bright red vein that runs through the heart of winter.

UMBRIAN ONION SOUP

La cipollata

FOR 4 TO 5 SERVINGS:

$\mathcal{A}$ comforting, mushy soup—this is almost play food—
that goes happily with a glass of red wine. It takes about an hour and
a half of effortless cooking, after a two-hour preliminary wait while
the onions soak and leach out some of their bite. The whole recipe
can be done in advance, however, stopping just before the addition
of the egg-cheese mixture. The basil leaves are an essential bright-
ener, which is why we've urged you to have a supply of summer's
best stashed in your freezer. Leftover *cipollata* is very good and can
be given a new twist by adding a little cooked pasta.

*A simple, hearty red wine goes
well here. Try Montepulciano
d'Abruzzo, Corvo, or simple
Chianti.*

1 pound mild onions, thinly sliced
2 ounces lard
1 tablespoon olive oil
½ teaspoon salt
Freshly ground black pepper
2 to 3 basil leaves
¾ cup drained canned
   Italian-style plum tomatoes,

chopped, pulsed in a food
   processor, or passed through a
   food mill
2 cups broth
1 egg, beaten with 3 tablespoons
   freshly grated parmigiano
4 slices crusty, country-style bread,
   lightly toasted

Soak the onions in a large bowl of cold water for 2 hours.

In a large casserole, melt the lard in the olive oil. Remove the
onions from the water, drain briefly, and transfer them to the
casserole. Add the salt, several grindings of pepper, and the basil
leaves. Stir, cover, and cook 10 minutes over medium-low heat.

Add the tomatoes and broth, stir, and bring the mixture to a
boil. Reduce to a simmer, cover, and cook over very low heat 1
hour. Set the soup aside at this point if not ready to serve.

When ready to serve, bring the soup back to a simmer. Off the
heat, beat in the egg-cheese mixture and serve at once, laying a slice
of toast in the bottom of each person's bowl. ∎

About Dried Beans

Italian cooking does wonderful things with shell beans, not the least of which are the myriad ways of *pasta e fagioli*—a name so often comically rendered as *pastafazool* in America that many people think that's the correct term. We venerate pasta e fagioli, but having offered three different recipes for it in our first book, *La Tavola Italiana,* we've resisted the impulse to present any more versions here. There is no shortage of other Italian bean recipes.

Those members of the legume family most often dried for cooking in Italy are cannellini, borlotti, ceci (chick-peas or garbanzos), and lenticchie (lentils—which are really pulses, but which for cooking purposes occupy the same ecological niche as legumes).

Cannellini are essentially our common kidney beans, red or white. Italian varieties are usually slimmer and more cylindrical than those grown here, but the flavors are much the same. Greenish-white French flageolets are like small white cannellini in appearance and flavor.

Borlotti are the favorite variety of bean-obsessed Tuscany. You're hard put to get a meal in Tuscany that doesn't include at least a side dish of beans, cooked very simply but laced with luscious extra-virgin olive oil. For American cooks, cranberry beans are as near as makes no difference to borlotti, and pintos or Great Northerns work well too.

A welcome new trend in our part of the world is the proliferation of bean varieties available in the markets. Fancy food stores are now even stocking what can only be called "designer beans." These are splashy speckled varieties with colorful names like Tongues of Fire, old-fashioned home-garden beans like Scarlet Runners, and special selections of the more familiar types such as pea and navy beans—all grown by specialized niche farmers and sold within a year of the harvest.

It comes as a surprise to many people that freshness matters, even in as durable a food as dried beans. If the beans you see in supermarkets look a little old and dusty, it may well be that they're actually several years old. By that point, they aren't simply dried: they're desiccated, and long, long cooking will be needed to reconstitute them. In many cases, very old beans burst and turn to pot-mush in the cooking—okay for thick soups and purees, but no good at all as a vegetable dish in themselves or a component in a mixed dish. And beans that have been stored too long lose flavor too—so there are good reasons to shell out the extra cash for top-quality, fresh products.

So great can the difference be, in fact, that some designer beans don't even need a preliminary soaking. (The label will tell you, if so.) They cook up almost as quickly as fresh-off-the-vine, newly shelled beans would. That's a convenience factor that, even without the added flavor, makes these specialty beans worth looking into.

When you have beans that do need soaking, there are two equally good ways to do it. The effortless one requires only that you pick over the beans (even the best of them can harbor little stones that are mighty hard on tooth enamel) and leave them overnight in a big bowl of cold water. Of course, you can only do that when you've decided or remembered that you're making a bean dish tomorrow. For those of us less foresightful or organized, the picked-over beans can be covered deeply with cold water, brought to a boil, boiled 1 to 2 minutes and then left to soak in the hot water 1 to 2 hours. Whenever a recipe of ours specifies one technique, the other can always be substituted. The less-violent overnight method is probably a bit better for beans that are very old. Lentils don't need a presoaking at all.

Beans, like pasta, shouldn't be overcooked. Firm, not mushy, is what Italians want, with sleek, plump shapes that say al dente to the eye as surely as a sample says it to the tooth. You really must fish out and taste a bean from time to time during the cooking. No matter how definite a recipe is about timing, if the beans are done an hour early, they're done. And if you're a traditionalist, never salt beans until the very end of the cooking: Italians swear that to do so earlier toughens them.

CALABRIAN BEAN AND PASTA SOUP

Millecosedde

FOR 8 SERVINGS

Y

This kind of dish responds well to everything but the absence of wine. A simple, dry red—Valpolicella, Chianti, Montepulciano di Abruzzo, Castel del Monte—would be fine.

The dialect name means "soup of a thousand things," hence you're encouraged to use as many kinds of dried beans as you can get. In southern Italy, this would always include fava beans, but we've found most of the dried favas available in the United States unpleasantly mealy, so we usually use baby lima beans instead. For the rest, kidney, pinto, navy, and Great Northern beans, plus lentils and chick-peas, are all good candidates. Select for color and shape contrasts—or use up odds and ends from the pantry.

This is an old-fashioned, long-cooked minestrone that comes out all thick and porridgy: terrific cold-weather fare. The cabbage, which can look like the dominant ingredient at the start, all but disappears into the cooking liquid—which is, truth to tell, more solid than liquid by the time the soup is ready.

Don't, under any circumstances, omit the olive oil and cheese and pepper at the end—the beans love them, and they make the dish. Extra-virgin oil is nice for the end dose, and ordinary olive oil is fine for the cooking dose.

10 ounces mixed dried beans (see
    headnote)
1 stalk celery, thinly sliced
1 carrot, thinly sliced
½ cup sliced onion
½ small head Savoy cabbage,
    shredded
¾ cup sliced mushrooms

5 cups broth (optional)
Salt
Freshly ground black pepper
10 tablespoons olive oil
¼ pound imported Italian pasta
    corta, e.g., ditali
Freshly grated pecorino romano

Pick over the beans, rinse them, and put them in a pot with cold water to cover by 2 inches. Bring to a boil, boil 2 minutes, then turn off the heat and let the beans sit in the water 2 hours. (If you're including lentils, omit the soaking for them.)

Drain the beans and put them in a large pot along with the celery, carrot, onion, cabbage, and mushrooms. Add 5 cups broth or water. Cover, bring to a boil, reduce to a simmer, and cook 1½ hours.

Stir in 1½ teaspoons salt, a generous quantity of black pepper, and 5 tablespoons olive oil. Cover and simmer 30 minutes. (The beans will absorb most of their liquid; if they take up too much, give them some extra hot water.)

Cook the pasta separately in boiling salted water until slightly less than al dente. Drain it briefly, add it to the beans, stir well, and cook 5 more minutes. Taste for salt.

Off the heat, stir in the remaining 5 tablespoons olive oil and let the soup sit covered 5 minutes before serving. Pass the grated pecorino and the pepper mill. ∎

FRIULIAN BEAN SOUP

Minestra di fagioli alla friulana

FOR 4 TO 5 SERVINGS:

*I*n Friuli, this recipe is made with a very localized variety of red beans. We use white cannellini, which behave and taste much the same, and which make a pretty, pale soup flecked with green from the parsley.

Most of the cooking can be done well in advance of serving, leaving only about 15 minutes for reheating and finishing. Those final steps are crucial ones for the flavor of the dish, however. The soup may seem thin after its first cooking, but it thickens very nicely at the end, when you add the aggressively flavored ingredients that really make the dish. (The technique isn't far different

Y

In Friuli, they would drink Tocai with this. If that's not available, try a Sauvignon, or even a Pinot bianco.

from the way Provençal cooks jazz up an otherwise humdrum vegetable soup with a last-minute infusion of pistou or rouille.)

Fatty bacon could be substituted for salt pork. In either case, go easy on additional salt until you see how much effect they have on the finished dish.

¾ pound dried white cannellini beans
1 stalk celery, finely chopped
2 small boiling potatoes (about 8 ounces), peeled and halved
2 carrots (about 4 ounces), peeled and halved
1 bay leaf
1 teaspoon salt

Freshly ground black pepper
2 tablespoons olive oil
2 ounces salt pork, blanched 2 minutes and finely chopped
⅓ cup minced flat-leaf Italian parsley
⅔ cup minced onion
1 clove garlic, minced
2 sage leaves, minced

Pick over the beans, rinse them, and put them in a pot with cold water to cover by 2 inches. Bring to a boil, boil 2 minutes, then turn off the heat and let the beans sit in the water 2 hours.

Drain the beans and return them to the pot along with 2 quarts cold water. Add the celery, potatoes, carrots, and bay leaf. Bring to a boil, reduce to a simmer, and cook covered until the beans are tender (about 1 hour).

Discard the bay leaf. Lift out the pieces of potato and carrot and mash them through a food mill or sieve back into the soup pot. Add the salt and a generous quantity of freshly ground pepper. Set the soup aside until ready to use.

Shortly before serving time, heat the olive oil in a small sauté pan. Add the salt pork and sauté 1 minute. Add the parsley, onion, garlic, and sage, and sauté 5 minutes. Bring the soup back to a simmer, stir in the entire contents of the sauté pan, and simmer 3 to 4 minutes. Check for salt and serve at once. ■

NEAPOLITAN CABBAGE, RICE, AND PROVOLONE SOUP

Minestra napoletana

FOR 4 TO 5 SERVINGS

Genial, comforting, mild, and savory cold weather food. While many winter soups call for stirring in grated cheese, this one actually cooks cubes of cheese in with the other ingredients. This makes it a soup for an informal occasion, because the melted cheese does have a tendency to solidify on your spoon as you eat, requiring vigorous labial and dental attentions—all, let us assure you, well worth the effort, but probably not what you want to put guests through.

One and a half to two hours of easy cooking, most of which can be done in advance, pausing either before adding the rice or, even later, before adding the cheese.

Simple, full-flavored, dry whites or reds will both go with this dish. Lacryma Christi, red or white, and Corvo, red or white, are both good options.

3½ ounces salt pork

½ cup chopped onion

1 clove garlic

1 tablespoon olive oil

1 pound Savoy cabbage, trimmed, washed, and shredded

½ cup Arborio rice

2 ounces provolone, cut in ⅛- to ¼-inch dice

Salt

Freshly ground black pepper

Freshly grated parmigiano or romano

Mince the salt pork, onion, and garlic together (or pulse them in a food processor). Put the mixture into a large casserole with 1 table-spoon olive oil over low heat and cook very gently 10 to 15 minutes, to render the fat and soften the onion. Meanwhile, bring 1½ quarts of water to a boil.

Add the shredded cabbage to the casserole and toss to coat it with the rendered fat. Pour in the boiling water, stir, cover, bring to a simmer, and cook 1 hour, stirring occasionally.

Stir in the rice and continue cooking 20 minutes. Add the diced provolone and cook 3 minutes more. Taste for salt and pepper and serve at once, passing the grated cheese at the table. ■

PASTA WITH CHICK-PEAS

Pasta e ceci

FOR 4 TO 5 SERVINGS:

Y

Dry white or red, according to your preference, but either should have a reasonably assertive flavor and good acidity. Lacryma Christi and Corvo both fit the bill; so do Verdicchio (white) and Ciro (red).

*W*hether you consider this a thick soup or a wet pasta, it is undoubtedly southern Italian soul food. It's a dish made from almost nothing; you'd think from reading the ingredient list that it would come out bland and monotone. Instead, it's richly subtle and intensely satisfying. But don't trust us; try it. We'll bet it enters your permanent personal cooking repertory, as it has ours.

Part of the reason it develops such a rich flavor is the long cooking. Between soaking the chick-peas and stewing them in tomato, garlic, and oil, we're looking at most of a day of cooking time. However, each step can be done separately and in advance, leaving only the addition of the pasta for the end. The rest of the reason why this dish is so brilliant is its embodiment of the principle that there is no such thing as a condiment on the Italian table: everything is an ingredient. Here, it's the last-minute lacing with oil and the mince of garlic, basil, and parsley that does the trick. They don't adorn or accent the dish; they complete it.

If you wanted to dress up this down-home minestra, you could start by using broth instead of water. You could also mash some of the chick-peas at the end, to thicken the liquid a bit and intensify its flavor. Red pepper flakes on the table wouldn't hurt: they're certainly a very authentic, very regional touch. (No grated cheese, though; it clogs the brightness of the flavor.) Another very traditional touch would be to use a mixture of pastas—ditalini, small shells, broken linguine, and fusilli. Finally, you can raise the gustatory ante by using extra-virgin olive oil for the last-minute dose. But all that is merely to indulge your sense of play in the kitchen. The basic recipe is paradise enow.

½ pound chick-peas

½ cup drained canned
   Italian-style plum tomatoes,
   coarsely chopped

2 cloves garlic, chopped

6 tablespoons olive oil

Salt

½ pound imported Italian short
   pasta, such as ditalini or shells

3 to 4 basil leaves, chopped

1 tablespoon chopped flat-leaf
   Italian parsley

Put the chick-peas into a large pot with cold water to cover by 2 inches. Bring to a boil, boil 2 minutes, then turn off the heat and let the chick-peas sit in the water 2 hours.

Drain them and return them to the pot with 2½ quarts fresh water, the tomatoes, half the chopped garlic, 2 tablespoons olive oil, and 2 teaspoons salt. Cover, bring to a boil, reduce to a simmer, and cook gently, covered, for 3½ to 4 hours, until the chick-peas are tender. Start testing after 2 hours, though, in case the chick-peas are very fresh and cook faster than usual. Uncover and set aside until ready to serve.

Return the soup to a boil, add the pasta and 1 teaspoon salt, and cook until the pasta is tender, about 20 minutes. Meanwhile, chop the remaining garlic, basil, and parsley to a fine mince. Stir this mixture into the soup along with the remaining olive oil and a generous quantity of black pepper. Serve at once. ∎

PASTA WITH LENTILS

Pasta con lenticchie

FOR 4 TO 5 SERVINGS:

Simple, dry, white or red—Corvo or Lacryma Christi, Verdicchio, Montepulciano d'Abruzzo, Castel del Monte, etc.

A good, satisfying dish, requiring little more of the cook than attention to its liquid level. As with the preceding pasta e ceci, this dish doesn't need any cheese. If you use extra-virgin olive oil to finish it, don't stir it into the pot, but pass it at table so people can have the fun—and the extravagance—themselves. But do make them use olive oil: the dish demands it.

One final bit of shopping advice: expensive lentils taste better than cheap lentils. With lentils more than any other legume, the price differential between run-of-the-mill stock and premium stock really reflects a perceptible quality difference.

½ pound top-quality lentils	5 ounces imported Italian
½ cup finely chopped carrot	bucatini, broken into 2-inch
½ cup finely chopped celery	lengths
1 cup finely chopped onion	Freshly ground black pepper
2 teaspoons salt	¼ cup olive oil

Carefully pick over the lentils, discarding any small stones. Rinse and drain them. Put them in a large pot together with the chopped vegetables, cold water to cover, and the salt. Cover and bring to a boil. At the same time, bring a kettle of water to a simmer. Cook the lentils slowly 1 hour, or until tender, checking them every 10 minutes or so and adding hot water from the kettle as necessary to keep them covered with liquid. (Lentils are very prone to sticking to pans if they get too dry.)

Stir in the broken-up bucatini and raise the heat until the mixture is simmering again. Cook gently 20 minutes, or until the pasta is al dente. Continue to check the liquid level as the pasta absorbs water, and leave the pot cover off if the dish seems too wet. The finished texture should be that of a thick soup.

When the pasta is done, taste the dish and add salt if necessary. Stir in a generous quantity of freshly ground black pepper and the olive oil. Serve at once. ■

RAVIOLI STUFFED WITH ENDIVE, PROSCIUTTO, AND RICOTTA

Ravioli con indivia, prosciutto, e ricotta

FOR SIXTY 2-INCH RAVIOLI:

T hese ravioli have an interesting bittersweet filling that derives from the traditional ricotta and spinach mixture. They are here accompanied by a quick tomato sauce—a 15-minute *pommarola*—heavily flavored with sage (the out-of-season sage leaves will be courtesy of your foresight and your freezer). The combination creates a very pleasing, light, modern-tasting harmony.

A light, bright red is the best choice here: a young Chianti Classico, for instance, or a Barbera, or a young Taurasi or Avellanio.

FOR THE FILLING:

1½ tablespoons butter

½ pound Belgian endive, chopped medium-fine

¼ pound prosciutto, ground or chopped fine

1 cup ricotta

3 tablespoons freshly grated parmigiano

Freshly grated nutmeg

Freshly ground black pepper

FOR THE SAUCE:

2 tablespoons butter

1 clove garlic, minced

24 sage leaves, tied in a bundle

2 cups drained canned

Italian-style plum tomatoes, pulsed in a food processor

½ teaspoon salt

Freshly ground black pepper

FOR THE DOUGH:

2 cups all-purpose flour

½ teaspoon salt

2 eggs

1 tablespoon olive oil

To make the filling:

In a skillet, melt the butter, add the endive and prosciutto, and sauté over moderate heat, stirring occasionally, 10 minutes. Transfer the contents of the pan to a bowl, let the mixture cool briefly, and stir in the ricotta, parmigiano, a pinch of nutmeg, and a generous quantity of black pepper.

To make the sauce:

In a nonreactive skillet, melt the butter, add the garlic and sage, and cook gently 1 to 2 minutes, until the sage is wilted. Stir in the tomatoes, salt, and pepper to taste. Bring to a boil, reduce to a simmer, and cook 10 minutes. Taste for seasoning and add more salt or pepper if needed. Discard the sage bundle just before using the sauce.

To form the ravioli:

Make the pasta dough as directed on page 54 in the Spring section. Divide it in four pieces. Set up a pasta machine and have a floured ravioli form ready (ours makes two rows of six ravioli, 1½ inches in diameter, which expand to 2 inches in cooking).

Roll one piece of dough to the next-to-last setting on the pasta machine and drape one end of it over the open grid of the ravioli form, leaving a little slack. Lightly press the solid piece of the form over the dough to make shallow depressions. Fill each pocket with about 1½ teaspoons filling. Fold the other half of the dough over the top and roll a rolling pin over the form to seal the ravioli. Turn them out onto the work surface and set them on a floured tray to dry.

Gather the excess dough into a ball. Make the next three batches of ravioli in the same way. If you have filling left at the end, re-knead the excess dough, roll it out, and make additional ravioli.

If you are not going to cook the ravioli immediately, turn them from time to time on their floured tray to be sure they are not sticking.

Final cooking:

Reheat the sauce. Bring a large pot of water to a boil with 1 tablespoon salt. Drop in the ravioli and cook them about 2 minutes, or until the edges of dough pierce easily with a fork. Drain, sauce, and serve. ∎

SHELLS WITH BEEF RAGÙ

Conchiglie con ragù

FOR 4 TO 5 SERVINGS:

*R*agù is only nominally a tomato sauce, though it tends to be classified as such. In reality, its primary flavors come from meat and mushrooms, as is the case in this thick, nubbly, and delicious example. Tomato is represented in the form of paste. (The brands imported from Italy in what look like toothpaste tubes are excellent.)

When an Italian recipe calls for ground beef, as this one does, you'd be well advised to buy stew beef—shin or similar lean, flavorful, long-cooking cuts—and grind it yourself or chop it in the food processor. Not only will you get better flavor, but you'll also avoid the excessive fat of preground meat.

The quantities given here make about 2½ cups of a very versatile sauce (you can use it in lasagna or cannelloni, or with risotto or polenta or gnocchi) that just loves grated cheese. Make sure you have plenty of good parmigiano on hand.

Y

A medium-bodied red wine of some complexity is called for here. Good choices include Barbera, moderately priced Cabernet (from the Veneto, for instance), Chianti Classico, Vino Nobile, Rubesco, Taurasi, and Regaleali.

¾ ounce dried porcini

4 tablespoons butter

1 tablespoon olive oil

½ pound lean ground beef

¼ cup thinly sliced onion

⅓ cup chopped celery

3 tablespoons tomato paste

Salt

Freshly ground black pepper

1 pound imported Italian
   conchiglie

Freshly grated parmigiano

Put the dried mushrooms in a bowl and pour 2 cups boiling water over them. Let them sit for 30 minutes, then drain them, reserving the water. Rinse the mushroom pieces thoroughly, chop them, and rinse again to remove all traces of grit. Line a sieve with a dampened paper towel and strain the mushroom-soaking liquid into a small bowl.

In a heavy-bottomed casserole, melt the butter in the olive oil. Add the ground meat, onion, and celery. Stir, cover, and cook over medium-low heat for 10 minutes, continuing to stir occasionally. Dissolve the tomato paste in 1½ cups hot water and stir it into the casserole. Then add the chopped mushrooms.

Set the cover slightly ajar on the casserole and simmer the sauce gently for 1 hour, stirring from time to time and adding up to ½ cup of the mushroom-soaking liquid, a little at a time, as the sauce thickens. Season to taste with salt and pepper.

When the sauce is nearly ready, bring 4 to 5 quarts water to a boil. Add 1 tablespoon salt and then the conchiglie. Cook until the pasta is al dente. Drain the pasta in a colander and place it in a warmed serving bowl. Toss with the ragù and serve, passing and using generous amounts of freshly grated parmigiano. ■

CORKSCREW PASTA, NEAPOLITAN STYLE

Fusilli alla napoletana

FOR 4 TO 5 SERVINGS:

This is a delicious-looking, spectacular-tasting dish, with its flecks of ricotta and nuggets of salami and shards of porcini caught up in the curls of fusilli (Naples' favorite pasta shape). It's another rich meat ragù, a classic long-cooked sauce, built this time around a single large piece of beef, which is gently and lengthily simmered and coddled into creating a rich, meat-flavored sauce around itself without losing all its own flavor. (This kind of sauce, remembered by most Italian immigrants to this country as the rarest of luxuries in the days of *la miseria*, is the ancestor of all those meaty, simmered-all-day-long tomato sauces that loom so large in Italian-American cooking today.)

Eye of chuck is a good cut to use: it rewards long, slow, moist cooking. In this case, we're talking about some four and a half hours, so you may want to start the recipe a whole day in advance. The technique for browning the beef may give you pause. Instead of taking care to seal the surface of the meat to keep its juices in, you're instructed to pierce it repeatedly with a fork to draw the juices out into the sauce. Don't hesitate to do it: the beef survives that brutal treatment very well.

For this primo, you don't serve the meat itself at all; you remove and reserve it for some (presumably) humbler purpose. Canny cooks, however, will recognize that a pasta course as tasty and rich as this one will go a far way toward satisfying everyone's appetite, so you might well save a bit of the sauce and serve it with the meat as a second course, if that doesn't seem to you too much of the same thing. Alternatively, reserve the meat whole for another day's secondo, or cut it up for great hot or cold sandwiches. Don't let its appearance fool you: the beef is pretty ragged-looking by the time it has finished cooking, but it's quite tasty still.

A fine red wine, with complexity and subtlety of its own: Taurasi Riserva, Corvo's Duca Enrico, Aglianico del Vulture Riserva, Chianti Classico Riserva, Carmignano Riserva, Rubesco Riserva, and other wines of that class.

1½ pounds stewing beef, in one
   piece, tied with kitchen string if
   necessary to hold it together
2 ounces lard
½ cup thinly sliced onion
½ cup thinly sliced celery
½ cup finely chopped carrot
1 clove garlic, minced
4 ounces pancetta, finely diced

½ cup dry white wine
2 tablespoons tomato paste
Salt
Freshly ground black pepper
2 tablespoons olive oil
1 pound imported Italian fusilli
3 tablespoons grated parmigiano
1 cup ricotta
4 ounces salami, finely diced

For the initial cooking of the sauce:

In a casserole large enough to hold the piece of beef comfortably,
melt the lard. Add the onion, celery, carrot, garlic, and pancetta.
Stir to coat the vegetables with the fat, then push them to the sides
of the casserole and put in the meat. Cook uncovered over low heat,
turning the meat every few minutes, until the vegetables are soft
and the meat brown—about 20 minutes. Each time you turn the
beef, pierce it deeply with a fork in several places. Meanwhile, bring
a kettle of water to a simmer.

Raise heat slightly under the casserole and pour a little of the
wine over the meat. Cook 5 to 10 minutes more, adding the wine
gradually and continuing to pierce and turn the meat.

When all the wine has been added and the vegetables are quite
soft, dissolve the tomato paste in 1 cup hot water and add it to the
casserole. Add more hot water from the kettle to cover the meat
completely. Add 1 teaspoon salt and a generous quantity of pepper,
cover, and cook at very low heat 2 hours, turning the meat often.

Add the olive oil and continue cooking another 2 hours, until
the meat is very tender, adding a little warm water if the sauce
appears to be getting too thick. (You can stop here, refrigerate the
casserole, and finish the cooking the next day.)

For the final cooking:

Remove the meat from the sauce—unless you plan to serve it as a
secondo—and reheat the sauce.

Bring 4 to 5 quarts water to a boil with 1 tablespoon salt. Add
the fusilli and cook until al dente.

Drain the fusilli, transfer them to a serving bowl, and toss them with half the sauce and all the parmigiano. Stir the ricotta and salami into the remaining sauce and spread it over the top of the pasta. Serve at once, passing additional grated cheese and a pepper mill. ∎

FUSILLI VESUVIUS

Fusilli alla vesuviana

FOR 4 TO 5 SERVINGS:

*W*hy is this dish named for Mount Vesuvius? One theory might be that when you live on the slopes of an active volcano, you learn to cook fast, just in case you have to leave in a hurry—and this is one of those lightning-fast sauces that you don't even start cooking until the pasta is on the boil. Alternatively, the mozzarella and pecorino, both of which are melted right into the sauce as it cooks, may have reminded someone of molten lava. (*Se non è vero, è ben trovato*. We categorically reject the prosaic likelihood that the dish was created by a cook from the eponymously named town situated near the foot of the volcano.)

The trick is to have the sauce ingredients all prepared and ready so you can move smoothly through saucing the pasta and popping it into the oven. In fact, since the dish is finished in the oven, this is one of the few cases where it's better if the pasta waits for the sauce, rather than vice versa. Otherwise, if the mozzarella cooks too long it can seize up and get rubbery. Those five minutes in the oven, by the way, imbue the fusilli with the sauce in a perfectly magical way.

A lightish, dry red is best here: Lacryma Christi, Barbera, and Chianti are all fine.

Salt

1 pound imported Italian fusilli

½ cup olive oil

1½ cups drained canned
   Italian-style tomatoes, chopped
   or pulsed in a food processor

6 ounces mozzarella, shredded

⅔ cup grated pecorino
   romano

½ teaspoon dried oregano

Freshly ground black pepper

Preheat the oven to 400°F. In a large pot, bring 4 quarts water to a boil with 1 tablespoon salt. Add the fusilli, stir, and cook until two thirds done. Drain and keep warm.

While the fusilli are cooking, put the olive oil in a shallow flameproof casserole with a lid, and heat it almost to the point of smoking. Add the tomatoes, mozzarella, pecorino, oregano, ½ teaspoon salt, and several grindings of black pepper. Stir energetically, reduce heat to low, and cook over low heat, stirring often, 5 to 7 minutes, or until the cheeses are just melted.

Drain the fusilli when they are still fairly firm, transfer them to the sauce casserole, and toss them well with the sauce. (Don't worry if the mozzarella tries to stick to the spoon; just scrape it off and drape it over the pasta.) Put the dish, uncovered, into the hot oven for 5 minutes. Remove it, toss the fusilli once more, and serve directly from the casserole. ■

PASTA BAKED WITH MEATS, CHEESES, AND HARD-BOILED EGGS

Maccaruni a lu furnu

FOR 4 TO 6 SERVINGS:

Calabrian in origin, and a bit labor-intensive (it will take about three hours from start to finish, but that is by no means nonstop work), this is a classic southern Italian special-occasion dish. The little meatballs look charmingly frivolous in the finished dish, along with the bull's-eyes of sliced hard-boiled egg and the diced cured meat. These are simple, satisfying, down-home flavors.

The traditional recipe calls for a dry soppressata, but any kind of dry or semidry *salumi* would do (for example, a hard salami, or, in U.S. parlance, pepperoni). Similarly, where we call for a combination of mozzarella and provolone, the traditional recipe uses *provola*, which is a semisolid cheese halfway between the two. By all means use provola if you can get it.

A reasonably full-bodied, dry red wine will work best here. Try Regaleali or Montepulciano d'Abruzzo, or even a young Nebbiolo.

FOR THE MEATBALLS:

1¼ to 1½ cups diced day-old
 country-style bread
6 ounces lean ground beef
½ cup grated pecorino
1 egg

1 tablespoon chopped flat-leaf
 Italian parsley
1 clove garlic, put through a press
⅛ teaspoon salt
Freshly ground black pepper

FOR THE DISH:

4 tablespoons olive oil
4 ounces dry soppressata, cut in
 ¼-inch dice
½ cup dry red wine
2 cups drained canned
 Italian-style plum tomatoes,
 roughly chopped

Salt
¾ pound imported Italian
 rigatoni
2 ounces grated provolone
2 ounces shredded mozzarella
3 hard-boiled eggs, sliced in rounds

Put the bread in a small bowl and sprinkle ¼ cup water over it. Let it sit until soft, then squeeze it fairly dry. Put it in a larger bowl and add the beef, pecorino, egg, parsley, garlic, salt, and a generous quantity of black pepper. Mix well. Wet your hands and roll the mixture into meatballs 1 inch in diameter. (There should be about 40 of them.)

In a large nonreactive skillet, warm 3 tablespoons olive oil. Add the meatballs and the diced soppressata and cook over moderate heat until the meatballs are browned on all sides. Raise the heat to medium-high, add the wine, and cook until it is almost entirely evaporated. Add the tomatoes and a sprinkling of salt. Bring to a boil, reduce to a simmer, cover, and cook gently 40 minutes.

In a large pot, bring 4 quarts water to a boil with 1 tablespoon salt. Drop in the rigatoni and cook until just short of al dente, then drain them. Meanwhile, mix the provolone and mozzarella together and oil a large baking dish (e.g., a 9- by 13-inch oval, 2½ inches deep).

Put a few spoonfuls of the sauce into the bottom of the baking dish. Make a layer of one third of the rigatoni. Top with half the egg slices, a scant one third of the mixed cheeses, and one third of the tomato sauce and its meats. Make another layer of rigatoni and toppings, then the final layer of rigatoni, all the remaining cheeses and sauce. Set aside until ready to cook.

Preheat the oven to 400°F. Bake the rigatoni uncovered for 20 minutes. Remove the dish from the oven and let it rest 5 minutes before serving. ∎

About Parmigiano

Many of our recipes for winter primi include grated parmigiano in the ingredient list—anywhere from a few tablespoons to half a cup. No other nation makes as effective use of cheese in its cooking as Italy, and no Italian cheese is more versatile than parmigiano. Indeed, Americans tend to use "Parmesan cheese" as a generic name for any grated cheese used in cooking. That, unfortunately, blurs some important distinctions, as well as ignoring the fact that parmigiano is also a marvelous eating cheese.

Parmigiano belongs to the class of cheeses known as *grana* for the characteristic hard, grainy texture they develop with age. Granas are made throughout Italy, especially in the north. Grana padano is one often seen in America, as is pecorino romano (specially under the proprietary name Locatelli Romano). All are good, and all distinctive in their flavors—in fact, there are many dishes in which pecorino romano is the only cheese that will deliver the desired effect. But it can't be denied that the Rolls-Royce of granas is parmigiano-reggiano.

This most conspicuous of cheeses is made in giant wheels as big around as truck tires, and the light-colored rind is stamped with its full name in a repeating pattern that guarantees authenticity. (Pecorino romano always has a black rind, and the rinds of other granas usually look like parmigiano but without the stamped name.) The parmigiano-reggiano name is strictly controlled by law, and was so long before the D.O.C. legislation was extended to cheeses. The name parmigiano-reggiano can be used for cheese made only in a small region around the cities of Parma, Modena, Bologna, and Reggio nell'Emilia; only in the period between April 1 and November 1 (when the milk is richest); only from skimmed cow's milk obtained from two successive milkings (morning and evening); and only by a process laid down in the laws of the Duchy of Parma seven hundred years ago.

Each wheel of parmigiano weighs from fifty to eighty pounds. It may be aged for up to twenty years, though three years is enough to classify a wheel as *stravecchio* (very old). Aging develops its incomparable nutty richness and a unique crystalline texture. When young, parmigiano can be used grated, for cooking, in paper-thin shavings to top various dishes, or in small chunks for eating in the hand.

The natural drying over time makes a well-aged parmigiano an exceedingly aggressive cheese for eating in the hand (one good-sized crumb will instantly draw all the moisture out of your mouth), but it's a heady experience with a glass of good red wine.

Excellent parmigiano is now widely available in this country, but that wasn't always the case. We used to make a point of bringing some back with us from every trip to Italy. We got into the habit after our first visit to Parma. As dedicated tourists, we had inspected the principal attractions of the city—the cathedral and baptistery, the Palazzo della Pilotta museums, the ducal gardens—and what we really wanted to do was look at cheeses. We picked out a neighborhood shop that had wheels of the cheese stacked in its window, went in and explained our desire for some parmigiano to take home to the United States.

The two brothers who ran the shop thought that was very funny—wasn't there any cheese in America? After a few more witty remarks, they decided that we ought to have a piece of their new thirty-kilo wheel of *stravecchione* (very very old), and they cheerfully set about the task of deconstructing that monument. Working with knives the size of sabers, a mallet, chisels, and a crowbar, it took them twenty-five minutes to pry open and cleave the huge, dense wheel. The operation drew an appreciative audience of local customers, each with advice on a better way to do it. By the time an eighth of the wheel had been separated and securely wrapped for transport back to the United States, we were fast friends with everyone in the shop.

Other than on such magical occasions, we don't recommend buying parmigiano in eight-pound lots. (We knew we'd be sharing our import with friends.) Once a wheel is cut open, the cheese tends to dry out, so you should generally buy only as much as you'll use over a period of a few weeks. Since it stales even faster after grating, don't buy it grated unless you know that your cheese store moves enough parmigiano to grate it fresh every day. And—need we say this?—never buy *any* grated cheese prepackaged in a cardboard tube! If it isn't dead stale from all the time it sat on the manufacturer's and distributor's and grocer's shelves, it'll be so laced with chemical preservatives as hardly to qualify as a natural food anymore.

If you buy grating cheese in chunks, you can have the pleasure of acquiring some of the many ingeniously designed graters now on the market, ranging from the standard metal hand-held rotary grater, through lucite devices like fat pepper mills, on up to cordless electric contraptions in space-age molded plastics. All of those that we've tried are pretty severely challenged by the texture of a truly aged parmigiano, so we tend to rely on the simplest, low-tech tool: a flat washboard-style metal grater, as wielded by white-gloved waiters in restaurants in Italy. You simply position it over the receiving dish and rub a chunk of cheese against it. Of course, when the cheese gets down past a certain size, you're in danger of adding grated fingertip to the dish too. (Those waiters wear gloves for protection as much as sanitation!) Then we switch to a rotary grater.

If you like to serve younger parmigiano, or any other grana, on an after-dinner cheese tray, there's another specialized tool that would be a worthwhile acquisition: a small, triangular-bladed knife with a stubby handle. Since even young parmigiano is hard to cut with a blade, you use this knife—which looks a bit like an Aztec sacrificial dagger—as a pry, inserting the tip and pulling forward to detach a piece of the cheese along its natural "fault lines." It's a bit of an affectation, of course, but it's really kind of fun to use and makes a good conversation piece for guests.

RISOTTO WITH FENNEL

Riso con finocchi

FOR 4 TO 5 SERVINGS:

A pale, creamy, ethereal-looking dish, but one with a decidedly sophisticated flavor. Long cooking of fresh bulb fennel transmutes its powerful licorice character into a mild, delicate fragrance and makes it meltingly tender. This dish diverges slightly from the standard risotto technique because the fennel needs a longer initial cooking and a larger quantity of liquid to begin with. It's finished in the traditional way, however.

If your fennel bulb retains any of the plant's feathery green leaves, you can chop them and add them to the simmering broth for a more robust fennel presence in the finished dish.

♈

This subtle dish wants a rich, full-bodied white wine. Good choices would include top-quality Friulian Tocai, Pomino bianco, Fiano di Avellino, Vintage Tunina, Torre de Giano Riserva, and Lombardy Pinot bianco.

6 tablespoons butter, in all	Salt
½ cup chopped onion	Freshly grated nutmeg
1 large fennel bulb (about 1	4 cups broth
pound), cored, washed, halved,	1½ cups Arborio-style rice
and cut in ⅜-inch slices	¼ cup freshly grated parmigiano

In a large, heavy-bottomed saucepan, melt 3 tablespoons butter. Over low heat, sauté the onion in the butter 2 to 3 minutes, until soft. Add the fennel, a sprinkling of salt, and a pinch of nutmeg. Stir to coat the fennel with the seasonings. Cover the pot and cook gently 10 minutes, stirring occasionally. Meanwhile, in another pot, bring the broth to a simmer.

After 10 minutes, add the rice to the fennel and onion, stirring to coat each grain with butter. Add enough broth to cover the rice (about 2 cups). Bring to a simmer and cook, uncovered, until the rice is just tender to the bite, approximately 20 minutes, adding more broth by ladlefuls as the rice absorbs it. If you run out of broth before the rice is tender, continue with hot water. The finished dish should be moist but not soupy.

When the rice is done, taste the dish and add more salt if necessary. Off the heat, stir in the remaining 3 tablespoons butter and the grated cheese, and serve at once. ■

THE COPS' RISOTTO

Risotto alla sbirraglia

FOR 4 TO 6 SERVINGS:

F olk etymology offers two explanations for the name of this rich-with-chicken risotto from the Veneto area, neither of them flattering to the nineteenth-century Imperial Austrian police force (*la sbirraglia,* in Venetian dialect) that occupied the region in those days and lent its name to the dish. The reference is either to the habit of the *sbirri* of stealing chickens to make this risotto for their dinner in the station house, or to the longing of the rebellious locals to chop the sbirri into as many little bits as the chicken in this dish. A more benevolent explanation might be simply that the forces of empire dined pretty high on the chicken.

Bright red-gold from carrot and tomato, warm and comforting from its ample quantity of white-meat chicken, this risotto is almost a secondo. If you're using it as a primo, follow it with the lightest of secondi.

Y

Choose a full-bodied white or a gentle red, as you prefer. Pinot bianco is a good option for the white, and Dolcetto or Merlot make nice choices for the red.

3 tablespoons olive oil	¾ teaspoon salt
1 onion, chopped	Freshly ground black pepper
1 carrot, chopped	6 cups broth, or mixed broth and
1 stalk celery, chopped	water
1 pound boneless chicken breast,	1½ cups Arborio rice
cut in 1-inch cubes	4 tablespoons butter
½ cup dry white wine	⅔ cup freshly grated
¾ cup drained canned	parmigiano
Italian-style plum tomatoes,	
coarsely chopped	

In a large, heavy-bottomed casserole, heat the olive oil, add the chopped onion, carrot, and celery, and sauté over medium-low heat 10 minutes, until the vegetables are soft but not browned. Add the chicken and cook 5 minutes, stirring often.

Raise heat to medium-high, pour in the wine, and cook briskly until it evaporates. Stir in the tomatoes, salt, and a generous quantity of black pepper. Cover tightly and simmer 20 minutes, stirring once or twice.

In another pot, bring the broth to a simmer. Stir the rice into the chicken sauce and cook 1 minute. Then start adding broth in the usual risotto manner, a ladleful at a time, stirring frequently and adding more as the liquid is absorbed. Regulate the heat to maintain a steady simmer.

After about 30 minutes, the rice should be tender and the broth entirely absorbed. Stir in the butter and grated parmigiano and cook 2 more minutes. Taste for salt and serve at once. ∎

POLENTA IN THE HIGH OLD ROMAN MANNER

Polenta alla vecchia maniera romana

FOR 6 SERVINGS:

Ⴘ

A good, assertive red will work best here. Try a Nebbiolo, or a Barbera and Nebbiolo blend, or a Veneto Cabernet.

Thanks to the dried mushrooms and prosciutto fat, this is an intensely flavorful, meaty-seeming sauce. In fact, so rich is the flavor here, and so satisfying in combination with the polenta, that it could easily serve as a main dish. Try the sauce on pasta too if you like highly assertive dishes.

As we've mentioned elsewhere, prosciutto fat may not be easy to come by. But since, in these unhealthily health-conscious times, even old-line Italian stores are reluctantly trimming most of the fat off their prosciutto before slicing it, they should be willing to sell you some fat for a nominal sum or even give it to you (along with, no doubt, a lecture about how the surgeon general thinks it will kill you).

½ ounce dried porcini

2 tablespoons olive oil

3 ounces prosciutto fat, chopped
   fine

¼ cup chopped onion

¼ cup chopped carrot

1 stalk celery, chopped

1 tablespoon chopped flat-leaf
   Italian parsley

¼ teaspoon dried marjoram

1 whole clove

¼ cup white wine

2 cups drained canned
   Italian-style plum tomatoes,
   roughly chopped

Salt

Freshly ground black pepper

1 recipe polenta (page 390)

1 cup freshly grated pecorino
   romano

Put the dried mushrooms in a bowl and pour 1 cup boiling water over them. Let them sit for 30 minutes, then drain. Rinse the mushroom pieces thoroughly, chop them fine, and rinse again to remove all traces of grit. (This recipe doesn't use the mushroom-soaking water, but you can reserve it for other purposes: line a sieve with a dampened paper towel and strain the liquid into a small bowl.)

In a nonreactive skillet, heat the olive oil, add the prosciutto fat, and sauté over low heat 2 to 3 minutes, until the fat is well rendered and brown. Add the onion, carrot, celery, parsley, marjoram, clove, and chopped mushrooms. Stir and sauté 5 minutes.

Turn heat to high, pour in the wine, and cook rapidly, stirring, until it is almost evaporated. Then add the tomatoes, a light sprinkling of salt, and a generous quantity of black pepper. Cover and cook 30 minutes. When the sauce is done, set it aside until ready to use. Then bring it back to a simmer.

Cook the polenta as directed in the basic recipe. Spread it out on a platter, pour the sauce over it, and top with half the grated pecorino. Serve at once, passing the remaining pecorino at the table. ■

SECONDI

Snow swirling outside the windows, chill winds howling around the eaves, darkness settling down quickly outside, while inside all is light and warmth and good smells from the kitchen.

Did we miss a cliché there? We hope not, because there's a real truth buried under that "family values" prose. The ancient reptilian cortex that we all carry around in our hindbrains knows that winter is for hunkering down, gathering the clan together, helping each other stay warm and fed through the lean, cold months ahead. Even if in fact some of us deal with cold weather by fleeing south to a tropical clime (or for that matter, by having given up entirely on cold weather and gone to live in a permanently frost-free zone), the body craves periods of hearty eating. These are the times for long-cooked stews, for boiled meats and roasts, for the dishes that perfume the house all day long as they cook quietly in a low oven or on a back burner.

OK, we know you work all day—who doesn't? And we know you can't spend several hours a day in the kitchen—who can? But hours of cooking means something different for the cooked than for the cook. Everything is happening to the chicken or beef or veal that is being transformed into your dinner, but once you've got them on the stove, your work is essentially over. Just because something's in the oven doesn't mean you have to sit on top of it all day like a broody hen on an egg. Long, gentle cooking—an instruction you'll see often in the next batch of pages—means undemanding cooking. Go write a letter, pay your bills, do a crossword puzzle, call your parents, call your children, wash the windows, or eat tonight's dinner while tomorrow's is taking shape on the stove: all that this kind of cooking requires is that you look in on it from time to time, stir it, sniff it, maybe taste it—nothing to make a fuss about, and a great deal to enjoy.

Our recipes in this section include a few fancy boiled items—a chicken stuffed with nuts and fruits; meats with bright, acid sauces—and stews or braises (the distinction in Italy may amount to personal preference about moistness or dryness) with deep, pungent, barely tomato-scented sauces. For family consumption, many of both sorts of dishes can easily become one-pot meals with the addition of a vegetable or potato.

With all of this moist, slow cooking going on, we've found it useful to keep a bit of made-up simple tomato sauce in the refrigerator or the freezer. Most of these dishes are not in any true sense of the words tomato-based, or even cooked in tomato sauces, but most of them want a small dollop of concentrated tomato flavor as part of their symphony. You can certainly use tomato paste from a handy squeeze tube, but a pint or half-pint of tomato sauce is an equally useful staple.

You won't find much fish here (and the one you do find may not be what you bargained for!): even in Italy, this is the meat season, the red wine time. So most of the recipes that follow are going to match well with red wines, ranging from the simplest to the subtlest. Some are pull-out-all-the-stops company dishes, but many are family dishes—though all share a harmonious richness of flavor that will make any of them, matched with an appropriate bottle of wine, a feast fit for the best of company and the dearest of kin.

BRAISED TINY OCTOPI

Moscardini in umido

FOR 4 SERVINGS:

For all the myriad of names that Italian has to differentiate these tasty creatures by size and species, English has only one poor noun, and an ugly one at that: octopus. No wonder so many Americans wrinkle their noses at the idea of eating them: an octopus scarcely sounds like the kind of beast we'd like to see on our plates. A *moscardino*, now, is an animal of a different stripe altogether: attractive, tiny (no more than 4 inches long, and the smaller the better, the tenderer and sweeter), with cute little tentacles and a nice, plump gray-brown sac. That sounds and looks appetizing.

In Italy, the really tiny ones (1 to 1½ inches long) are simply dredged with flour and deep-fried, usually along with equally tiny,

A dry white, as simple or as complex as your mood demands: the dish will accommodate them all. An excellent midrange choice would be Sauvignon from Friuli.

equally tasty squids and shrimps and fishes, as a component in a *fritto misto del mare*. Alas, we never get moscardini that small in this country—but we are increasingly seeing the next size up (approximately 3 inches) in our fish markets. When you see them, grab them: This is a recipe to keep on hand for when you can get those really small octopi—12 to 15 to the pound.

You probably won't be able to get your fishmonger (another ugly word: there's a bias against seafood built into the English language; nobody "mongs" vegetables) to clean the octopi for you, but be assured: it's really very easy to do. It will probably take you as long to read the directions as to perform the act. You can prepare them well in advance and keep them in the refrigerator until needed. Their actual cooking takes only about 20 minutes. As with all seafood, timing is critical in this dish: If you overlook the octopi, they'll turn to shoe leather and you'll have to cook on and on to get them soft again, which will in turn undo the lightness and freshness which is the charm of this recipe.

You don't have to rush the moscardini to the table, however: this dish is even better after it cools a little. Garlicked, toasted breads and raw fennel *in pinzimonio* (a vinaigrette dipping sauce) make excellent accompaniments to this lovely dish.

1½ pounds tiny octopi	4 tablespoons finely chopped
6 tablespoons olive oil	flat-leaf Italian parsley
1 large clove garlic, finely	½ cup dry white wine
chopped	1 cup canned Italian-style
¼ teaspoon crushed red	tomatoes, drained and chopped
pepper	Salt

To prepare the octopi:

Pick up an octopus and turn its body sac inside out. Pull away all the intestines (they come away neatly and hang by a thread). Cut off the head just above the eyes, freeing the sac from the intestines. Then holding the tentacles, cut just below the eyes. Flatten the tentacles into a rosette and look for a small hard beak at the center. Squeeze or poke it out and discard it. Turn the body sac right side out again and peel off any skin that hasn't already detached itself. Prepare the remaining octopi the same way, then rinse and drain them in a colander.

To cook the dish:

In a large, nonreactive skillet, heat the olive oil. Add the garlic, red pepper, and half the parsley, and sauté over medium-low heat 1 to 2 minutes, until the garlic begins to turn golden. Then add the octopi and sauté, stirring, 3 to 4 minutes.

Raise heat to medium-high and add the wine. Boil briskly until it is reduced to about one quarter of its volume, then add the tomatoes and a sprinkling of salt. Cover and simmer about 10 minutes, until the octopi are just tender. There should be some liquid remaining in the pan (i.e., the octopi should not be simply frying in the oil).

Transfer the contents of the pan to a serving dish, sprinkle on the remaining parsley, and serve at once. ■

VENETIAN BRAISED CHICKEN WITH MUSHROOMS

Pollastrello con funghi alla veneta

FOR 4 SERVINGS:

This lovely, satisfying recipe is probably very old: Those of a historical turn of mind will hear and taste, in its cinnamon and cloves, distant echoes of the Eastern spice trade that made the republic of Venice one of the great powers of Renaissance Europe. The tomatoes are probably a relatively modern addition; even so, they don't make a noticeably tomatoey sauce—it remains brown and meaty and subtle in style.

The traditional version of this dish calls for fresh funghi porcini, which would make it unutterably lavish. Plain cultivated mushrooms work quite nicely as substitutes. Cremini would be even better—and of course, if you can get any of the exotic woods mushrooms, by all means use them. You can also reinforce the flavor of domestic mushrooms by adding a bit of reconstituted dried porcini (and their strained soaking liquid) to the mix.

An uncanonical but good accompaniment to this dish (especially if you are not having a primo) is freshly made egg noodles, tossed with a bit of butter and the chicken's own sauce.

4 tablespoons butter, in all

3 tablespoons olive oil

¼ cup chopped onion

⅓ cup chopped celery

⅓ cup chopped carrot

One 3½-pound chicken, cut in
   serving pieces

Flour for dredging

2 whole cloves

¼ teaspoon ground cinnamon

¼ cup dry white wine

1 cup drained canned Italian-style
   plum tomatoes

Salt

Freshly ground black pepper

1 pound small white mushrooms,
   sliced ¼ inch thick

In a large casserole, melt 2 tablespoons butter with 2 tablespoons olive oil. Add the onion, celery, and carrot and sauté 3 to 5 minutes, until soft.

Rinse the chicken pieces, pat them dry with paper towels, and dredge them with flour. Push the vegetables to the side of the casserole and brown the chicken pieces on both sides, about 10 minutes. Add the cloves, cinnamon, and white wine. Raise heat to high and stir constantly until the wine is almost evaporated, scraping up browned bits from the bottom of the pan.

Put the tomatoes through a food mill fitted with the medium blade and add them to the pan. Stir, cover, and cook 20 to 25 minutes, until the chicken is tender. Turn the pieces over in the sauce once or twice during the cooking, adding warm water by tablespoonfuls if the sauce seems to be drying out. (But don't let it get soupy.) Halfway through the cooking, taste the sauce and add salt and pepper to taste.

While the chicken is cooking, heat the remaining butter and oil in a skillet and add the sliced mushrooms. Sauté over high heat, stirring constantly, until the mushrooms take up all the fat, about

1 minute. Turn heat to low, sprinkle the mushrooms with salt, and cook until beads of moisture begin to appear on them, about 2 minutes. Turn heat to medium and cook, stirring often, 5 more minutes.

When the chicken is tender, stir the mushrooms into the casserole, cook a final 5 minutes, and serve. ■

POACHED CHICKEN WITH WALNUT AND PIGNOLI STUFFING

Pollo ripieno alle noce

FOR 4 SERVINGS:

At once simple and complex, this wonderfully flavored dish demonstrates how a boiled chicken can be the food of kings. Remember the French King Henri IV, who made the first political promise of a chicken in every pot every Sunday. He of course had an Italian wife, Marie de' Medici, who is generally credited with inducing the French not to eat peas with a knife. (She introduced both peas and forks to France.)

The very rich stuffing of this bird virtually makes itself into a boudin, which you serve alongside the tender, moist flesh of the delicately poached bird. (If you're reluctant to spring for a sweetbread for the stuffing, you could substitute ground veal, but it will coarsen the texture somewhat.)

The poaching broth, which takes on wonderful flavor from what has been prepared in it, can be served as a first course with passatelli

A good white wine is the thing here, and any number of candidates will work: Fiano, Greco, Torre di Giano, cru Soave, full-bodied Arneis, top-quality Tocai or Sauvignon from Friuli, Pinot bianco, or Pomino Il Benefizio.

(page 41) or fresh egg noodles. Possible condiments for the finished bird—though none is strictly necessary—would be *salsa verde* (p. 383) or *salsa agrodolce* (p. 385)—or any of the spicy sauces commonly served with boiled meats.

1 chicken, 3 to 3½ pounds

SEASONINGS FOR THE BROTH:

½ carrot

1 stalk celery

1 small parsnip

½ small onion

1 bay leaf

5 whole peppercorns

1 teaspoon salt

INGREDIENTS FOR THE STUFFING:

4 to 5 slices day-old Italian or French bread, crusts removed, cut in 2-inch chunks (about 2 cups)

½ cup milk

4 ounces sweetbreads, trimmed and cut in 2-inch chunks

1 chicken liver, trimmed and cut in 3 to 4 pieces

⅓ cup shelled walnuts (1½ ounces), finely chopped

¼ cup pignoli (1½ ounces), finely chopped

1 egg

1 tablespoon freshly grated parmigiano

½ teaspoon salt

Freshly ground black pepper

Freshly grated nutmeg

Fill a large pot with enough water to eventually cover the chicken. Add all the seasoning ingredients, cover, and bring to a boil. Let this broth cook along while you do the remaining preparations.

Put the bread in a bowl, pour the milk over it, and leave it to soak. Pulse the pieces of sweetbreads and chicken liver in a food processor (or chop them finely together). Gently squeeze the milk out of the bread and put it in a large bowl. Add the meats, nuts, egg, parmigiano, ½ teaspoon salt, a generous quantity of freshly ground black pepper, and nutmeg to taste. Mix well. This will be a very wet stuffing.

Rinse the chicken. Fill its body cavity with the stuffing and sew the opening closed with a darning needle and heavy thread. Also sew closed any holes in the chicken's skin from which the stuffing might escape. Truss the chicken securely with kitchen string and slide it into the boiling broth. Adjust heat to maintain a gentle simmer and cook covered 1½ hours, until the chicken is perfectly tender.

Transfer the bird to a carving board and remove all the string and thread. Extract the stuffing whole, if possible, and cut it in thick slices. Carve the bird into serving pieces. Arrange chicken and stuffing on a heated deep platter and moisten it with some of the broth before serving. ∎

ROAST TURKEY WITH FRUIT-AND-CHESTNUT STUFFING

Tacchino arrosto alla lombarda

FOR 8 SERVINGS:

*T*his festive dish, a Christmas classic, is traditionally accompanied by boiled new potatoes browned in butter, sautéed spinach with raisins, and mostarda di Cremona, the spicy fruit relish that Italians dote on with roasted or boiled meats.

The real star of this recipe is its delightful, variegated stuffing, whose luscious fruit-nut-and-meat interplays give intriguing overtones to the normally bland turkey meat. Its base is chestnuts. For ease of handling, we've called for dried ones. Dried chestnuts, already peeled, are much easier to work with than fresh, but they need reconstituting. If you use fresh chestnuts, buy ½ pound, peel them, remove the brown inner skins (if you can without going mad), and skip the initial soaking-in-milk step.

A round and complex, not-too-aggressive red wine will match admirably with this roast turkey. Look for a 3- to 4-year-old Friuli Merlot, or slightly older Teroldego or Venegazzu. Carmignano Riserva or Chianti Classico Riserva will also serve well.

FOR THE STUFFING:

4 ounces dried chestnuts

2 cups milk, approximately

3 ounces pitted prunes

1 apple

1 firm-ripe pear

2 ounces shelled walnuts (about ¼
    cup)

2 ounces ground veal

1½ ounces pancetta, cut in
    matchsticks (or substitute
    blanched bacon)

½ teaspoon salt

2 tablespoons cognac

FOR THE TURKEY:

1 young turkey, 10 to 12 pounds

4 tablespoons softened butter

12 to 18 sage leaves

2 teaspoons rosemary leaves

½ cup broth

To prepare the chestnuts:

Put the chestnuts in a large pot with 1 cup of the milk and bring
to a boil. Boil 2 minutes, then turn off the heat and let the nuts sit
in the milk for at least 2 hours. Drain and rinse the nuts, discarding
the milk. Pick them over carefully, removing any remaining bits of
brown skin and cutting out any unsound parts.

Put the nuts in a clean pot with the remaining milk to cover.
Bring to a boil and simmer briskly, uncovered, about 15 minutes,
until the milk is entirely absorbed. Drain, rinse, and coarsely chop
them.

To make the stuffing:

Put the prunes in a bowl and pour boiling water over them to cover.
Let them soften 15 minutes, then drain, squeeze gently, and
coarsely chop them. Peel, quarter, and core the apple and pear. Cut
them crosswise into ¼-inch slices.

In a large bowl, mix together the chestnuts, prunes, walnuts,
apple and pear slices, ground veal, pancetta, salt, and cognac.

To cook the turkey:

Preheat the oven to 350°F. Rinse, drain, and pat dry the turkey.
Remove any pinfeathers. Fill the body cavity with the stuffing
mixture and sew it closed. Truss it with kitchen string so it will hold
its shape.

Rub the turkey's skin all over with the softened butter and set it on a rack in a roasting pan. Strew the sage and rosemary leaves around the bottom of the pan, and put the pan in the oven.

Roast the turkey for approximately 3 hours, basting every 20 minutes, first with the broth, then with its own pan juices. If the skin over the breast darkens too much, cover it lightly with a sheet of aluminum foil. The bird is done when its internal temperature reaches 175 to 180°F.

Transfer the turkey to a carving board and let it sit 20 minutes. Meanwhile, degrease the pan juices and strain them into a gravy boat. Remove the trussing string from the turkey, spoon out the stuffing into a dish, carve the bird, and serve. ■

VEAL BRAISED WITH POTATOES

Spezzatino di vitello con patate

FOR 4 SERVINGS:

*T*his homey dish employs an interesting technique: frying potatoes briefly before putting them into a braising liquid. That keeps them nicely intact by sealing their outsides so they don't break up in the cooking. At the same time, it lets them get very soft inside. (Don't be alarmed by the amount of oil called for below. It's for the frying and doesn't all end up in the dish. See About Frying in Olive Oil, page 128, if you need encouragement here.) You can fry the potatoes in batches if necessary, and the oil can be saved and reused.

By the end of the cooking, the veal will have used up almost all its liquid. That's fine, though you could add more water if you want a juicier dish; there's plenty of flavor to go around. This is one of

A not-too-aggressive red wine with some complexity will work best here. Try Vino Nobile or Rubesco, Dolcetto, or Barbera.

those traditional recipes for which there is no single canonical, you-must-do-it-this-way version: different cooks make it as moist or as dry as they and their families prefer.

2 tablespoons butter

1 cup olive oil

2 pounds boneless veal shoulder, cut in 2-inch pieces

Salt

Freshly ground black pepper

1 teaspoon rosemary leaves

1 tablespoon tomato paste

2 pounds potatoes, cut in wedges like apple segments, 1 inch at the thickest part

In a large nonreactive skillet, melt the butter with 1 tablespoon olive oil. Dry the pieces of veal with paper towels and brown them on all sides over medium-high heat, about 2 minutes.

Reduce heat to medium-low and sprinkle the meat with salt, pepper, and rosemary leaves. Dissolve the tomato paste in ½ cup warm water and stir it into the pan. Cover tightly and cook 40 minutes, regulating the heat to maintain a steady simmer. Turn the pieces of meat occasionally.

While the meat is cooking, heat the remaining oil in a heavy skillet to 360°F. Add the potatoes and mix to coat them all with the oil. Reduce heat to medium-low and cook 5 minutes, mixing the potatoes often, so all their surfaces are sealed. Set a sieve over a large bowl and pour out the contents of the skillet, leaving the potatoes suspended to drain off their excess oil.

When the veal has cooked 40 minutes, add the potatoes, stir all together well, cover, and cook 30 minutes more, mixing occasionally. If the cover does not seal tightly and the liquid evaporates so that the meat begins to fry, add small amounts of hot water.

Either serve at once or reheat when needed. ■

VEAL IN RED WINE

Vitello al vino

FOR 4 SERVINGS:

*M*ost Italian veal dishes suffer in American translation because our calves are so much bigger and older than Italian animals. This lusty dish is the exception: its rich, strong flavors are tailor-made—or butcher-made—for the kind of oldish veal we get in this country. One of the surprising presences in its harmony of tastes is the bay leaf, or rather bay leaves: their accent shines through quite pleasingly.

This is another of those Italian meat dishes that lie midway between a stew and a braise. The meat isn't meant to be swimming in sauce, only masked by it. Like all such dishes, this one can be made up well in advance and reheated when needed—just don't thicken the sauce until immediately before serving.

This dish wants a big red wine, both in it and alongside it, so it makes sense to use the same one for both purposes. Montepulciano d'Abruzzo works well, and so do the Lombardy reds (Inferno, Sassella, Grumello). A Rosso di Montalcino would also be fine.

6 tablespoons butter, in all

½ cup chopped onion

2 to 2½ pounds boneless stewing veal, cut in 2-inch pieces

Salt

Freshly ground black pepper

½ cup full-bodied dry red wine

2 to 3 tablespoons chopped flat-leaf Italian parsley

1 clove garlic, cut in 3 to 4 slices

2 bay leaves

1 cup broth, approximately

1½ tablespoons flour

In a large nonreactive casserole, melt half the butter and sauté the onion over medium heat 5 minutes. Pat the pieces of veal dry with paper towels.

Raise heat to medium-high, add the veal pieces, and cook them, turning, until they just lose their raw color, 1 to 2 minutes. Sprinkle the veal with salt and pepper and pour in the wine. Cook rapidly over high heat, stirring, 5 minutes. (Depending on the condition of your veal, the liquid will do either of two things: disappear—in part evaporating and in part being absorbed by the veal—or increase—

the wine may draw a good deal of liquid out of the veal. Either one is OK.)

Reduce heat to low, add the parsley, garlic, and bay leaves, stir, cover, and let simmer 1½ hours. Stir occasionally and, if necessary, add a few tablespoons of broth from time to time to keep the meat from drying out.

Mash the remaining butter in a small bowl and work in the flour to make a smooth paste. Reheat the veal to a simmer if necessary and stir the flour-butter paste into the sauce until it dissolves. Cook 4 minutes, stirring more or less constantly, then serve. ∎

BOILED VEAL SHANKS WITH GREEN SAUCE

Vitello bollito con salsa verde

FOR 4 SERVINGS:

A generous, full-bodied white wine will match best with these shanks and their piquant sauce. Try Pomino Il Benfizio, Torre di Giano Riserva, older Fiano, or Vintage Tunina.

*A*nother way of exploiting the marvelous succulence of veal shanks. Please see About Veal Shanks, page 279, for information on buying and portioning the meat. This is an altogether simpler recipe than either of the two in our Fall section, but the salsa verde—a mouth-tingling mixture of parsley, garlic, caper, anchovy, and vinegar, given body by fine bread crumbs—gives the dish real zing.

You can boil the shanks in broth or half broth and half water. Whatever you start with, the resulting brodo makes a nice medium for noodles or passatelli as a first course. And whatever you do, don't neglect the marrow. It's delicious spread on bread with salt and a crackling of pepper.

FOR COOKING THE VEAL SHANKS:

1 carrot, coarsely chopped

1 small onion, coarsely chopped

1 stalk celery, coarsely chopped

2 to 3 sprigs flat-leaf Italian
    parsley

½ teaspoon salt

3 whole peppercorns

4 meaty pieces veal shank, 2 to
    2½ inches long (about 3½
    pounds)

FOR THE SALSA VERDE:

2 anchovy fillets

2 cloves garlic

1½ tablespoon capers, rinsed and
    drained

¼ teaspoon salt

⅓ cup chopped flat-leaf Italian
    parsley

Scant ¼ cup fresh bread crumbs
    made from day-old Italian-style
    bread

2 teaspoons red wine vinegar

¼ cup olive oil

To cook the veal shanks:

In a large casserole, combine about 2 quarts water, or a mixture of water and broth, with the carrot, onion, celery, parsley, salt, and peppercorns. Bring to a boil over high heat and add the veal shanks, arranging them with the wider marrow opening facing upward. When the casserole returns to a boil, reduce heat to low, cover, and simmer 1¼ to 1½ hours, until the veal is perfectly tender.

To make the salsa verde:

Finely chop the anchovies, garlic, and capers together. Add the salt and parsley and chop again. In a small bowl, sprinkle the vinegar over the bread crumbs, and toss well. Stir in the parsley mixture, then add the olive oil to make a thick, nubbly sauce. Taste for seasoning and add more salt and vinegar if desired.

To serve:

Using a spatula, transfer the veal shanks from their cooking liquid to a warmed serving dish, handling them carefully to keep the marrow intact. Spoon a little broth over the shanks to keep them moist and serve at once. Pass the salsa verde separately, along with plenty of country bread (plain or toasted) to spread with marrow. ∎

BOILED BEEF WITH SWEET-AND-SOUR SAUCE

Bollito di manzo con salsa agrodolce

FOR 4 SERVINGS:

A red wine, but not too big or
assertive. Dolcetto or Barbera
would be fine; so would young
Taurasi or Aglianico, or a
young Gattinara.

The Italian partiality for serving simply boiled cuts of meat is part of the general Italian predisposition to simplicity in cooking and to the preservation of each ingredient's basic, natural flavors. Italian cooks, whether home cooks or restaurant chefs, insist on a level of freshness, quality, and flavor in those ingredients that we in the United States rarely ever see, for all our putatively higher standard of living.

In other words, boiled beef makes a wonderful, deeply satisfying dinner—if you have a wonderful piece of beef. We, being blessed with a local butcher with Italian standards—O. Ottomanelli & Sons, on Bleecker Street—enjoy it often. Our favorite cut is eye of chuck, not too easy to find in conventional butcher shops. Fresh brisket can also be fine. In Italy, short ribs are often used, but Italian beef is a lot leaner than ours, so be prepared to trim ruthlessly if you want to try that cut.

The salsa agrodolce takes only about five minutes to make and should be served fresh and warm. For us, the peperoncino rosso really perks up the sauce and we urge you to try it. The sauce is so simple that you could make up one batch with peperoncino and one without, and compare them.

FOR THE BOILED BEEF:

2 pounds eye of chuck or other
    boiling cut of beef, in a single
    piece
1 celery stalk, halved
1 carrot, halved lengthwise
1 small onion, halved

1 clove garlic
½ bay leaf
2 tablespoons chopped flat-leaf
    Italian parsley
1½ teaspoons salt
6 peppercorns

FOR THE SALSA AGRODOLCE:

1 tablespoon butter

1 tablespoon olive oil

1 peperoncino rosso (optional)

*2 tablespoons chopped flat-leaf
  Italian parsley*

⅛ teaspoon salt

1 clove garlic

1 tablespoon tomato paste

1 tablespoon red wine vinegar

1½ teaspoons sugar

Choose a pot large enough to hold the piece of beef and fill it with enough water to eventually cover the meat by 2 inches. Add all the flavoring vegetables and seasonings and bring the pot to a boil. Slide in the meat. When the water returns to a boil, adjust the heat to maintain a brisk simmer, and cook until the meat is very tender when pierced with a fork—2 hours or more, depending on the thickness of the cut.

While the meat is cooking, prepare the sauce. In a small pan over low heat, melt the butter in the olive oil. Add the peperoncino (if using), parsley, and salt. Put the garlic clove through a press into the pan and stir well. Sauté 3 minutes. In a cup, dissolve the tomato paste with ¼ cup water and the wine vinegar. Add it to the skillet. Add the sugar, stir, and cook 2 minutes. Remove the peperoncino and keep the sauce warm until ready to serve (or reheat it later).

When the meat is done, remove it from the broth to a heated deep platter. Bathe it with some of its broth. Carve thick slices at table (to keep the meat from cooling off too quickly). Pass a dish of the warm sauce. ■

TUSCAN POT ROAST

Manzo in umido

FOR 4 SERVINGS:

A red wine of medium body and medium complexity will work best here. We suggest Chianti Classico, Carmignano, Vino Nobile, or Rubesco for regional authenticity or near it. Dolcetto or young Gattinara would also be fine.

*T*his has got to be the world's simplest pot roast. You just sweat it along, covered, in its own juices—no other liquid for most of the time. It makes a richly flavored roast, very moist, with a good, dense, dark brown sauce, even though there isn't a speck of flour or any similar thickener.

You need to use a loose-textured cut of beef, like eye of chuck; we find that top or bottom round clenches under this type of cooking and never really tenderizes.

2 pounds stewing beef, preferably eye of chuck, in a single piece

3 tablespoons butter

1½ tablespoons olive oil

2 cloves garlic

4 sage leaves

Salt

Freshly ground black pepper

½ cup red wine

½ cup broth

In a Dutch oven just large enough to hold the meat, melt the butter with the oil. Add the garlic and sage. Pat the meat dry with paper towels and put it in the pan. Sprinkle it lightly with salt and pepper. Turn heat low, cover, and cook gently 1 hour, turning the meat after the first 5 minutes and then at intervals throughout the cooking.

After an hour, uncover the pot, raise heat to medium, add the wine, and boil it briskly 1 to 2 minutes, until nearly evaporated. Lower heat again, cover, and continue cooking until the meat is very tender, about 30 more minutes.

Bring the broth to a simmer in a small pot. When the meat is done, remove it to a serving platter and keep it warm. Degrease the pan juices carefully and discard the garlic and sage. Add the broth and boil rapidly, stirring and scraping up any browned bits from the bottom of the pot, until the sauce is nicely thickened.

Slice the meat fairly thick, ladle the sauce over it, and serve. ■

PIEDMONTESE BRAISED BEEF

Bruscit

FOR 4 SERVINGS:

This most unusual Piedmontese dish is pronouncedly spicy with wine and fennel. It's an extremely fine flavor, especially considering the few and relatively humble ingredients that compose it, but it's not going to be popular with those who don't like assertive flavors. *Bruscit* is a dialect name, and we haven't been able to find out what exactly it means. A reasonable bet is that the word is related to the standard Italian *bruscare*, meaning to brush or rasp, and the adjective *brusco*, meaning brusque, brisk, harsh, or assertive.

Serve bruscit with polenta and only polenta; it's much too strong for gnocchi or pasta. It also likes lots of pepper, so be sure to pass the pepper mill at the table.

What's called for here is a very high quality red wine, with plenty of assertion of its own and a good supply of tannin to match the bruscit's attack. Any of the fine Nebbiolo-based wines will do well, especially the Alban trinity—Nebbiolo, Barbaresco, Barolo.

3 tablespoons butter

2 pounds boneless beef stew, cut in ½-inch dice

2 ounces pancetta, cut in julienne strips

1 tablespoon fennel seeds, tied in a cheesecloth bag

Salt

½ cup dry red wine

Freshly ground black pepper

1 recipe polenta (page 390)

In a heavy casserole, melt the butter. Add the beef, pancetta, and bag of fennel seeds. Cook over medium heat, stirring, to brown the meat on all sides. Sprinkle it with salt. Add half the wine, cover tightly, and cook 2 hours, adjusting heat to maintain a gentle simmer. Check the pan every 15 minutes or so, and add the rest of the wine gradually, a tablespoon or so at a time, as each dose is absorbed.

At the end of the cooking time, the sauce should be dense and velvety and the meat extremely tender. If the sauce seems too thin toward the end, partially uncover the pan long enough to reduce the sauce sufficiently. At the end, remove the bag of fennel seeds and add a generous quantity of freshly ground black pepper.

While the meat is cooking, make the polenta as directed in the basic recipe. Pour it out onto a platter, make a slight depression in the center, and pour the bruscit and all its sauce onto the polenta. Serve at once, passing the pepper mill at the table. ∎

About Polenta

Now that Americans have given their hearts to pasta and risotto, there's no reason they can't extend their affection to the third Italian staple, polenta—especially since polenta is near kin to good old-fashioned American grits.

Like grits, polenta is inexpensive and rib-sticking. Like pasta and risotto, it's a culinary chameleon. You can serve polenta plain, with butter and salt and pepper, in place of mashed potatoes. You can dress it with sauces of all sorts—brown, red, white, and yellow. You can grill it and serve it with sausages or with game birds. You can melt sharp cheese on it. You can stir meats or vegetables or cheeses into it. And although it's made from corn, which often flattens a glass of wine, polenta gets along with wines just fine.

Polenta is one of the oldest foods known to man. The conquering legions of the Roman Empire subsisted on *pulmentum,* a sort of porridge made from various grains, which they learned about from the Etruscans. Polenta as we know it today, made with cornmeal, has been a staple of Italian peasant cooking ever since corn was introduced from the New World to the Old. In Italy, the techniques and utensils for making polenta are decreed by ancient custom and observed with reverence bordering on superstition.

According to the purest tradition, polenta must be cooked in a *paiolo,* a large copper pot shaped like a pail with a flaring rim. It's filled with water, which is brought to a violent boil (preferably over an open fire), and then coarse-ground cornmeal is showered in ever so gradually with one hand while the other hand stirs incessantly—and only in one direction!—with a long wooden stick called a *tarello.* (Chestnut and acacia are the only two woods sanctioned by the orthodox.) The polenta cooks for an hour, being stirred unremittingly, and then the seething lava is poured out onto a wooden board, or onto a linen cloth on a board. Mounded and set, the polenta is then sliced, either with a long wooden blade or a taut string—never a metal knife!—and served.

This is a charming portrait of the kitchen technology of a bygone age, and for those with an interest in culinary history and the leisure to experiment, it can be a pleasure to reconstruct the old ways. But few of us today have either the time or the equipment required, and so we pass it by.

But here's the good news. Polenta is not as demanding as all that. It does require a little more time and tending than pasta, but no more than risotto; and the range and versatility of the dishes you can make with polenta come close to those of pasta and rice.

Polenta may be a bit of an acquired taste for American palates—except for Southerners who grew up on spoon bread, hush puppies, and hominy grits—but it's very easily acquired once you discover all the interesting things that can be done with it. Here are some shortcuts we've found in our experiments:

- You don't have to scald your hand to trickle the meal through your fingers into boiling water; it mixes perfectly well with cool water.
- Calphalon or enameled cast iron transmits heat just as evenly as copper, and holds it well enough that it isn't necessary to stir unceasingly; once every couple of minutes will usually do it.
- Spreading the polenta shallow in a broad pot (as opposed to piling it deep in a pail-shaped vessel) both shortens the cooking time and permits stirring with an ordinary spoon, not the heavy rolling pin some modern recipes recommend.
- The finer the meal is ground, the quicker it cooks: 20 to 30 minutes is usually enough—though you can let it go longer if that's more convenient. For some people, the grittiness of very coarse-ground cornmeal is part of the pleasure of polenta. For others, the smoothness achieved only from finely ground meal makes a better foil for sauces, meats, or vegetables. *De gustibus.*

There are even recipes for cooking polenta in the oven or the microwave. But here we draw the line. Call it artisan pride, or call it ancient prejudice—but we like to keep in closer touch with our polenta than oven cooking allows.

Here's our preferred way to make polenta. The flavor and texture are identical to that produced by the most labor-intensive traditional techniques.

FOR 4 SERVINGS:

1½ teaspoons salt   1½ cups cornmeal
4 cups water

In a broad, heavy-bottomed pot, dissolve the salt in the water. Gradually add the cornmeal, stirring vigorously with a fork or wire whisk. Set the pot over medium heat and stir more or less continuously until the liquid comes to a simmer and begins suddenly to thicken. Turn heat to low and change to a large spoon or paddle-shaped scraper. Continue to cook and give a thorough stir, scraping all over the bottom of the pan, every minute or so.

The polenta will continue to thicken, and eventually will begin to stick to itself, rather than to the pot. As soon as it definitely pulls away from the sides of the pot—as little as 15 minutes, depending on the diameter of the pot and the depth of polenta in it—it's done.

If the polenta is to be served as is, use one of the following methods:

- Pour it into a heated dish and serve by scooping out individual portions (like mashed potatoes) with a spoon.
- Pour it onto a heated platter, mounding it slightly, and let it sit for a few minutes to firm. Cut vertical slices with a knife moistened with hot water.
- Pour it onto a heated platter, smooth the surface, and top it with the meat or other accompaniment. (If the accompaniment is a stew or something in sauce or gravy, make a basin-shaped depression in the polenta deep enough to hold the liquid and other ingredients.)

If the polenta is to be grilled, fried, or otherwise treated:
Take a large flat plate or marble and wet it down with cold water. Pour the polenta onto the surface and level it with a spatula or your hands, dipped in cold water as necessary to keep the polenta from sticking to them. (For most uses, the polenta should be about ⅜ inch thick.) Let it cool completely, then cut it into the desired shapes and proceed with the preparation. ■

THE BUTCHER'S STEW

Ragù del macellaio

FOR 4 SERVINGS:

*W*e had the policeman's risotto (page 367), with stolen chickens, no less; and the whore's pasta (page 160); now we have the butcher's stew, made with small amounts of several different meats. This dish is a specialty of Bari, where they dress *orecchiette* or *cavatieddi* with the sauce for a first course and serve the meat as a secondo. You could do it that way, but we like to serve gnocchi alongside. The dish also goes well with puree of potatoes or even polenta. A few sliced mushrooms browned separately and added to the sauce along with the tomatoes are another nice touch—not truly traditional, but very tasty.

Mixed-meat dishes seem to constitute an Italian culinary subspeciality, a minor oddity in a cuisine otherwise devoted to purity and singularity of flavor. The "noble"—i.e., costly—exemplars are bollito misto (always and only meats), *fritto misto* (may be meat or fish or vegetable), and *grigliata mista* (either meat or fish). *Ragù del macellaio* is the humble relative—what you make when the butcher gives you a price on odds and ends of meat accumulated throughout the day, or what the butcher's family gets to eat after all the good cuts are sold.

The roots of Italian cooking are in the cooking of the poor, and even the finest dishes reflect that heritage. Close kin to this southern example of the breed, for instance, is Piedmont's great *finanziera,* which is normally matched with the finest Barolos and Barbarescos, but is still essentially a stew of bits of veal and sweetbread and other offal. (We gave a recipe for it in *La Tavola Italiana.*) So, too, one of the specialties of the once great Ristorante Dodici Apostoli in Verona, *il piatto del taverniere,* which is a delicious braise of small pieces of kidney and liver—veal, beef, and/or horse—that matches exquisitely with the oldest Amarones.

A fine red wine is ideal here: Aglianico del Vulture Riserva, Salice Salentino Riserva, Taurasi Riserva, Regaleali Rosso del Conte, Corvo's Duca Enrico.

3 tablespoons olive oil
½ cup sliced onion
8 to 10 ounces each boneless veal,
   beef, lamb, and pork, cut in
   1½-inch cubes

1 cup drained canned Italian-style
   plum tomatoes, chopped
½ teaspoon salt
Freshly ground black pepper
1 recipe potato gnocchi (page 254)

In a casserole, heat the olive oil, add the sliced onion, and sauté over medium heat 3 minutes. Add the mixture of meats and brown the pieces well (in several batches if necessary). Stir in the tomatoes, salt, and a generous quantity of pepper. Cover and cook over low heat, stirring frequently, for 1½ hours, or until the meats are very tender. Taste for salt.

Cook the gnocchi as directed in the basic recipe. Transfer them to a heated serving dish, toss gently with the bruscit, both meat and sauce, and serve at once. ∎

SARDINIAN LAMB STEW

Petto di agnello al forno

FOR 4 SERVINGS:

*A*l forno in an Italian recipe name means baked, which is probably the original way this dish was cooked in Sardinia. Our mostly stove-top technique is a modern adaptation, convenient if you need the oven for another purpose. Either way, gentle cooking is the key, to allow those strong, wilds-of-Sardinia flavorings of juniper berry, rosemary, and garlic to blend into subtlety.

Lamb breast is a pleasant though little-used cut of meat in this country. If you can't find it, you can substitute 2 pounds of boneless lamb shoulder, cut into 1½ inch cubes, and allow at least 15 minutes' more cooking time. We find the dish goes particularly well with green beans.

2 tablespoons olive oil

2½ pounds lamb breast, cut in individual riblets

2 pounds small boiling potatoes, peeled and quartered

10 juniper berries, crushed in a mortar to a powder

1 teaspoon rosemary leaves, finely chopped

3 cloves garlic, finely chopped

1 teaspoon salt

Freshly ground black pepper

Film a flameproof casserole with a little of the olive oil. Put in the lamb and potatoes, and strew the juniper berries, rosemary, garlic, salt, and several grindings of black pepper over them. Moisten with the olive oil and 1 cup water.

Cover the pan and put it over medium heat. Bring the dish to a simmer, reduce the heat to low, and cook gently 45 minutes.

Preheat the oven to 400°F. When the 45 minutes are up, uncover the casserole and set it in the oven for 10 minutes to brown the lamb. After 5 minutes, turn the lamb pieces to brown their undersides. Serve at once. ∎

OXTAIL STEW

Coda di bue in umido

FOR 4 SERVINGS:

A generous, smooth red wine is needed here. Montepulciano d'Abruzzo would be excellent, and so would Rosso di Montalcino.

*T*his is a family dish, for people who don't mind watching each other take bones in their hands. It's also a great recipe to warm and perfume the house on a cold, dark winter day.

Oxtails are a sadly neglected resource. They have great flavor and terrific succulence, and all they ask to surrender both is to be cooked long and gently so they don't toughen up. The sauce in this dish takes on tremendous richness from the oxtails. Our theory is that Italian cooking does with red wine and tomato what French cooking uses brown stock and flour to achieve; that's why Italian is usually so much lighter on the palate and stomach.

As with the related Roman specialty, *coda alla vaccinara*, this recipe uses the acidity of celery to cut what would otherwise be the excessive "viscosity" (because of all the gelatine in the tailbones) of the meat. Oxtails, tomato (which has a fair amount of acidity of its own), and celery are a great traditional combination throughout Italy.

2½ to 3 pounds oxtails, cut up	2 tablespoons chopped flat-leaf Italian parsley
2 tablespoons olive oil	2 to 3 basil leaves
¼ cup thinly sliced onion	Salt
2 cloves garlic	Freshly ground black pepper
½ cup dry red wine	4 carrots, cut in 1½-inch logs
1 cup drained canned Italian-style plum tomatoes, chopped	4 stalks celery, cut in 1½-inch segments

Rinse and dry the pieces of oxtail. In a large, broad casserole, heat the olive oil, add the onion, garlic, and oxtails, and brown the meat over medium heat on all sides. Raise heat to high, pour in the wine, and cook uncovered until it evaporates, 5 to 10 minutes, turning the pieces of oxtail a few times.

Add the tomatoes, parsley, basil, ½ teaspoon salt, and a generous quantity of black pepper. Bring the mixture to a simmer, cover, and cook 2 hours.

Add the carrots, celery, and another ¼ teaspoon salt. Mix well and cook 1 hour more, or until the meat is tender enough to fall off the bone. ■

TRIPE BRAISED WITH POTATOES AND BEANS

Trippa alla milanese

FOR 4 TO 5 SERVINGS:

*T*his economical one-pot meal is wonderfully rich, savory, and satisfying on a cold winter evening. Its effect isn't strongly "tripey," which makes it a good way to introduce tripe skeptics to the pleasures of this unpretentious innard. The gravy alone is enough to make converts. (Have a lot of good crusty bread on hand.)

The directions may seem complicated, but each step is quite simple: the initial tripe preparation and the initial bean preparation amount to little more than boiling. Those two steps can be done ahead, at different times, over the course of a day or two. Just refrigerate the partially cooked components and bring them back to room temperature before proceeding with the 1¼ hours of cooking (or allow more time if they're cold). And don't be put off by the appearance of the dish-in-progress: it will be quite unprepossessing through most of the cooking time.

For a touch of elegance in serving—or to stretch the meal for

This understated dish responds remarkably well to a wide range of red wines, from simple fruity ones (such as Montepulciano d'Abruzzo and Castel del Monte) to more acidic, subtle wines (Chianti, Barbera) to rather aggressive tannic ones (Nebbiolo, Rosso di Montalcino).

a sixth person—you can put the stew in individual ramekins; top with a slice of onion, some grated parmigiano, and a veil of extra-virgin olive oil; and run them briefly under the broiler.

FOR THE INITIAL COOKING OF THE BEANS:

1¼ cups dried white beans

Green tops of 1 leek, roughly chopped

½ carrot, sliced

½ stalk celery, sliced

FOR THE INITIAL COOKING OF THE TRIPE:

2 to 2¼ pounds beef tripe

1 small onion stuck with 2 cloves

1 teaspoon salt

FOR THE MAIN ASSEMBLY:

2 tablespoons butter

4 ounces pancetta, chopped

½ cup chopped carrot

¼ cup chopped onion

White part of 1 large leek, chopped

6 to 8 sage leaves

1 cup drained canned Italian-style

tomatoes, put through a food mill or pulsed in a food processor

1½ teaspoons salt

1½ to 2 pounds potatoes, peeled and cut in 2-inch chunks

⅔ cup freshly grated parmigiano

To cook the beans:

Pick over the beans, rinse them, and put them in a pot with cold water to cover by 2 inches. Bring to a boil, boil 2 minutes, then turn off the heat and let the beans sit in the water 2 hours. Add the leek greens, carrot, and celery to the pot, bring it to a boil, reduce to a simmer, and cook covered 45 minutes, or until the beans are not quite tender. Drain them, discard the other vegetables, and set aside until ready to use.

To cook the tripe:

Rinse and drain the tripe. Pull off any pieces of fat adhering to it. In a large pot, bring 4 quarts water to a boil. Add the tripe, the onion stuck with cloves, and 1 teaspoon salt. When the water returns to a boil, reduce to a simmer, cover, and cook 1½ hours.

Drain the tripe and let it sit until cool enough to handle (or

spray it with cold water if you want to work with it immediately).
Then cut it into strips about 2 inches long by ½ inch wide. Set the
tripe aside until ready to use.

Final assembly and cooking:
In a very large casserole, melt the butter and sauté the pancetta over
low heat 5 minutes, until most of the fat is rendered. Add the
chopped carrot, onion, leek, and sage leaves and sauté 5 minutes
more.

Add the tripe to the casserole and stir well to coat it with the fats
and vegetables. Add the tomatoes, 3 cups hot water, and 1½ teaspoons salt. Stir, cover, and cook gently 30 minutes.

Add the potatoes and the cooked beans, stir, cover, and cook 20
to 30 minutes longer, until the potatoes are tender. Taste for salt.
Sprinkle the grated parmigiano over the tripe and serve at once,
straight from the casserole. ∎

CONTORNI

For cooking that remains true to the calendar, winter vegetable choices are few and familiar—primarily dried shell beans, the cabbage family, and the root vegetables. If that conjures up visions of heavy, sodden boiled foods (English cooking at its worst), the Italian repertory is going to surprise and delight you. Few cuisines have a lighter hand with "heavy" vegetables, and few do more to coax every last bit of flavor out of unpromising materials.

A kiss of ham and onion enlivens a cabbage. A sweet-and-sour sauce transfigures an onion. Garlic and peperoncino give a lilt to broccoli rape. Even recalcitrant red cabbage, a vegetable with a mind and a way of its own, responds to the blandishments of olives and capers. The more cultured members of the winter vegetable clan, brussels sprouts and radicchio, are even better students: their recipes are among the most charming and versatile of the whole winter menu.

Above all, let us not forget beans. The humble dried bean is a life sustainer. It's also a gastronomical treat. The many varieties of beans all have glorious flavor. Each part of Italy has a favorite variety and a special way of preparing it, but most bean recipes can be made with any beans you have in the pantry. Among their many virtues, dried beans are also very forgiving. Cook them a little bit longer or shorter, drier or wetter: they'll adapt and give you fine, homey, nourishing dishes every time.

HOME–STYLE SAVOY CABBAGE

Cavolo alla casalinga

FOR 4 TO 6 SERVINGS:

avoy cabbage is the lady of the family: delicately sweetish, with crinkly rather than flat leaves—the most interesting-tasting of the green cabbages. This excellent recipe lends even more flavor interest. Should you not have a food processor or blender, you'll have to sauté the ham and onions first, then pass them through a food mill.

Ⴘ

Choose according to your secondo.

1 head savoy cabbage (about 2 pounds), trimmed and quartered	*¼ pound boiled ham, roughly chopped*
Salt	*4 tablespoons butter*
½ cup roughly chopped onion	*½ cup broth*
	Freshly ground black pepper

Bring a large pot of salted water to a boil. Drop the cabbage quarters into it and cook 5 minutes. Drain, cool, and cut the cabbage into 1-inch pieces, discarding the tough core.

Put the onion and half the ham into a food processor or blender and process them to a fine mash. Melt the butter in a flameproof casserole and sauté the onion-ham mash over low heat 8 to 10 minutes. Raise heat to medium high, add the broth, bring to a boil, and simmer 5 minutes, uncovered.

Add the cabbage and the remaining ham. Mix well to coat the cabbage with the seasonings. Add salt and pepper to taste (depending on how salty the ham is). Cover and cook 5 minutes. Check seasoning and serve. ■

RED CABBAGE WITH OLIVES AND CAPERS

Cavolo rosso alla siciliana

FOR 4 SERVINGS:

Choose according to your secondo.

*I*f most red cabbage dishes are too sweet for you, try this one. It's brisk, yet rich from its unexpectedly smooth combination with wine vinegar, olives, and capers. The cooking technique is that typically Italian, quasi-risotto operation of adding only a little broth at a time until the vegetable absorbs it, so the flavors from the liquid concentrate in the cabbage, rather than the other way around.

1½ cups broth, approximately

4 tablespoons olive oil

1 pound red cabbage, thinly shredded (about half a large head)

Salt

Freshly ground black pepper

¼ cup red wine vinegar

2 ounces black olives, pitted and sliced or chopped

2 teaspoons capers, chopped

Have the broth at a simmer in a small pot. In a nonreactive skillet, heat the olive oil. Add the cabbage, salt and pepper to taste, and toss to coat it thoroughly with the oil. Sprinkle with the vinegar.

Cover and cook over moderate heat 5 minutes, or until the cabbage absorbs the vinegar. Add about ½ cup broth. Continue cooking covered, adding broth in small amounts as the cabbage absorbs it, about 30 minutes in all, or until the cabbage is tender. (If you run out of broth, use water.)

When the cabbage is tender and the dish fairly dry, stir in the olives and capers and cook 5 more minutes. Serve at once. ∎

GRATINÉED BRUSSELS SPROUTS

Cavolini gratinati al forno

FOR 4 SERVINGS:

*T*his is a picturesque and very tasty way to present sprouts. The *bandiera Italiana* colors (the green, red, and white of the Italian flag) advertise lively and complex flavors. Cooking in the oven brings out the sprouts' natural sweetness and lets them get meltingly tender without developing any cabbagy flavors, as they can when they are boiled even a little too long.

It's handy if you have béchamel sauce already made up, possibly stored in the freezer. If not, the ¾ cup needed here can be made in a jiffy. If the béchamel you have is any thicker than the consistency of thin cream, dilute it with a little of the sprouts' blanching water.

For fanatical vegetable lovers, this dish is a meal in itself. Otherwise, serve it with a simple meat or fish.

If the brussels sprouts are being served by themselves, accompany them with a medium-bodied, dry white wine, such as Arneis or Greco di Tufo or Torre di Giano. Otherwise, choose according to your secondo.

FOR THE BÉCHAMEL:

1 cup milk

1½ tablespoons butter

1½ tablespoons all-purpose flour

Pinch salt

Pinch freshly grated nutmeg

FOR THE SPROUTS:

1 pound brussels sprouts, trimmed

2 tablespoons butter

Salt

Freshly ground black pepper

2 ounces boiled ham, cut in julienne strips

¾ cup drained canned Italian-style plum tomatoes, finely chopped or pulsed in a food processor

1½ tablespoons grated parmigiano

1 tablespoon fine dry bread crumbs

To make the béchamel:

In a small pot, bring the milk to a simmer. In another pot, melt the butter over low heat. Stir the flour into the butter and cook, stirring, 2 minutes. Keep the heat low so the flour doesn't brown.

Still over very low heat, add the milk a tablespoon or two at a time, stirring vigorously with each addition. When all is incorporated and the sauce is a smooth cream, raise the heat slightly, bring it to a simmer, and cook 2 minutes. Stir in the salt and nutmeg and set the sauce aside until ready to use.

To blanch the vegetable:

Drop the brussels sprouts in a large pot of boiling salted water. When the water returns to a boil, cook 7 minutes, then remove the sprouts and spray them with cold water to stop the cooking. Set aside until ready to use.

To assemble and bake the dish:

Preheat the oven to 400°F. Butter a casserole just large enough to hold the sprouts in a single layer. Put them in the casserole and salt and pepper them lightly. Strew the ham over the sprouts. Spoon on the béchamel, then the tomatoes. Sprinkle on the grated cheese and bread crumbs. Finally, dot the remaining butter overall.

Set the dish in the oven and bake 20 to 25 minutes, or until it is nicely browned and crusty on top. For the best flavor, let it rest 10 to 15 minutes before serving. ∎

BRAISED BROCCOLI RAPE

Cima de rape affogato

FOR 4 SERVINGS:

*I*t's pronounced *rah*-pay, two syllables, unlike the word for sexual assault. In grocery stores here you'll see it spelled several ways, including rapp, rabe, and rabb, with or without the word "broccoli" attached to it. It looks like skinny broccoli shoots with a lot of leaves and a few small, broccolilike blossoms, and most people therefore think that it's the sideshoot of already harvested broccoli plants. In fact, it's the top—the flowering stalk and leaves (*cima*)—of a member of the turnip family—*rape*, in Italian. Sounds a bit like a W. C. Fields endearment, doesn't it: "And how are you today, my charming little turnip top?"

The recipe below is the Ur-treatment for any kind of strong-flavored, coarse-textured greens, including escarole, kale, dandelions, and mustard greens. Italian cooks seem to be born knowing how to perform this basic sort of cooking operation. Americans feel they have to parboil these greens first, but you don't really want to denature them: it's their intrinsic strength of flavor that makes them such great winter vegetables. Braising mellows them without sacrificing any of their characteristic pungency.

To trim broccoli rape, take off only the wilted, yellow leaves and the thick, tough stems. Cook all the rest: tender stems, leaves, flowers.

Broccoli rape braised a bit moister than directed here is often used to dress pasta. With a little grated cheese—a good sharp pecorino is best—the combination makes a very satisfying lunch or supper. Leftover broccoli rape and other such greens also make a fine topping for a schiacciata (see page 337). All in all, the "charming little turnip top" is quite a versatile friend.

If the dish is to be served by itself, a dry, acid white such as Verdicchio would be the best match. Otherwise, choose according to your secondo.

4 tablespoons olive oil	1½ pounds broccoli rape, trimmed
2 cloves garlic, halved	and roughly chopped
1 peperoncino rosso	Salt
	1 cup simmering broth or water

In a nonreactive skillet, heat the olive oil. Add the garlic and peperoncino. Sauté until the garlic turns a light golden brown, then press the pieces against the bottom of the pan with a fork and remove them. Discard the peperoncino if you wish.

Add the broccoli rape and sauté 5 minutes, tossing to coat it with the seasoned oil. Sprinkle with salt. Add the broth or water, cover, and cook 15 minutes, or until the broccoli rape is tender. Stir occasionally and add a little more water if the vegetable is drying out: the dish should be moist but not awash. Before serving, remove the peperoncino and taste for salt. ■

SWEET-AND-SOUR ONIONS

Cipolline in agrodolce

FOR 4 SERVINGS:

Y

Choose according to your secondo.

*I*n winter, Italian-neighborhood markets get very small (1 or 1½ inches in diameter), flat, nut-sweet yellow onions called *cipolline*, which have a flavor unlike any other onions. If they're not available, you can make the dish any time of the year with white pearl onions, but it'll be less ambrosial. If you absolutely can't get prosciutto fat, use rendered bacon fat and add it along with the butter. This preparation is equally good as part of a mixed vegetable antipasto.

Cipolline make excellent salad onions, both raw and boiled for Insalatone (see page 330). For that matter, they're great when simply peeled, put in a pan with butter, olive oil (2 tablespoons each for ¾ pound onions), and a sprinkling of salt, and stewed in their own juices until tender, about 30 minutes. They can be cusses to peel, however. If they don't give up their skins readily, drop them in boiling water for 10 seconds, then peel.

¾ pound fresh cipolline (10 to 20) or very small pearl onions (about 30), peeled	1½ tablespoons butter
	¼ teaspoon salt
	½ teaspoon sugar
1 clove garlic	½ cup red wine vinegar
2 ounces prosciutto fat	

Finely chop 2 of the cipolline (4 pearl onions) together with the garlic and prosciutto fat. In a shallow nonreactive casserole, melt the butter, add the chopped mixture, and sauté over low heat 5 minutes.

Add the whole cipolline and sauté them, turning often, 3 to 4 minutes (5 to 6 for pearl onions), until lightly browned. Sprinkle with the salt, then the sugar, rolling the onions around to coat them well. Add the vinegar and enough water to just cover the onions.

Bring to a simmer, cover tightly, and cook gently until the onions are tender—about 20 minutes for cipolline, 40 or more for pearl onions. Check frequently during the cooking, and add a few tablespoons hot water if the liquid is evaporating too fast: the onions shouldn't ever fry.

When the onions are tender, the liquid should be just a syrup in the bottom of the pan. If it is not, remove the onions and keep them warm while you boil down the liquid; when it is lightly syrupy, pour it over the onions and serve at once. ■

A POT OF BEANS

Fagioli alla maruzzara

FOR 4 SERVINGS:

*T*his tasty, hearty peasant dish is a cold-weather staple in and around Naples, where there are lots of versions and local variants of it, some leaner and some richer. The preparation also works well with red kidneys, or in fact almost any variety of bean. Cooking time may vary considerably depending on the age and dryness of your beans, but this doesn't present a problem since the beans and their flavoring vegetables first cook separately and can be made in advance, right up to the point of their joining and final 15 minutes of cooking together.

Those flavoring vegetables, by the way, produce a glorious, chlorophylly scent as they're sautéed. You'll be convinced you're getting all the winter vitamins you need, and you'll bless the basil leaves you stashed away in the freezer for just this kind of occasion!

Any leftovers—a rarity in our house—make a terrific soup, just pureed and extended with water or broth.

Choose according to your secondo.

½ pound dried cannellini

½ cup olive oil

1 stalk celery, sliced thin (½ cup)

1 clove garlic, minced

2 tablespoons chopped flat-leaf
   Italian parsley

2 tablespoons chopped basil

½ cup drained canned
   Italian-style tomatoes, chopped

Salt

Freshly ground black pepper

¼ teaspoon dried oregano

Pick over the beans, rinse them, and put them in a pot with cold water to cover by 2 inches. Bring to a boil, boil 2 minutes, then turn off the heat and let the beans sit in the water 2 hours. Bring them back to a boil, reduce to a simmer, and cook, covered, until the beans are almost tender (45 minutes to 1 hour).

In another large pot, warm the olive oil and sauté the celery, garlic, parsley, and basil over low heat 5 to 10 minutes, until the celery is just tender. Add the tomatoes and a generous sprinkling of salt, and cook 5 to 10 minutes more.

When the beans are ready, lift them out of their cooking water with a slotted spoon and transfer them to the pot with the vegetables. Stir in ½ teaspoon salt and a generous quantity of black pepper. Add enough of the bean cooking water to make the dish moist but not soupy. Cover and cook 10 to 15 minutes, or until the beans are perfectly tender. Stir in the oregano and serve at once. ∎

A DIFFERENT POT OF BEANS

Fagioli in umido

FOR 6 SERVINGS:

This dish starts out very much like the preceding *fagioli alla maruzzara,* but it turns out completely different. It's another remarkably homely, comforting dish, however, simple and satisfying. Adaptable, too: it's hard to mess up this recipe. You can use any kind of wine, blanched bacon instead of pancetta, any tomato sauce you happen to have left over in the refrigerator. If you have no sauce on hand, substitute ¾ cup of chopped canned tomatoes, and reduce the amount of broth to 1¾ cups.

Again, cooking time will vary according to the freshness of the beans.

Choose according to your secondo.

2 cups dried white beans—cannellini, Great Northern, or pinto	8 to 10 sage leaves
	1 teaspoon salt
	Freshly ground black pepper
1 ounce pancetta, diced	¼ cup dry wine, white or red
½ cup chopped onion	2 cups broth
3 tablespoons olive oil	½ cup tomato sauce (see headnote)

Pick over the beans, rinse them, and put them in a pot with cold water to cover by 2 inches. Bring to a boil, boil 2 minutes, then turn off the heat and let the beans sit in the water 2 hours. Bring them back to a boil, reduce heat to a simmer, and cook covered until the beans are not quite tender (45 minutes to 1 hour). Drain them, rinse in cold water to stop the cooking, and drain again.

In a pan large enough to hold all the beans later, put the pancetta, onion, and olive oil. Sauté over low heat until the onions are soft and the pancetta rendered. Add the drained beans, sage, salt, and a generous quantity of black pepper. Toss together and cook 2 minutes to imbue the beans with the seasonings. Add the wine and cook, stirring, 1 minute more.

Stir in 1½ cups of the broth and all the tomato sauce. Cover tightly and cook 30 minutes, stirring occasionally, until the beans are fully tender. Add more broth if necessary to keep the beans from drying out, and if the broth runs out before the beans are done, use water. Serve when the dish has reached the degree of moistness or dryness you like. ∎

HOME-STYLE POTATOES AND CARROTS

Patate e carote alla casalinga

FOR 4 SERVINGS:

Y

Choose according to your secondo.

*T*his is warm, comforting, homey food, just what you want to accompany a simply cooked meat or fish or fowl—though, for all its artlessness, the dish has enough flavor to match with more elaborate main courses too. We've served it at dinner parties, and guests have raved over it. The potato starches combining with the butter and broth make a nice glaze all by themselves.

If your carrots are at all old and tough, as midwinter carrots are prone to be, you may have to start cooking them sooner than the potatoes—or cut them smaller.

4 tablespoons butter

*1¼ pounds potatoes, cut in
    ½-inch cubes*

*1 pound carrots, cut in ⅜-inch
    rounds*

2 cups broth

Salt

Freshly ground black pepper

In a broad skillet, melt the butter, add the potatoes and the carrots, and sauté 5 minutes over moderate heat, stirring often. Meanwhile, in another pan, bring the broth to a simmer.

Sprinkle the vegetables with salt and pepper to taste and pour in the broth. When it returns to a simmer, cover the pan tightly (set a weight on the cover if it doesn't fit tightly enough to keep in all the steam) and cook until the vegetables are tender and have absorbed virtually all the broth—about 20 minutes. Check occasionally during the cooking, stir, and adjust the heat as necessary to maintain a very gentle simmer. Serve in a warmed bowl. ∎

GRILLED RADICCHIO WITH ANCHOVY-MUSTARD SAUCE

Radicchio alla veneta

FOR 4 SERVINGS:

*V*ivid garnet heads of radicchio are a comparatively recent arrival on American vegetable stands. Attractive in salads, they reveal an intriguingly bitter savor when grilled. The tastiest radicchio is the Treviso variety, with long, narrow heads shaped like loose-leaved Belgian endive. Round-headed Verona radicchio, looking like baby red cabbages, are less interesting in flavor, but this dish works well with either variety. We like to use it as a warm salad after the main course, though it can also be served as a contorno or even antipasto.

For this recipe, the sauce may be made well in advance, leaving only the grilling of the radicchio to be done at the last minute.

If served by themselves, choose a bright, acidic white wine such as a fine Soave or a Sauvignon; otherwise, choose according to your secondo.

2 anchovy fillets, chopped

1 tablespoon Dijon mustard

Juice of 1 lemon

1 clove garlic, lightly crushed

½ teaspoon chopped dried
rosemary leaves

1 tablespoon minced flat-leaf
Italian parsley

½ cup extra-virgin olive oil,
approximately

4 small heads radicchio (1 to 1¼
pounds), quartered lengthwise,
with enough of the core left on to
hold the leaves together

Salt

Freshly ground black pepper

In a small bowl, mash the anchovies to a paste. Whisk in the mustard and lemon juice. Add the garlic, rosemary, and parsley. Add 6 tablespoons olive oil in a thin stream, stirring constantly, to achieve a smooth sauce. This can be prepared well in advance and allowed to stand for several hours.

Heat a very large, heavy-bottomed skillet or griddle. Rub the pieces of radicchio with olive oil and sprinkle with salt and pepper. Lay them in the skillet and cook 8 to 10 minutes, turning occasionally and adding a little more oil if necessary, until they are tender when pierced with a fork.

Arrange the radicchio on a serving plate, cut sides up. Give the sauce a final stir, discard the garlic, and spoon the sauce over the radicchio. Serve at once. ■

DOLCI

Winter doesn't offer much new in the way of raw materials for desserts. Fall's fruits and nuts continue, and as the end-of-year holidays approach, they're worked into a multitude of special confections, according to the traditions and resources of the regions where they originate. But these are desserts that Italians purchase in bakeries, for the most part, and eat only on their associated feast days.

For the cook in the Italian home, the nonholiday winter meal is most likely to end, as at other times of the year, quite simply. Not that there's anything wrong with a dish of nuts and fruit. The choice, of course, is smaller than at other seasons: apples and pears, as long as they last, and then the imported exotics—oranges, bananas, and, above all, pineapples, on which Italians dote. Nuts, especially almonds and hazelnuts, and especially lightly roasted, are a favorite way of finishing off the last of the wine. And then there is dried fruit, which may be nibbled as is or reconstituted by steaming and then imbued with a little vermouth, a liqueur, or a grappa.

Among composed desserts, simple cakes and tarts are cheering on a cold day. They may well be filled with a fruit preserve that the provident cook put up during the glory days of the fruit harvest. And almost every family wants to mark the holidays with some special homemade sweet bread or fruit cake. We've provided several examples of these, the most typical and the most deeply Italian of all the winter desserts. And finally, just for fun, a thoroughly modern chocolate-almond-mascarpone "truffle" that alludes gracefully to the excitement of the Italian white truffle season.

Winter baking frequently relies on combinations of nuts and dried or candied fruits. A few words about technique may be helpful.

If you have almonds in their skins and a recipe calls for blanched, almonds skin easily. Drop them into boiling water for 20 seconds, run them briefly under cold water, then just squeeze them out of the skins. Let them dry—in a low oven if you're pressed for time.

Hazelnuts are more troublesome. Their bitter brown skins are maddeningly tenacious. Spread hazelnuts on a baking sheet and toast them in a 350°F oven for 10 minutes, then dump them on a dish towel, roll it up, and rub them vigorously against one another. This will take off as much skin as the nuts are willing to give up.

Sticky dried or candied fruits can be chopped more easily if dusted with a bit of flour. Avoid the mixed chopped candied fruits sold in supermarkets if you can. They're invariably stale and of poor quality. Specialty stores sell individual candied fruits, like citron and various citrus peels, in large pieces. These are much superior in flavor, and any you don't use at once will keep well for as long as a year in the freezer. ■

PEAR CAKE

Torta alle pere

FOR 6 TO 8 SERVINGS:

A glass of Asti Spumante will go nicely here, or a dryish Vin Santo.

*H*ere's a quick, moist, homey cake, perfect for frequent family consumption. Its simplicity of preparation also makes it useful for a last-minute sweet when you haven't many dessert ingredients in the pantry and don't have a lot of time to spare. The pear slices sink into the surface as the cake bakes, and the batter rises around them to make an attractive golden presentation.

Butter and flour for the pan	*2 teaspoons baking powder*
10 tablespoons butter, softened	*2 large pears (about 1 pound),*
1 cup all-purpose flour	*peeled, cored, quartered, and*
⅔ cup confectioners' sugar	*sliced lengthwise ¼ inch thick*
3 eggs, beaten together	*2 tablespoons granulated sugar*

Preheat the oven to 350°F. Butter and flour a 9- to 10-inch bake-and-serve cake dish.

In a bowl, cream the butter and confectioners' sugar. Beat in the eggs. Sift in the flour, mixed with the baking powder, and beat the resulting batter well. Transfer it to the prepared dish.

Arrange the pear slices in a circular pattern on top of the batter. Sprinkle the granulated sugar over the pears. Bake 40 to 45 minutes, or until the surface is golden and the edges of the cake pull away slightly from the rim of the dish.

Cool the cake on a rack and serve it directly from its dish. ∎

PEACH JAM TART

Crostata di marmellata di pesche

FOR 6 TO 8 SERVINGS:

This recipe illustrates a very standard Italian use of pasta frolla for a jam tart. We include it mainly as a reminder of the versatility of that sweet dough and the way a satisfying dessert can be made out of little more than a jar of fruit jam or preserves unearthed from the depths of the pantry. Nothing but the name need be changed if the jar you turn up contains raspberry, strawberry, or plum preserves instead of peach, as called for here.

♀
None needed, but a glass of Asti Spumante is perfectly acceptable.

Flour
1 recipe pasta frolla dough (page 110)

1½ cups peach preserves
1 egg

Preheat the oven to 350°F. Lightly flour a work surface. Flatten the dough on the work surface and flour it well. Roll it between two sheets of waxed paper into a circle ⅛ inch thick and about 12 inches in diameter. Peel off one sheet of waxed paper and position the dough loosely over a 9½-inch round pan, papered side up. Delicately peel off the remaining paper and fit the dough gently against the sides of the pan. Trim off the excess and gather it into a ball.

Spread the peach jam evenly over the surface of the dough. Flour and roll out the excess dough without enclosing it in waxed paper. Cut it in ¾-inch strips and form a lattice over the top of the jam.

Beat the egg in a bowl with 1 tablespoon water and paint the surface of the lattice and the edges of the tart. Wait a moment and paint again. Put the tart in the oven and bake 40 minutes. Cool on a rack. ■

CHOCOLATE SPICE CAKE

Certosina

FOR 1 CAKE:

♉

An Asti Spumante would be a good choice here; or try a still Moscato.

*T*his is a traditional Christmas cake from Bologna, where it is reputed to have been the speciality of the monks of the local charterhouse *(certosa)*, whence its name. Since it uses only baking soda for leavening, it makes a shallow cake and a fairly dense one—but its flavor and appearance are both delightfully chocolaty, and all the other good things in it give it a wonderful crunchy texture. Unlike many ancient holiday specialties, this one is quick and easy to make.

The result is similar in style and taste to some versions of the famous *panforte* of Siena. Like panforte, an uncut certosina will keep a long time if you keep it wrapped airtight. Once cut, however, it stales after a few days, even if you do rewrap it well.

½ cup sugar

½ cup honey

½ teaspoon baking soda

½ teaspoon anise seeds

1⅓ cups all-purpose flour

1½ ounces blanched almonds (¼ cup)

1½ ounces blanched hazelnuts (⅓ cup)

1½ ounces pignoli (¼ cup)

1½ ounces raisins (3 tablespoons), plumped in hot water and drained

1½ ounces candied orange peel, minced (¼ cup)

1½ ounces unsweetened baking chocolate, grated

Preheat the oven to 350°F. In a large bowl, mix the sugar, honey, baking soda, and anise seeds. Pour in 1 cup boiling water and mix well. Gradually beat in the flour to make a smooth batter. Add all the remaining ingredients and mix well again.

Butter a 10-inch round bake-and-serve dish. Pour in the batter and smooth the surface. Bake 30 minutes. Cool on a rack. ■

FRIULIAN FRUIT-AND-NUT ROLL

Putizza

FOR 8 TO 10 SERVINGS:

Friuli, the most northeasterly region of Italy, used to be part of Yugoslavia—back when Yugoslavia itself was not all apart, and when all of Yugoslavia was a part of the Austro-Hungarian Empire. The region has maintained strong Slavic traditions in its cooking. One of its traditional Christmas and New Year's sweets is this rich nut-and-fruit bread, with a filling similar to the other famed Friulian pastry, *La Gubana* (a recipe for which we gave in *La Tavola Italiana*). *Putizza* is not outrageously sweet, which makes it both an excellent coffee cake or teatime snack (either plain or lightly toasted and buttered) and a congenial companion to a glass of dessert wine.

A Vin Santo will work well here; dry or sweet really makes no difference. A Recioto di Soave is also a good choice. Likewise a slivovitz or a grappa, either of which might well be served with putizza on its home ground.

FOR THE DOUGH:

1 envelope active dry yeast

1⅓ cups warm milk

5 cups all-purpose flour

½ cup sugar

¼ teaspoon salt

Grated peel of ½ lemon

3 eggs, beaten together

6 tablespoons butter, melted

FOR THE FILLING:

2 tablespoons butter

2 tablespoons fine, dry bread crumbs

4 ounces shelled walnuts meats (1 cup)

1 ounce blanched almonds (3 tablespoons)

1 ounce candied citron, chopped (2 heaping tablespoons)

1 ounce candied orange peel,

chopped (2 heaping tablespoons)

2 ounces golden raisins (¼ cup), plumped in hot water and drained

2 ounces pignoli (3 tablespoons)

Grated peel of 1 lemon

Grated peel of 1 orange

1 egg yolk

FOR SHAPING AND BAKING:

Flour

2 egg whites

1 egg yolk

2 to 3 tablespoons sugar

To make the dough:

In a small bowl, dissolve the yeast in ⅓ cup milk. Mix in ½ cup flour to make a soft ball and knead briefly. Cover the bowl and let this sponge rise in a warm place until double in bulk, about 1 hour.

Put the remaining flour, the sugar, salt, and lemon peel into a large bowl. Make a well in the center and add the yeast sponge, eggs, melted butter, and remaining milk. Gradually incorporate the dry ingredients into the wet, to achieve a smooth dough. Knead the dough until it is supple and elastic, about 10 minutes by hand or 4 minutes if you have a heavy-duty mixer with a dough hook. Cover the bowl with plastic wrap and let the dough rise until double in bulk.

To make the filling:

In a small pan, melt the 2 tablespoons butter and sauté the bread crumbs 2 minutes or until lightly golden—but watch them: they burn easily. Transfer them to a large bowl. Finely chop together the walnuts, almonds, and candied fruits. Add them to the bread crumbs. Add the remaining filling ingredients and mix well.

Shaping and baking:

Preheat the oven to 375°F. Flour a work surface and roll out the dough into a sheet ⅛ inch thick and about 14 by 22 inches. Whip the 2 egg whites into soft peaks and fold them into the filling mixture. Spread the filling evenly over the entire surface of the dough, leaving 1 inch clear at the edges.

Roll up the dough jelly-roll fashion along one of its long edges. Pinch the trailing edge to seal the filling in. Pinch and seal the ends as well, and roll the cylinder gently under your hands to lengthen it slightly. Coil it like a snail shell onto a buttered baking sheet.

Beat the remaining egg yolk in a small bowl and paint the surface of the dough. Sprinkle it with sugar and bake 35 to 40 minutes, or until pastry is firm and golden brown. Cool on a rack. ■

MODENA ALMOND-SUGAR CAKE

Bensone

FOR 6 TO 8 SERVINGS:

*M*odena and the other small cities strung up and down the Po Valley have given the world an abundance of good eating. This simple, old-fashioned cake belongs on the region's honor roll. It's still made the way such sweets were made before modern baking powders came along, and it's all the tastier for that. Waverley Root reports that at one time potato flour amounted to about a third of its dry contents, to yield a smoother result, but we've found nothing at all wrong with the texture of this wheat-flour version. It develops a lovely sugar-almond crust.

Traditionally, bensone was made in a S shape, but it's just as good, and easier to handle, in a standard cake pan. While it is perfectly delightful by itself or accompanied only by a glass of Vin Santo, we like to serve it with a fruit sauce (e.g., the Strawberry Sauce on page 104.)

For bensone served by itself, try a Vin Santo; with strawberry sauce, try an Asti Spumante or a still Moscato.

8 tablespoons butter, cut into several small pieces	Grated peel of 1 lemon
2 ounces blanched almonds (5 tablespoons)	3 eggs
⅔ cup sugar	½ cup milk
2⅔ cups all-purpose flour	1 tablespoon baking soda
	1 tablespoon cream of tartar

Generously butter a 9½-inch cake pan with 1 tablespoon butter. Put the almonds and 2 tablespoons sugar into a blender or food processor and process them to a fine meal. Preheat the oven to 350°F.

Put the flour and lemon peel into a mixing bowl. Break in the eggs and add the remaining butter. Mix briefly. Put the milk in another bowl, dissolve the baking soda and cream of tartar in it, and add it all at once to the batter. (It will foam up vigorously.) Beat thoroughly, 3 to 5 minutes, until the batter is very smooth.

Pour the batter into the pan and spread the almond-sugar meal over the top. Bake 1 hour, until the bensone is domed and lightly golden and the edges begin to pull away from the pan. Cool on a rack. ■

LIGURIAN CHRISTMAS BREAD

Pandolce di Liguria

FOR 1 LARGE ROUND LOAF:

𝓘n all honesty, this isn't really a dessert, but sweets of this type are so much a part of Christmas feasting in Italy that we couldn't in conscience leave it out. Those who know Italian food will recognize at once that this *pandolce* is a close kin of the better-known panettone. In fact, its shaping technique is exactly how the original panettone was done, long before commercial bakeries took over the product. Pandolce, however, makes a denser loaf than panettone, and the fennel seed, pistachios, Marsala, and orange liqueur give it a very distinctive flavor. Like panettone, it's great toasted, with butter or jam.

We're giving you here a very traditional recipe and technique for making this ancient delight. Like most traditional methods, this one takes a long time: There are two rises of 18 and 12 hours. If you start early one afternoon, the loaf will come out of the oven late the next night. You could speed things up somewhat by doubling the amount of yeast, but the long mingling and development of the flavors is the essence of this preparation. Approach it in a leisurely fashion over a couple of days, and just stash the dough in the refrigerator at any time if it's ready for the next step before you are.

This is a very wine-friendly feast bread, quite sacramental in that respect. It will companion pleasantly with just about any wine, white or red, dry or sweet. Try it with a Malvasia di Lipari or a Passito from Pantelleria.

FOR THE STARTER AND THE FIRST DOUGH:

1 envelope active dry yeast	1¾ cups all-purpose flour
½ teaspoon sugar	

FOR THE SECOND DOUGH:

1¾ cups all-purpose flour

⅔ cup sugar

½ teaspoon salt

8 tablespoons butter, melted

½ cup dry Marsala

1 tablespoon orange liqueur

2 tablespoons golden raisins, plumped in hot water and drained

1 ounce candied citron, chopped (2 heaping tablespoons)

1½ tablespoons fennel seeds

2 tablespoons pignoli

1 ounce shelled pistachios (3 tablespoons)

To make the starter and the first dough:

In a small bowl, dissolve the yeast and sugar in ¼ cup warm water. Add 3 tablespoons flour and mix well. Cover the bowl with plastic wrap and let this starter work for 1 hour.

Add the starter to the remaining flour, along with ½ cup warm water. Knead 10 minutes by hand, or 5 in a heavy-duty mixer with a dough hook. Set the dough into a clean bowl, cover it with plastic wrap, and let it rise 18 hours (more or less).

To make the second dough:

Grease and flour a baking sheet. Put the flour, sugar, and salt in a large bowl and mix in the melted butter, Marsala, and orange liqueur. Add the risen dough and enough additional water (1 to 2 tablespoons should do) to make a soft dough. Add the raisins, citron, fennel seeds, pignoli, and pistachios and knead very well— 20 minutes by hand, 10 in a heavy-duty mixer.

Shape the dough into a ball and set it on the prepared baking sheet. Cut a strip of aluminum foil long enough to encircle the loaf with several inches' overlap. Fold it lengthwise twice and butter one side. Wrap it snugly around the loaf, pleating the ends together to seal them. Cover with a towel and let rise in a warm place 12 hours.

To bake:

Preheat the oven to 375°F. Cut a cross in the surface of the risen dough and put it in the oven. Bake 1¼ hours, or until the bottom of the loaf sounds hollow when tapped. Cool on a rack.

Pandolce will keep for a long time if tightly wrapped in aluminum foil. ∎

"WHITE TRUFFLES"

Tartufi bianchi

FOR TWENTY-FOUR 1-INCH BALLS:

*E*veryone knows chocolate truffles, which mimic the size
and color of French black *truffes*. Well, since the best Italian
truffles are white, it follows that Italian dessert truffles must also be
white. (As white as the truffles themselves, that is, which is to say
closer to white than black.)

These little confections are super-easy to make; and even
though they look nothing like the common chocolate truffles,
they'll satisfy even the most devoted chocoholic. They call for
amaretti cookies, which come wrapped in pairs. Amaretti are sold
loose, or in tins or bags, and are particularly easy to find in Italian
stores during the holiday season. A 3½-ounce bag contains 9 pairs,
ample for this recipe.

The other essential ingredient here is mascarpone, a luscious,
fresh buttery cheese. It's the binder that holds the truffles together
and the harmonizer of their various flavor elements.

*Chocolate is tough on wines,
but sparkling Brachetto
d'Acqui would go very nicely
with these tasty morsels.
Alternatively, have a small
glass of Frangelico or whatever
liqueur you used to flavor
them.*

4 ounces mascarpone	1 teaspoon unsweetened cocoa
2 tablespoons butter, softened	2 tablespoons Frangelico or other
7 pairs amaretti cookies	liqueur
1 ounce semisweet chocolate, grated	24 paper candy cups

In a medium-sized bowl, cream the mascarpone and butter together.
Grind 4 pairs of amaretti to fine crumbs in a cheese grinder (or
pulverize them under a rolling pin). Add them to the bowl along
with the chocolate and cocoa. Mix well. Add the Frangelico and mix
until it is absorbed by the cream. Chill this mixture well before
proceeding.

Pulverize the remaining 3 pairs of amaretti and spread the
crumbs on a small plate. Have the candy papers ready.

Working with wet hands, scoop up a portion of the chilled

truffle mixture and roll or pat it into a 1-inch ball. Roll the ball in the amaretti crumbs to coat it completely and set it in a candy paper.

Make the remaining truffles in the same way. Put them in a tin or covered dish and let them "ripen" in the refrigerator for at least 2 hours before serving. They'll hold well for several days. ∎

Menus

Gathering family and friends around a table, pouring them good, honest wine and feeding them good, honest food is, for the two of us, the most satisfying of all forms of entertainment.

The event doesn't have to be a five-star extravaganza (though, when we have the time, that's often what we'll aim for, for pure gastronomical play). The simplest menu can be as high a compliment to one's guests as an endless procession of delicacies. Balance and contrast are important to a just appreciation of food, and they often dictate a meal of no more than a single composed dish, along with the simplest of accompaniments—a boiled potato, a green salad, a loaf of bread. However, for those days when ambition or adventure or sheer joy of living move you to plan a more elaborate meal, here are a set of seasonal possibilities.

We've chosen dishes to showcase the best produce of each season and the styles of cooking that seem appropriate to each time of the year. Most of these meals consist of three or four Italian-style courses—antipasto, primo, secondo with contorno, and dolce. If that's more food than you care to eat, or more cooking than you feel up to, simply omit a course—each suggested meal will still be pleasing with any three of its four courses, or any two of its three. But don't instantly eliminate the menus that seem to involve too much cooking: if you check the individual recipes, you'll see that many of them can be done as much as a couple of days in advance, leaving you only a modicum of work to do after your guests have arrived. (Alternatively, you can invite your guests into the kitchen, give each one a glass of wine, and let them either watch or help. That way, making the dinner is as much a part of the evening's entertainment as consuming it.)

Not mentioned in the menus, but assumed as a part of almost any Italian meal, is a good crusty loaf of bread. (Not butter, though: to the Italian palate, it's superfluous.) And you can't go wrong by serving a cheese course after the secondo; or a dish of fruit, biscotti from a good Italian bakery, and/or tiny dark chocolates in place of the composed dessert.

Da bere—to drink with these menus—we've generally offered two alternatives: either a single wine to serve throughout the meal, or a pair of wines chosen to contrast with each other and complement the sequence of courses. These are not always the wines suggested for the recipes in the seasonal sections of the book—though you could certainly use those suggestions instead, if you want a multiple-wine meal. Any one of the menus can be made even more festive by serving glasses of a dry *spumante* as aperitif, such as a sparkling Prosecco. And any one can be rounded to a perfect conclusion with cups of strong espresso followed by a brandy or grappa.

SPRING MENUS

1

To capture the *leggerezza* of spring, here's an elegant meal you can whip up in about an hour of total kitchen time. If you're a novice pasta maker, perhaps you'll want to have the pasta ready in advance; or if time is really tight, buy it freshly made. Because so little is done to the ingredients, it's essential to have prosciutto, asparagus, and strawberries of the very best quality. (Quails and mascarpone are still uncommon enough in U.S. grocery stores that inferior specimens are rare.)

•

Prosciutto di Parma

Fresh egg noodles with mascarpone

Roasted quails
Asparagus with hazelnut butter

Strawberries with lemon and sugar

♀

Fiano di Avellino would accompany this entire meal to perfection.

2

Often it's necessary to give a dinner party for people whose tastes you don't know terribly well—colleagues from your new job, for instance, or your soon-to-be in-laws, or old school friends of your spouse who are passing through your part of the world after not having been seen for fifteen years. You want a meal that will give them lots of pleasure but not overwhelm them in case they're not dedicated food people like yourselves. Here's a menu that's as elegant as you could wish for such an occasion, but one that poses no challenges to timorous palates.

•

Asparagus with prosciutto rolls

Ligurian vegetable soup

Casserole roast of lamb stuffed with peas and mushrooms
Zucchini and spring onions with balsamic vinegar

Ricotta and almond torte

♀

A Gattinara can carry you from the antipasto right through the lamb.

♀♀

Or precede the Gattinara with an Arneis or Sauvignon for the first two courses.

It's really the most fun to cook for people whose tastes you know—especially when they're what Italians would call *buone forchette*—adventurous eaters who love strong, lusty flavors. Often, these are people who enjoy cooking themselves, so that sharing in making the dinner can be part of the evening's entertainment. Here's a menu that lends itself to assembly by as many willing hands as you have room for in your kitchen. (It's not too much for a single cook to handle, however.) The results are guaranteed to put sparkle in the eyes and color in the cheeks of all participants.

◆

Artichokes stuffed with tuna

Penne all'arrabbiata

Veal chops in red wine
Spinach with olive oil and lemon

Strawberry tart

♈

Barbera can happily take your group through the entire meal, including a glass or two for the cooks.

♈♈

For more variety, serve a Greco di Tufo with the first two courses; a Nebbiolo with the veal.

Dinner guests are not always summoned only on festive occasions. Sometimes you feed people for consolation (theirs or yours). Whether the slings and arrows of late twentieth-century stress are due to miserable weather, family feuds, unreasonable job demands, or any other physical or mental outrage, here's a soft, comforting menu calculated to soothe the spirits of those so exhausted that the very thought of chewing a lettuce leaf makes their gums hurt.

◆

Rice and peas

Golden braised chicken
Fennel braised with ham

Neapolitan chocolate mousse

♈

Connoisseurship takes too much effort at a time like this. Drink a Friulian Tocai throughout; it will forgive you for not thinking too much about it.

SUMMER MENUS

1

Should you be tempted by the thought of an Antipastissimo party, as described on page 122 of the Summer section, here's a blueprint for a delightful one. This can be an outdoor picnic buffet or an indoor cocktail party. The first three cold dishes and the schiacciata (more likely, several loaves of schiacciata) can be set out just before guests arrive, and the two heartier composed dishes served later and still warm from the oven. We haven't included a dessert in this menu, but that's not to say you couldn't. Similarly, you could add a platter of cured meats—salame, mortadella, prosciutto, soppressata—for confirmed carnivores.

•

Capri salad

Marinated zucchini with mint
Seafood salad

Tomato schiacciata

Eggplant Parmesan
Zucchini Bella Napoli

♟♟

You'll want at least two wines for this party, one red and one white. In fact, two of each for guests to sample would be in keeping with the spirit of the feast. Good choices for whites are Pinot grigio, Soave, Verdicchio, and Sauvignon. Valpolicella and Lacryma Christi are two relaxed reds that would fill the bill nicely here.

2

In contrast to the casual approach of the antipasto buffet above, summer sometimes calls for a more formal entertainment. The dishes served ought to pique appetites that may be languishing from the hot weather. The brightly accented flavors in each dish of this menu should do the trick. Overall, it's a light and elegant meal, easy on the cook and charming on the palate.

•

Scallops San Remo

Rigatoni with basil

Veal scallops with prosciutto, sage, and white wine
Green salad

Granita or gelato

♟

A Gavi would make pleasant, light drinking throughout.

♟♟

Or serve the Gavi with the first two courses, then a young, non-Riserva Chianti with the veal.

3

Heat or no heat, sometimes you need an important and festive meal in summer. To celebrate a graduation, wedding anniversary, birthday, or just the at-long-last arrival of vacation, here's a menu that will produce happy gustatory memories. (The cook's memories will be happiest if there's an air conditioner in the kitchen.)

◆

Batter-fried zucchini blossoms

Fresh egg noodles with prosciutto

Pizzaiola steaks
Neapolitan-style eggplant

Granita or gelato

♉

*If you want only one wine, make it red:
a young Taurasi or Aglianico.*

♉♉

*For more variety, serve a Pomino bianco
for the first two courses, then the red for
the beef and eggplant.*

4

If you're a family of dedicated fisherfolk, or have access to a good supply of fresh fish, here's a menu to showcase the ocean's bounty. The meal will make you feel you're spending the summer in a cottage by the sea, even if you're actually stuck in the heart of the city and purchased the wherewithal at the Fulton fish market.

◆

Gratin of mussels

Spaghettini with clams and shrimp

*Tuna steaks sauteed with olives and
capers*
Grilled tomatoes

Granita or gelato

♉

*A crisp Verdicchio can serve with all the
courses of this meal.*

1

There are still a lot of folks in this world whose knowledge of Italian food goes no further than spaghetti with meatballs and veal parmigiana. If you're acquainted with any such unfortunates, one day you might make a charitable contribution to their education by serving them this meal. We thought of dubbing this menu Breaking Away, in honor of the hero's father in the movie of that name, who went around complaining about having to eat "eeny food."

◆

Mushroom canapés

Zucchini egg-drop soup

Roasted veal shanks
Parmesan mashed potatoes
Green beans in green sauce

Autumn apples

Part of the learning experience of this dinner is the wine. Serve your students a cru Soave with their first two courses, and graduate them to a fine Barbaresco with the veal shank.

2

This is the first of two dinner parties designed to be served to homesick Italians—in this case, northerners. (Don't laugh: think of the first time you visited Europe, and how you pined for scrambled eggs or peanut butter.) This is the kind of meal a Venetian or a Lombard, a Piedmontese or a Friulian, would find *molto caratteristico*—very typical of the flavors of the northern Italian autumn. If you are really inviting Italians, make more polenta than you think you could possibly need: they'll vacuum it up!

◆

Ham and mushroom torte

Casserole-roasted pheasant
Grilled polenta

Poached pears with mascarpone and Gorgonzola

Y

Hard to think that Italians couldn't handle more than one wine, but if not, make them happy with a Dolcetto.

YY

Make them even happier by replacing the Dolcetto with a Nebbiolo when you serve the pheasant.

YYY

Make them happiest of all by bringing out a Picolit or Recioto di Soave when you serve dessert.

The second dinner party for homesick Italians—southerners, this time. Where the northerner in autumn eats heartily, the southerner dines piquantly. But consider making a double dose of that homely bean-and-escarole soup!

•

Spectacular stuffed peppers
Escarole and bean soup

Sweet-and-sour braised rabbit
Streamed broccoli

Baked pears
Walnuts, hazelnuts, almonds

♀

Try either of two fine Sicilian reds:
Rosso del Conte or Enrico IV.

♀♀

Or offer a Lacryma Christi bianco for the
first two courses, then bring out the red
with the rabbit.

So far with our fall menus, the cook has been pretty busy in the kitchen. Here's one that offers a breather: none of the dishes requires much time to prepare; and the secondo and contorno can share an oven while the cook shares an aperitif with the guests.

•

Prosciutto and pear rolls

Country wife spaghetti

Baked pork chops
Onions Castellare

Fruit and biscotti

♀

Pomino bianco or Pinot bianco can take
you through the whole meal.

♀♀

Or add a Barbera with the secondo.

WINTER MENUS

Serve this menu for a casual open house party and call it Souper Bowl Sunday. It's the simplest of foods: soups, cheeses, and breads. Set the breads out on a buffet table with the cold cheeses and condiments. Have the soups simmering on the stove, with a pile of bowls and spoons nearby. Serve the frico at a moment midway in the afternoon or evening, when most people have at least sampled the buffet but appetites are still brisk.

◆

Schiacciata with greens
Schiacciata with prosciutto
Black pepper biscuits
Olives, pickled peperoncini
Cheese board: taleggio, fontina, caciotta

Frico

Umbrian onion soup
Neapolitan cabbage, rice, and
provolone soup
Pasta with chick-peas

♈

To please everyone's taste, you'll need at least one red and one white wine. Montepulciano d'Abruzzo, Corvo, and Lacryma Christi all come in both colors, and any pairing would be fine with these simple foods.

Here's a melting pot of a holiday meal. It's a mixture of dishes from many Italian regions, north and south, not a combination that Italians—with their strong sense of traditional feast-day dishes—would ever be likely to serve. One trait it shares with those traditional feasts, though, is extreme richness: make it on a day when eating dinner is the day's main activity.

◆

Marinated winter vegetables

Fusilli Neapolitan style

Roast turkey with fruit-and-chestnut
stuffing
Red cabbage with olives and capers
Braised broccoli rape

Chocolate spice cake or Friulian
fruit-and-nut roll

♈

Pinot grigio could take you all the way
through.

♈♈

Add a Chianti Classico Riserva, with
either the fusilli or the turkey.

♈♈♈

It's a holiday; make it sparkle. Finish with an Asti Spumante or a Brachetto d'Acqui.

When the holiday is over, you still need to eat. Here's a comforting cold-weather dinner for family and old, old friends.

•

Friulian bean soup

Tuscan pot roast
Home-style potatoes and carrots
Home-style savoy cabbage

Pear cake

♀

One's enough. Make it Rubesco.

Winter Olympics: for big appetites after a day of ice-skating or snowball fights. This dinner is marked by complex but mostly gentle flavors, all very warming and nourishing. And the aromas of the cooking ought to attract the frostbitten throngs from afar.

•

Raw vegetables with creamy garlic
dipping sauce

Pasta baked with meats, cheeses, and
hard-boiled eggs

Boiled veal shanks with green sauce
Gratinéed brussels sprouts

"White truffles"

♀

Tocai or Vintage Tunina.

About Wine

Italian winemaking has changed more in the past three decades than it did in the three millennia that preceded them. A technological explosion has completely altered the way wines are made in Italy. There is so much experimentation going on—with monovarietal wines in Tuscany, with blended wines in Piedmont, with grape varieties and clone selections everywhere—that there's no way to learn everything about Italian wine in one lesson. There's too much information—fascinating, if you already like that sort of thing, but often difficult for Americans, who grow up without any grass-roots cultural or familial wine tradition to ground them in wine basics. Wine is simply a language most Americans don't speak, and Italian wine is one of its tougher dialects. So this little essay has no chance of making you an instant expert.

What it will do, we hope, is give you a general feel for Italian wines and their role with foods—which, let us hasten to assure you, is all that the vast majority of Italians have. The late Renato Ratti, a fine, innovative winemaker and a passionate scholar of Italian wine, once answered a query about the rarity of bottles from older Italian vintages and the paucity of long-established wine cellars in Italy with the wry remark: "You must understand, the Italian discovery of wine is quite recent."

What he meant was that, for centuries, Italians never thought about their wine. Wine was food. You drank it with meals, and you drank what there was, red or white, fresh or oxidized, dry or sweet, according to your region's traditions and your own means. Connoisseurship in the French sense and collecting in the American sense did not exist, and even now are hardly known in Italy. That's part of the reason why Italian wines invariably taste better with food than they do in the artificial circumstances of wine judgings. Italians are, to the eyes of American wine buffs, alarmingly casual about their great wines. World-class winemakers—men and women who are venerated like saints by American collectors—chain-smoke cigarettes during wine tastings, a vinous sin only a little short of spitting on the altar in church. Even the very best winemakers treat their very best wines like reliable old friends rather than manna from a divine visitation, and they insist on behaving toward them as if simple attention and common sense were all that were necessary to understand and enjoy them—an attitude that could put all wine writers out of work!

Here's an example of what we mean. A few years ago at Vinitaly, the nation's biggest wine exposition, we wanted to introduce a writer friend to the line of Mastroberardino wines, which we esteem highly. The Mastroberardino booth was presided over that day by Antonio Mastroberardino, who is a scholar of the ancient wines of his region, an inspired winemaker, and the head of the clan. As we tasted the various wines, Antonio described them and the effects he'd sought in them, and we nodded assent as his comments tallied with our own impressions.

Then came the pièce de résistance, his near-legendary 1968 Taurasi Riserva, a wine that we two (but not yet our friend) knew to be one of the best wines made anywhere in this century. The wine in our glasses was slightly but definitely oxidized: clearly once great, its freshness was fading, and its future prospects seemed bleak. As Antonio rhapsodized about the wine's complexity and elegance, its freshness and its potential for decades more of life, our hearts sank. We looked at each other in dismay, feeling embarrassment for our friend Antonio, disappointment for our friend the writer, and desolation for our friend the wine.

Then, a thought: Antonio had opened fresh bottles of all the earlier wines for us, but we hadn't seen him draw the cork from the 1968 Taurasi. Could we see the bottle? Of course. It was less than half full—far more missing than the small tasting portions we three had in our glasses. "Antonio, when did you open this bottle?" "Let me think: yesterday? No, Tuesday. Yes, Tuesday." We could see our writer-friend's face change immediately. Two days ago: forty-eight hours of standing around open, and this twenty-year-old wine was still this good? That's impressive.

It *was* impressive—even more impressive as a feat of wine stamina than that Taurasi would have been if shown under ideal conditions—but the point is that it was utterly uncalculated. The incident epitomizes for us the complexity of the Italian attitude toward wine: one of Italy's finest winemakers—passionate, learned, devoted—but refusing to fetishize even his greatest vintage. Wine is not a god, nor it is a thing to be collected, hoarded, displayed, and never consumed. Wine is a great, good thing to be sure, a thing to be proud of, to enjoy, to share, but a thing that ultimately dies. It is to be drunk, savored, appreciated, and—if it deserves it, if the winemaker has done his job well—remembered long after with pleasure.

The fact is, Italian wine is a love story, and like all true love stories, it's not simple, and it's not all happy. But, as in all true love stories, the good parts are glorious and make the whole experience unforgettable.

A Good Part: We are in the Piedmont, visiting Barolo and Barbaresco makers with a group of American wine-and-food journalists. An initially diffident Giuseppe Cola (Beppe, as everybody in Alba knows him), the long-time winemaker for Prunotto, grows more and more animated and enthusiastic as he discovers from our group's questions that we know something about wine and—what is clearly more important to him, since he willingly shares his years of wine knowledge—that we care about it. Our official visit is ending. We've tasted the array of wines that had been planned for us and need to move on to the next winery on our itinerary. Hesitantly, almost shyly, Beppe asks if it would be possible for us to return in a few hours? For a very short while? To taste something special that he would like us to know? We already think that his wines are something special, so there's no problem getting unanimous assent to taste a wine that he regards as out of the ordinary. When we return (after some bravura rescheduling efforts), Beppe has ready a cobwebbed magnum of Prunotto's 1951 Barolo, which he uncorks for us. Suddenly, the air is full of truffles: the overwhelming, appetite-stirring scent of white Alba truffles. (We recognize the aroma because it's truffle season and we've been smelling them everywhere, but never like this, rising right out of a wine!) The taste is even richer: truffles and tea and tar and black cherries, tobacco and leather and black pepper, a huge flavor, yet elegant and restrained. A wonderful, wonderful wine, and for many of the writers in the group a complete revelation of what mature Barolo from a great vintage can be: a wine education in a single glass. Beppe Cola, diffident again, scarcely says a word, but beams broad smiles as he sees the group's ecstatic reaction to his wine, his child.

A Bad Part: We are in the Veneto with another group of food-and-wine writers, visiting winemakers around Treviso. A young producer harangues us about the superlative qualities of his wine, which he describes as being as good as—in fact exactly like—Chablis. The sample he pours tastes like lemonade laced with Chardonnay. It turns out that this belligerent young man has tasted Chablis three times in his entire life, has scarcely traveled beyond the Veneto, and knows almost nothing about other Italian wines, much less French or American wines.

A Very Good Part: In Tuscany, traveling on our own, visiting makers of Brunello di Montalcino, trying to get the hang of that austere, splendid, difficult wine. At Fattoria dei Barbi, the impressive Signora Francesca Colombini-Cinelli, whose natural bearing is as aristocratic as her wines, has prepared for us a twelve-year vertical tasting of Brusco dei Barbi, a proprietary wine made entirely from the same strain of Sangiovese grapes that makes Brunello, but vinified by the process known as *governo toscano,* a second fermentation induced by the addition of reserved, semidried grapes. Barbi introduced Brusco in the early seventies as an experiment, hoping to create a wine that would be fresher, more forthcoming, and ready to drink sooner than the long-lived but often recalcitrant Brunello. A twelve-year vertical tasting—twelve different vintages of the same wine—is Something Special anytime, anyplace, but here particularly it was an honor, far more than we had expected, far more than seemed due to our modest status as writers. It was another whole wine education in miniature: we were able to trace back, year by year, the consistency of the wine's style (a supple muscularity supporting ripe, plummy fruit) and its development with age, from zesty fruitiness in its youth to depth and complexity in maturity, with—a real surprise—a redolence of black truffles. Signora Colombini-Cinelli, whose rapid, Tuscan-accented Italian had swept over us like a benevolent tidal wave all during the tasting, beamed a huge smile at our exclamations of *Tartufi neri!* "Apt pupils" seemed to be her thought, or at least we hoped it was: La Signora is a formidable lady, and a very knowledgeable one.

The kind of passion for their wines, generosity with them and eagerness to share their knowledge that the Signora and Signor Colla demonstrated on those two occasions are very characteristic traits among Italian winemakers up and down the peninsula. (Another typical trait is a penchant for choosing the coldest part of the cellars in which to deliver the lengthiest explanations. And you thought all these trips that writers get to take are unmitigated luxury!) Not so characteristic, but also, alas, not an extinct trait, is the kind of provincial smugness our Trevisano winemaker displayed. Not, mind you, that that sort of parochialism is exclusively Italian. You'll find it just as often in Napa and Bordeaux as you will anywhere in Italy. But the fact is that Italian winemaking is a complicated and often contradictory world, polarized between wines that are already world-class (and perhaps always were, though the world never knew of them) and wines that are of no more than local interest (and never will be, no matter what technological miracles are brought to bear on their making). From the professional and technical viewpoint, Italian winemaking is a microcosm of the country's absurd, convoluted, and impossible political and economic situation—and the coming of the European Economic Community is only going to confuse all three even more for many years.

That is Italian wine in Italy. In America, it's both more complicated and simpler. More complicated because so much of it is strange to us, the names and places and grape varieties all new and different; and simpler because the small fraction of Italian wine that comes to this country represents some of the very best of it. Even at the lower price levels, it is becoming rarer and rarer to get a bad Italian wine in America, or even an ill-made one. The general level of winemaking in Italy is now such that the wines that enter into international distribution are normally very clean, well-made specimens, as thoroughly policed by a highly competitive marketplace as they are by the regulatory agencies of the exporting and importing countries.

It's true that you can get Italian wines that aren't worth the price charged for them: In some cases, the combination of Italian inflation, the weakness of the U.S. dollar, and a particular winemaker's delusions of grandeur (think of our little Trevisano and his "Chablis") work to push a particular wine's prices to unrealistic levels. And a lot of importers are, we believe, concentrating on the wrong end of the wine market by aiming for the very top of the range. California winemakers seem prone to this same sin. Everyone forgets that the Alpine peaks of European fine wine are supported by the broad plains of thousands of years of wine as a daily beverage, a condition that has never existed in the United States. As near as we can see, expecting great wine to maintain a steady market in a nonwine-drinking environment has about as much future as trying to make foie gras without ducks and geese. America needs a sound, simple red wine to drink every day with hamburgers or spaghetti and a white to have with fishsticks and shrimp salad, and neither should cost more than the food they accompany. The winemakers who can begin filling that need will not only make themselves wealthy, but will also enrich the whole culinary culture of this country and strengthen the place of the finest wines in our lives.

End of sermon: back to Italian wine as it now is.

The best way to find out about any wines is the common-sense way: Taste them. Nothing substitutes for that. There are lots of books that can help you, if you want them, but the bottom line remains your evaluation of the wines, the simple, unarguable fact of whether they please you or not. And to find that out, you've got to drink them. Find a good wine dealer, buy a few different bottles, drink them with your ordinary meals, take a few notes to aid your memory, and follow your own preferences. The advantage of experimenting in this way with Italian wines is that they are such good "food wines." Not only are they great with their own foods, with dishes like those in this book, but they go well with other cuisines as well—especially with a lot of contemporary American cooking (a.k.a. Cal-Ital), which is so markedly influenced by the Mediterranean diet.

Chemistry can go a long way toward explaining why some particular wine and food combinations are more or less pleasing to most people's palates, and for some people that's a highly interesting subject. (If you want to pursue it, take a look at Tom's book, *The Right Wine*.) But in the end, if *you* like what's in *your* glass, there's nothing more to be said. All we can hope to do here is broaden your options for what you put in your glass and open your eyes to some wines you might well like if you get to know them.

In the recipe sections of this book, we've made a few wine suggestions for each dish. Most people will probably find these good matches. We'd like to encourage you to annotate these suggestions after making the dish and trying the wine: scribble notes in the margin about whether you liked the combination, or whether you want to try something different next time. But just in case you can't get any of the wines suggested, or if you'd like to try something different with a dish, we're going to offer first some "family portraits" of the major varieties of red and white wines and then give you some lists of Italian wines according to three general types—Light, Medium, and Big. You can then look for an alternative wine in the same group as the wine we've listed for the recipe, or, if you've found that wine too light or too heavy, you can try a wine of a different type.

The three classifications we're proposing correspond to the way you would use the wines in a meal:

- Light Wines: those you would use as aperitifs or serve with the simplest and lightest dishes (especially antipasti).
- Medium Wines: wines of medium body and assertiveness, to be served primarily with primi and not too delicate or too aggressive secondi.

- Big Wines: those to be served with the strongest or most complexly flavored dishes or with cheeses.

Let us say in advance, however, that these are guidelines, not absolutes. As you get to know the wines better, you should certainly want to branch out and try your own combinations of wine and food, whether or not they conform to the introductory guidelines we're offering here.

Our three classifications are of necessity generalizations. With any particular bottle, a cru designation, a Riserva status or a remarkably fine vintage year might qualify it for the next more substantial category—and vice versa: a wine from a poor year may be less substantial than its category suggests. Both of those kinds of changes will alter the kinds of food that wine will accompany. Note too that if you drink at two or three years of age a wine that ideally should be aged for ten or fifteen, you won't taste the complexity that authorities talk about—and that too will alter the kinds of foods that wine will accompany best.

We tell you all this not to discourage you or confuse you, but to emphasize the fact that circumstances alter cases. The cliché that wine is a living thing is remarkably true, and wines are as variable as people: that's part of their fascination. The more you know about the possibilities and variables in the wines you're choosing among, the higher your batting average of pleasing food-and-wine combinations is going to be, and the more enjoyment you'll take in it all—not just the meal and the wine, but even in your own cleverness in guessing just how well they were going to taste together.

One last tale to comfort you as you begin your exploration of all these foreign wines: One day in Florence we were talking with Piero Antinori, the head of the Antinori wine firm, an extremely sophisticated world traveler, and the man who more than any other pioneered the use of the "foreign" Cabernet Sauvignon grape in Tuscan wine. Piero was then experimenting, on the Antinori's Orvieto estates at Castello della Sala, with Chardonnay and Sauvignon and Gewürztraminer. So we asked which foreign grape he intended to try next. His perfectly serious answer floored us, and should comfort anyone confronting the unfamiliarity of Italian wines: "I would like to try to understand Nebbiolo [the most important red grape of the Italian Piedmont]. For me, it is the most foreign of all the grapes, and I can't comprehend the wine at all."

A GALLERY OF RED WINES

GRIGNOLINO AND FREISA

"Light" in a red wine doesn't mean the same thing that it does in a white. In weight on the tongue and intensity on the palate, the lightest red wines usually correspond to the middle range of whites. Perhaps the only Italian reds that are truly as light-bodied as a white are the rarely imported Freisa and Grignolino, both Piedmont wines made from grapes that can honestly be considered endangered varieties. If you ever get the chance to taste them, by all means take it. They are interesting, odd wines, genuinely charming and very light-bodied, the Grignolino with a distinctive strawberry tang and the Freisa with what is best described as a light cherry flavor, both comparatively high in acid and low in tannin, and capable of surviving pretty thorough chilling—in all respects, ideal summer reds for casual occasions and light foods. It would be a shame if they were allowed to go the way of the buffalo.

BARBERA AND DOLCETTO

These are the two most frequently drunk wines in the Piedmont, a great red wine region with plenty to choose from. Of the two, Barbera is unquestionably the lighter-bodied, though no one would ever take it for a wimp wine. It is also the least tannic and most acidic of the Piedmont reds. The latter trait, combined with its dry, slightly tart, clean fruit, makes it an excellent wine with all sorts of food, but especially with simply prepared entrees or the earlier, lighter courses of an elaborate dinner. Barbera in fact amounts to a fine, all-purpose, all-year-round companion for everyday cooking.

Dolcetto almost matches Barbera in utility. Usually a very fruity, easy-drinking wine of deep color, Dolcetto can take a few years of bottle age with some small loss of fruit and corresponding gain in complexity. Young Dolcetto is dry, light- to medium-bodied, and intensely fruity: think of Beaujolais with flesh, tannin, and fruit as its primary characteristics instead of acidity and fruit. Dolcetto makes a good dinner wine with pastas, simple meats both light and dark, and not-too-aggressive cheeses. It in fact will partner well with a wide range of foods, though (because Dolcetto is among the least acidic of Piedmont wines) very acid dishes will upset its balance. Like Barbera, Dolcetto rarely creates any palatal impression of great weight, though—again like Barbera—it almost always delivers a lot of flavor. This makes them very enjoyable warm-weather reds, for those times of year when a really serious red wine seems like more work than your palate is up to.

Most of the time, Barbera is a very pleasant wine-of-all-foods, light-bodied and acidic with a pleasing, black-cherry tang. In exceptionally fine vintages (such as 1982, 1985, 1988), or from particular fields and vinified with more than usual care, Barbera not only acquires greater body but also displays real complexity and character, while retaining its basic utility-infielder attitude toward food. Experiments with aging Barbera in *barriques* have shown great promise, and some makers are beginning to try their hand at blending Barbera with small quantities of the tannin-rich Nebbiolo, which yields a wine of exceptional structure and suppleness. In the right hands, this versatile, likable wine can get very near greatness. This is a wine that deserves a better and larger public.

In a few exceptional vintages (e.g., 1982 and 1985), Dolcetto too can make an important wine of great depth and complexity while still retaining its characteristic fruitiness. These unusual Dolcettos respond to food rather in the manner of full-bodied Burgundies: too much acid will undo them, but they have a tolerance for cream-based sauces that goes beyond that of many other Italian wines.

Both Barbera and Dolcetto serve perfectly as the introductory red wines of an important, multicourse, multiwine dinner: Interesting in themselves, they make useful, light- to medium-bodied foils for the big guns to follow.

BARDOLINO AND VALPOLICELLA

The area that stretches westward from Lake Garda past Verona and on to the Adriatic coast of the Veneto produces a great deal of red wine of widely varying character and quality. Among the very lightest of these reds are Bardolino and Valpolicella, wines whose appeal lies primarily in freshness and a delicate, berrylike character. Bardolino is sometimes so light as to look and taste almost like a rosé. In the recent past, Valpolicella was its practically indistinguishable twin, but some producers in the region have revived an even older way of vinifying the wine that gives it a darker color, deeper flavor, and more substantial presence. Valpolicella in this style is still by no means a huge wine—medium-bodied is as big as it gets—but it's no longer invariably the very light wine it was during the sixties and seventies.

If it's light to very light red wine you're looking for, choose the simplest appellations—no cru or vineyard designations, no special names or bottlings—plain Bardolino and Valpolicella, or, at most, Classico (which only indicates the heart of the zone) or Superiore (which only indicates a slightly higher degree of alcohol). Such bottles will be light, acidic, and fruity in a vaguely strawberry-and-grapes range, and will be able to take a fair degree of chilling without losing their charm. These make good, enjoyable picnic and barbecue wines. They match well with antipasti, primi, and light meats and fowls.

The special bottlings and the *cru* wines, on the other hand, will probably have undergone *ripasso*, a technique of inducing a secondary fermentation strengthened with the lees of Amarone (about which, see below). This yields a bigger, fuller, more substantial wine, still zesty and youthful but more able to stand up to red meats and other still simple but assertively flavored foods. If you're in doubt as to which kind you've got, price will probably tell you: all these "new old-style" Valpolicellas cost considerably more than the familiar light wine.

AMARONE

The Amarone zone lies in the heart of the Valpolicella zone, and the two wines incorporate the same grape varieties, though they couldn't be more different in their characters. Recioto della Valpolicella Amarone (to give it its full name) is a huge, velvety wine, Italy's biggest, and perhaps fullest-bodied unfortified dinner wine in the world. An unusual vinification process, involving the kind of semiraisined, very ripe grapes usually reserved for sweet dessert wines, yields a high-alcohol (14 percent is minimal), muscular, yet spectacularly fresh and intensely fruity wine of extraordinary aging potential. Its delicious, berrylike fruit is supported by an enormous body and an elegant texture that almost every taster describes as velvety and reminiscent of the feel of old Burgundy. Because of its size—its heft and authority—Amarone can only be compared to the biggest of the Rhône red wines, which it rivals in power and longevity (and value for dollar). Amarone needs a lot of time in bottle to achieve balance. Our preference is not to drink it until it is at least ten years old, and in fact to keep it as long after that as greed and gluttony will allow—the older Amarone is, the better it gets.

Because Amarone is so big a wine, many people are nervous about matching it with foods. Some prefer to treat it like port, serving it after the meal proper, with walnuts or hazelnuts. While Amarone is perfectly enjoyable that way, we think this is an opportunity lost. Despite its admittedly huge size and ample power, Amarone is an extraordinarily supple wine. It also characteristically retains a surprising freshness and fruitiness, even into its second and sometimes third decade, that balances and moderates its power, so it is usable and delicious with thoughtfully selected entrees or secondi—chiefly either those of assertive flavors themselves or composed dishes of great, balanced complexity. If you are able to obtain a chunk of top quality eating parmigiano, no wine in the world will do as much with it or for it as an Amarone. This is a gastronomical *ne plus ultra* comparable to a great Sauternes with foie gras.

CHIANTI, BRUNELLO, AND THEIR KIN

Chianti is far and away Tuscany's—and probably Italy's—best-known wine. Unlike Piedmont wines, which are almost always made entirely from a single grape variety, the wines of Tuscany are almost always blends of several varieties of grapes. The Sangiovese is the chief of these, and although it is capable of producing great wines by itself (we will have more to say of this below), centuries of local custom blend it with other varieties, including some white grapes, to produce the simplest and lightest (the light end of medium-bodied) versions of Chianti. The name Chianti was originally a geographical designation—a stretch of rugged, hilly land between Florence and Siena, which is now known as the Chianti Classico, the classic Chianti country, and the heart of the numerous Chianti appellations. Because the terrain of Tuscany is so varied and the clones of Sangiovese so numerous, Chiantis can differ markedly in quality and intensity, even within the same growing zone and appellation.

There are seven Chianti appellations: Chianti Classico, Chianti dei Colli Fiorentini (from the Florentine hills), Chianti dei Colli Senesi (from the Siena hills), Chianti dei Colli Aretini (the hills around Arezzo), Chianti delle Colline Pisane (the hills near Pisa), Chianti di Montalbano (an area northwest of Florence), and Chianti Rufina (an area northeast of

Florence). These zones differ from each other in significant ways. The Chianti of Siena, for instance, tends to be lighter-bodied and fruity, while that of Rufina is heavier, with more earth tones in its flavor. But the distinction that makes the greatest difference to the consumer is that between the simple Chiantis (from either a single designated zone or blended from several) and the Riservas (almost always from the Classico, with a few from Rufina).

Only the simple Chiantis and the non-Riserva bottlings can truly be considered light. Even among these wines, very good vintages will lift otherwise light wines into the middle category in terms of both weight and complexity. Just about the best indicator of lightness in a Chianti is price: The least expensive ones are usually the lightest.

Middle-range Chiantis—this will be most of the Riservas and cru bottlings—make very useful dinner wines. A Chianti Riserva is a select wine that has been given extra care and extensive barrel-aging. It contains fewer white grapes than the regular Chianti and needs more time to develop in the bottle. It is relatively high in acidity, with usually soft tannin, a lot of nice, sapid, Sangiovese fruit, and a fair degree of complexity. Such wines will match well with strongly flavored antipasti (especially meats), with spicy or aggressively flavored pastas and risottos, and with not-too-dramatic secondi.

This middle range is also the proper home for most vintages of Vino Nobile di Montepulciano and for the lighter vintages of Brunello di Montalcino—also Sangiovese-based wines (the Brunello entirely so). While Vino Nobile can for all practical purposes be regarded as a distinguished, usually softer and rounder, category of Chianti, Brunello is something else again. Brunello is vinified from a single, prized strain of Sangiovese grapes to make what may be the longest-lived wine in Italy. The best of all of these wines resemble clarets in their balance, but add a peculiarly Sangiovese juiciness and acidity that make them very versatile with all sorts of food. The clone of Sangiovese that makes Brunello has the same kind of tannic asperity as the Cabernet that forms the heart of clarets, but the Sangiovese's fruit is fuller, plummier, and more acidic, so over time it develops into a wine bigger in scale and surer in balance than all but the finest 100 percent Cabernets. Rosso di Montalcino is a younger wine from the same grapes, with considerably less wood aging. It can still be a very big wine, and always shows the same enormous Sangiovese fruit as Brunello.

In average vintages, a Brunello (just like a Barolo or a Barbaresco) should get at least five to eight years of aging before you drink it, and more won't hurt it. In a great vintage, a wine from one of the traditional makers will need twenty years to come around. If you think that is extravagant, a taste of mature Brunello will change your mind: deep and mouth-filling, with an aroma of truffles and forest earth and a flavor compounded of dry plums and cedar and black pepper and sometimes hints of tar and licorice, mature Brunello combines authority and suaveness in a way that makes it like no other wine. Brunello is a special-occasion wine: it needs big flavors as a foil—game, red meat roasts, wild mushrooms, big cheeses (especially parmigiano). It will take complex sauces in stride, whether they be redolent of tarragon, softened with cream, or rich with marrow. Rosso di Montalcino doesn't ask so much, but is still best served with robust foods—rich stews and braises, steaks, or that humble but savory Tuscan favorite, grilled sausages and Tuscan beans. In fact, Rosso di Montalcino reacts very well with the whole gamut of grilled meats and vegetables.

It's worth noting, by the way, that the very best vintages of Riserva Chianti from the Classico and Rufina zones, while not quite the equal of Brunello in body or longevity, are fully its match in complexity and elegance. And all Sangiovese-based wines share a capacity for long life and development. A Chianti Classico Riserva from a fine vintage and a good producer will take twenty years in stride and still taste live and supple.

Carmignano is another Tuscan wine notable for its fine balance and aging potential: A separate appellation, Carmignano has for decades (some claim centuries) been a blend of Cabernet—a grape just being introduced elsewhere in Tuscany—with the native Sangiovese to yield a wine of great poise and suppleness. Many Chianti-zone growers are now experimenting with similar blends (Antinori's Tignanello was the great pioneer in this) or with 100 percent Cabernet wines, some of which have achieved a wonderful lushness of fruit and great polish, while retaining a distinctively Italian acidity.

Neighboring Umbria also produces first-class wines on the Chianti model, both standard and Cabernet-blends. Lungarotti's Rubesco, Rubesco Riserva, and San Giorgio are the models there.

Riserva Chianti and all its kin respond very well to balanced and composed foods—small game birds and rich, lean meats (like squab) and fine cheeses. Because of their own characteristically great acidity (compared to, for instance, the red wines of France or California), the Sangiovese-based wines (indeed, Italian red wines in general) can deal quite satisfactorily with more acid foods than can any of the clarets: tomato-based sauces, for instance, pose no problems to Chianti, whereas they can undo most Bordeaux reds.

Finally, it is important to note that the very finest vintages of all these wines will normally promote them into our category of Big Wines—especially the Brunello, which can make as big and muscular a wine as anything California can produce.

Barolo, Barbaresco, and their kin

Nebbiolo is the star grape of the Piedmont, Val d'Aosta, and parts of Lombardy, where it makes the biggest, longest-lived red wines of the regions, and some of the world's best and most austere. The wines we get here come mostly from the Piedmont: Barbaresco, Barolo, Carema, Gattinara, Nebbiolo, and Spanna are all made of 100 percent Nebbiolo grapes, while Boca, Bramaterra, Caramino, Fara, Ghemme, Lessona, and Roero—place names all—are all blends of Nebbiolo (predominantly) with Barbera or Bonarda or other local grape varieties. We also receive some of Piedmont's experimental, non-D.O.C. blends of Nebbiolo and Barbera or Dolcetto: for example, Fontanafredda's Bardone, Granduca's

Barilot, Drago's Bricco del Drago, Valentino's Bricco Manzoni, Pio Cesare's Ornato. All of the Nebbiolo-based Lombard wines that we receive here come from the Valtellina zone. They include Grumello, Inferno, Sassella, Valgella, and Sfurzat. These Lombard wines, while they rarely reach the distinction of their Piedmontese cousins, are nevertheless fine wines and often excellent values.

In most vintages, the big three Nebbiolo wines—Nebbiolo d'Alba, Barbaresco, and Barolo—will emphatically belong in our category of big wines. Only light vintages of these and middling vintages of their lesser siblings will slip down into the medium class. Of these siblings, Gattinara is unquestionably the most distinguished. Lighter-bodied than either Barolo or Barbaresco, it nevertheless achieves very great elegance. Its somewhat less forceful impact in fact makes it a more useful and versatile wine, since it will match well with many foods that Barolo would overpower. For instance, you could conceivably serve a Gattinara with a *carne cruda all' Albese* (a veal tartare, ideally topped with slivers of fresh white truffle), whereas a Barolo wouldn't work with it (too much tannin, too big a flavor). A Gattinara will taste just fine with a simple veal cutlet too, while—at the other end of the spectrum—it will also interact beautifully with a standing rib roast or a ripe Gorgonzola. That kind of utility makes Gattinara and its cousins wines well worth seeking out.

Our Big Wine classification holds what we consider Italy's greatest red wines. In the Piedmont, these will always be the finest vintages of Nebbiolo and even average vintages of Barbaresco and Barolo—the latter two wines being not merely the greatest wines of the Piedmont but, in the opinion of many connoisseurs, the greatest wines of all Italy. Whether one accepts that evaluation or not, what is unquestionable is that the Nebbiolo grape, as cultivated around the small city of Alba, produces wines of a quality and longevity to rival any in the world. Full-bodied, rich with extract, possessing a good amount of acidity, a lot of tannin, and a very marked and assertive flavor (its descriptors usually include black cherries, old roses, tar, tobacco, leather, and pepper), these are red wines to match with grand and assertive dishes. The tannin, concentration, and complexity of the best Nebbiolo wines create palatal impressions of nobility and austerity that make them incomparable partners to red meats, roasts, and game—the whole category called in Italian *carni nobili*, the noble meats—and the great cheeses. Nebbiolo wines also match well with richly flavored pastas and risottos, particularly those incorporating wild mushrooms or the truffles whose aroma so many connoisseurs find in the wines themselves. Try them with a standing rib roast and sautéed funghi porcini, or with game and grilled porcini, or simply with some excellent Gorgonzola: those are extraordinarily satisfying combinations.

As with other kinds of Italian wine, Nebbiolo orthodoxy (long, slow, fermentation in huge wooden vats with lots of skin contact, years of barrel aging) is currently being questioned, revised, tinkered with, abandoned, and reaffirmed, all at the same time. The Nebbiolo grape seems not to notice: At least around Alba, it seems next to impossible to make a bad wine out of this incredible grape. Even more important, talented growers and winemakers seem to abound—again, at least around Alba. So the novice Barolo or Barbaresco drinker doesn't have to worry overmuch about the complications of vinification or the nuances of style. Just get in there and taste the wines: You'll find out quickly enough which style you like and who makes it.

Taurasi and Aglianico

Italy's third great red wine grape produces the finest red wines of southern Italy, Taurasi from the high hills east of Naples and Aglianico del Vulture from the ancient volcanic slopes of Basilicata. This is an extremely old variety, first brought to Italy by Greek colonists around 600 B.C. Its potential, unfortunately, is still vastly underrealized; in fact, it came close to being extinct. Its rescuer, and still its best producer, is Angelo Mastroberardino, whose distinguished Taurasi is a 100 percent Aglianico wine. In his hands, and in the hands of its other notable exponent, Donato d'Angelo, who produces a fine Aglianico del Vulture, the Aglianico can make a long-lived, full-bodied, tannic and austere but nevertheless harmonious and elegant wine. Its best vintages and its Riserva bottlings deserve to be ranked with other Big Wines, but so harmonious and supple are these two Aglianico-based wines that they don't overwhelm even relatively delicate dishes. They match well with all roasts (including fowl) and game, with cheeses, and even—perhaps especially—with meats or fowl prepared by moist cooking with marked acidity (e.g., *ragù alla napoletana, pollo alla diavola*). Like so many of the great Italian red wines, Aglianico and Taurasi are superb with wild mushrooms. Taurasi and Aglianico del Vulture will never feel as big in the mouth as Brunello, nor as tannic, but they are structured in much the same way, so Riservas from excellent vintages can live almost as long. Also, because of their great complexity, they can match happily with any of the foods you would pair Brunellos with. An Aglianico Riserva or a Taurasi Riserva can always find in itself some component to answer even the most aggressively flavored meals.

A GALLERY OF WHITE WINES

Italy produces scores of clean, brisk, light, white wines that can serve as universal aperitifs. Some names: Bianco di Custozza, Bianco di Toscana, Chardonnay, Frascati, Gavi, Lugana, Orvieto, Pinot grigio, Sauvignon, Soave, Verdicchio. The simplest and least-expensive classifications of all of these wines—not their cru bottlings or their barrel-aged specimens, but their broadest regional types—will be light-bodied, acidic, and clean, with a delicate fruit that will be barely distinguishable from one region or variety to another. That is both praise and disparagement: praise because these wines are well made, widely available, inexpensive, and pleasant quaffing; disparagement because that is all they are.

All of them will show very well with antipasti (especially vegetable ones or vinegared ones), simple pastas, seafood, fowl, and delicately flavored white meat dishes. Such wines make wonderful casual occasion sipping—picnics, backyard barbecues, afternoons at the beach, concerts in the park. They are ideal warm-weather wines: most of them can stand a good amount of chilling, and their typically high acidity and fresh fruit flavors are refreshing and revitalizing in the dog days.

In their place, these can be charming wines. But anyone who comes to, let us say, a Chardonnay of this class and expects to taste CHARDONNAY! is going to be grievously disappointed. For real varietal character—indeed, for real character of any sort in a white wine—you are going to have to climb a rung or rungs on the ladder of regional specificity, vinicultural care, and expense.

This is not to say that Italy doesn't produce any distinguished, light-bodied white wines. Ceretto's Blangé, for instance, a very light and lively version of the Arneis grape, makes a lovely aperitif and seafood wine. Many of the less expensive Gavis also give more flavor and character than, for example, Verdicchios of the same price—though in fairness we should also point out that there are single-vineyard Verdicchios (from Fazi Battaglia and Garofoli especially) and cru Soaves (from Anselmi and Bolla especially) that both fit and transcend the aperitif wine category. All of these latter will be distinguishable not only by their greater cost but by the addition of a vineyard name to (sometimes even its substitution for) the generic wine name.

The vast majority of the quality white wines made in Italy are of medium body and flavor intensity, fully dry, with relatively high acidity balanced by a fruitiness that is, usually at least, distinctive of the grape variety or varieties from which they are made or of the region from which they come. While they can be used as aperitifs, that isn't where they really shine. Rather, they show their best with foods, especially with primi and secondi of some substance and/or complexity. They can be overpowered by raw, aggressive flavors—none of these is the wine to have with bruscit or *lepre in salmi*—but they will work beautifully with all sorts of seafood and fowl and veal or pork, especially those dishes with acid sauces (from tomatoes or citrus or peppers).

The greatest variety of such wines originates in the two hyphenated northern regions of Trentino-Alto Adige and Friuli-Venezia Giulia, with the Veneto a fairly distant third. Among them, these three seem to account for most of the kinds of Italian white wines that reach these shores. These northern whites are usually vinified from and named for single grape varieties, some internationally known (Chardonnay, Gewürztraminer, Pinot bianco, Pinot grigio, Riesling, Sauvignon) and some purely localized (Tocai, Verduzzo). A few blended wines of interest are also made here: Soave, whose cru bottlings properly belong in this category, and also Breganze bianco, an interesting blend based on Tocai.

From scattered other parts of Italy you can also gather estimable middle-range whites. Most Gavi and Arneis (Piedmont), for instance, fall into this group, as do Pomino bianco (Tuscany), Torre di Giano (Umbria), Lacryma Christi (Campania), and several whites from Sicily (Alcamo, Corvo, Donnafugata, Regaleali bianco).

All of these are wines of more than passing interest, and, like such wines the world over, their quality as well as their characteristics will vary from harvest to harvest and from winemaker to winemaker. An off-year for any of them might well drop the wine back into our Light category, while an exceptional vintage might easily move any of them into our Big category. The latter is also true of any of these wines when bottled with a cru, vineyard, or Riserva designation: Any of those factors could indicate a wine that exceeds this middle classification.

The gulf between a good, interesting white wine and a genuinely distinguished one has been, to date, the hardest of all of wine's challenges for Italian winemakers to deal with, and it is these few, truly distinguished white wines that we designate in our Big category. What we mean by Big in white wines isn't just size, or heft, or weight, though all those characteristics obviously contribute to it. We're talking first and foremost about quality and distinctiveness, that compound of objectively present factors in a wine that induce a sit-up-and-take-notice response in the taster. We mean the kind of wine that seems to fill your mouth with flavor and reveal nuance under nuance as you start paying conscientious attention to it. This kind of wine you would never serve as an aperitif, though you might very well sit down to do some deep thinking with a glass of it.

Some Italian whites achieve this level intermittently, in very great vintages: Pinot bianco is a good example of this. Some Italian whites achieve it, not always, but often, in the hands of especially talented individual winemakers: Bruno Giacosa's Arneis, the Chardonnays of Angelo Gaja and Pio Cesare, Livio Felluga's Tocai, the Sauvignons of Abbazia di Rosazzo, Borgo Conventi, Gaja, Gradnik, and Russiz Superiore are all examples of this. And some few achieve that level of quality quite regularly, by a scrupulous adherence to the best of long-hallowed traditions combined with the tactful application of the best of modern technology: Examples of this—and they are among the very best white wines that Italy has to offer—are Frescobaldi's single-vineyard Pomino bianco Il Benefizio, Mastroberardino's cru bottlings of Greco di Tufo (Vignadangelo) and Fiano di Avellino (Vignadoro), and Valentini's Trebbiano d'Abruzzo.

To make such wines requires great grapes to start with, and the talent and tact, the feel for the grapes to know what can be made of them. More and more Italian winemakers are turning their attention to these problems, and they are starting to get results. Many of the resulting wines proclaim their uniqueness by bearing proprietary names rather than the conventional regional or varietal designations. Some of these, too, are among the most interesting of Italy's white wines, wines like Antinori's Cervaro della Sala, the Chardonnays from Castello Banfi (Fontanelle), Gaja, Lungarotti, and Pio Cesare, Ruffino's Libaio, Abbazia di Rosazzo's Ronco delle Acacie, Jermann's Vintage Tunina.

One final category of Italian white wines deserves mention. Italy produces many dry sparkling wines. *Brut spumante* is the Franco-Italian name by which they are generally designated. These range in character and quality from very pleasant, light party wines, usually made from local grapes—Prosecco Spumante, from the Treviso area, is an excellent example of the breed—up to full-bodied, austere sparklers made on the champagne model and often using the orthodox champagne grapes: Chardonnay and Pinot noir especially, with Pinot blanc frequently substituting for the red (but uninteresting) Pinot meunier. These latter can be very fine indeed, but they—like champagne—are never inexpensive.

DESSERT WINES

While Italians are not much given to elaborate desserts, they do like to finish up a fine meal or a special occasion with a little taste of something sweet. This often takes the form of a glass of dessert wine accompanied by a few simple biscotti or cookies or nuts. If the occasion is at all festive, a bottle of Asti Spumante frequently fills the bill.

Light, sparkling, heady with the aroma of the Moscato grapes from which it's made, Asti Spumante may be Italy's one truly national wine. American consumers who remember the rather inert, sticky-sweet specimens of the breed that afflicted our markets a decade or more ago will be happy to know that Asti makers have latched onto modern wine technology with enthusiasm. The wines they make now are consequently cleaner and lighter, with their natural Moscato lushness brightened and elevated by a healthy acidity. The many good makers include such old reliable firms as Cinzano, Fontanafredda, Gancia, Granduca, Martini & Rossi, and Riccadonna, and such fine smaller producers as Contratto and Vignaioli di Santo Stefano. The last-named also makes a small quantity of an exquisite nonsparkling Moscato, perhaps the best of its kind in Italy, which is exported by Ceretto.

The Moscato grape also figures largely in the other most popular group of Italian dessert wines, the *passiti*. These are still wines vinified from very ripe, sometimes even raisined, grapes. Most are of very local production, and the main grape often masquerades under local dialect names. Zibibbo, for instance, is the Sicilian name for Moscato, and there are many Sicilian versions of the wine—the most noted (deservedly so) being Moscato di Pantelleria.

Since we are speaking of Sicilian wines, we should mention here that other great Sicilian favorite, Marsala. Marsala is probably most familiar to Americans *in* desserts (basic zabaglione depends on it), but like many other once great and then debased Italian wines, this noble survivor is staging a magnificent comeback. It comes now in three grades: Fine, a sweet, fortified wine suitable to accompany dessert or biscotti; Superiore, aged longer, slightly higher in alcohol, and vinified either dry or sweet for dessert or aperitif—both styles smooth and aromatic—and Vergine, an exquisite, always dry fortified wine that is one of the world's great aperitifs. The sweet Marsalas—especially the Superiore grade—make fine companions to fruit, pastry, cream, or ice cream desserts. All Marsalas are vinified from blends of very traditional and localized Sicilian grape varieties. Marco DiBartoli is an excellent producer, whose Marsala Vergine and closely related Vecchio Sampieri are magnificent even at twenty years of age.

The other major dessert wine grape in Italy is Malvasia, which hundreds of years ago yielded the important export wine Malmsey, probably most familiar to English speakers today from Shakespeare's plays and the fate of his two unfortunate princes who drowned in a barrel of Malmsey. Malvasia isn't tremendously popular today, but the dessert wines made from it can still be fine indeed (though not, we feel, worth drowning in). In Italy, the most prized version of it is Malvasia delle Lipari—from grapes grown in the volcanic Lipari islands off the northwest coast of Sicily. Carlo Hauner is far and away the leading producer.

Malvasia grapes are also a major component in central Italy's complex Vin Santo, a wine that ranges in flavor from nutty and off-dry to spicy and very sweet, and in color from pale gold to the deepest amber. Especially popular in Umbria and Tuscany, Vin Santo is traditionally served with *biscotti di Prato*—small hazelnut or almond zweiback—for dunking. Almost all Chianti makers also produce small quantities of Vin Santo, and it is a matter of pride and fierce competition to maintain the quality and style of this ancient, traditional wine. Good makers include Antinori, Avignonesi, Badia a Coltibuono, Barbi, Brolio, Castellare, Frescobaldi, Lungarotti, and Monte Vertine.

One other, very local grape yields an exquisite off-dry to sweet (depending on the harvest) dessert wine: Picolit. A Friulian rarity, Picolit is often compared in style to sherry, but it has a distinctive flavor of its own as well as great style and nuance. Because the vines are shy bearers and prone to all sorts of ills, Picolit is unfortunately very expensive. One of the most consistent makers of lovely Picolit is Livio Felluga.

Finally, a very tiny amount of sparkling red dessert wine is exported from Italy. The one you are most likely to see is Banfi's Bracchetto d'Acqui, a sweet, light wine with a slight cherry flavor, which has the great virtue of partnering well with chocolate desserts, which not many other wines are willing to do.

WHITE WINES—LIGHT

Arneis

Bianco di Custozza

Chardonnay

Etna

Frascati

Galestro (and other
Chianti-zone whites,
depending on vintage)

Gavi

Orvieto

Pinot bianco

Pinot grigio

Riesling

Sauvignon

Soave

Trebbiano

Verdicchio

Verduzzo (only the secco)

Vernaccia

WHITE WINES—MEDIUM

Arneis (depending on style)

Breganze bianco

Chardonnay (depending on
region and/or maker)

Corvo bianco

Galestro (and other
Chianti-zone whites,
depending on vintage)

Fiano di Avellino

Gavi (depending on style)

Greco di Tufo

Lacryma Christi

Pinot bianco (depending on
region and maker)

Pomino bianco

Riesling (depending on region
and maker)

Sauvignon (depending on
region and maker)

Soave (cru bottlings only)

Tocai

Torre di Giano

Trebbiano (depending on
vintage)

Verdicchio (cru bottlings only)

Vernaccia (barrel-aged
specimens only)

WHITE WINES—BIG

Arneis (depending on style and vintage)

Chardonnay (depending on maker)

Fiano di Avellino (cru bottlings)

Greco di Tufo (cru bottlings)

Pinot bianco (depending on maker and vintage)

Pomino bianco (cru bottlings)

Tocai (depending on maker and vintage)

Torre di Giano (Riserva)

Trebbiano (depending on maker)

OUR FAVORITE WHITE WINE MAKERS

Abbazia di Rosazzo

Anselmi

Antinori

Borgo Conventi

Castello Banfi

Ceretto

Livio Felluga

Frescobaldi

Gaja

Bruno Giacosa

Gradnik

Jermann

La Scolca

Lungarotti

Mastroberardino

Pio Cesare

Pieropan

Ruffino

Russiz Superiore

Edoardo Valentini

RED WINES—LIGHT

Barbera

Bardolino

Dolcetto

Castel del Monte

Chianti

Ciro

Valpolicella

RED WINES—MEDIUM

Aglianico del Vulture

Barbera (cru or barrique-aged
    specimens)

Breganze

Cabernet

Carmignano

Chianti Classico (and some
    Riserva)

Chianti Rufina (and some
    Riserva)

Corvo

Dolcetto (cru bottlings)

Etna rosso

Franciacorta

Gattinara

Ghemme

Lacryma Christi

Merlot

Montepulciano d'Abruzzo

Nebbiolo d'Alba

Regaleali

Rosso Conero

Rosso di Montalcino

Rubesco

Spanna

Taurasi

Valpolicella (cru bottlings or
    ripasso wines)

Valtellina (Grumello, Inferno,
    Sassella, Valgella)

Venegazzu

Vino Nobile di Montepulciano

RED WINES—BIG

Aglianico del Vulture Riserva

Amarone

Barbaresco

Barolo

Brunello di Montalcino

Carmignano Riserva

Chianti Classico Riserva
    (depending on vintage)

Chianti Rufina Riserva
    (depending on vintage and
    maker)

Enrico IV (from Duca di
    Salaparuta)

Gattinara (depending on
    vintage)

Nebbiolo d'Alba (depending on
    vintage)

Rosso del Conte (from
    Regaleali)

Rosso di Montalcino
    (depending on vintage)

Rubesco (Riserva)

Salice Salentino

Spanna (depending on vintage)

Taurasi Riserva (and cru)

Teroldego

Valtellina (Sfurzat always,
    others depending on vintage)

Venegazzu

Vino Nobile Riserva

OUR FAVORITE RED WINE MAKERS:

CHIANTI AND KIN:

Avignonesi	Castello Banfi	Selvapiana
Badia a Coltibuono	Fossi	Spalletti
Barbi	Frescobaldi	Castello di Monte Antico
Berardenga-Felsina	Lamole di Lamole	Castello di Uzzano
Biondi-Santi	Monsanto	Fontodi
Boscarelli	Monte Vertine	Villa Cafaggio
Castellare	San Polo in Rosso	Villa di Capezzana

BAROLO, BARBARESCO, AND KIN:

Antoniolo	Cordero di Montezemolo	Produttori di Barbaresco
Luigi Bianco	Fenocchio	Alfredo Prunotto
Ceretto	Gaja	Ratti
Aldo Conterno	Bruno Giacosa	Vallana
Giacomo Conterno	Granduca	Vietti
Contratto	Pio Cesare	Voerzio

OTHER REDS:

Allegrini	Duca di Salaparuta	Nino Negri
Anselmi	Conte Loredan Gasparini	Quintarelli
Bertani	Lungarotti	Rainoldi
Donato d'Angelo	Masi	Regaleali
Leone de Castris	Mastroberardino	Maurizio Zanella

GRAPPA

Grappa is brandy—technically, pomace brandy, which is brandy distilled from the solids left over after the fermentation of wine. Every wine-making region and town in Italy is therefore capable of making a distinctive grappa, and right now it appears as if they are all doing so. An Italian embarrassment a decade ago—rustic firewater beloved only by transalpine truckers and backward *contadini*—grappa has now become an internationally chic *digestivo*. As a result, grappas have begun appearing in sleek designer bottles from more and more sophisticated origins: single grape varietals, single vineyards, especially prized parcels of land.

Grappa was and is a matchless after-dinner drink. Especially after a meal of heroic proportions, it is one of the great palatal pleasures and stomach soothers. Unaged grappa—readily identifiable by its crystal clarity—should be served ice-cold in a pony glass: the chill tames its fire and releases its aroma. Don't, however, ever put ice *in* grappa: Chill the whole bottle for about an hour in the freezer. A wood-aged grappa—which will show coloration ranging from pale gold to deep amber—should be served at room temperature in a brandy snifter, the better to savor its perfume. In either case, treat grappa just as you would any fine brandy: sip it slowly, rolling it all over your tongue before swallowing.

We should stress, for those new to the drink, that not only do different grappas taste very different from each other, but the *same* grappa will often taste different from one day to the next, according to the foods that have preceded it. We've never seen an explanation of the chemistry of this phenomenon, but it's undeniably true. A grappa that has an intensely floral aroma after a dinner featuring poultry and tomato sauce, say, may, when sniffed after consuming a rare roast beef, knock you back on your heels with a redolence of Parmesan cheese. And this is not to say that either the floral or the cheese aroma is unpleasant: It all depends on what you're in the mood for. In fact, when you have a selection of grappas to set out after dinner, you have all the additional fun of a ritual passing-around-and-sniffing of the bottles to see how each grappa is going to strike you and your guests today.

Grappa is primarily a northern Italian tradition, but it has caught on recently even in the south: The great Neapolitan wine house of Mastroberardino is now making grappas from the pomace of its prized white and red grapes, Greco di Tufo and Taurasi. Good Tuscan makers include Avignonesi, Badia a Coltibuono, Barbi, Felsina Berardenga, Castellare, Castello di Querceto and Monte Vertine. In the Piedmont and Friuli, almost every winemaker of any claim to authenticity and up-to-dateness produces at least one grappa, often several, from different pomaces (usually Nebbiolo, Dolcetto, or Barbera) or different locales and vineyards. There are also dedicated grappa distillers, ranging in size from the solitary, reclusive, and near-legendary Romano Levi, though larger artisan houses such as Nonino and Poli, to high-quality industrial establishments such as Nardini.

Index

A

Abbacchio in umido, 183–84
Abruzzese Lamb Stew, 286–87
Abruzzi-Style Fettuccine, 149–50
Agghiotta de pesce spada, 169–70
Agnello alla cacciatora, 82
Agnello alla montanara, 286–87
Agnello di Pasqua al forno,
    80–81
Agnello in umido all'abruzzese,
    83–84
Almonds, 411
    Chocolate Spice Cake, 414–15
    Fruit-and-Nut Roll, Friulian,
        415–17
    -Sugar Cake, Modena, 417–18
    Torte, Ricotta and, 115–16
Amarone, 440–41
Anatra alla romagnola, 270–71
Anchovies, 7
    -Mustard Sauce, Grilled Radicchio
        with, 409–10
    Peppers in a Pan, 193–94
    Spaghetti, Strumpet's, 160–61
Animelle al prosciutto, 90–91
Animelle in fricassea, 89–90
Antipasti, 8
    Artichokes
        Stuffed with Tuna, 24–25
        Tart, Stove-Top, 26–27
    Asparagus and Prosciutto Rolls,
        19–20

Beets with Balsamic Vinegar,
    220–21
Biscuits, Black Pepper, 340–41
Bread, Saint Clare's, 235–36
Canapés
    Mushroom, 230–31
    Polenta, with Gorgonzola,
        237–38
    Tuna and White Bean,
        137–38
Capri Salad, 123–24
Eggplant Parmesan, 134–36
Fennel-Flavored Cocktail Cookies,
    234–35
Frico, 336
Ham
    Bread, Saint Clare's, 235–36
    Fennel-Flavored Cocktail
        Cookies, 234–35
    and Mushroom torte, 232–33
Lentils on Bruschetta, Braised,
    332–33
Mozzarella
    Capri Salad, 123–24
    Eggplant Parmesan, 134–36
Mushroom
    Canapés, 230–31
    Torte, Ham and, 232–33
Mussels, Gratin of, 142–43
Onion
    Schiacciata, 37
    Tart, Stove-Top, 29–30

Peppers, Spectacular Stuffed,
    224–26
Polenta Canapés with Gorgonzola,
    237–38
Prosciutto
    Asparagus and, Rolls, 19–20
    and Pear Rolls, 226–27
    Radicchio with Scamorza, Grilled,
        335
Salad of Belgian Endive,
    Mushroom, and Ham, Warm,
    333–34
Scallops
    San Remo, 139–40
    Venetian Style, 38–39
Schiacciata
    Cheese, 236–37
    with Greens, 337
    Onion, 37
    Plain, 35–36
    with Prosciutto, 338
    Tomato, 138
Seafood Salad, 140–42
Tarts
    Artichoke, Stove-Top,
        26–27
    dough for stove-top, handling,
        28
    Easter, 33–34
    Onion, Stove-Top, 29–30
Torte, Ham and Mushroom,
    232–33

Antipasti *(continued)*
  Tuna
    Artichokes Stuffed with, 24–25
    and White Bean Canapés,
      137–38
  Vegetables
    Marinated Winter, 327–28
    Raw, with Creamy Garlic
      Dipping Sauce, 329–30
    Salad, Winter, 330–31
  Zucchini
    Battered-Fried, Blossoms,
      131–33
    with Mint, Marinated, 127–28
    Omelets, Small, 133–34
Appetizers, *see* Antipasti
Apples:
  Autumn, 311
  Baked, 310
Artichokes:
  about, 21–23
  Crêpes with Spring Vegetables,
    Timbale of, 67–69
  frozen, 22
  preparation for cooking
    large artichokes, 23
    tiny artichokes, 22–23
  Soup, Sicilian Pasta and, 48–49
  Stuffed with Tuna, 24–25
  Tart, Stove-Top, 26–27
Asiago, 303–04
Asparagi al parmigiano, 94
Asparagi fritti al prosciutto, 19–20
Asparagus:
  with Hazelnut Butter, 94
  Prosciutto Rolls and, 19–20
  Soup, Creamy Mushroom Style,
    46–47
  Spaghetti with, Tips, 60
Autumn Apples, 311

B

Bacon for Country-Style Scalloped
    Potatoes, 301–02
Bagna cauda, 329–30
Baked Apples, 310
Baked Bluefish with Scallions and
    Lime, 167–68
Baked Eggplant Sticks, 190

Baked Pears, 312
Baked Pork Chops, 87–88, 287–88
Balsamic Vinegar:
  Beets with, 220–21
  Zucchini and Spring Onions with,
    101
Barbaresco, 443–45
Barbera, 439–40
Bardolina, 440
Barolo, 443–45
Basil, 5
  Rigatoni with, 153
Battuto, 7
Bay Leaf, Grilled Pork Livers with
    Fennel and, 187–88
Beans, 293
  about dried, 344–45
  cooking, 345
  Cranberry, Tuscan-Style, 296–97
  Different Pot of, 407–08
  dried, about, 344–45
  Pasta Soup, Calabrian Bean and,
    346–47
  Pot of, 405–06
  soaking dried, 345
  Soup
    Calabrian Bean and Pasta,
      346–47
    Friulian, 347–48
    Tuscan-Style, 296–97
  White
    Canapés, Tuna and, 137–38
    Different Pot of Beans, 407–08
    Pot of Beans, 405–06
    Soup, Friulian Bean, 347–48
    Tripe Braised with Potatoes and,
      395–97
    Tuscan-Style, 296–97
Béchamel Sauce for Gratinéed
    Brussels Sprouts, 401–02
Beef:
  Butcher's Stew, 391–92
  Corkscrew Pasta, Neapolitan Style,
    357–59
  Crêpes with Spring Vegetables,
    Timbale of, 67–69
  Pasta Baked with Meats, Cheeses,
    and Hard-Boiled Eggs, 361–62
  Piedmontese Braised, 387–88

Pot Roast, Tuscan, 386
Ragù, Shells with, 355–56
Sauce, Lasagna with Spinach and
    Meat, 56–58
Steaks, Pizzaiola, 182–83
Stew, Home-Style, 79–80
  with Sweet-and-Sour Sauce, Boiled,
    384–85
Tripe, *see* Tripe
Beets with Balsamic Vinegar, 220–21
Belgian Endive, Warm Salad of
    Mushroom, Ham and, 333–34
Bel Paese, 304
Bensone, 417–18
Biscuits, Black Pepper, 340–41
Bistecche alla pizzaiola, 182–83
Blackberry Ice Cream, 211
Black Pepper Biscuits, 340–41
Bluefish:
  Gnocchi, 163–64
  with Scallions and Lime, Baked,
    167–68
  in Tomato Sauce, Baked, 166–67
Boiled Beef with Sweet-and-Sour
    Sauce, 384–85
Boiled Veal Shanks with Green
    Sauce, 382–83
*Bollito de manzo con salsa
    agrodolce*, 384–85
Bolognese Mushroom Caps, 285–86
Braciole di maiale al cartoccio,
    287–88
Braciole di maiale al forno, 87–88
Braised Broccoli Rape, 402–03
Braised Kid with Celery and
    Potatoes, 91–92
Braised Lamb, Abruzzi Style, 83–84
Braised Lentils on Bruschetta, 332–33
Braised Mallard Duck, 270–71
Braised Tiny Octopi, 371–73
Braised Veal with Spring Onions,
    77–78
Bread:
  Biscuits, Black Pepper, 340–41
  Bruschetta, Braised Lentils on,
    332–33
  Christmas, Ligurian, 419–20
  Easter Sweet Bread, 113–14
  Mushroom Canapés, 230–31

Pizza, *see* Pizza
Saint Clare's, 235–36
Schiacciata, *see* Schiacciatta
Soup
  Onion, Calabrian, 146
  Tuscan, 147–48
Broccoli Rape:
  Braised, 402–04
  Schiacciata with Greens, 337
Broth:
  about, 42–44
  Cheese Dumplings in, 41–42
  recipe, 44
Brunello, 442–43
Bruscit, 387–88
Brussels Sprouts, Gratinéed, 401–02
Bucatini:
  with Mushroom Tomato Sauce,
    245–46
  Pasta and Lentils, 352–53
Bucatini con pomodori e funghi,
  245–46
Butcher's Stew, 391–92
Butter:
  Asparagus with Hazelnut, 94
  Garlic, Veal Scallops with, 180

Cabbage:
  Red, with Olives and Capers, 400
  Savoy, Home-Style, 399
  Soup
    Calabrian Bean and Pasta,
      346–47
    Neapolitan Rice, Provolone, and,
      349–50
Caciocavallo, 304
Caciotta, 304
Cake:
  Almond-Sugar, Modena, 417–18
  Chocolate Spice, 414–15
  Pear, 412–13
Calabrese Potato Salad, 302
Canapés:
  Mushroom, 230–31
  Polenta, with Gorgonzola, 237–38
  Tuna and White Bean, 137–38
Capers, 6
  Red Cabbage with Olives and, 400

Spaghetti, Strumpet's, 160–61
Swordfish Steaks, Sicilian-Style,
  169–70
Tuna Steaks Sautéed with Olives
  and, 172–73
Capesanti in padella alla veneziana,
  38–39
Capretto in umido con verdure, 91–92
Caprino, 304
Carciofini ripieni all'abruzzese,
  24–25
Carmignano, 443
Carote al finocchio, 95
Carrots, 7
  with Fennel, 95
  Potatoes and, Home-Style, 408–09
Casserole-Roasted Pheasant, 273–74
Casserole Roast of Lamb Stuffed with
  Peas and Mushrooms, 84–86
Cauliflower in Marinated Winter
  Vegetables, 327–28
Cavolini gratinati al forno,
  401–02
Cavolo alla casalinga, 399
Cavolo rosso alla siciliana, 400
Ceci in umido, 294
Celery, 7
  Kid with Potatoes and, Braised,
    91–92
  Linguine, Seven Savors, 152
Certosina, 414–15
Cheeses:
  about, 303–08
  Dumplings in Broth, 41–42
  Schiacciata, 236–37
  as seasoning, 6
  see also specific types of cheese
Chestnut Stuffing, Roast Turkey with
  Fruit-and-, 377–79
Chianti, 441–42, 443
Chicken:
  with Cinnamon and Cloves, 269–70
  gizzards for Egg Noodles Roman
    Style, 243–44
  Golden Braised, 71–72
  with Mushrooms, Venetian Braised,
    373–75
  Procida Style, Sauté of, 173–74
  Risotto, Cop's, 367–68

Stew of Vegetables and, Summer,
  175–76
with Walnut and Pignoli Stuffing,
  Poached, 375–77
Chicken Livers, Spaghetti with
  Mushrooms and, 61–62
Chick-Peas:
  Pasta with, 350–51
  with Tomato and Onion, 294–95
Chocolate:
  Honey-Nut Balls, Spiced, 318–19
  Mousse, Neapolitan, 106
  Spice Cake, 414–15
  "White Truffles," 421–22
Christmas Bread, Ligurian, 419–20
Ciambotta, 198–99
Cima de rape affagato, 402–03
Cima ripiena alla genovese, 74–75
Cinnamon, 5
  Chicken with, and Cloves,
    269–70
  Pear Tart, Spiced, 313–14
Cipollata, 343
Cipolle alla Castellane, 295–96
Cipolline, Sweet-and-Sour, 404–05
Cipolline in agrodolce, 404–05
Clams, Spaghettini with Shrimp and,
  158–59
Cloves, 5
  Chicken with Cinnamon and,
    269–70
  Pear Tart, Spiced, 313–14
Coda de bue in umido, 394–95
Coffee Ice, Espresso, 205
Coffee Ice Cream, 210
Conchiglie con ragù, 355–56
Coniglio in agrodolce, 277–78
Cop's Risotto, 367–68
Costarelle in graticola, 185–86
Costolette di vitello in vino rosso,
  76–77
Country-Style Scalloped Potatoes,
  301–02
Country-Style Zucchini, 196
Country Wife Spaghetti, 247–48
Courses of an Italian meal, 8–10
  see also individual courses, e.g.
    Antipasti; Desserts
Coviglie al cioccolato, 106

Creamy Asparagus Soup Milanese
    Style, 46–47
Crêpes with Spring Vegetables,
    Timbale of, 67–69
Crescenza, 304
Crostata di fragole, 112–13
Crostata di marmellata de pesche,
    413–14
Crostini ai funghi, 230–31
Crostini di fagioli e tonno, 137–38
Crostini di polenta con gorgonzola,
    237–38
Cured meats as seasoning, 6

D

Desserts:
  Apples
    Autumn, 311
    Baked, 310
  Bread
    Easter Sweet, 113–14
    Ligurian Christmas, 419–20
  Cake
    Almond-Sugar, Modena, 417–18
    Chocolate Spice, 414–15
    Pear, 412–13
  Chocolate
    Honey-Nut Balls, Spiced, 318–19
    Mousse, Neapolitan, 106
    Spice Cake, 414–15
    "White Truffles," 421–22
  Christmas Bread, Ligurian, 419–20
  Easter Sweet Bread, 113–14
  Fruit-and-Nut Roll, Friulian,
    415–17
  Ice Cream, 208–09
    about, 206–08
    Blueberry, 211
    Coffee, 210
    Peach, 212
    Ricotta, 213
  Ices
    about, 203–04
    Espresso Coffee, 205
    Lime-Grapefruit, 206
  Mousse, Neapolitan Chocolate, 106
  Nut
    Balls, Spiced Honey-, 318–19
    Roll, Friulian Fruit-and-, 415–17

Pasta frolla, 108–12
Peach
  Ice Cream, 212
  Jam Tart, 413–14
Pears
  Baked, 312
  Cake, 412–13
  with Mascarpone and
    Gorgonzola, Poached, 315–16
  Tart, Spiced, 313–14
Strawberries
  with Lemon and Sugar, 103
  Sauce, 104
  Tart, 112–13
Tarts
  Peach Jam, 413–14
  Pear, Spiced, 313–14
  Sand, 316–17
  Strawberry, 112–13
Torte, Ricotta and Almond,
  115–16
"White Truffles," 421–22
Zabaglione with Vin Santo, 105
Zeppole, 107–08
Dessert Wines, 448–49
Different Pot of Beans, A, 407–08
Dipping Sauce, Raw Vegetables with
  Creamy Garlic, 329–30
Dolcetto, 439–40
Dolci, *see* Desserts
Duck, Braised Mallard, 270–71
Dumplings in Broth, Cheese, 41–42

E

Easter Sweet Bread, 113–14
Easter Tart, 33–34
Egg Noodles:
  Lamb, Braised, Abruzzi Style,
    83–84
  with Mascarpone, Fresh, 55
  with Prosciutto, Fresh, 148–49
  Roman Style, 243–44
Eggplant:
  in Egg-Tomato Sauce, 298–99
  Neapolitan-Style, 191–92
  Parmesan, 134–36
  Southern Mixed Vegetables,
    198–99

Spaghetti Norma, 250–51
Sticks, Baked, 190
Stuffed Peppers, Spectacular,
  224–26
Eggs:
  Omelets, Small Zucchini, 133–34
  Pasta Baked with Meats, Cheeses,
    and Hard-Boiled, 361–62
  Soup, Zucchini Egg-Drop, 240–41
  Tart, Easter, 33–34
  Zabaglione with Vin Santo, 105
Endive, Ravioli Stuffed with,
    Prosciutto, Ricotta and,
    353–55
Enraged Penne, 58–59
Espresso:
  Coffee, Ice, 205
  Coffee Ice Cream, 210

F

Fagiano ai sapori veneziani, 273–74
Fagioli alla maruzzara, 405–06
Fagioli alla toscana, 296–97
Fagioli in umido, 407–08
Fagiolini in salsa verde, 297–98
Faraona al cartoccio, 272–73
Fats, cooking, 6
Fava Bean Soup, Pea and, 45–46
Fegatelli alla fiorentina, 187–88
Fennel:
  Beef, Piedmontese Braised, 387–88
  Carrots with, 95
  -Flavored Cocktail Cookies, 234–35
  Ham, Braised with, 96
  Pork Livers with Bay Leaf and,
    Grilled, 187–88
  Risotto with, 365–66
Fettuccine, Abruzzi-Style, 149–50
Fettuccine all'abruzzese, 149–50
Finocchio al prosciutto, 96
Fiori fritti, 131–33
Fish:
  Bluefish
    Gnocchi, 163–64
    with Scallions and Lime, Baked,
      167–68
    in Tomato Sauce, Baked, 166–67
  Flounder Sauce, Linguine with,
    62–63

grilling, 165
Sardines Baked with Tomato,
    267–68
Swordfish Steaks, Sicilian-Style,
    169–70
Tuna
    Artichoke Stuffed with, 24–25
    Canapés, White Bean and,
        137–38
    Poached, Steaks, 170–71
    Sautéed with Olives and Capers,
        172–73
Flan, Parmesan Cheese, 31–32
Flan al parmigiano, 31–32
Flounder Sauce, Linguine with,
    62–63
Focaccia:
    Schiacciata, see Schiacciata
Fontina, 304
    Sauce, Tripe in Golden, 288–89
Food mill, 41, 157
Fragole al limone, 103
Freisa, 438–39
Fresh Egg Noodles with Parmesan,
    148–49
Fricase(ed):
    Sweetbreads, 89–90
    Turkey, 178
Frico, 336
Frittatine ai zucchini, 133–34
Friulian Fruit-and-Nut Roll, 415–17
Frollini al finocchio, 234–35
Fruit, 188
    Cake, Chocolate Spice, 414–15
    dried or candied, 411–12
    ices, see Ices
    macedonia, 203
    -and-Nut Roll, Friulian, 415–17
    selecting, 188–89
    Stuffing, Roast Turkey with
        Chestnut-and-, 377–79
    see also specific types of fruit
Frying in olive oil, 128–31
Fusilli:
    Corkscrew Pasta with an Uncooked
        Sauce, 151
    Neapolitan Style, 357–59
    Vesuvius, 359–60
Fusilli alla napoletana, 357–59

Fusilli alla vesuviana, 359–60
Fusilli con salsa crude, 151

G

Garlic, 7
    Butter, Veal Scallops with, 180
    Dipping Sauce, Raw Vegetables
        with Creamy, 329–30
    Vermicelli with, and Olive Oil,
        161–62
Gatto Santa Chiara, 235–36
Gelato, about, 206–08
Gelato di caffè, 210
Gelato di crema, 208–09
Gelato di mirtille, 211
Gelato di pesche, 212
Gelato di ricotta, 213
Genovese Stuffed Breast of Veal,
    74–75
Giardiniera, 327
Gnocchi:
    about, 253–56
    basic recipe, 254–55
    Bluefish, 163–64
    Gratinéed Polenta, 258–59
    Gratinéed with Tomato and
        Mozzarella, 256–57
    with Lamb and Pepper Sauce,
        257–58
Gnocchi alla sorrentina, 256–57
Gnocchi con ragù di agnello e
    peperoni, 257–58
Gnocchi di pesce, 163–64
Gnocchi di polenta con prosciutto,
    258–59
Golden Braised Chicken, 71–72
Gorgonzola, 305
    Pears with Mascarpone and,
        Poached, 315–16
    Polenta Canapés with, 237–38
Granita, about, 203–04
Granita di caffè, 205
Granita di limone verde e pompelmo,
    206
Grapefruit Water Ice, Lime-, 206
Grappa, 454
    Apples, Autumn, 311
Gratinéed Brussels Sprouts, 401–02

Gratinéed Polenta Gnocchi, 258–59
Gratin of Mussels, 142–43
Green Beans in Green Sauce, 297–98
Green Sauce:
    Green Beans in, 297–98
    Veal Shanks with, Boiled, 382–83
Grignolino, 438–39
Grilled Pork Livers with Bay Leaf
    and Fennel, 187–88
Grilled Radicchio with
        Anchovy-Mustard Sauce,
        409–10
Grilled Radicchio with Scamorza, 335
Grilled Spareribs, 185–86
Grilled Tomatoes, 194–95
Guinea Hen, Roast, 272–73

H

Ham:
    Bread, Saint Clare's, 235–36
    Fennel
        Braised with, 96
        -Flavored Cocktail Cookies,
            234–35
    and Mushroom Torte, 232–33
    prosciutto, see Prosciutto
    Salad of Belgian Endive,
        Mushrooms, and, Warm,
        333–34
    see also Prosciutto
Hare, Stewed, 290–92
Hazelnuts, 411
    Chocolate Spice Cake, 414–15
Hen, Roast Guinea, 272–73
Herbs, 5–6
Home-Style Beef Stew, 79–80
Home-Style Potatoes and Carrots,
    408–09
Home-Style Savoy Cabbage, 399
Honey-Nut Balls, Spiced, 318–19
Hors d'oeuvres, see Antipasti

I

Ice Cream, 208–09
    about, 206–08
    Blueberry, 211
    Coffee, 210

Ice Cream *(continued)*
   Peach, 212
   Ricotta, 213
Ice cream machines, 208
Ices:
   about, 203–04
   Espresso Coffee, 205
   Lime-Grapefruit Water, 206
Insalata belga saporita, 333–34
Insalata caprese, 123–24
Insalata di mare, 140–42
Insalata mista, 201
Insalatone, 330–31
Involtini all'abruzzese, 283–84

J

Juniper berries, 5
   Lamb Stew, Sardinian,
      392–93

K

Kid with Celery and Potatoes,
   Braised, 91–92

L

Lamb:
   Braised, Abruzzi Style, 83–84
   Breast of, Hunter's Style, 82
   Butcher's Stew, 391–92
   Gnocchi with, and Pepper Sauce,
      257–58
   Leg of, Casserole Roast of, Stuffed
      with Peas and Mushrooms,
      84–86
   Roasted Easter, 80–81
   Stew
      Abruzzese, 286–87
      Butcher's, 391–92
      Sardinian, 392–93
      Summertime, 183–84
Lasagna pasticciata con spinaci,
   56–58
Lasagna with Spinach and Meat
   Sauce, 56–58
Lavender, 5
Lemon, 7

Spinach with Olive Oil and, 100
Strawberries with, and Sugar, 103
Lenticchie all'umbra, 332–33
Lentils:
   Braised, on Bruschetta, 332–33
   Pasta with, 352–53
Lepre in salmi, 290–92
Licurdia, 46
Light Tomato-Zucchini Soup, 145
Ligurian Christmas Bread, 419–20
Ligurian Vegetable Soup, 49–50
Lime:
   Bluefish with Scallions and, Baked,
      167–68
   -Grapefruit Water Ice, 206
Linguine:
   with Flounder Sauce, 62–63
   Seven Savors, 152
Linguine ai sette sapori, 152
Livers:
   Chicken, Spaghetti with
      Mushrooms and, 61–62
   Pork, Grilled with Bay Leaf and
      Fennel, 187–88

M

Macaroni with Baked Tomatoes,
   246–47
Maccaruni a lu furnu, 361–62
Maccheroni con pomodori al forno,
   246–47
Manzo in umido, 386
Marinated Winter Vegetables,
   327–28
Marinated Zucchini with Mint,
   127–28
Marjoram, 5
Mascarpone, 305
   Egg Noodles with, Fresh, 55
   Pears with Gorgonzola and,
      Poached, 315–16
   "White Truffles," 421–22
Mazze de tamburo alla bolognese,
   285–86
Melanzane alla partenopea, 191–92
Mele al forno, 310
Mele d'autunno, 311
Menus, 423–31

Milanese Braised Veal Shanks,
   282–83
Millecosedde, 346–47
Minestra di fagiole e scarole, 241–43
Minestra di fagioli alla friulana,
   347–48
Minestra di piselli e fave, 45–46
Minestra di pomodoro e zucchini,
   145
Minestra di zucchini e uova, 240–41
Minestra napoletana, 349–50
Mint, 5
   Zucchini with, Marinated, 127–28
Modena Almond-Sugar Cake, 417–18
Montasio, 305
   Frico, 336
Moscardini in umido, 371–73
Mousse, Neapolitan Chocolate, 106
Mozzarella:
   about, 124–26
   Bread, Saint Clare's, 235–36
   Buffalo, 126
   Capri Salad, 123–24
   Fusilli Vesuvius, 359–60
   Gnocchi Gratinéed with Tomato
      and, 256–57
   the making of, 125–26
   Pasta Baked with Meats, Cheeses,
      and Hard-Boiled Eggs, 361–62
   Zucchini Bella Napoli, 197–98
Mushrooms:
   about, 227–30
   Bolognese, Caps, 285–86
   Canapés, 230–31
   Chicken with, Venetian Braised,
      373–75
   cremini, 229
   Lamb Stuffed with Peas and,
      Casserole Roast of, 84–86
   Pizza, 265
   Porcini, 229, 230
      Polenta in the High Old Roman
         Manner, 368–69
      Ragù, Shells with Beef, 355–56
   as seasoning, 6
   Salad of Belgian Endive, Ham,
      and, Warm, 333–34
   Spaghetti with, and Chicken
      Livers, 61–62

Tomato Sauce, Bucatini with,
    245–46
Torte, Ham and, 232–33
Veal Rolls Filled with Pork, and
    Parmigiano, 283–84
ussels, Gratin of, 142–43
ustard Sauce, Grilled Radicchio
    with Anchovy-, 409–10

eapolitan Cabbage, Rice, and
    Provolone Soup, 349–50
eapolitan Chocolate Mousse, 106
eapolitan-Style Eggplant, 191–92
utmeg, 5
uts, 411
Balls, Spiced Honey-, 318–19
Fruit-and-Nut Roll, Friulian,
    415–17
see also specific types of nuts

ctopus:
Braised Tiny, 371–73
Seafood Salad, 140–42
live Oil, 218
frying in, about, 128–31
pomace, 130
reusing, 130
Spinach with, and Lemon, 100
Vermicelli with Garlic and, 161–62
lives, 6, 217–18
Marinated Winter Vegetables,
    327–28
Pork Stewed with, 86–87
Red Cabbage with Capers and, 400
Spaghetti
    Country Wife, 247–48
    Strumpet's, 160–61
Swordfish Steaks, Sicilian-Style,
    169–70
Tuna Steaks Sautéed with Capers
    and, 172–73
Ziti, Palermo-Style, 249–50
melets, Small Zucchini, 133–34
nions, 7
Castellare, 295–96

Chick-Peas with Tomato and,
    294–95
Peas with, Sage, and Salami, 98
Potatoes, Country-Style Scalloped,
    301–02
Schiacciata, 37
Soup
    Calabrian, 146
    Umbrian, 343
    Sweet-and-Sour, 404–05
    Veal with Spring, Braised, 77–78
    Zucchini and Spring, with
        Balsamic Vinegar, 101
Oregano, 5
Potatoes Sautéed with, 192–93
Ossibuchi alla milanese, 282–83
Oxtail Stew, 394–95

P

Palermo-Style Ziti, 249–50
Pancetta, Warm Salad of Belgian
    Endive, Mushrooms, and,
    333–34
Pandolce di Liguria, 419–20
Pan pepato, 318–19
Pappa al pomodoro, 147–48
Pappardelle alla romano, 243–44
Parmesan Mashed Potatoes, 300
Parmigiana di melanzane, 134–36
Parmigiano:
    about, 363–65
    Asparagus with Hazelnut Butter,
        94
    Dumplings in Broth, 41–42
    Eggplant Parmesan, 134–36
    Flan, 31–32
    Mashed Potatoes, 300
    Rigatoni with Basil, 153
    Risotto, Saffron, 252–53
    Veal Rolls Filled with Pork,
        Mushrooms and, 283–84
Parsley:
    Green Beans in Green Sauce,
        297–98
    Green Sauce
        Boiled Veal Shanks with, 382–83
        Green Beans in, 297–98
Passatelli in brodo, 41–42

Pasta:
    Artichoke Soup, Sicilian Pasta and,
        48–49
    Baked with Meats, Cheeses, and
        Hard-Boiled Eggs, 361–62
    Bucatani
        with Mushroom Tomato Sauce,
            245–46
        Pasta with Lentils, 352–53
    with Chick-Peas, 350–51
    Egg Noodles
        Lamb, Braised, Abruzzi Style,
            83–84
        with Mascarpone, Fresh, 55
        with Prosciutto, Fresh, 148–49
        Roman Style, 243–44
    Fettuccine, Abruzzi-Style,
        149–50
    fresh, 51–54
    Fusilli
        Corkscrew Pasta, Neapolitan
            Style, 357–59
        Corkscrew Pasta with an
            Uncooked Sauce, 151
        Vesuvius, 359–60
    homemade, 51–54
    Lasagna with Spinach and Meat
        Sauce, 56–58
    with Lentils, 352–53
    Linguine
        with Flounder Sauce, 62–63
        Seven Savors, 152
    Macaroni with Baked Tomatoes,
        246–47
    Mascarpone, Fresh Egg Noodles
        with, 55
    Penne, Enraged, 58–59
    Ravioli Stuffed with Endive,
        Prosciutto, and Ricotta,
        353–55
    Rigatoni with Basil, 153
    Shells with Beef Ragù, 355–56
    Soup
        Artichoke, Sicilian Pasta and,
            48–49
        Bean and, Calabrian, 346–47
    Spaghetti
        with Asparagus Tips, 60
        Country Wife, 247–48

Pasta *(continued)*
    with Mushrooms and Chicken
       Livers, 61–62
    Norma, 250–51
    Strumpet's, 160–61
    Spaghettini with Clams and
       Shrimp, 158–59
    Tomato Sauce for, *see* Tomato
       Sauce
    Uncooked Sauce
      Corkscrew Pasta with an, 151
      Seven Savors Linguine, 152
    Vermicelli with Garlic and Olive
       Oil, 161–62
    Ziti, Palermo-Style, 249–50
Pasta con lenticchie, 352–53
Pasta e carciofi alla siciliana,
    48–49
Pasta e ceci, 350–51
Pasta Frolla, 108–12
    to bake filled, 112
    to bake unfilled, 111–12
    ingredients, 110
    Peach Jam Tart, 413–14
    preparing, 108–11
    shaping and baking, 111
Pasta machines, 51–54
Patate al forno alla contadina,
    301–02
Patate all'origano, 192–93
Patate e carote alla casalinga,
    408–09
Peach:
    Ice Cream, 212
    Jam Tart, 413–14
Pears:
    Baked, 312
    Cake, 412–13
    with Mascarpone and Gorgonzola,
       Poached, 315–16
    Rolls, Prosciutto and, 226–27
    Tart, Spiced, 313–14
Peas:
    Lamb Stuffed with Mushrooms
       and, Casserole Roast of, 84–86
    with Onion, Sage, and Salami, 98
    Rice and, 64–65
    Soup, Fava Bean and, 45–46
    Tomato, Braised with, 97

Pecorino romano, 305–06
    Cheese Schiacciata, 236–37
    Fusilli Vesuvius, 359–60
    Rigatoni with Basil, 152
Penne, Enraged, 58–59
Penne all'arrabbiata, 58–59
Peperoncini for Marinated Winter
    Vegetables, 327–28
Peperoncino rosso, 6, 223
    Penne, Enraged, 58–59
Peperoni imbottiti, 224–26
Pepper Biscuits, Black, 340–41
Peppers:
    about, 221–23
    Bell
      about, 221–22
      Chicken and Vegetables,
       Summer Stew of, 175–76
      Corkscrew Pasta with an
       Uncooked Sauce, 151
      Gnocchi with Lamb and, Sauce,
       257–58
      in a Pan, 193–94
      Southern Mixed Vegetables,
       198–99
      Spaghetti, Country Wife, 247–48
      Stuffed Spectacular, 224–26
    frying, Italian, 222–23
    hot cherry, 223
    peperoncino rosso, 6, 223
      Penne, Enraged, 58–59
Pere al forno, 312
Pere al mascarpone e gorgonzola,
    315–16
Pesce al forno, 166–67
Pesce azzurro alla scalogna, 167–68
Petto di agnello al forno, 392–93
Pheasant, Casserole-Roasted, 273–74
Piccillato di Pasqua, 113–14
Piedmontese Braised Beef, 387–88
Pignoli:
    Apples, Autumn, 311
    Chocolate Spice Cake, 414, 415
    Fruit-and-Nut Roll, Friulian,
      415–17
    Stuffing, Poached Chicken with
      Walnut and, 375–77
Piselli alla napoletana, 97
Piselli alla rustica, 98

Pizza:
    about, 260–61
    dough, 261
    Mushroom, 265
    Schiacciata, *see* Schiacciata
    Tomato, 263–64
Pizza al pomodoro, 263–64
Pizza dolce, 115–16
Pizza equipment, basic, 262–63
Pizzaiola Steaks, 182–83
Pizza 're carcioffole, 26–27
Pizza 're cepodde, 29–30
Plain Schiaciatta, 35–36
Poached Chicken with Walnut and
    Pignoli Stuffing, 375–77
Poached Pears with Mascarpone and
    Gorgonzola, 315–16
Poached Tuna Steaks, 170–71
Polenta:
    about, 388–90
    Canapés with Gorgonzola,
      237–38
    Gnocchi, Gratinéed, 258–59
    in the High Old Roman Manner,
      368–69
    method for making, 389–90
    serving, 390
    shortcuts, 389
Pollastrello con funghi alla veneta,
    373–75
Pollo alla canevesana, 269–70
Pollo alla procidana, 173–74
Pollo in potacchio all'anconetana,
    71–72
Pollo in umido con verdure, 175–76
Pollo ripieno alle noce, 375–77
Pork:
    Bacon for Country-Style Scalloped
      Potatoes, 301–02
    Chops, Baked, 87–88, 287–88
    Ham, *see* Ham; Prosciutto
    Livers with Bay Leaf and Fennel,
      Grilled, 187–88
    Spareribs, Grilled, 185–86
    Stewed with Olives, 86–87
    Veal Rolls Filled with, Mushrooms,
      and Parmigiano, 283–84
Potatoes, 293
    Country-Style Scalloped, 301–02

Gnocchi
  about, 253–56
  basic recipe, 254–55
  Bluefish, 163–64
  Home-Style, and Carrots, 408–09
  Kid with Celery and, Braised,
      91–92
  Mashed, Parmesan, 300
  with Oregano, Sautéed, 192–93
  Parmesan Mashed, 300
  Salad, Calabrese, 302
  Southern Mixed Vegetables,
      198–99
  Tripe Braised with, and Beans,
      395–97
  Veal
    Braised with, 379–80
    with Zucchini and, 181
t of Beans, 405–06
t Roast, Tuscan, 386
osciutto:
  about, 339–40
  Asparagus and, Rolls, 19–20
  Egg Noodles with, Fresh, 148–49
  Mushroom Caps, Bolognese,
      285–86
  and Pear Rolls, 226–27
  Polenta in the High Old Roman
      Manner, 368–69
  Ravioli Stuffed with Endive, and
      Ricotta, 353–55
  Schiacciata with, 338
  Sweetbreads with, 90–91
  Veal Scallops with, Sage, and
      White Wine, 179
  see also Ham
rovolone, 306
  Eggplant, Neapolitan-Style, 191–92
  Pasta Baked with Meats, Cheeses,
      and Hard-Boiled Eggs, 361–62
  Soup, Neapolitan Cabbage, Rice,
      and, 349–50
untarelle, 200
urea al parmigiano, 300
utizza, 415–17

)

aglie al forno, 73
aglie al pomodoro, 176–77

Quails:
  Braised, on a Bed of Risotto,
      275–76
  Roasted, 73
  with Tomatoes and Rosemary,
      Braised, 176–77
  Quick Summer Tomato Sauce,
      156–57

R

Rabbit, Sweet-and-Sour Braised,
    277–78
Radicchio:
  with Anchovy-Mustard Sauce,
      Grilled, 409–10
  with Scamorza, Grilled, 335
Radicchio alla veneta, 409–10
Radicchio con scamorza, 335
Ragù, Shells with Beef, 355–56
Ragù del macellaio, 391–92
Raisins:
  Apples, Autumn, 311
  Chocolate Spice Cake, 414–15
  Fruit-and-Nut Roll, Friulian,
      415–17
  Swordfish Steaks, Sicilian-Style,
      169–70
Rape saltate in padella, 99
Ravioli con indivia, prosciutto, e
    ricotta, 353–55
Ravioli Stuffed with Endive,
    Prosciutto, and Ricotta,
    353–55
Raw Vegetables with Creamy Garlic
    Dipping Sauce, 329–30
Red Cabbage with Olives and Capers,
    400
Red pepper (spice), 4–5
Rice:
  Peas and, 64–65
  Risotto, see Risotto
  Soup, Neapolitan Cabbage,
      Provolone, and, 349–50
Ricotta, 306
  Ice Cream, 213
  Lasagna with Spinach and Meat
      Sauce, 56–58
  Ravioli Stuffed with Endive,
      Prociutto, and, 353–55

Tart, Easter, 33–34
  Torte, Almond and, 115–16
Ricotta salata, 306
  Spaghetti Norma, 250–51
Rigatoni:
  Baked with Meats, Cheeses, and
      Hard-Boiled Eggs, 361–62
  with Basil, 153
Rigatoni al basilico, 153
Rinforzata, 327
Risi e bisi, 64–65
Riso con finocchi, 365–66
Risotto:
  with Fennel, 365–66
  Quails on a Bed of, Braised,
      275–76
  Saffron, 252–53
  with Spring Greens, 65–66
Risotto alla milanese, 252–53
Risotto alla sbirraglia, 367–68
Risotto con verdura, 65–66
Roasted Easter Lamb, 80–81
Roasted Quails, 73
Roasted Veal Shanks, 280–81
Roast Turkey with
      Fruit-and-Chestnut Stuffing,
      377–79
Robiola, 306
  Prosciutto and Pear Rolls, 226–27
Rollato d'agnello alla ragusana,
    84–85
Romano, pecorino, see Pecorino
    romano
Rosemary, Quails Braised with
    Tomatoes and, 176–77
Rotolini di prosciutto e pere, 226–27
Rucola, 200–01

S

Saffron, 5
  Risotto, 252–53
Sage:
  Chicken with Cinnamon and
      Cloves, 269–70
  Peas with Onion, and Salami, 98
  Veal Scallops with Prosciutto, and
      White Wine, 179
Saint Clare's Bread, 235–36

Salad:
about, 200–01
Capri, 123–24
mixed, 201
pinzimonio, 201
Potato, Calabrese, 302
Seafood, 140–42
Vegetable, Winter, 330–31
Warm, of Belgian Endive,
    Mushrooms, and Ham, 333–34
Salami, Peas with Onion, Sage, and,
    98
Salsa di fragole, 104
Saltimbocca alla romana, 179
Sand Tart, 316–17
Sarde all'anconetana, 267–68
Sardines:
Baked with Tomato, 267–68
cleaning, 267
Sardinian Lamb Stew, 392–93
Sauce:
Anchovy-Mustard, Grilled
    Radicchio with, 409–10
Béchamel, for Gratinéed Brussels
    Sprouts, 401–02
Creamy Garlic Dipping, Raw
    Vegetables with, 329–30
Flounder, Linguine with,
    62–63
Green
    Green Beans in, 279–98
    Veal Shanks with, Boiled,
        382–83
Meat, Lasagna with Spinach and,
    56–58
Ragù, Shells with Beef, 355–56
Strawberry, 104
Sweet-and-Sour, Boiled Beef with,
    384–85
Tomato, *see* Tomato Sauce
Sautéed White Turnips, 99
Sauté of Chicken, Procida Style,
    173–74
Scallions, Baked Bluefish with Lime
    and, 167–68
Scallops:
San Remo, 139–40
Venetian Style, 38–39
Scaloppine con burro d'aglio, 180

Scamorza, 306
Radicchio with, Grilled, 335
Schiacciata, 35–36
Schiacciata:
Cheese, 236–37
with Greens, 337
Onion, 37
Plain, 35–36
with Prosciutto, 338
Tomato, 138
Schiacciata alla campagnola, 37
Schiacciata al pomodoro, 138
Schiacciata al prosciutto, 338
Schiacciata con formaggio,
    236–37
Schiacciata con verdura, 337
Seafood:
Clams, Spaghettini with Shrimp
    and, 158–59
Octopi
    Braised Tiny, 371–73
    Seafood Salad, 140–42
Salad, 140–42
Scallops
    San Remo, 139–40
    Venetian Style, 38–39
Shrimp
    Seafood Salad, 140–42
    Spaghettini with Clams and,
        158–59
Seasonings, 4–7
Shells with Beef Ragù, 355–56
Shrimp:
Seafood Salad, 140–42
Spaghettini with Clams and,
    158–59
Sicilian Pasta with Artichoke Soup,
    48–49
Sicilian-Style Swordfish Steaks,
    169–70
Soffrito, 7
Soppressata for Pasta Baked with
    Meats, Cheeses, and
    Hard-Boiled Eggs, 361–62
Soups:
Artichoke, Sicilian Pasta with,
    48–49
Asparagus, Creamy, Milanese Style,
    46–47

Bean
Escarole and, 241–43
Fava Bean and Pea, 45–47
Friulian, 347–48
and Pasta, Calabrian, 346–47
Bread
Onion, Calabrian, 146
Tuscan, 147–48
Broth, 44
about, 42–44
Cheese Dumplings in, 41–42
Cabbage
Calabrian Bean and Pasta,
    346–47
Neapolitan Rice, Provolone and,
    349–50
Egg-Drop Zucchini, 240–41
Escarole and Bean, 241–43
Fava Bean and Pea, 45–46
Onion
Calabrian, 146
Umbrian, 343
Pasta
and Artichoke, Sicilian, 48–49
Bean and, Calabrian, 346–47
Pea and Fava Bean, 45–46
Tomato-Zucchini, Light, 145
Vegetable, Ligurian, 49–50
White Cannellini Bean, Escarole
    and, 241–43
Zucchini
Egg-Drop, 240–41
Tomato-, Light, 145
Southern Mixed Vegetables, 198–99
Spaghetti:
with Asparagus Tips, 60
Country Wife, 247–48
with Mushrooms and Chicken
    Livers, 61–62
Norma, 250–51
Strumpet's, 160–61
Spaghetti alla ciociara, 247–48
Spaghetti alla Norma, 250–51
Spaghetti alla puttanesca, 160–61
Spaghetti con fegatini, 61–62
Spaghetti con punti d'asparagi, 60
Spaghettini with Clams and Shrimp,
    158–59
Spareribs, Grilled, 185–86

ectacular Stuffed Peppers, 224–26
ezzatino con zucchini e patate, 181
ezzatino di bue alla casalinga,
   79–80
ezzatino di maiale con olive,
   86–87
ezzatino di vitello con cipolle,
   77–78
ezzatino di vitello con patate,
   379–80
iced Honey-Nut Balls, 318–19
iced Pear Tart, 313–14
ices, 4–5
inach:
   Crêpes with Spring Vegetables,
     Timbale of, 67–69
   Lasagna with, and Meat Sauce,
     56–58
   with Olive Oil and Lemon, 100
inaci all'olio e limone, 100
ew:
   Beef, Home-Style, 79–80
   Butcher's, 391–92
   Chicken and Vegetables, Summer
     Stew of, 175–76
   Hare, 290–92
   Lamb
     Abruzzese, 286–87
     Butcher's, 391–92
     Sardinian, 392–93
     Summertime, 183–84
   Oxtail, 394–95
   Pork Stewed with Olives,
     86–87
inco di vitello arrosto, 280–81
ove-Top Tarts:
   Artichoke, 26–27
   handling the dough, 28
   Onion, 29–30
racchino, 306–07
rumpet's Spaghetti, 160–61
mmer Stew of Chicken and
   Vegetables, 175–76
mmertime Lamb Stew, 183–84
eet-and-Sour Braised Rabbit,
   277–78
eet-and-Sour Onions, 404–05
eet-and-Sour Sauce, Boiled Beef
   with, 384–85

Sweetbreads:
   Chicken with Walnut and Pignoli
     Stuffing, Poached, 375–77
   Fricasseed, 89–90
   with Prosciutto, 90–91
Swiss cheese for Fennel-Flavored
   Cocktail Cookies, 234–35
Swordfish Steaks, Sicilian-Style,
   169–70

T

Tacchino arrosto alla lombarda,
   377–79
Tacchino brodettato, 178
Tagliatelle al prosciutto, 148–49
Taleggio, 307
Taralli col pepe, 340–41
Tarragon, 5
Tarts:
   Artichoke, Stove-Top, 26–27
   dough for stove-top tarts, handling,
     28
   Easter, 33–34
   Onion, Stove-Top, 29–30
   Peach Jam, 413–14
   Pear, Spiced, 313–14
   Sand, 316–17
   Strawberry, 112–13
Tartufi bianchi, 421–22
Taurasi, 445
Tegamino di cozze, 142–43
Thyme, 5
Timbale of Crêpes with Spring
   Vegetables, 67–69
Timballo di crespelle al verde, 67–69
Timballo di pere, 313–14
Toma, 307
Tomato:
   Bucatini with Mushroom, Sauce,
     245–46
   Capri Salad, 123–24
   Chick-Peas with, and Onion,
     294–95
   Egg-, Sauce, Eggplant in, 298–99
   Eggplant Parmesan, 134–36
   freezing, 239–40
   Fusilli Vesuvius, 359–60
   Grilled, 194–95

Lamb
   Braised, Abruzzi Style, 83–84
   Stew, Summertime, 183–84
   Linguine, Seven Savors, 152
   Macaroni with Baked, 246–47
   Pizza, 263–64
   Quails Braised with, and
     Rosemary, 176–77
   Sardines with, Baked, 267–68
   Sauce, see Tomato Sauce
   Schiacciata, 138
   Soup
     Bread Soup, Tuscan, 147–48
     Light Zucchini-, 145
   Southern Mixed Vegetables,
     198–99
   Spaghetti
     with Asparagus Tips, 60
     Country Wife, 247–48
     Norma, 250–51
   Swordfish Steaks, Sicilian Style,
     169–70
   Uncooked Sauce, Corkscrew Pasta
     with an, 151
   Ziti, Palermo-Style, 249–50
Tomato paste, 7
Peas Braised with Tomato, 97
Tomato Sauce:
   about, 154–55, 157
   Bluefish Baked in, 166–67
   canned tomatoes, use of, 157
   Eggplant in Egg-, 298–99
   Gnocchi Gratinéed with, and
     Mozzarella, 256–57
   Mushroom, Bucatini with, 245–46
   Quick Summer, 156–57
   Schiacciata, Tomato, 138
   Seven Savors Linguine, 152
   Spaghetti, Strumpet's, 160–61
   Uncooked Sauce, Corkscrew Pasta
     with an, 151
   Zucchini, Country-Style, 196
Tonno alla stimpirata, 172–73
Tonno lessato, 170–71
Torta alle pere, 412–13
Torta di funghi e prosciutto,
   232–33
Torta pasqualina, 33–34
Torta sabbiosa, 316–17

Torte:
  Ham and Mushroom, 232–33
  Ricotta and Almond, 115–16
Trenette al mascarpone, 55
Tripe:
  Braised with Potatoes and Beans,
    395–97
  in Golden Fontina Sauce, 288–89
Trippa alla milanese, 395–97
Trippa alla valdostana, 288–89
"Truffles, White," 421–22
Tuna:
  Artichokes Stuffed with, 24–25
  Canapés, White Bean and, 137–38
  Poached, Steaks, 170–71
  Sautéed with Olives and Capers,
    172–73
Turkey:
  Fricassee, 178
  with Fruit-and-Chestnut Stuffing,
    Roast, 377–79
Turnips, Sautéed White, 99
Tuscan Bread Soup, 147–48
Tuscan Pot Roast, 386
Tuscan-Style Beans, 296–97

U

Umbrian Onion Soup, 343
Uova con melanzane, 298–99

V

Valpolicella, 440
Veal:
  Breast of, Genovese Stuffed, 74–75
  Butcher's Stew, 391–92
  Chops, in Red Wine, 76–77
  Potatoes, Braised with, 379–80
  in Red Wine, 381–82
  Rolls Filled with Pork,
    Mushrooms, and Parmigiano,
    283–84
  Scallops
    with Garlic Butter, 180
    with Prosciutto, Sage, and White
      Wine, 179
  Shanks
    about, 279

and Green Sauce, Boiled, 382–83
  Milanese Braised, 282–83
  Roasted, 280–81
  with Spring Onions, Braised, 77–78
Sweetbreads
  Fricasseed, 89–90
  with Prosciutto, 90–91
  with Zucchini and Potatoes, 181
Vegetables:
  Chicken and, Summer Stew of,
    175–76
  Crêpes with Spring, Timbale of,
    67–69
  Marinated Winter, 327–28
  Raw, with Creamy Garlic Dipping
    Sauce, 329–30
  Salad, Winter, 330–31
  Soup, Ligurian, 49–50
  Southern Mixed, 198–99
  Winter, Salad, 330–31
  see also specific vegetables
Venetian Braised Chicken with
  Mushrooms, 373–75
Vermicelli con aglio e olio, 161–62
Vermicelli with Garlic and Olive Oil,
  161–62
Vermouth:
  Scallops San Remo, 139–40
  Strawberry Sauce, 104
Vinegar:
  Balsamic, *see* Balsamic Vinegar
  wine vinegar, 7
Vin Santo, Zabaglione with, 105
Vitello al vino, 381–82
Vitello bollito con salsa verde,
  382–83

W

Walnuts:
  Fruit-and-Nut Roll, Friulian,
    415–17
  Stuffing, Poached Chicken with
    Pignoli and, 375–77
Warm Salad of Belgian Endive,
  Mushrooms, and Ham, 333–34
White Beans:
  Canapés, Tuna and, 137–38
  Different Pot of Beans, 407–08

Friulian Bean Soup, 347–48
  Pot of Beans, 405–06
  Tripe Braised with Potatoes and,
    395–97
  Tuscan-Style, 296–97
"White Truffles," 421–22
Wine, 7, 433–54
  as a course, 10
  Dessert, 448–49
  Grappa, 454
    Apples, Autumn, 311
  Red, 438–45, 451–53
    Beef, Piedmontese Braised,
      387–88
    Veal Chops in, 76–77
    Veal in, 381–82
  White, 445–48, 450–51
    Veal Scallops with Prosciutto,
      Sage, and, 179
Wine vinegar, 7
Winter Vegetable Salad, 330–31

Z

Zabaglione al Vin Santo, 105
Zeppole, 107
Ziti, Palermo-Style, 249–50
Ziti con salsa alla palermitana,
  249–50
Zucchini:
  Batter-Fried, Blossoms, 131–33
  Bella Napoli, 197–98
  Chicken and Vegetables, Summer
    Stew of, 175–76
  Country-Style, 196
  with Mint, Marinated, 127–28
  Omelets, Small, 133–34
  Soup, Egg-Drop, 240–41
  Southern Mixed Vegetables,
    198–99
  and Spring Onions with Balsamic
    Vinegar, 101
  Veal with, and Potatoes, 181
Zucchini alla Bella Napoli, 197–98
Zucchini alla contadina, 196
Zucchini a scapece, 127–28
Zucchini e cipolle saltati, 101
Zuppa di verdura all'agliata, 49–50